A SOCIOLOGY OF JUSTICE IN RUSSIA

Much of the media coverage and academic literature on Russia suggests that the justice system is unreliable, ineffective and corrupt. But what if we look beyond the stereotypes and preconceptions? This volume features contributions from a number of scholars who studied Russia empirically and in depth, through extensive field research, observations in courts and interviews with judges and other legal professionals as well as lay actors. A number of tensions in the everyday experiences of justice in Russia are identified and the concept of the 'administerial model of justice' is introduced to illuminate some of the less obvious layers of Russian legal tradition, including file-driven procedure and extreme legal formalism combined with informality of the pre-trial proceedings, followed by ritualistic format of the trial. The underlying argument is that Russian justice is a much more complex system than is commonly supposed, and that it both requires and deserves a more nuanced understanding.

MARINA KURKCHIYAN is a Senior Research Fellow at the Centre for Socio-Legal Studies and a Fellow of Wolfson College at the University of Oxford.

AGNIESZKA KUBAL is a Lecturer in Sociology at Department of Social Science, University College London.

CAMBRIDGE STUDIES IN LAW AND SOCIETY

Founded in 1997, Cambridge Studies in Law and Society is a hub for leading scholarship in socio-legal studies. Located at the intersection of law, the humanities, and the social sciences, it publishes empirically innovative and theoretically sophisticated work on law's manifestations in everyday life: from discourses to practices, and from institutions to cultures. The series editors have longstanding expertise in the interdisciplinary study of law, and welcome contributions that place legal phenomena in national, comparative, or international perspective. Series authors come from a range of disciplines, including anthropology, history, law, literature, political science, and sociology.

Series Editors

Mark Fathi Massoud, *University of California, Santa Cruz*

Jens Meierhenrich, *London School of Economics and Political Science*

Rachel E. Stern, *University of California, Berkeley*

A list of books in the series can be found at the back of this book.

A SOCIOLOGY OF JUSTICE IN RUSSIA

Edited by

Marina Kurkchiyan
University of Oxford

Agnieszka Kubal
University College London

CAMBRIDGE
UNIVERSITY PRESS

University Printing House, Cambridge CB2 8BS, United Kingdom

One Liberty Plaza, 20th Floor, New York, NY 10006, USA

477 Williamstown Road, Port Melbourne, VIC 3207, Australia

314-321, 3rd Floor, Plot 3, Splendor Forum, Jasola District Centre, New Delhi - 110025, India

79 Anson Road, #06-04/06, Singapore 079906

Cambridge University Press is part of the University of Cambridge.

It furthers the University's mission by disseminating knowledge in the pursuit of education, learning and research at the highest international levels of excellence.

www.cambridge.org
Information on this title: www.cambridge.org/9781316648285
DOI: 10.1017/9781108182713

© Cambridge University Press 2018

This publication is in copyright. Subject to statutory exception and to the provisions of relevant collective licensing agreements, no reproduction of any part may take place without the written permission of Cambridge University Press.

First published 2018
First paperback edition 2019

A catalogue record for this publication is available from the British Library

Library of Congress Cataloging in Publication data
Names: Kurkchiyan, Marina, 1954– editor. | Kubal, Agnieszka, 1983– editor.
Title: A sociology of justice in Russia / edited by Marina Kurkchiyan, University of Oxford; Agnieszka Kubal, University College London.
Description: Cambridge, United Kingdom ; New York, NY, USA : Cambridge University Press, 2018. | Series: Cambridge studies in law and society
Identifiers: LCCN 2018009839 | ISBN 9781107198777 (hardback) | ISBN 9781316648285 (paperback)
Subjects: LCSH: Justice, Administration of–Social aspects–Russia (Federation)
Classification: LCC KLB1572 .S66 2018 | DDC 340/.1140947–dc23
LC record available at https://lccn.loc.gov/2018009839

ISBN 978-1-107-19877-7 Hardback
ISBN 978-1-316-64828-5 Paperback

Cambridge University Press has no responsibility for the persistence or accuracy of URLs for external or third-party internet websites referred to in this publication, and does not guarantee that any content on such websites is, or will remain, accurate or appropriate.

*To Michael and Ashish
with thanks*

CONTENTS

List of Figures	page ix
List of Tables	x
List of Contributors	xi
Acknowledgements	xii

1 Introduction: Exploring the Diversity of Experiences of Justice in Russia   1
MARINA KURKCHIYAN AND AGNIESZKA KUBAL

2 The Professionalisation of Law in the Context of the Russian Legal Tradition   12
MARINA KURKCHIYAN

3 To Go to Court or Not? The Evolution of Disputes in Russia   40
KATHRYN HENDLEY

4 The Everyday Experiences of Russian Citizens in Justice of the Peace Courts   68
VARVARA ANDRIANOVA

5 In Search of Justice: Migrants' Experiences of Appeal in the Moscow City Court   92
AGNIESZKA KUBAL

6 When Business Goes to Court: Arbitrazh Courts in Russia   118
TIMUR BOCHAROV AND KIRILL TITAEV

7 Journalists, Judges and State Officials: How Russian Courts Adjudicate Defamation Lawsuits against the Media   141
MARIA POPOVA

8 Accusatorial Bias in Russian Criminal Justice   170
PETER H. SOLOMON, JR

CONTENTS

9   Decision-Making in the Russian Criminal Justice
    System: Investigators, Procurators, Judges and
    Human Trafficking Cases   205
    LAUREN A. MCCARTHY

10 The Richelieu Effect: The Khodorkovsky Case and
    Political Interference with Justice   231
    JEFFREY KAHN

11 Administerial Justice: Concluding Remarks on the
    Russian Legal Tradition   259
    MARINA KURKCHIYAN AND AGNIESZKA KUBAL

Index   278

FIGURES

4.1	Comparison of civil, criminal and administrative cases heard in Courts of Justices of the Peace from 2005 to 2014	page 72
4.2	Categories of cases – according to the parties involved – decided in Russian Courts of Justices of the Peace from 2007 to 2014	73
5.1	Immigration law cases in District Courts in Russia, 2007–2016	98
6.1	The current structure of Arbitrazh courts in Russia	120
7.1	Number of civil defamation cases in Russia, 1997–2015	144
7.2	Plaintiff success rate, 1997–2011 (in %)	155
7.3	Share of municipal officials among plaintiffs (in %)	156
7.4	Share of regional officials among plaintiffs (in %)	157
7.5	Share of federal officials among plaintiffs (in %)	157
7.6	Share of *siloviki* among plaintiffs (in %)	157
7.7	Share of *byudzhetniki* among plaintiffs (in %)	158
7.8	Median Compensation Award (in rubles), 1997–2011	160
7.9	Median Moral Compensation Award (in rubles)	160
7.10	Predicted probability of victory in court by plaintiff group (%)	164

TABLES

6.1	The outcome of administrative cases in the Arbitrazh courts (%) from 2007–2011	page 129
7.1	Regions represented in the sample by percentage and number of cases	154
7.2	Moral compensation awards by plaintiff group	161
7.3	Logit coefficients for the probability of success in court by plaintiff group, 1998–2011	163
7.4	Logit coefficients for the probability of success in court by plaintiff group, 1998–2011	166
7.5	FGLS coefficients for size of moral compensation award by plaintiff group, 1996–2011	167
9.1	Human trafficking (Article 127.1) definition as of 2003	209
9.2	The use of slave labour (Article 127.2)	210

CONTRIBUTORS

Varvara Andrianova
Centre for Socio-Legal Studies, University of Oxford

Timur Bocharov
Institute for the Rule of Law, European University at St Petersburg

Kathryn Hendley
Law School, University of Wisconsin

Jeffrey Kahn
Law School, Southern Methodist University

Agnieszka Kubal
Department of Social Science, University College London

Marina Kurkchiyan
Centre for Socio-Legal Studies, University of Oxford

Lauren A. McCarthy
Department of Political Science, University of Massachusetts Amherst

Maria Popova
Department of Political Science, McGill University

Peter H. Solomon, Jr
Munk School of Global Affairs, University of Toronto

Kirill Titaev
Institute for the Rule of Law, European University at St Petersburg

ACKNOWLEDGEMENTS

We would like to thank the Foundation for Law, Justice and Society, with special appreciation for the contribution of its chairman, John Adams, who has been generous in his sponsorship of our research. His continued interest in and support of the work carried out at the Centre for Socio-Legal Studies in Oxford provided the opportunity for years of study of Russian law and society. In many ways this book emerged from a set of workshops supported by the Foundation. Our appreciation goes to all our contributors for their excellent contributions, their forbearance in the face of occasionally stern editing, and their collegiality, especially during the trips that they were asked to make to Oxford while we were developing the book and its themes. During the final stages we had the privilege of experiencing the high professionalism of the Cambridge University Press production team. They have brought the book to life with their combination of courteous and insightful suggestions for improvement, along with an impressive efficiency and scrupulous adherence to deadlines. Our gratitude goes to all of them.

CHAPTER ONE

INTRODUCTION
Exploring the Diversity of Experiences of Justice in Russia

Marina Kurkchiyan and Agnieszka Kubal

Much of the academic literature, analytical reports and media commentary suggest that the justice system in Russia is unreliable, corrupt and therefore ineffective (Freeland 2000; Pastukhov 2002; Solomon 2005; Transparency International 2007). Scholars and practitioners alike stress the numerous dysfunctionalities of the Russian justice system. They say it does not provide equal access to justice, it does not treat its litigants fairly, its enforcement of rights and obligations is erratic and it suffers from what some scholars describe as 'telephone law' (Ledeneva 2008; Sakwa 2009). The judiciary is deemed to be dependent on the state and is often thought to be pressured to deliver specified outcomes (Kononenko and Moshes 2011; Ledeneva 2008; Pastukhov 2002). The legal culture in Russia is described as being afflicted by legal nihilism, leading many citizens to avoid the law altogether if they can. Some cases – Yukos, Pussy Riot, the Greenpeace 'piracy' in the Arctic – have become so notorious that people tend to regard them as typical of the entire system. Most recently, Russia's treatment of NGOs and refugees, and its military advances in the international arena, notably the annexation of Crimea and involvement in the civil war in Eastern Ukraine, have led many observers to seriously question the country's commitment to both international law and the principles of human rights.

However, perhaps the full picture is not as discouraging. In this book we want to move beyond the stereotypes and ideological preconceptions. The scholarship presented here is intended to overcome the tendency to exaggerate the image of the Russian justice system as a flawed, homogenised monolith that imposes inadequate adjudication upon an ill-served populace.

We position this volume against a backdrop of empirical research that brings to light a more nuanced picture of how the legal system in Russia works for the vast majority of ordinary people. Evidence-based analysis of Russian justice shows that it is highly misleading to generalise about it. The politicised cases, with their high stakes and well-known defendants, are not typical. And it is questionable whether 'telephone law' assumptions are relevant to ordinary cases that have no political implications. One might wonder, if the justice system is really so unreliable, why does each year see more and more people actually going to court and voluntarily using the law to solve their disputes.

We are not suggesting that the legal system in Russia is free of corruption, and we acknowledge that it is certainly problematic in several other ways. But in this book we argue that Russian justice is a much more multifaceted system than is commonly supposed, and it both requires and deserves a more in-depth understanding. In our attempt to arrive at such an understanding, we have posed more subtle questions than are usually discussed. In what circumstances do distortions take place? What is distinctive about the social context of a particular case? What are the accepted rules of the game in a particular part of the legal system? How do ordinary Russian citizens feel about lawyers, courts and judges? These issues have long awaited proper academic scrutiny and discussion that draws on accurate information. This book is a step in that direction, and we hope that it is a significant step.

To help us in this pursuit we have invited a number of scholars who have studied Russia first-hand, through extensive field research. The intention was to map out the delivery of justice at every level of the Russian court system in order to assemble an empirical base from which to infer common characteristics of the Russian delivery of justice. In doing so, our volume identifies a number of tensions in the everyday life experiences of justice that illuminate some of the not at all obvious layers of what law means and how it works in Russia. These findings are summarised in the concluding chapter. For instance, the cases we report on show the culture of extreme formalism, found both in the literal-minded interpretation of statute law and in the way that officials and courts alike rely heavily on written documents, and the informality that is at the same time a legitimate part of the legal procedure in at least the low level courts where most of the cases are initiated. There is a mismatch between what people expect of their judges and the role that those judges feel they have to play in the overall delivery of justice.

Within a system that lacks uniformity and clearly defined boundaries, it is hardly surprising that people tend to become convinced that others around them are breaking the law with impunity, or at least getting around it somehow. However, such perceptions do not necessarily stem from an actual disrespect for law and legality. An excessively high expectation of what can be achieved by the letter of the law can also contribute to the legal cynicism that is widespread in Russian society. For example, if a judge exercises discretion his action can easily be misinterpreted as corruption. The public is then likely to suspect that the victorious party has either 'bought the judge' directly or drawn upon a network of connections and mutual favours of some non-monetary kind.

The evidence-based accounts presented in this book also aim to go beyond the commonly applied rule of law logic. Typically that logic measures Russia against a Western standard and finds that it falls short. Our viewpoint is that the Russian legal tradition should be judged on its own terms, a viewpoint that is commonly unheeded because Russia's historical development has been so jerky and turbulent. Every period of Russian history has been marked by drastic social change, often indeed by a full-scale revolutionary transition with a pronounced intention to break away from the dominant traits of whatever has come before. In such an environment of conflicting legacies it is admittedly quite difficult to arrive at a clear picture of any coherent legal tradition. Our contributors have treated that difficulty as both a challenge and an opportunity. Our ambition has been to appreciate not only the radical changes but also the deep-lying continuities in Russia's history. An in-depth empirical focus has enabled us to embrace this patchy legal tradition, and to see it as a source of legacies, recurring traits and nuances that are too often brushed aside by scholars. Where others may see mere idiosyncrasy, we see a unique legal culture that is significant and complete in itself. Empirical research on the ground in contemporary Russian society has compiled a stock of knowledge that transcends the normative assessment typical of the rule of law approach and replaces it with an evaluation of legal processes that takes full consideration of the Russian legal context.

To study Russia from within in this way does not mean that we avoid comparisons with the legal practices of other jurisdictions. Throughout its entire history, Russia has borrowed legal institutions extensively from the Roman law tradition, making it a close relative of the family. In fact, the similarities are so pronounced that they distract attention from the unique features of the Russian tradition. However, the comparisons in this book do not use the language of evaluation, and we are not interested in the degree of Russia's adherence to the Western rule of law yardstick. Our concern is to capture the everyday reality of Russian life, with all its instinctual practices and subtleties. This non-normative comparative perspective helps us to avoid yet another pitfall in Russian studies – the epistemological 'dead end' of Russian exceptionalism – in other words, orientalising Russia, seeing it as dark, secretive and corrupt. Instead, a meaningful, evidence-based and impartial comparison enables the argument put forward in this book to avoid extreme positions. Where international similarities and differences are noted and discussed, the authors also question where they come from, why they occur and with what consequences.

Methodologically, the book presents a series of case studies which are selected systematically, allowing the contributors to consider examples from almost the entire hierarchy of the Russian structure of courts. The studies range from the courts of the Justices of the Peace upward to the appeal courts and the Arbitrazh courts. Between them the authors examine a wide variety of cases: from petty claims such as a mundane civil dispute with little of value at stake, up to major commercial confrontations involving giant corporations and vast sums of money. Some cases are administratively or criminally significant and affect the entire lives of those involved. Others are highly politicised and are decided by different rules from the rest of the institution of justice. The intention here is to give a 'thick' (Geertz 1975), thoroughly researched description of each case procedure, rather than to opt for broad generalisations about the outcomes of whole classes of cases.

To collect their primary source material, the contributors have drawn upon a mixture of quantitative and qualitative methods. Typically these include first-hand observations of court proceedings followed by interviews with the judge, litigants, witnesses and legal professionals; focus group discussions bringing together cross-sections of the general public; and statistical analyses of large data sets. The interviews were in depth, digging beyond the straightforward evidence and legal argumentation of a case, to inquire into the background of the problem at issue and the various assumptions and expectations on the part of those involved in the case. This approach has the advantage of reaching outside the courtroom and gaining some insights into the ways in which all parties involved in the process experience law. The rich and insightful array of individual contributions explores ideas about the various relationships that the actors hold vis-à-vis the different levels of the justice system hierarchy. These insights allow the editors to go beyond particular cases and tease out regularities that are common throughout the Russian institution of justice.

The volume starts with two chapters that look at the broader legal environment and experiences of justice in everyday life. In Chapter 2, Marina Kurkchiyan poses questions pertinent to the core purpose of *A Sociology of Justice in Russia* by examining the importance of the transformation of 'lay' law into a professionalised and autonomous legal space, and the implications that semi-professionalised conception of law has on the Russian legal culture. Kurkchiyan traces the evolution of the legal profession through the major stages of Russian history, before concentrating on the organisational form and identity of the legal profession today. She asks a number of crucial questions: What does the legal profession in contemporary Russia look like? How do its members operate? What kind of identity have they developed? What interests do they prioritise? What is the informal code of conduct within the profession that the members accept in their mutual dealings? What is the current trend in the professionalisation of law in Russia? This case study is based on historical sources in combination with original data that the author has collected over a number of years.

In Chapter 3, Kathryn Hendley focuses on the ideas that lay people hold about the access that is available to them to redress their grievances in her analysis of the handling of disputes in contemporary Russia. She asks why, when and under what circumstances people go to court in Russia. Her answer to that question is based on discussions with ordinary Russians during a series of focus groups conducted in 2014 in Moscow, Voronezh and Novosibirsk. The consensus that arises from this case study is that Russian people, just like those in other jurisdictions, see litigation as a last-ditch alternative. However, the participants' reluctance to go to court was not due to fears of potential external interference or corruption. Instead, they worried about the time and emotional energy required to see a lawsuit through to its conclusion. There was agreement among the participants in the focus groups that if informal negotiations failed, then litigation was a viable option. These results are generally consistent with the findings of legal sociologists in other countries, suggesting that the rhetoric about the dysfunction of Russian courts is overblown, at least for mundane civil cases.

Each of the subsequent chapters focuses on a different level of the pyramid of the justice system and each provides an intensive study of a specific case that is typical of that level. The lowest level court in Russia is the Court of Justices of the Peace. This is where Varvara Andrianova (Chapter 4) situates her inquiry into the experiences of justice by ordinary Russian citizens. Courts of Justices of the Peace are the local institutions of justice that deal with more than 90 per cent of all cases initiated in Russia. As the lowest and most accessible layer of courts in the country, these courts hear the majority of small civil, criminal and administrative cases. Such issues are deemed not to require legal assistance, which puts the pressure of dealing with the legal process solely on the court-users and judges. An examination of how court-users work through the maze created by these courts sheds light on the nature of the relationship between citizens and state institutions in Russia.

Andrianova's findings indicate a number of factors that contribute to creating particular experiences for Russian citizens who petition the lower courts. The first distinctive feature is the availability of direct access to judges during pre-trial sessions. These informal, non-recorded sessions give claimants an opportunity to assess the strength of their case and, even more importantly, to evaluate the judge's opinion of it. Numerous pre-trial sessions lead to most cases being decided before the hearings. As a result, the subsequent public hearings become mere formalities for the announcement of decisions, while in practice court-users' ability to participate in the legal process is limited to the pre-trial sessions and informal conversations with the judges. Andrianova's examination of people's experience of the Courts of Justices of the Peace reveals fully legitimate, relaxed procedural standards at the pre-trial stage and the lack of barriers between court-users and decision-makers. These features contribute to existing images of the favouritism and corruption attached to Russian state institutions, which in turn reflects a deeply rooted and pervasive attitude of distrust in the delivery of justice.

The next case study, by Agnieszka Kubal (Chapter 5), moves up a level in the Russian justice system hierarchy and focuses on the courts of general jurisdiction at district and regional levels. This first-hand empirical, ethnographically informed study looks at a specific type of legal case, the immigration law case. Russia is the third largest destination for migrants globally (after the United States and Germany) and with this chapter, Kubal contributes to a more complex picture of how law works in practice in Russia and how it is experienced by Central Asian migrants within the courtroom setting. This in-depth examination and analysis serves to open up a broader question: What do immigrant experiences tell us about the Russian justice system?

Kubal's findings indicate that the great majority of these immigration cases are adjudicated according to the so-called case file model, wherein the judges arrive at their decisions on the basis of the written evidence presented to them by civil servants. They do not seek to build up a full picture of the facts of the case, for example, by questioning the defendant about the circumstances and listening to his or her version of the relevant events. The written evidence produced by the Federal Migration Service seems to be unquestionable. It consists of material such as photographs of people working on a construction site, protocols from immigration raids and elaborate affidavits signed by the defendants, all of which appears to make these cases technically and legally simple to adjudicate. Through the prism of the immigration law cases, Kubal analyses the mechanisms of decision-making in Russian courts and investigates the potential new role of Russian judges as immigration law enforcers. Furthermore, these cases contribute to our understanding of how, in a situation where the law is not clearly determined and open to discretionary application, factors such as ethnicity and migrant status complicate a person's experiences of the justice system.

With the next case study we leave the different levels of the courts of general jurisdiction and turn to a specific kind of dispute in Russia, the commercial dispute in an Arbitrazh Court. In contrast to the popular understanding that the Arbitrazh Court system involves mainly commercial disputes where 'big money' is at stake, Timur Bocharov and Kirill Titaev (Chapter 6) also discuss the various types of disputes that fall under the jurisdiction of the Arbitrazh Court. Their mixed-methods analysis, combining qualitative with quantitative sources, demonstrates that the largest group of cases in the Arbitrazh courts is made up of mundane disputes in which the authority of the court is used to sort out petty contractual disagreements or simply produce documentation for administrative records.

What emerges from the analysis of the Arbitrazh courts in Russia is that the system enjoys a significantly high level of independence with no obvious evidence of corruption. These courts are relatively well developed in comparison with other branches of the Russian legal system; they attract the most qualified professional resources available in the country, and they make good use of advanced technology. Yet, the direction of the future development of Arbitrazh courts is far from being certain.

The next case study, by Maria Popova (Chapter 7), remains within the broad area of civil cases but narrows its focus to the particular issue of judicial independence in the context of defamation complaints against the media. Popova uses an original longitudinal data set containing close to 2,000 civil defamation complaints against media outlets that were adjudicated by Russian courts from the majority of Russian federal regions between 1997 and 2011. This rich data set allows her to investigate whether the various types of plaintiffs have different probabilities of winning in court. Do politicians win more often than ordinary plaintiffs? If political office does help, are regional or federal incumbents the more privileged in court? The analysis takes into consideration the significant changes in the media environment that occurred during the period being studied, as well as relevant innovations in both legislation and judicial practice.

Popova's findings contribute to the already nuanced picture of Russian civil justice. On the one hand, the data suggest that defamation cases are not foregone conclusions and that the likelihood of victory is not predetermined by external interference. Political affiliation, Popova argues, is not a significant factor determining the outcome of defamation cases. The plaintiff success rate in Russia has declined over time from about 75 per cent to around 50 per cent, bringing the ratio in line with the probability of success in the American context. On the other hand, scrupulous analysis does indicate that the judgments are not free from bias and that what is often referred to as 'administrative resources' do interfere with the legal process. This scrutiny of selected cases does tell us about the nuances of the Russian legal procedure, such as an extreme formalism and the tendencies to avoid using discretion among judiciary. Also, the absence of 'public interest' arguments in defamation disputes makes it problematic to strike a reasonable balance between the protection of dignity and the freedom of the press.

The following two chapters, by Peter H. Solomon and Lauren A. McCarthy, deal with the types of relationships discernible to a socio-legal scholar studying criminal justice in Russia. Peter H. Solomon's analysis (Chapter 8) focuses on the accusatory bias that is embedded, arguably, in the Russian criminal justice system. Historically, both the

Soviet Union and post-Soviet Russia had extremely low rates of acquittal in criminal cases, a pattern that conventional wisdom associates with an accusatorial bias. However, when we extend the initial viewpoint and adopt a broader comparative perspective, we find that other countries like Canada, Germany, the Netherlands and France also have low rates of acquittal. This comparison suggests that this indicator alone cannot be used as evidence of a predisposition of the Russian judiciary to convict the defendant. Therefore, Solomon argues, in order to test whether Russian criminal justice does indeed suffer from accusatory bias, one has to examine the absence or presence of pre-trial screening, dispositions imposed by prosecutors such as the withdrawal of charges, or some other diversion.

After a brief history of the low acquittal rate in Russia, Solomon examines the use of prosecutorial discretion to screen cases before trial in Germany and other Western countries, especially through the exercise of quasi-judicial functions by prosecutors. These practices are juxtaposed against the absence of significant pre-trial filtering of cases and allows him to explore their implications for understanding the statistics of the outcomes of criminal cases in Russia. The analysis highlights the impact of new measures to avoid full trials (reconciliation and plea arrangements), as well as the continuing weakness of judges in Russia, the nature of the role of investigators and the absence of meaningful changes in criminal procedure.

Lauren A. McCarthy's case study (Chapter 9) focuses on a unique type of case resulting from a significant legislative change: the introduction of human trafficking laws into the Russian Criminal Code in 2003. She uses evidence from court documents in over 100 cases of human trafficking to explore how decision-making processes play out in reality when judges are provided with space for a novel approach. In effect they are invited to adopt 'outside the box' interpretations of the new legal concepts and determine how to apply them. McCarthy's study traces how the criminal system responds when judges and prosecutors find themselves on untested ground. She argues that over time the system tends to move away from a bold and novel approach towards a conservative 'safety zone', where trafficking crimes are defined in such a way that well-established and tested laws can apply. She explains this trend as a concern of both judges and prosecutors, to avoid having their judgments overturned on appeal because that would reflect unfavourably on their careers. However, as McCarthy points out, such a tendency is not unique to the Russian justice system. In almost all Western jurisdictions, cautious approaches towards new laws, in particular trafficking laws, are often the norm. Nor is Russia unique in the use of quantitative indicators to assess the performance of legal actors. But it certainly is true that the Russian mindset of legal positivism exacerbates the practice.

The last case study uses a backdrop of ordinary, everyday cases to highlight the high-profile cases that the Russian legal system is so infamous for: cases in which politics may and indeed does interfere with justice. Jeffrey Kahn (Chapter 10) follows the case of Mikhail Khodorkovsky, one of Russia's wealthiest citizens, who was first arrested for various 'economic crimes' in October 2003. Many observers believe that his fall from grace was meant only to warn his fellow oligarchs that their Yeltsin-era wealth would remain safe only as long as they stayed out of politics. Khodorkovsky paid the price for breaching that understanding. Under that interpretation, his fate was perhaps unjust, but it is not broadly replicable. However, the very fact that the justice system can be manipulated by politicians to achieve predetermined outcomes necessarily generates a 'Richelieu effect', as Kahn terms it. This effect occurs when political pressure corrupts and weakens the internal 'checks and balances' mechanism of the system, while nevertheless doing so under a veneer of formal legality. To make his argument, Kahn places under microscopic analysis the final verdict read out by the judge at the Khodorkovsky trial, testing it against the principle of the right to a reasonable judgment. Kahn's perspective on the matter is unique, having been directly involved in drafting a report that was ultimately delivered to President Dimitry Medvedev, arguing for the annulment of Khodorkovsky's second conviction.

The concluding chapter (Chapter 11) highlights the main themes that emerge from the empirical studies included in this volume. It adopts a bottom-up approach, concentrating on the underlying themes that guide the discussion in each chapter. This technique allows the editors to go beyond familiar arguments such as the culture of autocracy or the impact of the post-Soviet transition in describing the characteristics of Russian legal culture. The main contribution that links this book's accounts of the different corners and contexts of the Russian justice system is the emergence of a specific and unique model of justice delivery, which we dub 'the administerial model of justice'.

References

Freeland, C. (2000) *Sale of the Century: Russia's Wild Ride from Communism to Capitalism*. New York: Crown Publishers.

Geertz, C. (1975) *Interpretations of Culture*. Oxford: Oxford University Press.

Kononenko, V. and Moshes, A. (2011) *Russia as a Network State: What Works in Russia When State Institutions Do Not?* Basingstoke: Palgrave Macmillan.

Ledeneva, A. (2008) 'Telephone justice in Russia', *Post-Soviet Affairs*, 24(4): 324–350.

Pastukhov, V. (2002) 'Law under administrative pressure in post-Soviet Russia', *East European Constitutional Review*, 11(3): 66–74.

Sakwa, R. (2009) *The Quality of Freedom: Khodorkovsky, Putin, and the Yukos Affair*. Oxford: Oxford University Press, 185–206.

Solomon, P. (2005) 'Informal practices in Russian governance: courts and law enforcement'. Paper given at the conference Europe – Our Common Home? Berlin: ICEEES VII World Congress, 25–30 July.

Transparency International (2007) *Global Corruption Report 2007: Corruption in Judicial Systems*. New York: Cambridge University Press.

CHAPTER TWO

THE PROFESSIONALISATION OF LAW IN THE CONTEXT OF THE RUSSIAN LEGAL TRADITION

Marina Kurkchiyan

When legal historians describe families of legal traditions, it is routinely assumed that Russian law belongs to the Roman law group. However, it has also been acknowledged that Russian law has atypical characteristics (Berman 1963: 187). The Russian legal tradition differs from core Roman law in a number of ways, one of which is the remarkably late and still only partial professionalisation of law in Russia. By the 'professionalisation of law' I mean the abstraction of law into a distinct social sphere, with lawyers demarcating their jurisdiction and being in exclusive control of legal affairs. 'Professionalised law' refers to a specific legal culture that has grown out of a culture of 'lay law' or, to use Bourdieu's terminology, a 'vulgar vision' of law (Bourdieu 1987: 828). It is a far-reaching social effect of the emergence of the legal profession as an organised group with protected group boundaries, a shared common identity and a set of socially orientated goals (Abel and Lewis 1989). Such professionalisation is fundamental to the Roman law tradition.

In Western Europe, legal actors organised themselves in the early Middle Ages into corporate groups with a monopoly over studying, interpreting, developing and applying law. These legal professionals cultivated what Friedman calls an 'internal legal culture' (Friedman 1975: 194). Ordinary citizens came to rely on the professionals to make sense of their cases, to format them into files that were legally sound and to help them to find their way through the labyrinths of the law's technical language, elaborate procedures and distinctive way of reasoning.

Meanwhile, the Russian legal tradition followed quite a different trajectory. It will help if we first place the issue of the professionalisation of law in Russia on a broader historical canvas. An appreciation of how law evolved in Russia can contribute to the understanding of what law is and how it is seen and used by legal actors and the public alike. This will enable us to strike the right balance in our assessment of the current state of Russia and to go beyond the common tendency to judge the performance of the Russian legal system only by contrasting it to the 'rule of law' culture, which is arguably a distinct outcome of the professionalisation of law in the Western legal tradition. In making such an analysis, it becomes apparent that the process of professional institution-building in Russia is still a work in progress and at an early stage.

This does not mean that Russia does not have properly qualified lawyers or that Russians do not know how to deal with the law professionally; far from it. Many of the practising lawyers and judges in Russia are at least as skilled and knowledgeable as their Western colleagues. Even so, while knowing how to put law into action is a necessary condition for the construction of a professionalised legal sphere, it is not sufficient. To transform law from being a 'lay' social phenomenon into a professionalised institution, it is first necessary for legal actors to be consolidated into independent groups, with gatekeeping rules, internal procedures and a distinct identity.

In this chapter, I trace the numerous twists and turns in the evolution of the legal profession through the major stages of Russian history before concentrating on the organisational form and identity of the legal profession today. I base some of the analysis on secondary historical sources while using original data that I have collected in Russia in recent years to underpin the main points.

LAWYERS IN THE CONTEXT OF THE ROMAN LEGAL TRADITION

In his examination of the foundation and growth of the Roman law tradition from antiquity onward, Fries (1985: 272) tells us about the early emergence of a group of people, the jurists,

> who began to study and manipulate the materials of private law in a disciplined fashion. They articulated and organised existing legal rules, they identified and described the systematic boundaries and internal

articulation of private law, they deduced fundamental principles and concepts of law, and they applied these principles and concepts in the coherent development of new rules and institutions.

The effect was that, by the time the Roman Empire reached its height, law had been transformed into a self-consciously autonomous field of study and activity.

With the decline of the Roman imperial structure the lawyers suffered, too, and Europe experienced several centuries of 'law without lawyers' (Brundage 2008:1). Yet, the established Roman concepts of what law is, how it should be dealt with and, most importantly, by whom, persisted and slowly spread across medieval Europe. Reinforced by the traditions and texts preserved and taught in the leading universities of Bologna, Paris, Oxford, Valencia and elsewhere, the Roman tradition of law in Western Europe gradually came back and shaped itself, between the eleventh and thirteenth centuries, into a distinct institution with a strong identity. Brundage tells us that, around the year 1150, only a scattering of jurists were teaching Roman law in a small number of cities but, by 1250, professional lawyers had set up offices in almost all European cities and some smaller towns as well, offering specialised advice across the range of legal matters (Brundage 2008). Within this overall pattern, a variety of ways to organise the internal structure of the profession emerged, reflecting local contexts across the societies of Western Europe and bringing together members of the various specialities – such as advocates, solicitors, barristers, notaries, coroners, proctors, judges and so forth. Over time, some of these organisations have been transformed and others have disappeared, while new ones have emerged to fit the conditions prevailing at different periods of history (Abel 1988). Rules and regulations, formal and informal, were introduced to govern professional behaviour by means of the relevant corporate organisations. Reynolds argues that the shift from unprofessional to professional law that began in much of Europe during what she describes as the 'long twelfth century' constitutes a major turning point in legal history (Reynolds 2003: 348).

Different forms of association became fixtures of the legal landscape across the continent from the twelfth and thirteenth centuries onwards, gate-keeping entry into the profession and policing their monopoly over the legal domain. To join the group, one had to go through specified rites of passage, such as extensive formal education in law, examination, pupillage or apprenticeship. It is mostly due to this development that, in Western Europe, law grew to become a highly sophisticated institution. It is, to a large extent, its early professionalisation that eventually elevated law to the status it has today, where it is recognised as the central force in organised society, wielding unquestioned legitimacy in its power to structure social relationships. It is difficult to imagine the emergence of a 'rule of law' culture without law having first been spun into a distinct and specialised domain.

LAW WITHOUT LAWYERS: A LONGSTANDING RUSSIAN LEGAL TRADITION

In this respect, the contrast between the Western and the Russian legal tradition is sharp. One could argue that to be 'a lawyer' as a defined social role was not known in pre-modern Russia at all. It was alleged that, during his visit to England in 1698, Peter the Great noticed a group of people in the courtroom he was visiting and asked who those people were and why they were there in such big numbers. When he was told that they were lawyers, he proclaimed in astonishment: 'What are they there for? In my entire kingdom there are only two lawyers, and I am thinking of hanging one of them when I get back' (Troitsky 2000: 27).

It has to be stressed that the absence of a legal profession does not imply that law has not played an important role in Russia. Its use for constitutional arrangements and as a 'lay' instrument for dispute resolution has been evident throughout the country's history and sometimes in pure Roman law form. In approximately the same historical period in which Roman law was experiencing its renaissance in Europe, its influence could be seen in Kiev Rus' (as early medieval Russia was commonly referred to) during the tenth, eleventh and twelfth centuries. However, the channels, the drives and the forms of the transfers were specific to the local circumstances. The main contexts in which Russians were exposed to the principles of Roman law were their conversion to Christianity in the tenth century and their ongoing trade relationships with neighbouring Byzantium.

The earliest legal texts in Russia hint at the impact Roman law had in Russia. The texts appeared in the tenth century in the form of treaties between Rus' and Byzantium, dated 911, 944 and 971 respectively. The treaties carry a strong imprint of the Byzantine style of legislation and the original documents were written in Greek. The agreed view of them among historians is that the Russian side appears to be a reactive partner who was complying with the Byzantine practises of document-writing and record-keeping (Franklin 2002: 90). One could argue that this early experience of treaty-making later developed into a power-sharing medium within the polity, effectively using it as a constitutional device. Among the examples of this practice were charters defining the jurisdiction and status of the Church, provision for merchants and their entitlements, outlines of the rights and obligations of the Princes of Novgorod, treaties between princes about who would rule where and charters defining the powers of the Grand Prince's judges. It could be argued that this line of influence seeded the Russian interpretation of the role of law in the centuries that followed. Treaties came to be seen as a legal tool in the hands of the rulers, to be used for the purposes of making deals, sealing agreements and setting institutional boundaries.

The more significant import of Roman law texts into Rus' was through the Church of Rus', which was originally set up as a branch of the Patriarchate of Constantinople. While introducing Christianity into Kiev Rus', Greek clergymen brought Byzantine canon law with them. The early Christian texts were in the Greek language and thus unintelligible for ordinary people, who continued to be excluded when the documents were later translated into Church Slavonic and thus forced to rely on the priesthood. Referring to this as the root of the legal borrowing in Russia, Berman (1963: 188) suggests that Russia and the West shared the same language of Roman law from the start. However, law, as he reminded us, is much more than just a language. It also expresses values, practises, institutional principles and the accumulated experience of the actors who deal with the law (Berman 1963: 190). It is this distinction that throws a revealing spotlight onto the gulf between the two legal traditions. By the sixteenth century, English lawyers were consulting rich collections of books and legal records (Berman 1994; Holt 1992) while, in Europe, Dutch and Austrian legal philosophers were engaged in arguments about the abstract principles of natural law and the concrete practise of positive law (Boucher 2009). At the same stage, Russia only exhibited the very first signs of having a national legal code in the *Sudebnik* of 1551.[1] The foundation of the Russian administrative system of law, together with any meaningful

---

[1] Although the earlier compilation was dated 1497, it was adopted by the Stoglav Assembly in 1551.

discussion about law as an organised institution in the country, can begin only with that code (Butler 2009: 17).

It then took centuries before the Russian legal tradition moved closer to the Western legal system in terms of the institutional framework of delivering justice, a movement that was achieved after extensive legal borrowings from the West. In the seventeenth century, the transformative reforms of Peter the Great began the process when he 'cut a window through to the West' (Pushkin 1998, translated by Dewey). The Petrian reforms consisted of new legal institutions, lawmaking, law enforcement and even vocabulary, such as the words 'jurist' and 'jurisprudentsia' (jurisprudence), introduced in a manner that was intended to squeeze out 'the old way' of doing things. They exposed the Russian intellectual elite to new ideas of the running of social affairs. Among a new but still small cadre of Westernised Russian thinkers, awareness of the need for educated lawyers became a recognised social necessity.

Despite the growing demand for a professional representation of the interest of the people, all of the succession of Russian sovereigns who followed Peter remained suspicious of the lawyers. For instance, the Empress Ekaterina II attributed her success in governance to her skill in keeping lawyers at bay and declared, 'As long as I am alive there will be no lawyers and no prosecutors in Russia' (Collection of the Imperial Russian Historical Society 1878: 489, cited in Troitsky 2000).

By the end of the eighteenth century, Ekaterina's negative attitude towards the legal institution was very much in tune with the parallel autocratic regimes in Western Europe. And indeed, all authoritarian regimes have the inclination to keep legal actors under tight control (Solomon, 2010: 352). Governments in Western countries, however, had no option but to negotiate with professionally organised legal structures that had been there for centuries whereas, in Russia, rulers had no such problem and could enjoy the exercise of unrestricted power (Wortman 1976: 9).

By the mid-nineteenth century, Russia could still be accurately depicted as a society of 'law without lawyers'. Legal functions were performed by people without professional training and drawn from all corners of society:

> bankrupt nobility, landlords and merchants; among them were clerks, who before that used to run the affairs of their masters; there were retired military personnel and even keepers of taverns and beer shops; there

were bureaucrats who had been dismissed from the service; and others; one cannot name all of them.

(Pomekhin 1900: 2217)

In short, any literate person in need of earning a living could get involved in legal affairs and play a role in the litigation process. The roles themselves were narrowly bounded and no predictable procedure was in place. For instance, in many cases the function of a judge was to prepare a trial record by writing down the materials of investigation and passing the file upwards within the hierarchy. The decision was then made on the basis of that written file (Vas'kovskii 1893: 310). Legal representatives were not expected to appear in court and their role came down to drafting petitions on behalf of claimants.

It has to be said that Russia as a society governed by 'law without lawyers' is not an exception within the global pattern; in fact, the opposite is true. The Western European model of having an independent legal institution that monopolises the interpretation and implementation of law does stand out from the general pattern across the world. Yet, the similarities in form and legal texts between Russian law and Roman law do obscure the manner in which the partial professionalisation of law in Russia came about in non-linear fashion and several centuries late. This peculiar history is of profound importance for the analysis and assessment of today's Russian legal culture. After all, it is acknowledged that the legitimacy of law is not grounded in its intrinsic quality. Arguably law is legitimate because of the existence of a professional legal group that has successfully created a boundary between laypeople and law itself. When law is abstracted from daily life, laypeople tend to deal with law as it is, rather than to question its substance (Fries 1985: 281). This pulling of law out of everyone's reach has never been part of the Russian historical experience.

THE EMERGENCE OF PROFESSIONALISED LAW IN RUSSIA

The move from non-professional to professional law came with the judicial reforms of 1864, when a unified system of justice was introduced, setting up a new court structure and modernised rules for legal proceedings. Although the reforms marked a new stage in the development of the Russian legal institution, the long build-up to the professionalisation of law should be traced back to the Petrian era, when

Russian formal legal education began. In effect, the pattern of the professionalisation of law resembles the process that had taken place in the West some five centuries earlier. The first Russian educational and research establishment, the Academy of Science, was launched in St Petersburg in 1725, followed by Moscow University in 1755, with law as one of its few subjects. However, for years thereafter, only small groups of professors from Germany and France went to teach law in these educational centres, sometimes attracting only a small number of Russian students, and at other times, none at all.

It was only at the end of the eighteenth century that a handful of Russian lawyers, who had travelled to Scotland in order to read law at Glasgow University, came back to take up newly established positions as professors of law at Moscow University (Butler 2009: 28). Thereafter, just as in medieval Europe, domestic legal education produced a small elite who were initially few in number but well connected and vocal, and who shared a real sense of professional identity. To a great extent, it was this group of jurists who later pushed for the significant 1864 reform (Wortman 1976: 237–240).

The Judicial Statute enacted in 1864 established an advocacy bar. The new bar was to be a corporate self-governing body with high entry thresholds and strict rules. Overall, it was constructed in a part-English, part-French image of the legal profession. Membership was open only to those with higher education in law and with not less than five years of apprenticeship in legal practice. In the process of joining, members were required to take an oath that would bind them to a code of conduct (Huskey 1986: 13).

For Russia, this was a dramatic innovation. In a single legislative stroke, it transplanted onto Russian soil an institutional framework that, in other countries, had taken centuries to evolve. It is indicative that the newly professional generation of lawyers created by it repeatedly tried to distance themselves from those who had gone before them. As one prominent advocate stated at the time, 'We have emerged not from that lot, not even from their ashes; we are absolutely new. We do not have any historical links, nothing is inherited by us from the past, and we are proud of that' (Pomekhin 1900: 2220).

Despite a number of attempts to derail the group formation of lawyers by the ruling regime, the bar was able not only to survive in the hostile political environment of the late-nineteenth century but also to expand and build a strong sense of identity and social purpose. The emerging profession played a significant role in the turbulent political life of Russia as the nineteenth century turned into the twentieth (Troitsky 2000: 187–230).

However, the professionals never succeeded in squeezing out their non-professional predecessors in the key role of legal representative. By the end of its half-century of existence, the bar was providing only a small part of the legal services available to the public. The professionals were still forced to operate alongside private advocates, some of them without any formal education despite being licenced by the local courts. Private advocates remained a scrappy group with no professional identity and no organisational structure. Although the balance between sworn advocates and their private competitors was changing quickly, by the end of the Tsarist period, the number of private advocates still remained substantial.[2]

In addition, a significant number of *podpol'nie* (underground) – uncertified legal actors – continued to operate, particularly in small towns and villages. They consulted clients, drew up documents and made representations in the courts. A *podpol'nie* advocate had no difficulty in earning a living. The tranquil operation of lay legal actors across the country could be seen as the result of an insufficient supply of educated lawyers. However, another way to look at it is to acknowledge that there was probably not a high demand for professional services among the population. Overall, the 'lay' consumption of law continued to be a sufficient means of communication between the public, the courts and the bureaucracy at large.

To add to this, customary law remained a substantial part of the legal landscape. It was practised in *Volost'* courts. Set up in 1861 in rural districts to deal with the most common problems among peasants, both civil and criminal, *Volost'* courts were outside of the general court structure and formal written law had little relevance to them (Frierson 1986).

Overall, reflecting on the evolution of Russian legal tradition, it is difficult to overstate the importance of the final fifty years of Tsarist Russia in regard to the professionalisation of law. Knowledge of law was accumulating, legal education was expanding, legal associations were being formed and the overall impact of these three processes was the forming of a profession with a distinct group identity. Yet the would-be

---

[2] Whereas, in 1890, there were twice as many private advocates as sworn ones (3,407 private vs. 1,830 sworn), the ratio was reversed by 1913 (5,658 sworn vs. 2,099 private). See Gernet (1916: 57).

profession's brief period of institutional existence was not nearly long enough for it to monopolise the legal domain, change the public's mentality and construct a new meaning to law. In the society at large, law continued to be seen simply as a 'lay' instrument for sorting out everyday problems.

LAWYERS WITHOUT LAW: THE DE-PROFESSIONALISATION OF LAW IN THE SOVIET ERA

The *Bol'shevik* revolution of 1917 changed, once again, the trajectory of the evolution of the Russian legal domain, tailoring it to an ideologically driven approach to law. During the first two decades of social engineering, the consumption of law shifted back and forth between legal nihilism and extreme legal instrumentalism. Sometimes there was a vision that the newly constructed egalitarian society would have no need for law at all and consequently all activities related to law would die out. At other times, the policy was based on the assumption that law existed in society to advance political goals.

According to the early revolutionary ideology, a communist society was one in which there was no need for lawyers and in which justice would be delivered 'by the people and for the people'. The Revolutionary Decree on the Courts, issued in December 1917, abolished the entire Tsarist legal system – the bar, the procuracy and the courts. A new People's Court was set up, based on the assumption that anyone who was considered to be a man of good standing could deliver justice without the involvement of legally trained people. Legal education was removed from the university curriculum.

This was a big step towards the de-professionalisation of law. However, it should be added that, against the historical background, it was merely a swing back to the vision of law that had endured throughout the entire Russian legal tradition. After all, even in the early twentieth century, the vision of the legal domain as an autonomous institution run by professionals was still far from being established in the country.

However, it turned out that even a relatively weak legal profession could not be eliminated overnight. The Revolutionary Decree was followed by a powerful confrontation between the legal cadres of the old regime and the new authorities. The majority of the members of the old bar, particularly members of the Moscow and Petrograd bars, continued to function as before and ignored the formal ruling.

Meanwhile, the Bolsheviks created alternative institutional structures with the intention of driving the disloyal professionals out of legal practice. They ordered regional Soviets to set up Colleges of Accusers and Defenders, with members regulated by them, and placed them under the supervision of the local People's Courts. The outcome of this undertaking was patchy, to say the least. There was little understanding at the local level of what the new colleges should look like, and there were insufficient resources to make the system work. Huskey comments that, by the start of the Civil War a year after the Communists took power, 'neither the de-professionalization of legal practice nor the subsequence provision for the establishment of colleges of legal representatives succeeded in fundamentally altering the method of delivering legal services to the population' despite drastic changes in the courtroom environment (Huskey 1986: 52).

The outbreak of the Civil War in the autumn of 1918 put an end to the forbearance of the authorities. Security organisations such as the Cheka reduced the already compromised role of the People's courts. The practice of having a legal presence in court proceedings, which was already being brought down to a minimum, was eventually deemed unnecessary. Private legal practice was banned. Many lawyers of the older generation left the country. Those who remained in Russia had to take up whatever source of earnings came their way. A small number of the educated cadres of the former regime continued to practise law in the service of the state, while others went 'underground', earning fees for advising clients in private and drafting legal documents for them unofficially. The organised professional community of around 13,000 educated and practising advocates, which had existed across Russia prior to the revolution, had been reduced to around 650 members who were eking out a precarious living by 1921 (Huskey 1986: 77).

The years of the Civil War and the devastating impact of the 1918–1921 economic policy known as 'War Communism' forced the Bolsheviks to shift to a more market-friendly approach, known as the 'New Economic Policy'. Society was in urgent need of a legal order that could restore the dwindling legitimacy of the government and provide the people with a sense of stability. For the legal sphere it meant relative elevation of the role of the People's courts. Some of the pre-revolutionary institutions such as the Procuracy were relaunched. Local associations of advocates were brought back under the new name of 'Colleges of Defenders'. These bodies were granted a semi-autonomous status and placed under the supervision of the local court, the local Soviet and the Procuracy. A substantial number of lawyers trained in pre-revolutionary Russia were able to get back into legal practice (Jordan 2004: 31–32).

However, this short phase of partial restoration of legitimacy to the legal institution should not be taken as a step towards professionalisation. The reform offered little more than a breathing spell during which the small group of previously trained lawyers could once again earn their living by practising law in a few big cities. They were merely the surviving rump of the pre-revolutionary legal profession, trying to manage in a non-professional legal environment that lacked identifiable shape and predictability. According to Huskey's assessment, almost 90 per cent of court proceedings lacked legal representation, although 'underground' lawyers, particularly in the countryside, did continue to consult and to provide services to the Russian peasantry (Huskey 1986: 17).

The next anti-law wave began in 1928, when the immediate pressure of the economy began to ease and social life was lifted out of misery. Official policy bounced back once more towards intensified class war. The return to revolutionary fundamentalism meant a renewed legal nihilism. Purges were introduced by the security agencies from 1928 onward and implemented with increasing severity against 'anti-Soviet elements of the bourgeoisie who are unable to comprehend soviet morality'. These campaigns were effective in clearing out most of the lawyers who cherished the memory of their former professional identity. By 1933, the eradication of the pre-revolutionary generation was complete and was slowly replaced by a new generation of Soviet-educated lawyers whose professional identity was that of state employees with internalised norms of self-censorship.

This second wave of legal nihilism came to its logical conclusion when the regime reached the stage at which its aggressive social engineering had to be replaced by a self-preservation approach. Scholars of the legal history of the Soviet period viewed the promulgation of the 1936 Constitution as the benchmark of that transition (Berman 1963). In terms of legal ideology, it meant an acknowledgment that law was there to stay, even when society would step into the inevitable communist phase. At this point the Soviet model of Soviet law, legality and the legal profession was established and, with only slight fluctuations, remained in place until the final years of the USSR. It was then inherited by contemporary Russia.[3]

Within this Soviet model, the possession of a legal education became the norm to secure employment in law. Successful completion of the training period entitled the holder to be certified as a 'jurist' and opened the way to salaried state employment in a great variety of law-related jobs. Jurists could become notaries, registrars (handling marriages, estates and so forth), *jurisconsults*,[4] judges, procurators or investigators. According to Soviet statistics, whereas in 1940 there were 20,900 jurists in employment, by 1987 their number had increased to 230,300 (Statistical Annual Report 1988).

Jurists also had the option to take up an advocacy job representing clients in criminal cases and providing legal advice to the population. Given the Soviet context, advocates were granted an anomalous status. Private practice was abolished but the advocates were not strictly state employees either. In this study of the Soviet advokatura, Huskey commented that although it was strikingly small and did not meet Western standards, it was one of the most autonomous institutions in the Soviet Union (Huskey, 1982). Advokats worked in consultancy offices set up under the umbrella of the local colleges of advocates. The colleges were supervised by the regional offices of the Ministry of Justice and also had to negotiate party interference, with the result being that their self-governance was rudimentary. Even so, it was noticeable that some colleges, such as those in Moscow, managed to exhibit more independence than others (Barry and Berman 1968). However, in the Soviet model, the lawyers, as a profession, were more like trained technicians operating the law under the guidance of political authorities. In that sense the Soviet model of the legal profession is a situation in which there are lawyers without jurisdiction over law.

To sum up, prior to the post-Soviet transition, lawyers in all the assorted legal roles, including advocates in pre-revolutionary Russia, had never gained full 'ownership' of their jurisdiction. As Russia moved

---

[3] This is not to say that there were no developments of the legal institution in the Soviet Union. Periodically, legal reforms were initiated and public debates took place. However, the conceptual approach to the status of lawyers in society remained stable.

[4] *Juristconsults*, the largest group of Soviet jurists, were legal advisers employed to serve management as well as employees in almost all sufficiently large institutions. These included major branches of government, productive enterprises and social institutions such as education, health, etc.

into its post-Soviet phase in the 1990s, the legal culture that it brought into the transition was a combination of a deeply rooted ideology of law as a 'non-professional' sector, a historical memory of extensive borrowing of Western forms, plus the Soviet experience of trained legal specialists who distrusted formally organised structures.

There are, therefore, good reasons to argue that, at the start of post-Soviet society, the internal legal culture was Roman in its form but deeply Russian in its substantively normative level of the institution. An understanding of this pattern allows us to appreciate the perspective within which current developments must be assessed. It seems that the interesting question is not why some lawyers continue to move casually between the boundaries of legal and illegal, nor why being a lawyer often means only having a licence for employment rather than belonging to a profession, nor why distrust in the institution of justice is so deep in Russia. The more relevant issues are the direction in which Russian legal culture is now moving and whether there are, as yet, any clear signs of a Western-type professionalisation of law.

POST-SOVIET DEVELOPMENTS IN THE PROFESSIONALISATION OF LAW

As the 1980s turned into the 1990s, the whole Soviet institutional landscape crumbled when the country's trajectory made yet another sharp turn, this time towards marketisation. Making far-reaching changes in the law – in content, procedure and institutions – had been both an objective of the transition and an instrument for achieving it.

A set of reforms was implemented by the new authorities to bring the provision of justice up to the standards expected in any democratic order. The 1992 Law on the Status of Judges established the principle of lifetime appointments for judges, stipulating that a judge could be removed only by a judicial qualification committee. An attempt was made to ensure that judges would be adequately paid from public funds, so that they could function independently – an anticipation that has proved to be difficult to achieve (Kurkchiyan 2007). The direct institutional link between investigators and prosecutors was dismantled to reduce accusatorial bias and the adversarial process was reinstated to strengthen the role of lawyers in the court room (Solomon 2005). A number of commentators have observed that the establishment of an adequate institutional infrastructure has largely been completed (Lewinbuk 2010: 35–7).

On the other hand, shifts in professional, commercial and social relationships triggered new types of conflict, exacerbated minor disputes and increased behavioural deviance. As the transition progressed, the demand for legal services greatly increased. Pushed into finding solutions for this range of novel issues, people at every level became more and more inclined to bring law into play. It is safe to state that the perceived value of law in Russian society has been consistently increasing since the start of the transition (Hendley 2012).

Now that these changes have taken place, it is appropriate to ask what they amount to in terms of the professionalisation of law. With lawyers now multifarious in Russia, what shared meanings, conventions and self-regulated norms of behaviour are emerging among them? At the deepest level of identity within the profession, is a consolidation of professional values now detectable? In other words, is the trajectory of development of the post-Soviet Russian legal tradition turning towards closer integration with the Roman law family, or does the inherited vision of law continue to ensure that Russian law remains at odds with Western culture?

To address these questions I now examine the essential provisions for the professionalisation of law to occur: The competence of legal actors (limited in this chapter to practising lawyers), the growth of their professional identity and their consolidation into a co-operative infrastructure, the *advokatura*. As this is the only organised legal branch I will consider the strength of the informal rules within it and the building and protecting of professional boundaries around it.

Competence
Competence, built up through intensive and extensive education, with care for its quality, is crucial for any professionalised social sphere (Evetts 2011: 26). It is commonly achieved by peers having control over university admissions and by curricula and setting a high threshold for final certification, with various forms of pupillage and post-university training set up and assessed by corporate bodies.

During the Soviet period, university education was already a necessary requirement for employment as a lawyer, albeit tightly homogenised, controlled by the state and overloaded with mandatory ideological subjects such as the History of the Communist Party or Marxist-Leninist Philosophy. The rapid release of market forces into the educational sphere led to an unregulated expansion of the existing law schools and the formation of many more private educational establishments of questionable quality. In the early decades, the number of young people who were studying law increased approximately twentyfold. Many institutions started to offer certificates to whomever was able to afford the fee, without any quality control. This chaotic increase in the number of people who possessed an official certificate to practise law drove down even further a general standard of legal competence that was already uneven and poorly protected. By the early 2000s, although the total number of lawyers exceeded demand to a significant extent, there was a shortage of skilled lawyers in the Russian market. As Hendley and her colleagues noted after studying the lawyers, in the 1990s it was doubtful that law-school graduates were any better than those without any legal education (Hendley et al. 2001). My own interviews with practising lawyers in 2003 confirmed this observation. I was repeatedly told that:

> 'the quality of education fell significantly after the Soviet system was dismantled. Formal education does not mean much nowadays. Everything is based on self-education and practical experience'.
>
> (Moscow, April 2003)

One cannot help but ask why people would pay for a certificate which is not backed by actual knowledge and, furthermore, why anyone would expect to go into practice with it and find clients for their services. I would argue that one answer lies in the vision of law that was still strong in society. People still assumed that law is a straightforward thing, a matter of general knowledge and not of specialised or complex expertise. Laypeople often did not hesitate to discuss and make judgments on any issue of legality. I witnessed this instinct at work on a research project about the institutional transplant of two UK-modelled Press Complaints Committees into two Russian towns, Rostov and Nizhny Novgorod. In both places, the newly set up councils comprising people with non-legal backgrounds intended to resolve disputes informally, using common sense and guided by a code of conduct. Instead, they quickly turned themselves into interpreters of law and issued law-like judgments (Kurkchiyan 2009).

The mentality of ordinary people in treating law as a non-professional, common-sense matter was exemplified by the manager of a middle-sized business firm, interviewed in the mid-2000s:

> I do not need a lawyer in my business. I would not trust his judgment anyway and would still make all the necessary inquiries myself. I can read, which means I can work out what the law says. I do not need lawyers for that.
>
> (Moscow, November 2004)

This ingrained conception of law as a field that can easily be grasped by a non-professional layman formed the environment in which an essentially fake educational certificate could be regarded as legitimate permission to practise.

After the first decade of chaotic legal growth in the 1990s, the government did introduce laws to establish various quality control mechanisms such as assessment procedures and formal accreditation (Turturica 2006). To some extent, these measures have had a positive impact. Research in 2015 made it possible to detect a change in mood in the legal community compared with that revealed by data from 2003 and 2004. The earlier research found deep pessimism, spontaneous negative remarks and general frustration. These comments were typical:

> The trade is dominated by people who offer their services only to extort money from the client, often even under the pretext that it is needed to bribe the judge, and then disappear taking huge sums of money with them. And they usually have an official certificate of being a lawyer.
> (Moscow, March 2003)

In the data collected in the later research, one can pick up a mild change of tone, as illustrated by this comment from a lawyer who specialises in commercial disputes:

> There are many highly qualified lawyers with high moral standards in all branches of the legal field. But along with them there are certified people who do not even come close to being what one would call a professional lawyer. The situation has improved in recent years. Still, the competition within the profession remains unhealthy.
> (Moscow, February 2015)

Or consider these remarks, offered by a lawyer working mostly with criminal cases:

> One should not blacken all prosecutors and judges hastily. Among them are many competent, decent and honest professionals whom we all respect.
> (St Petersburg, April 2015)

Inferences from research point out that a threshold (albeit a low threshold) has now been established for professional competence. This change has been driven by improved state regulation of the educational system, backed up by demand in the market for competent legal services. Meanwhile the highest standard of training, comparable to the international level, has become available in a few elite law schools, mainly in Moscow and St Petersburg. However, there is no doubt that competence at the lower level remains far too low. In the absence of internal regulation within the profession at large, entry into the profession, too, is still wide open. As a result, the professional potential is unevenly distributed through the system, with high competence concentrated at the lucrative commercial end of the spectrum while leaving everyday disputes and low-level courts exposed to poor service. The lack of a reliable standard for measuring the level of competence and insufficient consistency in actual performance prevent far-reaching advances towards the professionalisation of law.

Organisational Autonomy and the Monopoly of Legal Practice
Self-governance is a fundamental condition for a group with specialised knowledge to develop a sense of shared identity, to project a clear message to the rest of society about its social mission and to demarcate and then ring-fence a sector of the social sphere as its professional domain. The only segment of the legal community that can be considered as having evolved in that direction is the Russian bar (the *advokatura*). It is no accident that it is considered to be the core of the legal profession, even though only a minority of practising lawyers in Russia are members (ICJ 2015). As noted earlier, even in Soviet times, Russian advocates worked within institutional structures that, at least in appearance, could claim partial autonomy. During the years of *perestroïka* they were even granted an opportunity to go further and create an independent national union – an opportunity that was lost as a consequence of internal disagreements and the turbulent sociopolitical environment (Jordan 2006).

The post-Soviet drive to open up competitive markets in as many sectors as possible created an unrestricted playing field for anyone with an ambition to be a lawyer. Private practices were legalised and sprouted in every city in a variety of forms, from individual practices to partnerships, hierarchically managed firms and loose associations. In that competitive context, 'alternative' colleges of advocates came into existence. They presented themselves as forward-looking, flexible and market-oriented, in contrast to the old colleges of advocates, but they reduced their access requirements to almost nothing, mostly took on commercially lucrative cases and in practice, stayed away from unpaid legal aid. Meanwhile the 'traditional' colleges of advocates covered almost 90 per cent of all criminal cases (Bocharov and Moiseeva 2016). The confrontation between 'traditional' and 'alternative' forms and ideologies did not help to strengthen the profession as an interest group. Instead, the tension between them led to disorder in the legal profession, intensified by the general lack of quality control and the uncontrolled expansion of private practice outside both *advokaturas*. Reflecting on the early years of the transition, one of my interviewees remarked in 2015:

> 'Nihilism deepened in the 1990s, after the breakdown of the U.S.S.R. Those were rakish years of legal anarchy. Everything was turned upside down and now everyone is surprised that there is no trust and respect for law. After the experience of that chaos it will take time to recover'.
> (St Petersburg, April 2015)

Meanwhile, work started as early as 1992 on preparing new legislation to regulate the *advokatura* but it took a decade to bring the draft to the stage when it was signed into law in May 2002. The law required that a single Federal Chamber of Advocates should be set up and linked to regional chambers, and specified that it should be independent and self-regulated. All lawyers who already held the status of advocate automatically became members of the united chamber, including members of the 'alternative' as well as the 'traditional' bars. However, new membership was to require five years of practical experience followed by the passing of entrance examinations. The 2002 law gave exclusive rights to the members of the *advokatura* to appear in the courtroom to represent a client, with the only exception being that corporate lawyers employed by companies were to be allowed to represent their firms.

Initially, the formation of the united *advokatura* was met with resentment and deep distrust by almost all the lawyers who stayed outside of the new *advokatura* and whom I interviewed in the months after the publication of the Advocacy Act. The main issue was the requirement that a lawyer must be a member to represent a client in court. For lawyers who were not already members of the old *advokaturas*, it meant either a reduction in their practice, or an entry examination if they chose to join the bar. During my interviews, the issue was usually packaged in terms of 'Who will be controlling the controllers?' The typical reactions were along the following lines:

> They [the examiners] will just let their own people in and keep the rest of us out.

> I have a PhD and I have taught and practised law for years. And now some people with questionable reputations will be given the power to judge me. I do not trust them,

> What is happening now is that a small group of old advocates who are close to the government pushed this law through to make money out of the power that the law will give them to decide who is in and who is out.
>
> (Moscow, September 2002)

For these reasons it is not surprising that, rather than making plans to join the bar, many lawyers concerned themselves with finding ways to get around the provisions of the new Advocacy Act – even before it came into effect. It did not take long before the law was challenged and then, in 2004, abolished by a decision of the Constitutional Court. Since then, advocates have not had a monopoly of courtroom representation. The success of the challenge can be explained by the resistance of, as Bocharov and Moiseeva phrase it, 'independent professionals' as opposed to the 'independent profession' (2016: 40). However, the court's judgment is also telling in relation to the shared vision of how law should be viewed. It shows that the traditional mentality of the 'lay' concept of law remains very much alive in Russia. It seems that neither the solid knowledge of the courtroom procedure itself nor the professional performance of the actors is expected to produce much of value.

Nevertheless, the Russian post-Soviet *advokatura* has proved to be a living organism. Its membership is expanding. In 2002, there were 48,800 advocates who became members by default when the bar was established. By 2015 the number had risen to around 70,414 (ICJ 2015). In that time, the *advokatura* had been performing the kind of task that one would expect of a professional organisation in any country, such as demarcating the group's boundaries, protecting the members' interests and holding disciplinary hearings in response to complaints against its members. The initial scepticism about the examination procedure proved to be unfounded and, in my interviews in 2015, there was no mention of unfairness in how it had been done. I was also told about various activities initiated proactively by the *advokatura* from which my informants had benefited personally, such as holding useful lectures, arranging professional conferences, setting up exchange programmes with peers abroad and reaching out to the law schools by offering courses and internship arrangements.

However, the number of advocates remains several times less than the number of lawyers practising overall. Most lawyers remain outside any organisational umbrella and do their work unhindered by the constraints of regulation. It was evident in the 2015 findings that the incentives for practising lawyers to join the *advokatura* were not thought to be strong. On the contrary, there are disincentives to consider and not just the obvious one that there is no need to obtain membership in order to represent a client in court. For example, an advocate is required to do some unpaid work for a not-for-profit organisation and, at least in theory, comply with the code of conduct. Consequently, as one lawyer put it:

> It is not important to join the bar. To be successful one simply has to build up a social network and keep it active. Your worth is determined by your network, not by the bar membership. Often, resolving a problem comes down to knowing whom to make a call to.
> (St Petersburg, April 2015)

Overall in Russia today the balance is still on the side of the 'glass is half empty', rather than 'half full'. The *advokatura* brings together only a small segment of the total number of practising lawyers. The lack of a professional overview of all the practitioners unquestionably holds back the formation of a profession as it is recognised in the West and, without this, there is little chance of the professionalisation of lawyering as an ideology.

Even so, it is indeed the case that, within the post-Soviet legal community, a professionally organised group is slowly emerging. The question now is how successful it has been in shifting the underlying assumptions of the internal legal culture. Within their organisation, have the *advokatura* been effective in introducing informal norms of acceptable behaviour or in shaping professional ethics?

Informal Norms and the Code of Conduct within the *Advokatura*

Service to the public is considered to be a fundamental characteristic of any profession. For the legal profession, it necessarily generates tension between allegiance to the client and the social duty to uphold specific values and the integrity of justice. In all jurisdictions, the boundary between the two obligations is a misty zone that all lawyers have to negotiate (Barry and Berman 1968). In the Western tradition, a commitment to the interest of the client sits deeply in the professional ethic, while the opposing ethos of commitment to society at large is maintained by the professional body which lays down a code of conduct, imposes procedural rules and draws an assortment of red lines that prevent a lawyer from acting against the profession's interests.[5] How do Russian advocates deal with this dilemma?

'The client first' side of the conflict of principles has become an unquestioned rule for advocates in contemporary Russia. The 2015 data showed that the dominant mentality was that everything should be done to deliver what the client asks for. This was the defining criterion to distinguish between good and bad lawyers. I was repeatedly told that an advocate is not judged among colleagues by the success rate of his cases but by the way in which he treats his clients. Bad advocates are those who let down their clients, those who are 'regularly late for court hearings or simply do not turn up at all', who 'appear in court without having properly prepared their line of defence', who 'take money and do nothing for the client' or who 'take cases in an area of law in which they have no knowledge whatsoever and, even after that, do not bother to look up the law and learn it properly' (Moscow, February–March 2015).

In contrast to the situation in other countries, this commitment to clients was not offset by norms of self-regulation and by group pressure to protect the profession's integrity. As one advocate put it to me:

> I often use informal methods to achieve results. That is unavoidable in this profession. If I have an important client who is willing to put down big money, then I would use that money to achieve results any way I can. If, as a lawyer, you do not use all possible means and resources to get results you will not be understood, either by your clients or by your colleagues.
>
> (Moscow, March 2015)

The main explanation which the advocates use to justify this behaviour is that it is not possible to operate by rules other than those that prevail across society. By the nature of their job, advocates frequently have to deal with an inefficient and corrupt state bureaucracy, especially when they need to access information, to secure a particular document or to obtain expert assessment for a case. To be able to deliver such things, they have to find shortcuts. This was an argument that came up repeatedly, as in this example:

---

[5] There are Western examples in which lawyers step outside the law, such as in a conflict when a defence lawyer shares an ideological cause with the defendant in acting against the state (McEvoy 2011). However, such cases are exceptionally rare.

> The environment is corrupt and there is no escape from it. The state bureaucracy pushes you in that direction. Your case could go into the archive and you would still be waiting for a simple document for your client.
>
> (St Petersburg, April 2015)

There was also a rationalisation that it is okay to play outside the law if that is the only way to achieve a just outcome; one cannot deliver justice while maintaining professional integrity. The logic came down to the view that, if the player is not playing by the rules established in the game, then it is better not to be in the game to start with. This attitude was expressed in statements such as this:

> Things are more complicated than the 'illegal' or 'informal' labels might suggest. For instance, if the opposite side is making a move, you have to respond in the same way in order not to disadvantage your client. Or, in criminal cases, it can be tempting to make a deal [informal approach, bribe] with an investigator or a judge. Often that is done for the sake of justice because we cannot achieve it by legal means. For example, when the accused is being kept in detention without having been convicted, there is no other way. But I would not do it for a defendant that I believe to be guilty. For some clients I would bend a law to get justice; for others I would not.
>
> (St Petersburg, April 2015)

Seen in its context, this version of a lawyer's code of conduct is lucid. It also specifies boundaries or limits that are seen as unacceptable. In my study, straightforward criminal behaviour such as intimidation of a witness was considered to be taboo, even if it was in the interest of the client. My interviewees admitted that, nevertheless, it does occasionally happen, but it is always condemned by the advocates. The advocate community was also indignant about so-called 'pocket lawyers' – legal professionals who co-operate with investigators who offer them cases in return for closing their eyes to the shortcomings of the process of preliminary investigation. There was also an outcast group of advocates whose membership was used only for the sake of personal protection. These were people who obtain status to secure the immunities enjoyed by advocates.

The Western notion that, as legal professionals, it is incumbent upon the advocates to set the rules of legality and force them upon society, was not even mentioned, by any advocate to whom I talked. However, a general sense of frustration came across strongly and a clear longing for a regulated ethic was apparent as well. There was a feeling that things were improving, albeit slowly. This notion was exemplified by comments like these:

> We are far from feeling that we are working in a legal environment that is regulated by a code of conduct, but there is a clear tendency towards it. Violations are widespread, but at least we do not think of them as normal any more.
>
> (Moscow, March 2015)

> Our community is trying hard to keep the house clean. Unfortunately that is proving to be difficult.
>
> (St Petersburg, May 2015)

To put this in the context of professional development, there is no doubt that the informal rules that would enhance the integrity and prestige of the legal profession in Russia are underdeveloped. That is the case even among the *advokatura*, the small proportion of the legal community which operates under an organisational umbrella. However, this has to be seen in perspective. When the situation is placed in its historical context, it can be seen not as a failure but as an early stage of evolution. Traditions, informal norms and internalised social restrictions do not emerge overnight. The interesting issues here are the direction in which the group formation is evolving and whether or not the sense of professional identity is strengthening.

Identity

In the 1990s, the need to find a niche in the shaky post-Soviet environment of wild competition compelled lawyers to search for their identity (Hendley *et al.* 2001). My data show that the preferred way to build that identity was to look far back and emulate the nineteenth-century bar. Almost every member of the *advokatura* to whom I spoke mentioned having roots in the first Russian bar and expressed pride in that heritage. At the same time, the most recent past was rejected. One might expect that, after successfully preserving their special status throughout the entire Soviet time against all the odds, the advocates would feel pride in that period of their organisational history. However, it was not mentioned once in my interviews.

Some advocates also proclaimed their commitment to the normative vision of the *advokatura*: what it is for and its social mission. Phrases such as 'The task of the *advokatura* is to originate, preserve and pass our traditions on to the next generation' (St Petersburg, April 2015) or

'A strong *advokatura* will raise the prestige of our profession and people will start to trust us' (Moscow, February 2015) were not exceptional, although not common either. In a few cases, professional identity came across as something much stronger, involving a commitment to law as a moral calling that empowers an advocate to serve justice and promote the cause of social responsibility:

> 'It is more than an occupation. It is style of life. It is even more than that. It is the whole of our lives. It is not true that we cannot make a difference. That is an excuse. Good and hard work does bear fruit'.
> (St Petersburg, April 2015)

Nevertheless, when it came to belonging to a professional community with a sense of solidarity and a group identity, there was deep frustration at the state of the profession. The advocates bemoaned the lack of a reliable standard that would allow group formation to progress and encourage a sense of belonging to the group. The prevailing view was that, as it is, the profession cannot attract respect. As one advocate phrased it:

> It is not possible to develop a shared solidarity in my profession. I have seen and worked with many excellent lawyers, highly competent and responsible, but also with some who do not follow ethical rules in dealing with people and do not know how to behave in court. They get into quarrels and exchange insults during hearings. Some advocates exhibit behaviour unacceptable anywhere, let alone in court. How could I identify myself with them?.
> (Moscow, September 2014)

CONCLUSION

To understand the contemporary development of the Russian legal institution one has to consider it against the background of its legal tradition. In Russia the legal sphere has never (or not yet) succeeded in separating itself fully from its social context. Its professionalisation is still a work in progress.

Currently we are observing a phase in which, once again, a Westernised vision of professionalised law is re-emerging in Russia and strengthening visibly. However, it still clashes with the traditional popular mentality that law is merely a text which carries a single, clear meaning that any layperson can read and understand. This interplay between 'professional' and 'lay' approaches to law has numerous implications for both internal and general legal cultures.

Internally, we have to appreciate that, although the professionalisation of law is happening and there are clear indications that the fundamentals are now in place, it remains a work in progress. It will undoubtedly take time before the balance tilts towards 'the glass is half full' rather than 'half empty'. Until then, one should not expect to see effective self-cleaning forces within the profession, or a general commitment to moral principle, or even an adequate appreciation of the value of strict procedural requirements in a courtroom.

Within the general legal culture, it is difficult to see how a full respect for and trust in the legal institution can be established. The 'lay' consumption of law creates an environment of ongoing scepticism about justice, regardless of how it is delivered. As Bourdieu pointed out: '[t]he establishment of properly professional competence, the technical mastery of a sophisticated body of knowledge that often runs contrary to the simple counsel of common sense, entails the disqualification of the non-specialists' sense of fairness, and the revocation of their naïve understanding of the facts, of their "view of the case"' (Bourdieu 1987: 828).

If a legal case in Russia has an unexpected outcome, as often occurs in any jurisdiction, it is not regarded as a matter for expert interpretation or as a professional reading of the law's subtlety. Instead, it is routinely explained away as the arbitrary application of a principle by a court. In such an interpretation, neither the skills of lawyers nor the formalities of legal procedure have particular significance. The dominant conception of law remains purely instrumental and is seen to be a product of informal agreements. In Russia, the law continues to be devoid of the powerful mystique that, in the West, turns it into an unconditional social good in its own right.

References

Abel, R. L. (1998) 'Lawyers in the civil law world', in Abel, R. L. and Lewis, S. C. (eds.) *Lawyers in Society*. Vol. 2. Berkeley: University of California Press, 1–53.

Abel, R. L. and Lewis, S. C. (1989) 'Putting law back into the sociology of lawyers', in Abel, R. L. and Lewis, S. C. (eds.) *Lawyers in Society*. Vol. 3. Berkeley: University of California Press, 478–526.

Barry, D. D. and Berman, H. J. (1968) 'The Soviet legal profession', *Harvard Law Review*, 82(1): 1–41.

Berman, H. J. (1963) *Justice in the U.S.S.R: An Interpretation of Russian Law*. Cambridge, MA: Harvard University Press.

(1994) 'The origin of historical jurisprudence: Coke, Selden, Hale', *Yale Law Journal*, 103(7): 1651–1738.
Bocharev, T. and Moiseeva, E. (2016) *Byt' advokatom v. Rossii: sotsiologicheskoe issledovanie professii*. St Petersburg: European Institute in St Petersburg.
Boucher, D. (2009) *The Limits of Ethics in International Relations: Natural Law, Natural Rights, and Human Rights in Transition*. New York: Oxford University Press.
Bourdieu, P. (1987) 'The force of law: toward a sociology of the judicial field', *The Hastings Law Journal*, 38: 805–853.
Brundage, J. A. (2008) *The Medieval Origin of the Legal Profession: Canonists, Civilians, and Courts*. Chicago: University of Chicago Press.
Butler, W. E. (2009) *Russian Law*. Oxford: Oxford University Press (3rd edn).
Collection of the Imperial Russian Historical Society (1878) [Сборник императорского русского исторического общества], Vol. 23.
Evetts, J. (2011) 'Sociological analyses of professionalism: past, present and future', *Comparative Sociology*, 10(1): 1–37.
Franklin, S. (2002) *Writing, Society and Culture in Early Rus, c. 950–1300*. Cambridge: Cambridge University Press.
Friedman, L. M. (1975) *The Legal System: Social Science Perspective*. New York: Russell Sage Foundation.
Frierson, C. A. (1986) 'Rural justice in public opinion: the Volost' court debate 1861–1912', *The Slavonic and East European Review*, 64(4): 526–545.
Fries, B. W. (1985) *The Rise of the Roman Jurists*. Princeton: Princeton University Press.
Gernet M. N. (1916) *Istoria Russkoi Advokatury [History of the Russian Advokatura]*, Moscow, Izd. Sovetov prisiazhnykh povierennykh, Vol. 3.
Hendley, K. (2012) 'The puzzling non-consequences of societal distrust of courts: explaining the use of Russian courts', *Cornell International Law Journal*, 45(3): 517–567.
Hendley, K., Murrell, P. and Ryterman, R. (2001) 'Agents of change or unchanging agents? The role of lawyers within Russian industrial enterprises', *Law and Social Inquiry*, 26(3): 685–715.
Holt, J. C. (1992) *Magna Carta*. Cambridge, MA: Cambridge University Press.
Huskey, E. (1982) 'The limits to institutional autonomy in the Soviet Union: case of Advokatura', *Soviet Studies*, XXXIV(2): 200–227
  (1986) *Russian Lawyers and the Soviet State*. Princeton: Princeton University Press.
ICJ (2015) *Towards a Stronger Legal Profession in the Russian Federation*. Geneva: International Commission of Jurists.
Jordan, P. A. (2004) *Defending Rights in Russia: Lawyers, the State, and Legal Reforms in the Post-Soviet Era*. Vancouver: University of British Columbia Press.

Kurkchiyan, M. (2007) 'The impact of the transition on the role of law in Russia', in Bruinsma, F. and Nelken, D. (eds.) *Explorations in Legal Cultures*. Gravenhage: Reed Elsevier, 75–94.

(2009) 'Russian legal culture: an analysis of adaptive response to an institutional transplant', *Law and Social Inquiry*, 34(2): 337–365.

Lewinbuk, K. P. (2010) 'Perestroika or just perfunctory? The scope and significance of Russian's new legal ethics laws', *The Journal of the Legal Profession*, 35(1): 25–80.

McEvoy, K. (2011) 'What did the lawyers do during the "war"? Neutrality, conflict and the culture of quietism', *Modern Law Review*, 74(3): 350–384.

Pomekhin, P. A. (1900) 'Fragments from an advocate's memo', *Pravo*, 47: 2220–2217.

Pushkin, A. S. (1998) 'The bronze horsemen', *Translation and Literature*, 7(1): 59–71 (Trans. J. Dewey).

Reynolds, S. (2003) 'The emergence of professional law in the long twelfth century', *Law and History Review*, 21(2): 347–366.

Schuz, F. (1951) *Classical Roman Law*. Oxford: Clarendon Press.

Solomon, P. H. (2010) 'Authoritarian legality and informal practices: judges, lawyers and the state in Russia and China', *Communist and Post-Communist Studiers*, 43: 351–362

(2005) 'The criminal procedure code of 2001: will it make Russian justice more fair?' in *Ruling Russia: Law, Crime and Justice in a Changing* Society, Pridemore, W. (ed.), Lanham: Rowan and Littlefield, 77–100.

Statistical Annual Report, National Economy of U.S.S.R. in 1987 (Statistichaeskii Ejegodnik, Narodnoe Khoziaistvo S.S.S.R. v. 1987). (1988) Moscow: Finances and Statistics.

Troitsky, N. A. (2000) *Advokatura v. Rissii i Politicheskie Protsessi v. Rossii v. 1866–1904*. Tula: Avtograph.

Turturica, C. (2006) 'Law school accreditation in the new independent states of the former Soviet Union: what steps for the future?' *International Journal of the Legal Profession*, 13(2): 152–183.

Vas'kovskii (1893) *Organizatsiia Advokatury*. St Petersburg: Soikina.

Wortman, R. S. (1976) *The Development of a Russian Legal Consciousness*. Chicago: Chicago University Press.

CHAPTER THREE

TO GO TO COURT OR NOT? THE EVOLUTION OF DISPUTES IN RUSSIA

Kathryn Hendley

Life everywhere is beset by challenges. In Russia, as elsewhere, some of these challenges ripen into fully fledged disputes, while most are not pursued. The reasons for this tend to be opaque. The problems that fall by the wayside are like the proverbial trees that fall, unheard, in the forest. Disputes that end up in court are much noisier and easier to study. Yet they tell an incomplete story. In any society, unpacking the motivations for not going to court is just as important as understanding what happens in court. Russia is no exception.

In this chapter, I analyse the reactions of Russians to two hypothetical problems that might arise in their daily lives. First I sought their responses to a malfunctioning mobile phone. Then I asked them to contemplate a disagreement over real estate in the wake of a family death. The advantage of posing stylised facts is that everyone is responding to the same situations. This approach draws back the curtain on the process of deciding what road to take, or, perhaps more accurately, whether to take any road at all. What emerges is a strong aversion to litigation. The reasons defy the common wisdom. Despite the steady drumbeat of concern over political interference and corruption in the post-Soviet courts in the mass media and scholarly literature, such fears are entirely absent from the discussions. Instead, much like their counterparts elsewhere, Russians' hesitation is fuelled by their fears of the cost, time, energy and emotional sacrifices required for litigation (Engel 1984; Merry 1990). For them, filing lawsuits was viewed as a last resort; their consistent preference was for finding a way to resolve problems without involving the courts. Their discussions reveal a myriad of possibilities, along with glimpses into their pluses and minuses.

METHODOLOGY

Critical to understanding Russians' decision-making process is an ability to eavesdrop as they work out their responses. Absent the possibility of being a fly on the wall in the lives of ordinary Russians, focus groups provide the next best vehicle. Although artificial in that they bring together strangers for heartfelt discussions, they have the advantage of allowing the participants to speak their mind rather than being limited to the predetermined answers of a survey. The disadvantage of working with hypothetical situations was blunted by the fact that a number of the respondents and/or their friends had experienced similar problems (even though they were not recruited on this basis) and shared their actual reactions as well as the rationales behind them.

Working with Moscow-based Russian colleagues, I organised nine focus groups in 2014, divided equally between Moscow, Voronezh and Novosibirsk.[1] The discussions were facilitated by an experienced Russian sociologist. Because most of the participants had full-time jobs, the meetings were held in the evenings and at weekends, and lasted about two hours. Each group included eight to twelve to participants, whose names have been changed here to protect their anonymity. An effort was made to ensure diversity in terms of gender, employment and education. Almost evenly divided by gender, with forty-six men and forty-five women, their ages ranged from 23 to 66, with an average age of 41. From a financial point of view, the participants were comfortable. Two-thirds said that they could easily afford big-ticket items, such as refrigerators and televisions, while the remainder said that such purchases would be a struggle for them, but that they had no trouble covering their daily expenses.

---

[1] The project was originally designed to investigate popular attitudes toward mediation in Russia. These venues were selected to reflect their receptivity to mediation. Voronezh is the home of Elena Nosyreva (2010), the head of the working group that drafted the 2011 law introducing mediation. She has established a mediation center at Voronezh State University. Novisibirsk has no discernable profile regarding mediation. Moscow, as usual, is *sui generis*. It is home to mediation activists and mediation centers, but is not known for this. As the focus groups progressed, it became evident that the participants were unaware of the advent of mediation. The discussions nonetheless provided rich source material on the process of disputing.

Hypothesising that attitudes towards dispute resolution would be coloured by prior court experience, I divided the groups accordingly. In each locale, one group was composed of court veterans, another of those who had never been to court and the third was mixed. Almost all of those with experience had been through civil processes.[2] Most (87 per cent) had been the instigators of their court cases. Reflecting the docket of Russian courts, the most common types of case were housing (33 per cent) and family (27 per cent) disputes, with cases involving labour claims, personal injury, business problems and debt collection also represented.

The focus groups were organised around three hypothetical scenarios. The goal was to pose mundane problems that could, but need not, be solved through litigation.[3] They were designed to ratchet up the complexity of the problem – in terms of both substance and emotion – as the discussions proceeded. The first problem involved a recently purchased mobile phone that had stopped working. The second posited a residential water leak. The third explored a sticky inheritance dispute. In this chapter, I analyse the focus groups' discussions of the first and third scenarios. I have elsewhere explored Russians' reactions to water leaks in their apartments (Hendley 2011a). By focusing on the arenas of consumer and inheritance law, I am able to examine how Russians approach problems involving both strangers and intimates. Socio-legal theory predicts that willingness to use the courts is correlated with social distance – i.e., that, as a relationship grows more remote, people tend to be more willing to pursue disputes (Engel 1984). Prior Russia-based research has produced mixed results. The social distance hypothesis was confirmed when it comes to mundane disputes among neighbours (Hendley 2011a), but not to disputes between firms (Hendley 2001). It is, however, just one of several explanatory factors that emerged from the focus group discussions.

My analysis relies on the so-called 'pyramid of disputing' framework, developed by Felstiner et al. (1980–81). Its triangular shape recognises that relatively few of the multitude of annoyances of daily life are

---

[2] The only exception was Vera, a 40-year-old Muscovite who worked in a technical capacity at a university, who had been the victim of a crime. She represented her own interests at the subsequent trial. Like most European countries (e.g., McKillop 1997), victims are parties to criminal cases in Russia, where they can weigh in on the treatment of the defendant and seek civil damages (Maggs et al. 2015).

[3] For a discussion of more politically charged complaining in Russia, see Henry (2012).

pursued. In other words, as the stakes rise, an increasing number of these nuisances fall away.[4] Indeed, many victims do not perceive themselves as such and do nothing. Others recognise or name the injury but still opt to stay silent (Sandefur 2007). Those who pursue the injury will identify or blame the perpetrator. Some stop there, satisfied with the knowledge of who did them wrong. A very few push further, and make a claim against the wrongdoer. Such claims can take many forms, ranging from a request for an apology to litigation. The reasons why potential disputes languish unpursued or proceed up the pyramid vary according to the surrounding circumstances and the character and capabilities of the victim. The underlying institutional environment and legal culture also play a role, which allows the Felstiner et al. framework, which is grounded in the US experience, to be adapted to remarkably different settings, including China (Michelson 2007), Kyrgystan (Cormier 2007) and Russia (Hendley 2001, 2010).

HANDLING CONSUMER DISPUTES

The first task tackled by each focus group was the discussion of a situation in which a schoolteacher puzzled over what to do about a malfunctioning mobile phone. Cards on which a Russian-language version of the following scenario was printed were distributed to the participants. They were given time to read and absorb the facts.

> Irina Ivanova, a 44-year-old teacher, bought a new mobile phone in the "Evroset"[5] store near the school where she teaches. She is not tech savvy. Previously, she had a very basic mobile phone, which she lost. The salesman persuaded her to buy a smartphone for $150, assuring her that, if problems arose, she could easily exchange the phone for a

---

[4] For example, a US-based study of disputing behaviour found that '71.8 per cent of individuals with grievances complained to the offending party, and that a dispute arose in 63 per cent of those situations. Of these disputes, 11.2 per cent resulted in a court filing'. They concluded that 'It is clear that litigation ... is by no means the most common response to disputes' (Trubek et al. 1983: 86–7). In a 1997 survey of Russian firms, we found that, for every 100 sales transactions, twenty-four experienced difficulties. Of these, sixteen were resolved informally, seven were resolved through threats of litigation and/or the imposition of penalties, and only one was litigated (Hendley et al. 2000: 652, n. 52).

[5] Evroset' (https://euroset.ru/) is a chain of stores that is ubiquitous throughout Russia, which sells mobile phones and other electronics.

new one. He also convinced her to buy a two-year extended warranty for $50.[6] Two weeks after the purchase, her phone stopped working. When she took it back to the store, she was told that she would have to buy a new phone. The manager explained that the problem with her phone arose due to improper use, invalidating the warranty.

The participants' initial reactions confirmed the relevance of the scenario to Russians' daily lives. Oleg, a 37-year-old Novosibirsk programmer, commented that, 'in reality, many have confronted this sort of situation'. No one disputed that Irina Ivanovna had suffered an injury. In Felstiner *et al.* parlance, the focus group participants agreed that she had named her injury. The fact pattern also clearly identified her tormenter, namely Evroset', which meant that blame had been assigned. The real question here was whether to make a claim and, if so, what sort of claim.

Do nothing. At some point in every group's discussion, one or more of the participants advocated that Irina Ivanova let it go and buy a new phone. In other words, they recommended that she not make any sort of claim. For some who took this position, the cost of the phone simply did not warrant investing the time and energy needed to get Evroset' to live up to its word. On the other hand, Gennadii, a 31-year-old Voronezh entrepreneur whose wife was a schoolteacher, reminded the group that the modest salaries of teachers made the cost of the phone more significant. He said that he would weigh the cost of pursuing a claim against the price paid for the phone.

Many saw making a claim against a retail outlet as quixotic. Larisa, a 35-year-old who worked for a Voronezh construction company, reflected the feelings of customers everywhere when she said that, 'It seems to me that salespeople have been given strict instructions to give customers the runaround as much as possible ... First they tell you that you are a fool, then they tell you that it's all your fault'.[7] Others were more fatalistic. Nadia, a 33-year-old Voronezh doctor, said that she would chalk it up to bad luck and move on. Others echoed her sentiments, noting that the teacher would need a strong backbone to

---

[6] Several of the focus groups got bogged down in squabbles over the best way to handle this extended warranty. This was most pronounced in the groups with prior court experience. Across the board, most participants saw Irina Ivanovna's purchase of the warranty as foolish.

[7] Larisa's comments were grounded in her unsatisfactory experience of buying a computer at Media Market, a chain of 'big box' stores in Russia.

defend her rights, whether at the store or in court. Alla, a 34-year-old Moscow bookkeeper who was a veteran of multiple lawsuits, spoke of the toll it took on her wellbeing. In her view, most would do nothing. Elena, a 58-year-old Voronezh teacher, spoke for many when she said, 'If a person has plenty of time; if he has nothing to do; if he is free, then let him go to court somewhere – write to everyone. But she is a teacher – she has to behave rationally.' When asked what she would do in Irina Ivanovna's position, Elena said, 'I wouldn't do anything. I would give this phone to my grandson and let him try to figure it out. I'm not interested in running around. I don't want to do it.'

However, not everyone agreed. When responding to Elena, Boris, a 39-year-old Voronezh factory worker, took a different tack, saying, 'I believe that you need to fight for your rights ... in any situation ... if you are in the right, then you need to see it through to the end'. Few were as bristly as Boris, but most conceded that, if Irina Ivanovna saw this as a question of principle, then she ought to make a claim.

Seek recompense from the store. For those who advocated making a claim, there was general agreement that returning to the Evroset' store where she bought the phone ought to be her first step. Few saw any point to utilising the complaint book (*zhalobaia kniga*) that all retail outlets are required to make available to consumers.[8] Instead, the participants thought she should approach the store manager and ask to exchange the phone or, if that proved impossible due to a model change, ask for her money back.

Some were sure that the store would do right by Irina Ivanovna. For example, Matvei, a 28-year-old supervisor at a Moscow trading company, commented that, 'If she paid, then she should simply take her receipt ... and everything will proceed normally'. Several of his fellow participants shared stories that ended with them being able to return items such as phones, tablets and CD players months after the purchase. Similar stories emerged from the other groups. Others' confidence stemmed from the sheer size and reputation of Evroset'. One Moscow

---

[8] The only group that mentioned complaint books was the Moscow group, which included both those with and those without court experience. It was raised towards the end of the discussion and felt like an afterthought. The group agreed that salespeople generally discouraged customers from using these books. Some thought this might be because complaints recorded in these books could negatively impact on salespeoples' bonuses. Having these books is a practice that, as Chekhov (1982) reminds us in his short story, 'The complaints book', dates back to the Tsarist era. They were also ubiquitous during the Soviet era (Bogdanova 2015; Hilton 2009).

participant was convinced that Evroset' had an informal policy providing that, as long as you had a receipt, you could exchange your phone at any time for any reason.[9] Unaware of this policy (which, at best, was not binding), others felt that Evroset' would be loath to risk bad publicity by thwarting the desires of their customers. Several contrasted the likely response of Evroset' with that of a kiosk, and all agreed that Irina Ivanovna would have less luck at a more fly-by-night enterprise.

However, the majority of the focus group participants were doubtful about Evroset's willingness to comply with her demands at face value. A fair number felt that the store's concern over its reputation would cut the other way, namely that management would fear an avalanche of returns if they were too accommodating. At every site, there were a few participants who told horror stories about their experiences with Evroset' and other big chain stores. They came away believing that such stores could not be pressured by consumers; that they were too big to care. Those in this camp were firmly convinced that talking to the original salesperson would be a waste of time. They advocated taking the claim to the store manager and, if that failed, going public, either in the store or more publicly. Some women suggested that the very fact that Irina Ivanovna was a woman and a teacher could be a benefit if she were willing to 'create a scandal' (*ustroit' skandal*) by approaching customers, telling them what had happened to her and encouraging them not to buy a phone at Evroset'. Olga, a 39-year-old Muscovite who worked at an advertising agency, recounted her response after buying a sofa at Ikea that was infested with bugs. After the store personnel refused to help her, she mounted a multi-pronged attack. Not only did she take up a position near the cash registers and loudly caution customers against buying anything, but she also began spamming Ikea's potential customers with emails about the bugs. Within days, officials from Ikea's corporate office reached out to her to reopen negotiations. She achieved her dual goals of shaming Ikea and getting her money back. Her fellow group members were astonished by the

---

[9] He attributed this policy to Evroset's founder, Evgenii Chichvarkin. By 2014, when the group was conducted, Chichvarkin had fled Russia ahead of a criminal indictment for tax evasion and had sold the company. He successfully fought efforts to extradite him from his new home in London. His co-founder, Boris Levin, was less nimble and was held for many months in pre-trial detention. Eventually, he was released after being acquitted in a jury trial (Arlidge 2012).

TO GO TO COURT OR NOT? THE EVOLUTION OF DISPUTES IN RUSSIA

story. Most said that they lacked the courage to follow her example.[10] The more common suggestion was to approach one of the many television programmes that take on consumer complaints, though no one had actually tried this option.[11] Everyone agreed with Olga as to the need to push the claim up the corporate ladder when stymied by store management.

The fact pattern stipulates that the store manager told Irina Ivanovna that she was responsible for the problems with the phone. Precisely how this could be proved and who should have the burden of proof was the subject of lengthy debate in every group.[12] Few thought that Evroset' would take Irina Ivanovna's word that she had done nothing wrong. Instead, most realised that the phone would have to be put through a process that produces a written finding (*zakliuchenie*) that would assign blame. This so-called 'expertise' (*ekspertiz*) process has become commonplace in recent years, which explains why what might seem to be a fairly technical legal requirement is so familiar to ordinary Russians. Nevertheless, their knowledge tends to be only skin-deep. Groups consistently argued over who would have to pay for this process and where it would take place. Most firmly believed that the customer had to bear the financial burden. In reality, it is the store that is required to cover these costs, though if the customer is found to be at fault, s/he has to reimburse the store. Of all the participants, only Marina, a 44-year-old Novosibirsk bookkeeper with no court experience who reported no prior personal skirmishes with retail outlets, was fully conversant with the details of the law. Quite matter-of-factly, she told her colleagues that not only does the store have to pay, but also that the customer has the right to be present when the evaluation takes place.

Although most participants knew that *ekspertiz* would be needed to substantiate Irina Ivanovna's claim, many were nervous about pursuing it on their own. They spoke of the inherent advantage for Evroset', given that it deals with dissatisfied customers on a daily basis.

---

[10] In several groups, it was suggested that a university education tended to inhibit a willingness to throw public tantrums. Most (80 per cent) of the focus group participants held university degrees.
[11] *Kontol'naia zakupka* (Test purchases) is a program that was mentioned in several groups. http://zakupka.tv/ (accessed 14 March 2016).
[12] See Belov (2015) for an analysis of the burden of proof in consumer cases under Russian law.

Even those who had succeeded on their own begrudged the time required and the attendant inconvenience.[13] A fair number of participants doubted the integrity of retail outlets. The remark of Vitalii, a 47-year-old Novosibirsk state worker, that 'Any trade organisation counts on the fact that, if they mislead a person, s/he will give up' was emblematic.

Seek assistance from centres set up to protect consumer rights. In every group, someone brought up the possibility of seeking help from centres created to protect consumer rights. Usually the participant who raised the idea had personal experience with such centres. For those who were unfamiliar with them, they quickly came around to the idea when their more experienced colleagues explained how they empowered consumers. In socio-legal terms, involving these centres acted to transform 'one-shotters' into 'repeat players' (Galanter 1974), thereby levelling the playing field. These centres offer practical advice on how to approach retail establishments, explaining that managers are just as eager as their customers to avoid litigation. Raisa, a Moscow pensioner, sought counsel when her water meter was improperly installed and was advised that she 'simply needed to scare [management] a bit at the start'. When necessary, the staff of these centres – who include lawyers – also prepare written documents ranging from formal claims (*pretenzii*) to be presented to management, to complaints designed to initiate lawsuits (*iskovye zaiavleniia*). Polina, a 47-year-old manager of a Novosibirsk furniture store who had been on both sides of consumer disputes, pointed out that the *pretenzii* prepared by such centres lay out the basis for the claim in clear terms, relieving customers of the burden of articulating their concerns verbally. Participants generally believed that stores took their claims more seriously when they came with the imprimatur of one of these centres, and several reported that management capitulated immediately once one became involved.

---

[13] Nikolai, a 36-year-old Voronezh construction worker, recounted a situation very similar to Irina Ivanovna's. He had bought a smart phone for his daughter that, in relatively short order, stopped working. His initial entreaties to the store came to naught; he was told that his daughter had damaged the phone. He then pursued expertise at an independent service centre. Its conclusion was that the phone had been faulty from the outset. Armed with this evidence, the store replaced his daughter's phone. The ordeal took months.

State-funded centres to protect consumer rights can be found in each of the locales of the focus groups.[14] Most stories about them were positive. Typical was Anton, a 39-year-old construction worker from Novosibirsk. He had no court experience and was keen to maintain his track record. Having previously benefitted from free advice from a consumer rights centre,[15] he insisted that, if confronted by a situation analogous to that of Irina Ivanovna, his first step would be to return to the centre, even before going to the store. Yet some participants who had used these centres reported less favourable treatment. One bone of contention was whether the services were free. Among the Voronezh participants, for example, several reported receiving free services while others complained about being expected to pay for advice. The consensus seemed to be that initial consultations were free, but that fees were charged when staff lawyers drafted documents. Some questioned the quality of these lawyers, pointing out that they tended to be young and inexperienced due to high turnover. Dmitrii, a 41-year-old Voronezh manager who had initiated several civil lawsuits, complained of being overcharged, saying that having a lawyer prepare a complaint for court typically costs 1,500 rubles (about $30), but that the centre lawyers charged him 5,000 rubles.[16]

File a lawsuit. Everyone agreed that court was a last resort (*kraiinii sluchai*). As Oleg put it, 'Of course, if she's really been turned away everywhere, then naturally she ought to go to court.' Implicit within his comment is a recognition that Irina Ivanovna ought to appeal to store management and the consumer rights centre before initiating litigation. Court veterans and neophytes agreed that, even if management had initially given her the cold shoulder, she ought to share the complaint

---

[14] E.g., http://mozp.org/ [Moscow]; http://ozppvrn.ru/ [Voronezh]; www.kalinnsk.ru/industry/consumer-protection/ [Novosibirsk] (accessed 14 March 2016). Some centres also operate hotlines, provide on-line advice and have in-house *ekspertiz* services. The website for the Moscow centre states that, during 2015, they provided 9,260 oral consultations, prepared 3,250 *pretenzii* and conducted *ekspertiz* in 740 cases. It further notes that they prevailed in 95 cases, recovering over 32 million rubles for their clients.

[15] Anton's prior case involved faulty shoes. When he tried to return them, the seller refused, citing improper use. The centre prepared a *zakliuchenie* for him and the store promptly refunded the sale price.

[16] Despite his experience, Dmitrii was unaware that such expenses could be reimbursed if he prevailed in the subsequent court case. When this was raised, others piped up to remind everyone that this was a big 'if' and that Irina Ivanovna would be liable if she lost in court.

with them before filing it with the court because it might prompt a last-minute settlement. Oleg, among others, was more sceptical, arguing that a company like Evroset' would not back down.

The reasons why the focus group participants were reluctant to go to court mirror those previously identified among Russians and are similar to those voiced by grudging litigators elsewhere (Engel 1984; Hendley 2010; Merry 1990). Those with prior court experience complained bitterly about the time and emotional energy needed to see a lawsuit through to the end. Alla, who had survived several housing cases, invoked the infamous McDonald's hot coffee case (Haltom and McCann 2004), though she thought it revolved around a hot tart (*pirozhka*), saying that, in contrast to the US, you could not win millions in Russia. In her words, 'If you're willing to waste time and . . . if you have an inner rod of strength, then maybe, I don't know, you can achieve a great deal.' She reported that, although she was no longer as terrified of litigation as she was at first, she still felt ill effects on her health due to the stress. Another court veteran said that Irina Ivanovna would need the strength of 'reinforced concrete' to survive the ordeal. As a general matter, the participants, regardless of their prior experience, questioned whether a middle-aged female teacher could be tough enough. Although they conceded that some enjoy litigation as a kind of sport, no one admitted to sharing these feelings.

Others were discouraged by proof problems. Most believed that Irina Ivanovna would have to affirmatively prove that she had not damaged the phone. Tatiana, a 29-year-old manicurist from Novosibirsk who had sued her insurance company after it failed to pay her claim following a car accident, pointed out the difficulty of proving a negative. Only a very few participants understood that Evroset', not Irina Ivanovna, would bear this burden. Those who did, however, were more sanguine about her prospects, though not about the time that would have to be devoted to the case. Tatiana also noted the difficulty of preparing for battle, saying that, 'When you show up in court, they'll immediately ask you "Where is the refusal of the store to return the item?" . . . You need written evidence of the refusal.' She cautioned her fellow participants, 'In the present day, to prove something . . . you need to consult in advance with a bunch of lawyers (*advokaty*), read everything thoroughly on the internet in order to approach the issue properly and to cite to the relevant legislation. Only then can you accomplish anything.' Though she had represented herself in court, she had gone to a lawyer for help with preparing her complaint.

Her comments reflect a larger concern with legal literacy. Few felt sufficiently knowledgeable about either the substantive law or the procedural requirements for bringing a lawsuit to proceed on their own. Like Tatiana, many spoke positively about the bounty of information available on the internet.

The cost and competence of lawyers were further constraints on litigating. There was a consensus that Evroset' would have good lawyers who are experienced at repelling consumer claims. In most groups, someone would ask whether Irina Ivanovna ought to consult a lawyer about her options. Inevitably, this idea would be shouted down, either due to doubts about lawyers' skill levels or their cost. Few thought lawyers, especially those who were unknown, were worth consulting. When the prospect of using a free clinic was raised, the response was disdainful, though a few did admit to relying on free help from law students. The only universally acceptable option was to consult a friend who happened to be a lawyer. Only then could you be sure that the advice could be trusted.

Despite this chorus of negativity regarding lawyers, about half of the participants with court experience had hired lawyers to represent them. An additional 30 per cent took Tatiana's road and paid for a lawyer to draft their complaints. Although the sample gathered for these focus groups is not representative, it is still a sad commentary on the state of the Russian legal profession to be able to find so few clients who were willing to speak out in support of their lawyers. Interestingly, those without court experience were more open to consulting lawyers, arguing that any financial outlay would reap benefits in the long run.

HANDLING INHERITANCE DISPUTES

In addition to considering how to deal with the faulty mobile phone, the focus groups were also asked to contemplate how they would handle a problem that arose after the death of a beloved family member.[17] In contrast to the first situation, this scenario required them to think about how their calculations might change if their disagreement was with family members rather than faceless salespeople and managers.

---

[17] See Butler (2014) for an analysis of the twists and turns of inheritance law during the Soviet and post-Soviet eras.

> Daria Nikolaevna is a 20-year-old secretary. She spent her summers in the countryside at her grandparents' *dacha*.[18] Her own parents died tragically when she was young, so her grandparents brought her up. In addition to her father, they had two other children, each of whom had a child. None of them lives nearby, and so have not recently visited the *dacha*. Her grandmother died a few months ago. Her aunts and uncles and cousins are keen to sell the *dacha*. It is located near a river and real estate developers have already bought up adjacent properties. Daria is determined to keep it. Although she does not yet have children, she wants the *dacha* to be there when she has a family.

As with Irina Ivanovna, the focus group participants agreed that this was not an uncommon problem. They immediately saw the complication raised by the familial setting. Gennadii put it best, 'In my opinion, it is useless to negotiate with family ... To be honest, I have found it easier to deal with strangers.' His comments, like those of many of the participants, reflected his own sad experiences. Towards the end of his grandmother's life, her daughter (Gennadii's aunt) wanted to sell her apartment. Gennadii refused to allow it, reasoning that his grandmother should not be forced to move. They 'butted heads' for many years, culminating in a court case that satisfied no one.

Do nothing. Daria Nikolaevna's problem does not fit as neatly into the 'naming, blaming, claiming' framework of Felstiner *et al.* (1980–81) as Irina Ivanovna's dispute with Evroset' did. At the same time, most participants agreed that it presents a dilemma that needs to be resolved, suggesting the need to make a claim.

A few participants disagreed. In essence they advocated that Daria Nikolaevna bury her head in the sand and hope for the best. Ksenia, a 45-year-old Moscow housewife, suggested that she should continue using the *dacha* as if nothing had changed. Her opinion is grounded in her firm belief that Daria is entitled to the dwelling because she (unlike the other relatives) had spent time there in recent years.

---

[18] A *dacha* is a summer dwelling. In the Soviet period, *dachas* tended to be modest, due to limitations on construction and the unavailability of building materials. In the post-Soviet period, the rich have built ostentatious 'cottages'. According to a 2010 survey by VTsIOM, 48 per cent of Russians own *dachas* (Elkov and Cherniak 2013). Zavisca (2003) reminds us that, in addition to vacationing at their *dachas*, many Russians cultivate the land surrounding them.

Her fellow participants disagreed, both with her legal reasoning and her logic.[19] Aleksei, a 28-year-old Moscow bank manager, noted that she could certainly live there, but wondered what would become of her if her relatives dragged her into court or the developers pounced on the property.

Negotiate a settlement with the relatives. The participants saw finding a compromise that satisfied both Daria Nikolaevna and her relatives as a more realistic option. Although all conceded that this would be an uphill battle, most concurred with Eduard, a 42-year-old Moscow construction foreman, when he said that, 'relatives will come to terms with each other sooner or later'. The odds of doing so hinge on the character of those involved and their prior relationship. As Eduard put it, 'We can contemplate thousands of alternatives, but it all depends on the human factor (*chelovecheskii faktor*).' Some thought it would be possible for Daria Nikolaevna or the relatives to find the 'golden words' (*zolotye slova*) that would bring the other side around, while others mocked the very idea that there might be some key to unlocking an agreement. All agreed that, in this case, stubbornness and greed would be the enemy of compromise. Some attributed the obstinacy suggested by the scenario to the low level of civil society in contemporary Russia, saying that Russians do not know how to compromise.

Obviously the simplest way to reach an accord is for one side to give in. Elena thought that the out-of-town relatives ought to give up their interest in the *dacha*. 'They should show mercy (*miloserdie*) to their niece and give her everything because they don't need it. They live far away. She lived without parents. They should show mercy.' Others in her group were skeptical that these relatives would walk away from a valuable asset simply because, in Elena's view, it was 'the right thing to do'. Like many others, she felt strongly that family members should not take each other to court; that the family ties ought to be sacrosanct. Berta, a 49-year-old financial director from Novosibirsk, whose relationship with her niece had been destroyed when they could not come

---

[19] In an amusing aside, Vasilii, a 27-year-old administrator at a gambling salon, asked Ksenia whether, if he stole her phone and held it for a year, he would be entitled to keep it. As in all the focus groups, the participants in this Moscow group, which mixed those with and those without court experience, had only a cursory and often inaccurate understanding of the law. The Civil Code provides a preferential right for an heir who is living in a disputed property at the time of the decedent's death (Art. 1168, GK RF 2001). It goes on to grant such an heir the right to buy out the other heirs (Art. 1170, GK RF 2001).

to an accord in a situation similar to Daria Nikolaevna's, likewise advocated capitulation. Not surprisingly, she identified with the older generation and thus argued that Daria should give up her share to them. Most respondents viewed capitulation by either side as unlikely.

The possibility of selling the property coloured much of the discussion. Most thought that having Daria Nikolaevna buy out her relatives would be an ideal, but unrealistic solution for a 20-year-old secretary. They doubted that she had sufficient money saved or that a bank would give her a loan. A more feasible option would be for the three heirs to join forces and put the *dacha* on the market. They pointed out that, with the proceeds, Daria would be able to purchase her own place. Few paid much attention to Daria's strong emotional attachment to the *dacha* dating back to her childhood. When a Moscow participant raised it, her concerns were dismissed as trivial. One of her male colleagues said that Daria should 'swallow' [*progolit'*] it, meaning that she needed to get over it. Others agreed.

One of the reasons why the prospect of selling dominated the conversations was because the low level of knowledge about the legality of the various options gave rise to heated arguments. As Ellickson's (1991) seminal work on Shasta County farmers and ranchers reminds us, people tend to order their behaviour based on what they believe the law to be, even when they are incorrect. Russians are no different (Hendley 2010). Some were firmly convinced that, without the consent of all involved, none of the heirs could sell their shares. These participants offered up the possibility of partitioning the land and the house itself and sharing it. Although Russian law would allow such an outcome,[20] it would fully satisfy no one. Others thought that each heir had the right to sell his share, irrespective of whether his co-owners had acquiesced. Some thought that a physical partition would precede any such sale, while some thought that the remaining owners would have to accommodate themselves to their new co-owners. Needless to say, the latter could give rise to untold complications. The prospect of a sham sale to patently undesirable elements, such as drug addicts, in order to force Daria Nikolaevna into a fire sale at a below-market price, was raised, as were many other wild scenarios.[21]

---

[20] In this regard, the Civil Code embraces freedom of contract. Parties can agree among themselves as to how to divide up real estate (Art. 252, GK RF 1994).

[21] For example, one of the Voronezh participants recounted a scheme whereby a company buys random shares in real estate, and then sends in Uzbeks to live there

Only a few participants were aware of the technical requirements of the law. In an odd twist, the most well versed was one of the younger participants. At the age of 28, Pavel was an experienced Novosibirsk real estate agent, who cheerfully shared his hard-earned knowledge with his colleagues.[22] He explained, 'If she doesn't want to sell, that's her business, but she needs to understand the legal rules. If they sell their shares and notify her before that, this is all legal. Maybe it is unfair (*nespravidlivo*), but it is legal (*zakonno*).' To clarify, the law requires an appraisal of the property. It then gives Daria the right of first refusal. If she sticks to her guns, her relatives are free to sell their shares to any willing buyer at the appraised price (Articles 252–254, GK RF 1994).[23] This could open the door to the sort of nightmare scenarios suggested by Pavel's less well-informed colleagues.

Pavel wondered whether the question of how Daria Nikolaevna and her relatives would deal with each other was rendered moot due to the interest of developers. The spectre of developers on her doorstep made most participants apprehensive.[24] They were sympathetic to her plight, but saw her situation as profoundly hopeless. Indeed, they worried for her physical safety. Nina, a pensioner in the same group of court veterans as Pavel, commented that, 'Developers have already bought up the neighbouring properties. They won't stand on ceremony with respect to this *dacha*'. Pavel later noted that developers have 'special (*osobye*) methods of convincing [homeowners] why they should buy the property. Believe me, they work extremely well.' No one had a good word to say about developers; they were uniformly seen as unscrupulous. Most groups shared horror stories of the extra-legal methods employed by developers to get their way. Examples included arson, cutting off utilities and even murder.[25] It is worth

---

with instructions to make it so unpleasant for the remaining owners that the latter will sell out.

[22] At the conclusion of the session, several of his older colleagues asked for his business card.

[23] Several members of the mixed Novosibirsk group were aware of the general parameters of the law, but they believed that any sale would have to go through the court, which is not required by the law.

[24] In two groups – the Moscow and Novosibirsk groups without court experience – no one mentioned the developers.

[25] Such claims harken back to the sorts of self-help solution embraced by peasants during the Tsarist era, often referred to as *samosud* (e.g., Frank 1999; Frierson 2002).

noting that no one had any personal experience with developers, but felt free to pass along third-hand stories.

File a lawsuit. Law loomed larger for this scenario. Participants were quicker to invoke the law and to suggest consulting with a lawyer and/or pursuing a claim in court. In contrast to the mobile phone hypothetical, where lawyers were seen as superfluous because participants were confident that, between the Internet and consumer rights centres, they could piece together their legal position, inheritance law was viewed as denser and less susceptible to quick web-based diagnoses. Daria Nikolaevna's youth also played a role in participants' advocacy for seeking legal advice. Nevertheless, their distrust of lawyers continued unabated. Timofei, a 55-year-old Novosibirsk entrepreneur, reflected this apprehension: 'I would go to one legal consultation office and receive a written answer as to how to resolve this problem. Then I would go to a completely different legal consultation office and get the same from another lawyer. I would then draw my own conclusion.' Because he did not believe that a voluntary solution would be viable, his next step would be to initiate a lawsuit. Though many saw the wisdom in talking through the nuances of the situation with a lawyer, few were as impetuous as Timofei about court.

As before, the time and energy needed for litigation discouraged many. Moreover, Elena's view that suing relatives is unseemly swayed many, both as a matter of principle and of experience. In almost every group, someone shared a Dickensian saga of battling with relatives for years with little to show for it other than hard feelings.[26] As Maksim, a 36-year-old Voronezh taxi driver, put it, 'As a rule, when relatives start to litigate, they rarely stop.' Hence, most advocated trying to come to an amicable resolution rather than making a dash for the courthouse. Litigation was seen as an option to be pursued if all else failed.

The complexity of the situation convinced a fair number of participants that, absent a settlement, court would be the only option. The fact that those without court experience held out the greatest hope for the courts is perhaps to be expected. They believed that only the Russian courts have the power to divide the property. In reality, however, notaries play a more central role in managing estates in Russia than do judges (Bespalov and Bespalova 2013; Butler 2014). Yet only a

---

[26] Berta's battle with her niece dragged on for more than four years. One Voronezh participant told of a case that lasted for more than eighteen years. Another shared a story of friends who litigated over the ownership of a house for more than ten years.

handful of the focus group participants brought up notaries. Those with court experience were sceptical that Daria Nikolaevna had a compelling case. Some questioned whether she could muster a viable cause of action.[27] The court veterans agreed that, if she somehow ended up in court, then the judge would encourage her to find an accommodation with her relatives that would avoid clogging the docket. They understood that Russian judges are keen to process cases quickly and try to avoid those in which the issues are more emotional than legal (Hendley 2017). A case like Daria Nikolaevna's, in which the parties are at stalemate, would be anathema. Maksim put it more bluntly: 'Here the court can do nothing; going to court is useless (*bezpolezno*).'

EXPLAINING THE DECISION TO LITIGATE (OR TO BYPASS THE COURTS)

The focus group discussions remind us of Russians' distaste for litigation. At the same time, they reveal a nuanced attitude. The very fact that Russians are using the courts in ever-increasing numbers suggests that, while courts may not be anyone's first choice, they constitute a viable alternative.[28] Indeed, in contrast to the common wisdom perpetuated by the media and much of the social science literature, their reasons for shunning the courts in the sorts of mundane cases discussed have nothing to do with their fears of political interference or corruption in the courts. Indeed, neither issue came up. Instead, their antipathy was fueled by a complicated mix of factors that are familiar to socio-legal scholars around the world.

Likely outcome. It is hardly surprising that the focus group participants raised the likelihood of success as a factor to be considered in whether to file a lawsuit. They uniformly saw the costs associated with litigation as high and were reluctant to move forward unless they had some assurance of success. This concern was more pronounced with regard

---

[27] The more knowledgeable participants cautioned that Daria Nikolaevna should not dawdle if she wanted to use the courts. They knew that she had only six months from the date of her grandmother's death to make her claim (Art. 1163, GK RF 2001). A few were aware that, after that time, she could petition to have the statute of limitations reinstated, but that it would be an uphill battle.

[28] The number of civil cases decided more than doubled between 2012 (5.1 million) and 2014 (13.9 million). The data for the first half of 2015, which documented 8.1 million civil cases decided, indicate that this trend is continuing (Otchet 2012, 2014, 2015).

to the first scenario. The price of the phone left many participants on the fence as to whether to make any sort of claim. Ratcheting up the stakes troubled them. By contrast, few questioned the propriety of asserting a claim to the *dacha*. The consensus among the participants as to Daria Nikolaevna's right to a share in the dwelling made them less apprehensive about the probable outcome.

Costs. With respect to both scenarios, the focus group participants' reluctance to go to court was fuelled by their perceptions of the costs of doing so. Like many Russians, they believe that court cases tend to drag on endlessly.[29] According to the 2012 round of the Russian Longitudinal Monitoring Survey – a nationally representative panel survey – over two-thirds of respondents cited delays as a constraint on their willingness to use the courts. While it is true that cases occasionally drag on for years, these are the exceptions rather than the rule. The procedural codes contain deadlines for every category of case, which tend to be measured in weeks and months.[30] Detailed statistics of judges' ability to live up to these rules are maintained. They reveal that fewer than 2 per cent of civil cases violate these deadlines.[31] These data play a critical role in determining salaries and promotions and, not surprisingly, judges rarely tarry. Indeed, their need for speed risks sacrificing substantive justice at the altar of efficiency (Pomorski 2001).

The discussions of the inheritance claim were replete with examples of cases that took years longer than anyone thought necessary. It is not surprising that many of these stories involved friends or the friends of friends. The length of time involved may have been exaggerated through the retelling, but the very fact that the participants could recite these details is indicative. The duration of cases cited during the discussions of the consumer complaint tended to be shorter, but

---

[29] Although most participants wondered how Irina Ivanovna would find time to pursue a lawsuit, Elizaveta, a 41-year-old Moscow housewife, disagreed. She spoke with some authority, having suffered through a lawsuit over property lines with a neighbour. She pointed out that, as a teacher, Irina's workday ended at 3 p.m. and that she had a long summer vacation.

[30] For example, Art. 154 of the Civil Procedure Code (GPK RF) mandates that civil cases heard by district courts be resolved within two months of being filed. Justices of the peace, who have jurisdiction over simpler civil cases, are given only a month from the date a case is accepted to issue a decision.

[31] As the number of cases has increased, the incidence of violations of the statutory deadlines for resolving civil cases has inched downwards. In 2012, it was 1.9 per cent, which decreased to 1.6 in 2013 and 1.4 in 2014. For the first six months of 2015, 1.2 per cent of cases fell into this category (Otchet 2012, 2013, 2014, 2015).

were no less annoying to those involved. For example, Egor, a 65-year-old Muscovite who chaired his housing committee, told of a lawsuit brought against him several years ago by the former chairman, on the grounds that he refused to pay her a bonus. 'I didn't spend a *kopeck* on this idiotic complaint, which she lost. But I lost an entire summer. Every week we went to deal with this nonsense. I sat there in court, waiting three or four hours.' Others were similarly galled by what they saw as the indifference of judges and court staff to the inconvenience such delays caused to working people. On the other hand, a 2008 Levada Center survey of Russian court-users reveals that they were generally satisfied with the timing of their hearings (Hendley 2016), leaving open the question of whether the focus group participants might be outliers.

The monetary cost of litigation also played a role. As I noted earlier, participants bemoaned the cost of lawyers. Not everyone believed that the advice and/or services on offer were worth the price. Attitudes diverged when it came to the two scenarios. As to the *dacha*, the need for legal expertise was more obvious and participants were more willing to pay the going rate for it (rather than relying on lawyer-friends). By contrast, going it on their own or relying on law-related websites were more palatable options when it came to the consumer claim. Indeed, many advocated simply discarding the faulty phone and buying a new one. The relatively low ($150) value of the phone pushed many to question whether activating the judicial process was worth it. A full understanding of the regime for court fees was beyond the ken of almost all of the participants. A few knew that Russia has a loser pays system that would allow Irina Ivanovna to be reimbursed for her legal expenses (including the cost of a lawyer and *ekspertiz*) if she prevailed. However, only one participant knew that filing fees (*gosposhlina*) are waived for consumer claims initiated by consumers (Article 17, O zashchite 1992), and he was atypical. When explaining to his group that bringing consumer claims was basically free for the plaintiff, Sergei, a 46-year-old Moscow computer specialist, cited the law governing consumer rights by name. Though he did not bring this up in the group meeting, he had initiated a case alleging falsified election results, which is strikingly different from the mundane claims made by others with court experience.

However, the cost that was most troubling to the focus group participants was emotional. Even when the potential lawsuit would target a faceless stranger, as in the first scenario, the likely toll on the claimant's physical and psychic wellbeing troubled participants. When talking about her then pending lawsuit, Elena's comments about the damage to her health were reminiscent of what Alla said in her Moscow group (discussed earlier). Maksim reminded his colleagues that, 'If you don't want to damage your nerves, you can hire a lawyer (*advokat*) at the outset and empower him to act on your behalf, then you don't have to go.' For many, the decision to pursue the claim to court hinged on the amount at issue. Although Vera (a 40-year-old Muscovite who worked in higher education and was part of the same group as Alla) saw herself as the sort of person who, when wronged, pursued the matter to the end, she conceded that, in Irina Ivanovna's shoes, she probably would not file a lawsuit over such a small sum. Protecting her nerves would be more important.

Social distance. Concerns over the psychological costs of litigating only deepened when the context shifted to a dispute among family members. As the socio-legal literature predicts, the focus group participants were more skittish about confrontational strategies, such as litigation, when it involved people known to them (Engel 1984; Hendley 2011a; Merry 1990). Egor expressed the sentiments of many when he said that, when it comes to family disputes, 'Reconciliation is always better than court.' Reflecting on his experience, Gennadii noted that not only are such cases difficult for the parties, but they also try the patience of judges. He recalled that, after several years of hearings in which neither side was willing to budge, the frustration of the judge boiled over. She told them, 'You have worn me out. Haven't you figured out a solution yet?' Her remark hints at the tendency to turn to the court in despair when all efforts to solve a problem have failed. When the problem is rooted in a legal question, this makes sense. When, as in Daria Nikolaevna's situation, the legal issues are masking a deeper interpersonal problem, the parties often come to the court with unrealistic expectations. As the judge in Gennadii's case implied, the resolution ought to come from the parties themselves.

Estrangement is not an uncommon consequence of litigation over inheritance claims. Recall Berta's story of how her relationship with her niece was ruined due to their court battle. Along similar lines, Gennadii's relationship with his aunts did not survive their lawsuit. These are representative of the many stories told of relational damage in the wake of litigation after the death of a loved one. The evidence presented at the hearings tends to be intensely personal, painting a picture of a relationship with the deceased that may be at odds with that of the opposing party. Charges of deceit and lying tend to fly fast and furiously. The psychological damage is not always assuaged by the court's decision; it can sometimes exacerbate the underlying tensions. On the other hand, Galina, a 40-year-old school administrator from Voronezh, contended that the court can provide a level of clarity that is often impossible for family members to attain as their disagreements devolve into verbal mud wrestling. She laments the fact that, in the wake of such disputes, when family members 'see each other on the street, they will turn away – they won't even greet each other. Given that, it seems to me that it's better to go to court'. Her comments echo Yngvesson's (1985) argument that lawsuits can act to reframe the relationships among intimates.

As the social distance between the parties increases, relational damage is less likely. Irina Ivanovna, for example, has no longstanding relationship with Evroset'. She may come away from a lawsuit determined never to return to the store, but the overall impact on her life is minimal. My research on debt collection among industrial firms in the economic (or *arbitrazh*) courts suggests that relational damage may also be muted when the key evidence is document-based rather than testimony-driven. I found that Russian firms come away from lawsuits with few hard feelings towards one another. In contrast to their counterparts in legal systems with stronger adversarial traditions, these Russian firms typically continue doing business together (Hendley 2004). As veterans of many court proceedings (or 'repeat players', in Galanter's 1974 terms), the petty annoyances of court that the focus group participants harped on had receded to background noise. The participants' court experiences tended to be limited to one or two cases that loomed large in their memories. Even so, as far as the mobile phone scenario was concerned, none of them were worried about the danger of damaging the relationship with the retail outlet.

Legal literacy. The focus group participants frequently referred to themselves as legally illiterate (*iuridicheskie negramotnye*). They came to the same conclusion as to Irina Ivanovna and Daria Nikolaevna. They were particularly tough on the former. Like many of her colleagues, Ekaterina, a 52-year-old Novisibirsk grocery store manager, condemned Irina, as an educated person, for relying on the promises of the salesperson and not reading the fine print of the sales contract, saying 'She is at fault herself'. Similar sentiments were expressed in the other groups. Yet, when pressed by the moderator, most participants admitted that they rarely read consumer contracts carefully before signing them.

This is hardly unique to Russians, though some participants were quick to attribute it to the 'mentality' of Russians.[32]

Despite describing themselves as largely ignorant of the law, the participants did not hesitate to put forward their views of the law as gospel. The discussions were peppered with squabbles over the specifics of law in which neither side had it quite right, but both sides were confident of their positions. Typical is the response of Valentina, a 56-year-old Moscow state bureaucrat who, when challenged, responded, 'It is not my opinion, it is the law'. I earlier noted the fact that most participants did not realise that filing fees are not assessed on consumer complaints and that they did not know that losers pay the legal expenses of winners in court. Along similar lines, only one participant pointed out that Irina Ivanovna would be entitled to recover punitive (*moral'nye*) damages under the law (Article 15, O zashchite 1992). As to the second scenario, examples include Daria Nikolaevna's legal right to inherit. Because she was a grandchild, rather than a child of the deceased, some were convinced that she would have to take a back seat to her aunts and uncles. Others thought that her right to inherit would depend on whether her grandparents had taken on the formal role of guardian after the death of her parents. Still others thought that it would hinge on whether she had been living at the *dacha* when her grandmother died. To be fair, every group had vocal members who interpreted the facts correctly, understanding that Daria Nikolaevna took her father's share.

Discussions of the letter of the law featured more prominently in the groups populated by those with court experience. While the other groups eventually wound their way around to questions of what the law allowed, such issues tended to be brought up at the outset by court veterans. Their knowledge was broader and more accurate than that of their less experienced colleagues. As a group, however, they were not more likely to agitate for litigation.

Personal experience. Even more telling in shaping participants' attitudes towards disputes were their own personal experiences. For some, such as Pavel (real estate agent) and Egor (housing committee chair),

---

[32] In earlier focus groups that gathered together Russians who had recently made substantial repairs to their homes, the participants also confessed to failing to read contracts before signing them. Some attributed it to 'laziness', while others saw it as a consequence of their busy lives (Hendley 2010: 674). For a comparison with the US, see Ayres and Schwartz (2014).

these experiences stemmed from their jobs whereas, for most, the defining moments grew out of prior disputes. Those who had benefited from consultations with consumer rights agencies enthusiastically recommended this avenue. They saw it as a way of levelling the playing field when challenging big retail outlets. When it came to court, most participants saw their experiences as cautionary tales. A few came away disillusioned with the integrity and competence of judges. Not surprisingly, these participants warned their colleagues away from using the courts. The more common reaction to the courts was a recognition of the importance of being well prepared and patient when initiating a lawsuit. None of them saw litigation as the ideal outcome; most saw it as a last-ditch solution.

CONCLUSIONS

The narrative of Russian courts within the mass media (both Russian and Western) and much of the social science literature is one of dysfunction (e.g., Dawisha 2014; Gessen 2015, 2016; Hedlund 2005). Courts are typically described as politicised, corrupt and incompetent, leading to the conclusion that they are unusable. While not disputing the existence of these phenomena in Russian courts, my analysis of the discussion of how to solve problems among the focus group participants suggests that such concerns do not dominate the thinking of Russians when faced with routine problems. Much like their counterparts elsewhere, few of the focus group participants were eager to go to court. However, their reluctance stemmed not from a dread (or expectation) of extralegal pressure being applied on judges, but from more mundane fears of the stress associated with litigation. These include the time and energy needed to see a lawsuit through to the end as well as the emotional and financial costs. Their self-diagnosed legal illiteracy and lack of trust in legal professionals only redoubled their misgivings. They recognised the danger of ruptures in personal relationships when litigating with friends and family. Even so, going to court is clearly seen as a viable option if efforts to resolve problems resist negotiated settlements.

A very different picture might emerge if Russians were asked about their likely course of action in response to a less routine problem. My prior research (Hendley 2011b) suggests that Russians tend to avoid the courts when faced with a dispute involving the state or a well-connected individual (regardless of whether such connections are political or financial). It is in these categories of dispute, which are relatively rare, that Russians see a genuine risk of political interference. As a result, they tend to stay silent and absorb damages passively rather than risk rocking the boat and bringing down the wrath of their powerful enemies on themselves.[33] This serves to remind us of the multiple narratives of law and courts in contemporary Russia. Like potential litigants elsewhere, Russians' willingness to use the courts depends on a multiplicity of factors, including the merits of their claims as well as the context in which they arise.

ACKNOWLEDGEMENTS

Funding for the research underlying this article was provided by grants from the Eurasia Foundation, the International Research and Exchanges Board and the Graduate School of the University of Wisconsin-Madison.

References

Arlidge, J. (2012) 'Mayfair's most wanted: ES meets Yevgeny Chichvarkin', *Evening Standard,* 14 December. www.standard.co.uk/lifestyle/esmagazine/mayfair-s-most-wanted-es-meets-yevgeny-chichvarkin-8411511.html (accessed 12 March 2016).
Ayres, I. and Schwartz, A. (2014) 'The no-reading problem in consumer contract law', *Stanford Law Review,* 66(3): 545–610.
Belov, B. A. (2015) 'Raspredelenie bremeni dokazyvaniia v sporakh s potrebitelem', *Rossiiskaia iustitsiia,* 12: 13–15.
Bespalov, Iu. F. and Bespalova, A. Iu. (2013) *Dela o Nasledovanii: Nekotorye Spornye Voprosy Pravoprimeneniia.* Moscow: Prospekt.
Bogdanova, E. (2015) 'The Soviet consumer: more than just a Soviet man', in Vihavainen, T. and Bogdanova, E. (eds.) *Communism and Consumerism: The Soviet Alternative to the Affluent Society.* Boston: Brill, 113–38.
Butler, W. E. (2014) *Russian Inheritance Law.* London: Wildy, Simmonds and Hill.
Chekhov, A. (1982) 'The complaints book', in *Chekhov: The Early Stories, 1883–1888.* New York: Macmillan, 36–7 (transl. P. Miles and H. Pitcher).
Cormier, K. E. (2007) 'Grievance practices in post-Soviet Kyrgyz agriculture', *Law and Social Inquiry,* 32(2): 435–66.

---

[33] Cautionary tales abound, ranging from those who ran afoul of Putin to those who were on the losing side of battles for corporate control. The former include Aleksei Naval'nyi and Mikhail Khodorkovskii (e.g., Herszenhorn 2014; Sakwa 2009). The latter include the many entrepreneurs languishing in jail on the basis of manufactured evidence (e.g., Romanova 2011).

Dawisha, K. (2014) *Putin's Kleptocracy: Who Owns Russia?* New York: Simon and Schuster.
Elkov, I'. and Cherniak, I'. (2013) 'Kvartirnyi vopros', *Rossiiskaia gazeta*, 4 July, http://rg.ru/2013/07/04/socio.html (accessed 15 March 2016).
Ellickson, R. (1991) *How Neighbors Settle Disputes*. Cambridge, MA: Harvard University Press.
Engel, D. M. (1984) 'The oven bird's song: insiders, outsiders, and personal injuries in an American community', *Law and Society Review*, 18(4): 551–82.
Felstiner, W. L. F., Abel, R. L. and Sarat, A. (1980–81) 'The emergence and transformation of disputes: naming, blaming, claiming ...', *Law and Society Review*, 15(3–4): 631–54.
Frank, S. P. (1999) *Crime, Cultural Conflict, and Justice in Rural Russia, 1865–1914*. Berkeley, CA: University of California Press.
Frierson, C. (2002) *All Russia Is Burning! A Cultural History of Fire and Arson in the Late Imperial Russia*. Seattle: University of Washington Press.
Galanter, M. (1974) 'Why the "haves" come out ahead: speculations on the limits of legal change', *Law and Society Review*, 9(1): 95–160.
Gessen, M. (2015) 'Is it 1937 yet?' *New York Times*, 5 May. www.nytimes.com/2015/05/06/opinion/masha-gessen-putin-russia-is-it-1937-yet.html (accessed 10 April 2016).
  (2016) 'Putin's year in scandals', *New York Times*, 6 January. www.nytimes.com/2016/01/06/opinion/putins-year-in-scandals.html?_r=1 (accessed 10 April 2016).
Grazhdanskii kodeks Rossiiskoi Federatsii, chast' pervaia, No. 51_FZ, 30 November 1994 [GK RF 1994] www.consultant.ru/document/cons_doc_LAW_5142/ (accessed 10 April 2016).
  chast' tret'ia, No. 146-FZ, 26 November 2001 [GK RF 2001] www.consultant.ru/document/cons_doc_LAW_34154/ (accessed 10 April 2016).
Grazhdanskii protsessual'nyi kodeks Rossiiskoi Federatsii, No. 138-FZ, 14 November 2002 [GPK RF] www.consultant.ru/document/cons_doc_LAW_39570/ (accessed 10 April 2016).
Haltom, W. and McCann, M. (2004) *Distorting the Law: Politics, Media, and the Litigation Crisis*. Chicago: University of Chicago Press.
Hedlund, S. (2005) *Russian Path Dependence*. New York: Routledge.
Hendley, K. (2001) 'Beyond the tip of the iceberg: business disputes in Russia', in Murrell, P. (ed.) *Assessing the Value of Law in Transition Economies*. Ann Arbor, MI: University of Michigan Press, 20–55.
  (2004) 'Business litigation in Russia: a portrait of debt collection in Russia', *Law and Society Review*, 31(1): 305–47.
  (2010) 'Mobilizing law in contemporary Russia: the evolution of disputes over home repair projects', *American Journal of Comparative Law*, 58(3): 631–78.
  (2011a) 'Resolving problems among neighbors in post-Soviet Russia: uncovering the law of the *Pod"ezd*', *Law and Social Inquiry*, 36(2): 388–418.

(2011b) 'Varieties of legal dualism: making sense of the role of law in contemporary Russia', *Wisconsin International Law Journal*, 29(2): 233–62.

(2017) *Everyday Law in Russia*. Ithaca: Cornell University Press.

(2016) 'Justice in Moscow?' *Post-Soviet Affairs*, i32: 491–511.

Hendley, K., Murrell, P. and Ryterman, R. (2000) 'Law, relationships and private enforcement: transactional strategies of Russian enterprises', *Europe-Asia Studies*, 52(4): 627–56.

Henry, L. A. (2012) 'Complaint-making as political participation in contemporary Russia', *Communist and Post-Communist Studies*, 45(1): 243–54.

Herszenhorn, D. (2014) 'Aleksei Navalny, Putin critic, is spared prison in a fraud case, but his brother is jailed', *New York Times*, 30 December www.nytimes.com/2014/12/31/world/europe/aleksei-navalny convicted .html?_r=0 (accessed 10 April 2016).

Hilton, M. (2009) 'The customer is always wrong; consumer complaint in late-NEP Russia', *Russian Review*, 68(1): 1–25.

Maggs, P. B., Schwartz, O. and Burnham, W. (2015) *Law and Legal System of the Russian Federation*. Huntington, NY: Juris Publishing (6th edn).

McKillop, B. (1997) 'Anatomy of a French murder case', *American Journal of Comparative Law*, 45(3): 527–83.

Merry, S. E. (1990) *Getting Justice and Getting Even: Legal Consciousness among Working-Class Americans*. Chicago, IL: University of Chicago Press.

Michelson, E. (2007) 'Climbing the dispute pagoda: grievances and appeals to the official justice system in rural China', *American Sociological Review*, 72(3): 459–85.

Nosyreva, E. I. (2010) 'Spetsial'noe pravovoe regulirovanie posrednichestva (analiz zakonoproekta)', *Treteiskii sud*, 2: 39–44.

Otchet o rabote sudov obshchei iurisdiktsii o rassmotrenii grazhdanskikh del po pervoi instantsii za 12 mesiatsev 2012 g. www.cdep.ru/index.php?id= 79 (accessed 15 March 2016).

Otchet o rabote sudov obshchei iurisdiktsii o rassmotrenii grazhdanskikh del po pervoi instantsii za 12 mesiatsev 2013 g. www.cdep.ru/index.php?id= 79 (accessed 15 March 2016).

Otchet o rabote sudov obshchei iurisdiktsii o rassmotrenii grazhdanskikh del po pervoi instantsii za 12 mesiatsev 2014 g. www.cdep.ru/index.php?id= 79 (accessed 15 March 2016).

Otchet o rabote sudov obshchei iurisdiktsii o rassmotrenii grazhdanskikh, administrativnykh del po pervoi instantsii za 6 mesiatsev 2015 g. www.cdep.ru/index.php?id=79 (accessed 15 March 2016).

'O zashchite prav potrebitelei'. Zakon Rossiiskoi Federatsii ot 7 fevralia 1992, No. 2300–1, with amendments through 13 July 2015. 1992. www.consultant.ru/document/cons_doc_LAW_305/ (accessed 15 March 2016).

Pomorski, S. (2001) 'Justice in Siberia: a case study of a lower criminal court in the city of Krasnoyarsk', *Communist and Post-Communist Studies*, 34(4): 447–78.

Romanova, O. (2011) *Butyrka*. Moscow: Astrel'.

Russian Longitudinal Monitoring Survey-Higher School of Economics, www.cpc.unc.edu/projects/rlms-hse (accessed 10 April 2016).

Sandefur, R. (2007) 'The importance of doing nothing: everyday problems and responses of inaction', in Pleasence P., Buck, A. and Balmer, N. (eds.) *Transforming Lives: Law and Social Processes*. Ontario: Legal Services Commission, 112–32.

Sakwa, R. (2009) *The Quality of Freedom: Khodorkovsky, Putin, and the Yukos Affair*. New York: Oxford University Press.

Trubek, D., Austin, S., Felstiner, W. L. F., Kritzer, H. M. and Grossman, J. B. (1983) 'The costs of ordinary litigation', *UCLA Law Review*, 31(1): 72–127.

Yngvesson, B. (1985) 'Dispute processing: re-examining continuing relations and the law', *Wisconsin Law Review*, 3: 623–46.

Zavisca, J. (2003) 'Contesting capitalism at the post-Soviet dacha: the meaning of food cultivation for urban Russians', *Slavic Review*, 62(4): 786–810.

CHAPTER FOUR

THE EVERYDAY EXPERIENCES OF RUSSIAN CITIZENS IN JUSTICE OF THE PEACE COURTS

Varvara Andrianova

This research describes the experiences of ordinary Russian citizens in Justice of the Peace courts, the local institutions of justice that hear more than 90 per cent of all cases initiated in the Russian Federation.[1] My intention is to examine how Russian court users work through the maze of lower courts without relying on any legal assistance, to look at the images of the institution that emerge through interaction with the administration and the judges and to reflect on the resulting assessment of justice as a summary of the whole experience of the court.

The research was conducted in Justice of the Peace courts in Moscow and two courts in one of Moscow's satellite cities. Four Justice of the Peace courts in Moscow were randomly selected from a list of judicial districts in residential areas.[2] The city in Russia was randomly selected

---

[1] 'Statisticheskie Pokazateli Deyatelnosti Sudov Obshey Yurisdiktsii' [Statistical Indicators of Activity of Courts of General Jurisdiction], *Sudebniy Departament pri Verhovnom Sude Rossiyskoy Federatsii*, [Judicial Department of the Supreme Court of the Russian Federation], searchable database of court statistics arranged by year, available at www.cdep.ru/index.php?id=79.

[2] I refer to the courts in Moscow as Justice of the Peace courts in Moscow' or 'the Moscow court'. Respondents' names will be kept anonymous; they will be referred to as Respondent, Attorney, Assistant, etc., #, MC. I conducted interviews with five judges in Moscow, who will be referred to as Judge #, MC. There are currently 438 judicial districts in Moscow. For the relevant legislation, see the website of the President of the Russian Federation, with the most recent updates on the number of judicial districts in Moscow and the Moscow Region. 'V Mosckve Uvelicheno Kolishestvo Mirovih Sudey' [The Number of Justices of the Peace Has Been Increased in Moscow], available at http://kremlin.ru/events/president/news/16115.

from a large number of Moscow satellite cities with populations ranging from 20,000 to 40,000 people, which entitles them to two Justices of the Peace (or JPs).[3]

My research used an assortment of mixed methods, which consisted of observations, semi-structured interviews with all participants of the process of justice, focus groups with ordinary citizens and judges, and the analysis of secondary sources, most of which were existing large-scale research projects on citizens' attitudes towards legal institutions. My initial goal was to listen and to be a non-obtrusive observer in the courtroom in order to capture all the nuances of people's experiences. However, as the research project developed, it became apparent that it was necessary to speak to people in order to capture their perceptions and evaluations of what was happening to them. Most interviews in this study followed case observations and were conducted with the litigants and their families, judges, the court administration and legal professionals if they were present. I aimed to elicit people's perceptions of their experiences in the courtroom, their opinions of the court process and its main participants and their overall evaluation of their experiences in the lower courts.

INSTITUTIONAL SETTINGS AND JURISDICTIONS

The original Russian institution of Justices of the Peace was established as part of the Judicial Reform of 1864. It was set up as a court for minor civil and criminal cases and was meant to apply both customary and statutory law, to use mediation where possible and to instruct the public in formal law. JPs did not have a formal legal education and their decisions could not be appealed to the higher courts. It was expected that the Justice of the Peace courts would become a forum where ordinary people could bring their daily disputes and, in return, receive a common-sense approach to their legal problems and a rudimentary understanding of the principles of formal law. However, the institution did not last long – it did not survive the sweeping reforms of the Soviet revolution and was abolished by the Bolsheviks in 1917 (Solomon 2002, 1997).

---

[3] The name of the regional city is withheld in order to protect the identity of the judges and litigants. This city will be referred to as 'the regional city', or 'the city in the Moscow region'. Respondents will be numbered as Respondent #, RC.

It was this institutional model, however, that inspired the (re)introduction in 1991 of the Courts of Justices of the Peace as part of the post-Soviet democratisation of the Russian system of justice (Solomon 2008). Initially, legislators had hoped to revive the idea of JPs who would be close to the people; elected, yet without the requirement of a formal legal training. However, over time, the emphasis of the legal reforms shifted from the establishment of a less professional, simpler form of local justice to the creation of a new branch of the state legal system. With the expansion of the jurisdiction of JPs through their takeover of criminal cases punishable by incarceration, the legislators introduced the requirement of a formal legal education and five years of professional experience for judicial candidates. As it stands now, JPs have the same status and responsibilities as federal judges, with minor differences in salaries and court administration (Hendley 2012a).

The jurisdiction of current Russian Justice of the Peace courts includes three types of case:

- civil, where the amount in dispute does not exceed 50,000 rubles and which includes most family matters and divorces where there is no conflict over children or division of property, property disputes for values not exceeding 500 days' minimum wage, labour disputes (recently limited) and disputes on the use of land;
- criminal, where the maximum punishment does not exceed three years of imprisonment; and
- administrative, i.e., violations of federal administrative law entrusted to courts, taxation violations (recently limited), petty hooliganism, public drunkenness and serious non-criminal traffic violations.[4]

In addition to the traditional 'peace-making' nature of the role of JPs, the institution is charged with the objective of bringing Russian courts within *'shagovaya dostupnost'* – or immediate reach of the Russian population – and of reducing the case load of district judges, thus improving the efficiency of the adjudication of small civil, criminal and administrative claims (Shaposhnikov 2006).

Due to the limited administrative staff of the courts, which I discuss in greater detail shortly, most of the administrative duties of day-to-day court operation fall on the judges themselves. JPs are also responsible

---

[4] 'Kompetentsiya Mirovogo Sudyi' [The Competence of a Justice of the Peace], Fed. Law No. 188-FZ (Dec. 17, 1998), SZ RF 1999, Art. 3, http://base.garant.ru/12113961/#block_3.

for personally guiding litigants through the process of case preparation during the pre-trial sessions. As a result of this judge-centred institutional structure, it could be said that the institutions themselves are largely identified with the judges.

JP districts have been created according to the ratio of one judge per 15,000–23,000 people.[5] Currently there are around 7,500 JPs in Russia.[6] Their case load depends on the specifics of each district. In large cities, legal disputes tend to be more significant in monetary value and thus tend to fall more often within the jurisdiction of district courts, leaving the JPs to deal mostly with small administrative disputes and civil claims (Hendley 2012a). In residential areas, the majority of the cases tend to be family disputes, divorces and property claims whereas, in commercial areas, most cases are related to debt collection and business disputes. The workload of JPs in busy districts can reach 700 cases per month, whereas some judges can hear as few as fifty-four cases per month. Overall, JPs hear about 3,800,000 cases a year, up to 98 per cent of which are resolved within the time allocated by law (Bogdanova et al. 2008; Chechina 1999).[7]

Figure 4.1 presents a graphic view of cases brought to the Courts of Justices of the Peace by the type of dispute involved.[8]

Analysis of case loads brought to the Courts of Justices of the Peace from 2005 to 2014, according the area of law involved, shows a consistent increase in the number of civil cases. The most notable changes within this category are a steady rise in claims by the tax

---

[5] 'Ob Obshem Chisle Mirovih Sudey i Kolichestve Sudebnih Uchastkov v Subjektah Rossijskoy Federtsii' [On the total number of Justices of the Peace and the number of judicial districts in the subjects of the Russian Federation], Fed. Law No. 188-FZ (Dec. 17, 1998), SZ RF 1999, Art. 4, available at http://base.garant.ru/12113961/#block_4.

[6] 'Obzor Rezultatov Deyatelnosti' [Review of Activity], VKKSRF [Supreme Qualification Panel of the Judges of the Russian Federation] 2015) available at http://vkks.ru/publication/39178/.

[7] 'Kompetentsiya (jurisdiktsiya) mirovih sudey' [The Competence (Jurisdiction) of Justices of the Peace], *Department of The Courts of Justices of the Peace of the City of Moscow*, available at http://mos-sud.ru/courtsrf/competention/.

[8] 'Sudebnaya Statistika', *Upravleniye Sudebnogo Departamenta v g. Moskve*, available at http://usd.msk.sudrf.ru/modules.php?name=stat&rid=2. Statistics describing the yearly activities of the Justice of the Peace courts were available for each district, as well as nationwide, until early 2014. Reports published since 2014 offer a statistical breakdown according to judicial district, without providing overall numbers nationwide.

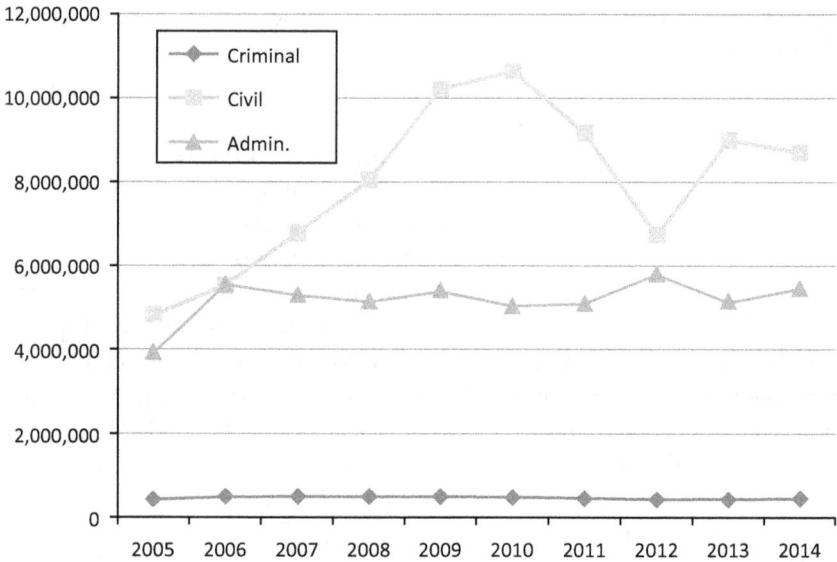

Figure 4.1 Comparison of civil, criminal and administrative cases heard in Courts of Justices of the Peace from 2005 to 2014.

authorities against private citizens, the recovery of overdue rent and utility payments, private claims related to pension payments and claims related to payments for labour. All cases that reached the stage of official decision can be classified according to the parties involved: physical persons, legal entities and the state.

Figure 4.2 shows a general increase, from 2007 to 2010, in cases of legal entities against private citizens (including cases of state agencies against private citizens, covering such fields as taxation and the recovery of debts for the use of utilities). As Figure 4.2 shows, both cases involving two physical parties and those involving physical parties against legal entities remained relatively stable, with just minor fluctuations. It is important to note a relative under-representation in the category of cases of private citizens against the state, showing a reluctance among Russian citizens to initiate claims against state authorities. This also shows that cases initiated by the state undergo substantial fluctuations, which may be explained by political changes in the country and perhaps suggesting that tendencies in Russian lower courts reflect general directions in the operation of the overall Russian state apparatus, as well as ongoing jurisdictional changes.

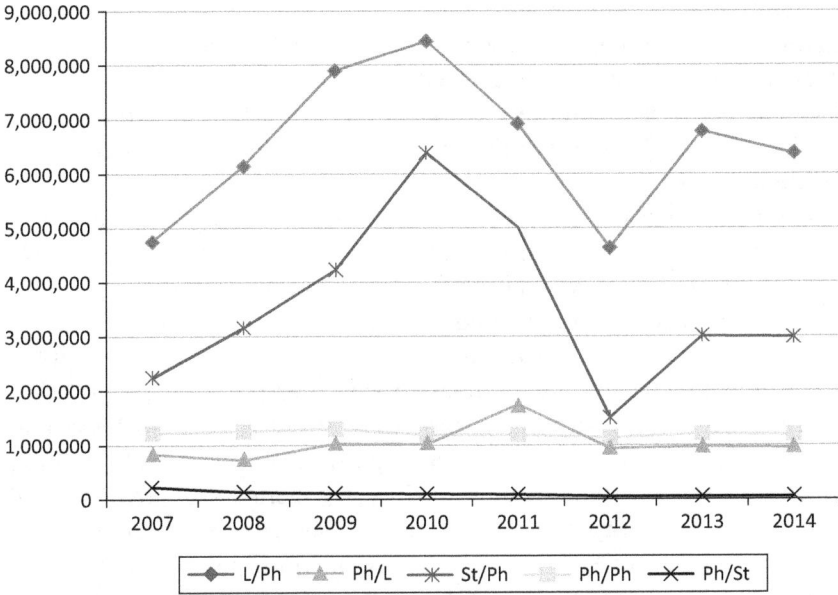

Figure 4.2 Categories of cases – according to the parties involved – decided in Russian Courts of Justices of the Peace from 2007 to 2014.
Note: the categories listed in the key are L=Legal Entities, Ph=Physical Persons and St=State, starting with the initiating party.

CONSTRUCTING THE IMAGE OF THE COURT

What image does the Justice of the Peace court give to people when they find themselves under its roof? What impression do they form from just being in the physical space of the court and learning how to find their way around? What expectation of justice results from the initial experience of going to court?

The architectural organisation and symbolic adornment and operation of any institution play a significant role in constructing a public image of it. Visually, Russian lower courts do not have prominent independent architectural images associated with the law. They blend into the general vision of official state buildings – such as city councils, police stations or utilities management offices. Buildings that housed the Justice of the Peace courts in my study had a utilitarian administrative purpose – one of the regional courts was located in a minimalist 1970s brick building shared with the local police station and small hair salon. In fact, most of the regional lower courts were located in buildings that had been repurposed after the fall of the Soviet Union.

Another trend among Justice of the Peace court buildings was for them to be located on the ground floor of ordinary residential blocks of flats. All the court buildings that I visited in Moscow were thus located, often in quite recent constructions. These locations gave Justice of the Peace courts the appearance of cramped, low-ceilinged residential corridors without windows; they were, in fact, very common spaces planned as flats but used as legal offices. The larger rooms served as public courtrooms and the smaller ones as offices for the judges and court staff. The narrow and windowless corridors and the residential feel of the spaces communicated the mundane and ordinary nature of these courts. As a result, Russian Justice of the Peace courts resembled local bureaucratic agencies similar to state Passport and Registration offices – which deal with mandatory registrations at local addresses and the issuing of internal and foreign passports – or Local Housing Authority offices, which collect utility payments and provide local public services. This general atmosphere was closely associated with what people experience in other state institutions. As one of my respondents commented: 'You come here, and there are no instructions on who to go to see first or what to do – it is like a labyrinth' (Respondent 5, MC).

The public areas of the Russian courts usually had no members of court staff assisting court users – judicial assistants and court secretaries would briefly walk through the public area to the courtrooms for the scheduled hearings, but would not normally interact with the public. Most of my respondents expressed deep frustration about the difficulties of dealing with the Russian courts' administration. As one of them grumbled, 'One has to know one's way around here; no one will just open the door and give you what you want' (Respondent 17, MC). After a long wait in a dimly lit corridor, another respondent commented, 'They treat us like they are big bosses, and we have to do everything they say; they either have lunch, or have more important people to see' (Respondent 12, RC). Russian court users were frustrated by the accepted rules of operation of the lower courts yet, despite this, had no option but to interact with the courts according to these widely accepted norms of behaviour – as when in any state institution and when navigating through state bureaucracy.

The perception of being in a bureaucratic space was also reinforced by the presence of state regalia in most courtrooms and offices of the judges and usually included Russian and local flags, coats of arms and quite frequently, portraits of the president. The resulting image is that of a distant, non-customer-friendly institution, lacking – most importantly – any visible outward expression of its association with law and justice.

What can this tell us about Russian legal culture? It could be said that, traditionally, Russians interacted with state institutions as the sources of good and bad – from protection and punishment to the distribution of goods, jobs and opportunities. As one regional judge commented, 'People still see courts as they were in Soviet times: they expect that the state will do everything for them. We do not work like this now, we can only help people to help themselves' (Judge 2, RC). Indeed, my interviews with court users suggest that the latter have developed an expectation that local courts will act as 'one-stop shops' where all their legal needs can be met. One could argue that this traditional relationship with the Soviet state created a certain expectation that the state would not only control every aspect of people's lives but would also take care of all their problems; however, the relationship did not encourage citizens to be proactive themselves in protecting their legal interests. In present-day Russia, nevertheless, there are many situations in which people have to take the initiative and turn to the courts in order to reach the result they want. Most people in Russia take this initiative in a way that is familiar to them. They see the Justice of the Peace court as one of the bureaucratic institutions of the state, dealings with which are typically done in a personalised way, with the main effort being on maintaining outward formality while internally relying on establishing relationships of 'understanding' and building informal contacts.

CHASING JUSTICE IN THE CORRIDORS OF POWER

Most civil cases start with a petition from a plaintiff, submitted in the required format and accompanied by any relevant supporting materials. Recent changes in their operation mandate that all Justice of the Peace courts must maintain a website with general information about court jurisdiction, location, opening and reception hours, a list of hearings and decisions and downloadable, printable forms of any required petitions. This reform aimed to make the operation of lower courts in Russia transparent and accessible, while improving the overall image of courts and judges. However, while most of the lower courts have now created official websites, their maintenance is lagging behind due to the lack of trained court staff and the heavy workloads of the judges. The administration of Russian Justice of the Peace courts seems thus to be limited to the bare functional minimum. It typically consists of a judicial secretary, an archives officer and more rarely (depending on the size of the district), a judicial assistant, all of whom are required to keep track of scheduled hearings and invite litigants into courtrooms.

It is important to stress again that the institutional model of Russian Justice of the Peace courts does not include a well-defined administrative body that facilitates and expedites case resolution. As a result, JPs have to perform a great number of administrative functions and are seen both as ultimate decision-makers and as heads of court administration. They do delegate some of the paperwork and organisational duties to their secretaries but remain in almost complete control of their courts and case files. This means that all responsibility for preparing cases, updating files, communicating with the relevant authorities and general administrative and secretarial duties usually falls on the JPs, who can then distribute them down the line of authority. This observation reflects a general tendency towards centralised institutional structures in Russia, which creates and reinforces traditional vertical relationships of power and authority.

After a petition has been filed, the judge can accept it and thus initiate a case, deny the petition for lack of substance, return it for its failure to meet the formal or substantive requirements or remain without action until the petition is corrected. JPs are required to take an active role in case management: they have to assist the parties with formal discovery and subpoenas, which usually requires them to have a number of pre-trial meetings and discussions regarding the merits of the case. However, at this stage, a great many disputes initially brought to the courts are abandoned due to their legal or procedural complexity, the settlement of the parties or a change in the intention of the parties to go through with the formal hearing.

This brings me to another important observation: an established tradition in the Russian lower courts allows for an additional informal step in the procedure of case resolution which allows litigants to have unlimited meetings with the judge at any time before the petition is filed or adjudicated. These pre-trial hearings take the form of personal consultations and offer court users a number of opportunities to receive personal advice from the judge and to form a personal relationship with him/her, which is a strong distinguishing feature of this uniquely post-Soviet legal procedure. The judges are easily accessible on a 'first-come, first-served' basis during daily reception hours. These consultations are very informal in nature, allowing the parties to ask the judge for advice on any procedural and legal aspects of their claims. The sessions take place in the judges' offices, are not considered as a formal stage in the proceedings and are not recorded verbatim. After a claim has been officially accepted by the court, these sessions are noted as pre-trial meetings but no formal transcripts are maintained.

This highlights the duality of the everyday operation of Russian lower courts (Hendley 2011). While the outwardly projected image of Russian courts as unfriendly and dismissive creates concern among court users, a different picture emerges when we consider the nature of the relationship between the latter and JPs that forms during the pre-trial sessions I described earlier. The growing use of lower courts suggests that Russian citizens are not deterred by the closed doors and bureaucratic difficulties. Most of my respondents understood that personal effort and persistence were the most appropriate and effective strategies for obtaining guidance and fully benefiting from pre-trial sessions.

My interviews and observations in court suggest that most of my respondents took advantage of this direct access to the judge. As one of the respondents in the regional city commented,

> I came to see the judge twice – the first time he looked over my petition to make sure that everything was in order and that I had all the documents I needed to start the claim. The second time, we looked at the answer from the other side. I think it was very important that I had some kind of idea of how my case would go.
>
> (Respondent 11, RC)

A litigant in a property division case in a regional city also stated:

> At first the judge tried to talk me out of filing a claim: it is a family issue, he said it would be better to settle it by ourselves. But I see no other way here, so I filed anyway.
>
> (Respondent 9, RC)

What was normally discussed in these sessions? The judges stressed that, during the pre-trial meetings, they could comment only on the procedural steps and evidence required for filing claims in their courts. As one regional judge stated:

> I cannot give legal advice; but I can try to talk to the people and see if their problem can be solved out of court. It is my duty to try and prevent the claim.
>
> (Judge 2, RC)

Further conversations with the judges and claimants suggested that standard pre-trial discussions of potential claims involved both legal and procedural advice, mostly because people struggled to separate the substantive and procedural elements of their claims from the emotional side of their arguments. One of the judges in Moscow commented:

> Sometimes you have to explain to people in plain words that they do not have a claim here, or that they will not win just because they feel strongly. We have to educate people.
>
> (Judge 4, MC)

From the perspective of court users, pre-trial sessions were considered important in helping them to navigate through the uncertainties of the legal process. As one claimant in a regional city stated, 'It is good that you can talk to the judge; at least, you understand your case better and know what to do. The judges can tell you how it is' (Respondent 3, RC). Another claimant in Moscow described his meeting with the judge:

> He tried to talk me out of going to court; he said that it would be difficult, and I would not get as much as I want. But I have to do it, so he said that I need to think it over, come back, and then he will explain which documents I need to assemble.
>
> (Respondent 5, MC)

From these and similar statements we can see that the judges perform multiple functions in the Russian Justice of the Peace courts: they listen, advise, educate and manage the timing and preparation of cases, all of which is done while formally upholding the black letter of Russian law. They are seen as 'one-stop shops' for small legal matters, inseparable from the perception of the justice process itself, which unfolds as a multi-stage process of satisfying legal requirements in personal meetings with the judges.

The JPs commented that, on average, they have at least one meeting with each party in civil cases. In their experience, it was quite rare for the litigants not to take advantage of these meetings, because discussing their cases with the judges personally gave them some peace of mind about their claims.

> Sometimes people come two, three times, and hope that it makes their case better. All we can do is help them understand what is necessary to prepare their cases. We can help them understand better what they need to do.
>
> (Judge 2, RC)

The court users valued these meetings quite highly:

> I would rather come here five times and be ready for everything than lose my case.
>
> (Respondent 8, MC)

> If you have this opportunity, you have to use it. I came at first expecting this and that, but the judge tells you how things really are in your case.
>
> (Respondent 11, RC)

Forming a better understanding of their legal causes, necessary evidence and forthcoming procedural steps allows Russian court users to prepare for their cases more thoroughly and to form a concrete expectation of the outcome based on the evaluation of the actual decision-maker in their cases.

This suggests that pre-trial sessions give Russian court users an opportunity to shape the trajectory of their cases from the very beginning of their court experiences. This extended pre-trial stage also allows them to be more involved in the management of any information that goes into their files. While the judge has the ultimate role of managing and updating files with the help of the limited court staff, court users have an active role in the collecting of any necessary evidence and presenting it in the required format. JPs normally advise claimants on which documents are necessary for their particular case – although claimants have to go to other bureaucratic offices to obtain them – often with the precise wording requested by the judge; the documents then find their way into the file. The existence of pre-trial sessions creates an incremental procedure in file creation and gives litigants a chance to participate at every stage of this process. However, this ability to participate in the creation of case files, together with direct access to the judges, reinforces a partial and corrupt image of Russian courts in general. This experience of dealing with court administration and case management informally confirms people's existing belief that every citizen – especially those with higher social status – is able to use courts in this way, thus strengthening their perception of corruption and favouritism in Russian institutions of justice (Ledeneva 1998).

EXPERIENCE IN THE COURTROOM: FROM INFORMAL MEETINGS TO THE EXTREMES OF FORMAL RITUALS

The informal pre-trial stage is followed by a judicial courtroom procedure. All public hearings in Russian lower courts are held formally and decided unilaterally by the judge. This judgment, or indeed any order of a JP in relation to a proceeding, can be appealed in the district court within ten days of the hearing. One of the indicators of the quality and reliability of JP performance, it could be argued, is the low rate of reversal – 3 per cent in criminal cases and 0.8 per cent in civil cases. Some studies also link high levels of effectiveness of Justice of the Peace courts with their increased appeal among the population (Hendley 2012a, 2012b).

There is no requirement that hearings be recorded in an audio or stenographic format – the records of public proceedings are usually dictated by the judge to the secretary. Two narratives usually develop in a normal proceeding: the actual narrative of exchanges between the judge and the parties, and the official narrative dictated by the judge for the record.

So how do people experience the formality of the courtroom hearing that follows after the informally arranged pre-trial meetings? From the perspective of my respondents, everything that happened in the courtroom was dictated by the judge, and they had no other option but to relinquish any control or initiative they expected to have in presenting their cases. Typical comments that I was repeatedly given were:

> I did what the judge said – sit, stand, then answer. This was my first time in court, so I just wanted to do what the judge said.
>
> (Respondent 3, MC)

> It was difficult because the judge wanted me only to answer his specific questions; it was very fast, and I did not have time to think, it all went very quickly.
>
> (Respondent 11, MC)

Although all respondents anticipated that the hearing itself would be important, in the overall process of decision-making they realised that the judge already knew the outcome before the formal hearing even started. One claimant in a regional city commented, while the judge was out of the courtroom preparing the decision,

> The judge has seen all the documents; he knows the case because he told me what documents I needed so I think he knows what decision to take. I am just worried in case there were any changes or if the other party did something [extralegal means of influence].
>
> (Respondent 16, MC)

The JPs confirmed that, as a rule, they knew which decision to take ahead of time because the applicable law was clear and they had all the necessary documentation to support their decisions; new and unexpected evidence or statements by the parties would rarely emerge during the hearing itself, as a senior judge in the regional court said:

> I decide cases according to the law: it is important to determine all the facts of the case – done in pre-trial investigation, in civil cases – in pre-trial hearings. So the case has to be very clear before the day of the hearing.
>
> (Judge 2, RC)

Because, at the hearing, the case is already clear to the judge and there are very few, if any, questions to clarify, proceedings usually run in a fast, formalised manner, mostly to comply with the requirements of procedural regulations. Predictably, the abruptness and shortness of interactions with the judge in the courtroom created the impression that the hearings were held only for formal purposes and not in order to reach a fair judgment. My respondents commented that they wanted to be able to speak more in court; it was important for them to tell their story:

> I could not even explain anything to the judge. I think it was unfair, the judge asked questions, and when I wanted to speak, he said it was not relevant to the case.
>
> (Respondent 11, MC)

> I thought I could tell my side of the story, but it seems like it was all already decided, so why did I have to appear at all?.
>
> (Respondent 18, RC)

These statements came from both winning parties and those who lost their case. A defendant who received a suspended sentence in a criminal case commented:

> I am glad that it all ended well; I was very worried because I could not say anything in the courtroom; you just have to answer questions when the judge asks, but it is good that it ended positively.
>
> (Respondent 9, RC)

Another successful claimant in the regional city stated:

> I thought I would need to explain the situation in the beginning or somehow make a statement, but the judge already had my statement and just read it. I guess that is how the hearing goes.
>
> (Respondent 13, RC)

These statements indicate that Russian court users, just like anywhere else, valued the ability to tell their story and to be heard by the decision-maker. However, in the context of the courtroom, Russian litigants faced the reality of formal procedures which allowed them very little personal speaking and participation time.

JPs, on the other hand, had pragmatic explanations for what was happening in the courtroom. As one of them put it:

> People want to tell their story, but they have to do it in the way that is correct according to the procedure. They had plenty of opportunities to talk, to express their complaints, or to describe the facts of their cases in the pre-trial hearings. In the courtroom I just need to determine the facts on the basis of which the decision will be made, and to give people a chance to admit or deny them; that is what I want to hear, not the whole story from beginning to end.
>
> (Judge 3, RC)

Another judge in a Moscow court said:

> People do not know about court procedure; they come thinking that it will be like on TV programmes. I have eighteen cases from the Taxation Service to resolve – and I have to do all the calculations – then three criminal offences and, if I listen to everybody, we will be here until 10 p.m.
>
> (Judge 6, MC)

As a result of this interaction with the lower courts, Russian litigants did not feel that they were treated with respect and dignity by the court, with the exception of their private meetings with the judges. Yet, they had no other option than to follow the procedure imposed on them for the sake of their case reaching a successful outcome, as one litigant in the Moscow court said:

> I can tell you that it is incorrect when you cannot even talk openly in the courtroom; it was my opportunity to tell the truth. But you know how it works, the rules are the rules. I did not want to argue ('*konfliktovat*') with the judge. It all could end badly.
>
> (Respondent 19, MC)

This treatment in the lower courts seemed to be accepted by court users, even though they found it unjust and disrespectful. Sensing injustice, however, does not empower them to demand other treatment from decision-makers or state employees. Instead of demanding fair and respectful treatment, Russian citizens take a gaming attitude towards the courts and find ways of dealing with the particularities of this institutional arrangement. I would argue that the unwillingness of Russian court users to oppose judicial authority, in addition to the high level of formality in the hearings coexisting with the informality of pre-trial sessions, are the main characteristics of the legal process in Russian lower courts.

LEGAL ASSISTANCE IN RUSSIAN JUSTICE OF THE PEACE COURTS

Perceptions of competent legal assistance have been recognised as one of the main factors shaping people's overall perceptions of organisational justice (Tyler 2008). Empirical studies suggest that litigants' evaluations of their experiences of the justice system depend in part on their relationship with their legal counsel.

> If lawyers are viewed as agents of the legal system and if they are the agents which whom the litigant has the most contact, then a favourable impression of the lawyer might generalize to produce favourable impressions of the system. In addition, evaluations of lawyers might influence perceived fairness and satisfaction by virtue of the importance of the lawyer for successful litigation.
>
> (Lind et al. 1989: 20)

As Russian lower courts are designed to deal with the legal problems that are considered simple enough to be resolved without legal representation, there is no expectation that lawyers would play any role in the courts of Justices of the Peace. It is assumed that disposing with the need for legal representation in small cases would make courts more attractive financially and more accessible to people with no specific legal knowledge or previous court experience. Indeed, the majority of cases in Russian lower courts are filed and resolved without any involvement by legal representatives. Only a small number of litigants who participated in my research turned to the help of external legal professionals on those occasions when they believed the cases to be too difficult for them to handle alone. One litigant, a defendant in a divorce case, stated: 'It is serious, so I had to find an attorney; you need to treat this seriously' (Respondent 9, RC). Another litigant in an inheritance claim in Moscow said:

> I thought I could do it by myself at first; then I talked to the judge, and it became clear that I did not know the laws and the deadlines. He said

> that, in these cases, it is better to have an attorney. You need to pay, but at least you know that it will go well.
>
> (Respondent 12, RC)

Another group of cases involving external legal assistance were those in which people, based on the pre-trial meetings with the judges, did not expect a good outcome or had been told that their cases were not sufficiently strong.

> I came to talk to the judge, but it was very confusing; it seemed that he already had a negative opinion about my case. I went to the local attorney to double-check and then filed the case. It is a pity that I cannot take my case to another judge, but the attorney said that we have a strong case.
>
> (Respondent 11, RC)

This suggests that Russian lower-court users largely turned to attorneys after they had tried to evaluate their cases themselves in pre-trial sessions and realised that they needed additional support. The availability of pre-trial sessions in Russian courts puts attorneys in a secondary advisory position; people rely on the latter when they cannot rely on the judges to give them any certainty about the outcome of their case.

A short note needs to be added here about the availability of free legal aid for Russian court users. Free legal assistance is available to any Russian citizen who qualifies according to a federal law that came into force in 2011.[9] The groups of citizens who qualify for this assistance include pensioners, people with disabilities, minors and other disadvantaged citizens. However, my research suggests that none of my respondents were aware of the existence of free legal assistance. The judges themselves referred to it as a very complicated scheme, as evidenced by this judge in the regional city: 'People have to request free legal assistance from the court, which means that they need to know about it, but if we (judges) don't tell them, they don't know about it. This whole idea does not work in reality' (Judge 2, RC).

Therefore, although independent, privately obtained legal assistance in the lower Russian courts was generally seen as a way to

---

[9] 'O Besplatnoy Juridichesstkoy Poloshi v Rossiyskoy Federatsii' [About Free Legal Aid in the Russian Federation], Federalniy Zakon Rossiyskoy Federatsii, 21 November, 2011, N324 – FZ, available at 9. Федеральный закон Российской Федерации, 21 ноября 2011 года, N324 - ФЗ.

secure the desired outcomes in difficult cases, it was not considered necessary and was not normally paid for because court users expected legal clarification and procedural assistance from the judges. My findings show that Russian court users perceived the judges themselves to be sources of legal advice, as one pensioner in the Moscow court stated: 'That is why you come before the hearing: the judge can explain what you don't understand (Respondent 11, MC). The judges themselves commented that, despite not having this responsibility and, in fact, despite being precluded from giving legal advice, they often do have to clarify the legal aspects of cases to people who need their help.

> I know it is not my responsibility, but I don't want anybody's time to be wasted and I have to explain the legal aspects of complaints quite often.
> (Judge 2, RC)

Although the overall number of people seeking legal representation in court remains low, the use of paid legal services in Russia has been growing, as a claimant in Moscow stated.

> I went to an attorney to make sure that I had a strong claim; it is not that expensive if you don't want to be represented in the hearing but only. want some advice
> (Respondent 9, MC)

The increased willingness of the Russian public to consult attorneys before court appearances was mentioned by the Russian judges as well:

> People are still very sceptical about appearing in court with attorneys, the cost being one of the main reasons, but we have many more attorney offices here now, so more people are taking advantage of that.
> (Judge 2, RC)

It is apparent that the availability of professional legal advice in Russia has increased. However, only a small number of my respondents actually turned to attorneys for help, and even fewer were represented in the courtroom.

One explanation may be the generally low quality of legal services available for small cases in which the payout is expected to be small, combined with the deep mistrust of lawyers that has been verified in almost all surveys (Rimskiy 2009). Nevertheless, it seems that the main reason for the almost non-presence of lawyers in the Justice of

Peace courts is the availability of pre-trial sessions, which gives court users an opportunity to gain legal and procedural advice directly from the judges.

When summarising the role that legal professionals play in shaping people's perceptions of courts, my respondents expressed the need for professional legal assistance even at this lowest level of legal institutions. Since legal counsel was not required, the tendency was to obtain it in the form of helpful information from the source that would – officially or unofficially – be responsible for providing it. While the use of courts without legal advice is considered complicated, intimidating and stressful, Russian court users deal with these complications by relying more on the personal interaction they have with the judge during the pre-trial sessions, which is then occasionally backed up by the opinion of external legal professionals. With free legal aid being virtually unused in the lower Russian courts, the cost of professional legal services and external attorneys is considered a deterrent. The informality of communication between court users and judges allows for a more informal flow of information and thus greater clarification and explanation during the pre-trial meetings, probably due to the traditional way in which Russian people perceive state institutions, including courts.

USERS' REFLECTIONS ON THE OUTCOME OF THEIR CASES

When asked to evaluate their experiences immediately after the hearings, court users stated that they were shocked and shaken by the proceedings. Even in cases with favourable outcomes, people did not describe their immediate reaction and feelings as positive –

> 'I am just glad it's over; I feel relieved that it ended' (Respondent 9, RC); 'How can you be happy after this? You saw how stressful it was' (Respondent 17, MC); 'It was so difficult, I feel like I was just very lucky'. (Respondent 22, MC)

– were the most common comments made by court users. The brevity and reserved nature of comments following successful outcomes were usually accompanied by a general feeling that something rather unusual or lucky had just taken place. Litigants often did not want to discuss the outcome of their case, as though they feared that, if examined, the outcome would be reversed or somehow taken away from them. The overall perception of justice was of a rather fleeting and ephemeral nature.

In some cases which ended favourably, court users praised the judge but did not extend their praise to the courts themselves:

> The judge was good. It is important, you know, for a judge to be a human being ('*chelovek*'). You can talk to him, and he can understand you.

Another interviewee commented:

> I was lucky to have a good judge; he helped me to prepare my case. Otherwise, I would not have known what to do.

The emerging theme is that people perceived their success in court as something lucky and unusual, something that happened despite the system being unwelcoming and unfair, as this respondent in Moscow commented:

> I really hope to never have to do it again. All this going to the court and worrying and not knowing how to behave in the courtroom – it is really difficult.

The situation was somewhat different for cases with a negative outcome. Russian court users commonly stated that the negative outcome was expected and that they did not keep their hopes up because the system as such was unjust and corrupt. There were repeated comments such as:

> What else could you expect from courts?.
>
> (Respondent 8, RC)

> It would be unrealistic to expect to get justice – obviously those who arrange it get justice.
>
> (Respondent 18, MC)

> I don't know why the judge just took their side. I even had an attorney, I paid for legal help and it was useless. The judge had decided it all beforehand.
>
> (Respondent 9, RC)

> If I were somebody, it would have been decided differently. I am just a pensioner. I don't know legal things, I don't have money or children in high places.
>
> (Respondent 19, MC)

Some respondents also attributed their negative outcomes to a lack of preparation and lack of clarity of communication with the court:

> I live on the other side of town. I had to come here four times because, each time, they told me to get different documents; they don't want to do anything.
>
> (Respondent 14, RC)

> One day the judge says you need this document, then you need an expert opinion, then they say you need something else, and they always tell me that it's unknown if that's enough documentation.
>
> (Respondent 13, RC)

These signs of frustration are not unique to Russia; the distinguishing feature, however, is that the Russian court users perceived the negative experiences to be the norm, while cases with favourable outcomes were classified as aberrations from the general norm.

Another important observation in the Russian lower courts is that the evaluation of case outcomes seemed to differ between those who had pre-trial consultations with the judges and the small number of those who did not. Those litigants who took advantage of the pre-trial meetings with the judge were generally more composed and realistic about their expectations:

> I met with the judge two times to prepare. He explained what documents I need, it took me a long time to collect them, hope all this hassle pays off.
>
> (Respondent 9, RC)

> I think the judge was very helpful, I came a couple of times because I was really unsure about my documents. He took the time to explain it to me.
>
> (Respondent 19, RC)

People who did not have pre-trial sessions with the judge and hoped to win purely through their own preparation felt very strongly about their case but were more agitated:

> I have done everything myself, I researched all the forms, I know what I am asking for in this case. I am not going to ask for it from the judge in private, the other party has done it, it is not right.
>
> (Respondent 11, RC)

Parties who did not have private consultations with the judge felt that they lost an opportunity to influence their case. This respondent, clearly suggesting that the judge was taking sides, complained:

> I did not know that I could come and discuss my case with the judge. I live far [away] and have to work all day; it's not fair that others come and talk to him, and they now know each other.
>
> (Respondent 19, RC)

Evidently, people had undervalued expectations of what they could achieve in the lower courts primarily due to their lack of trust in the state institutions overall. Mixed with people's belief that decisions usually depend on the social status and personal connections of litigants, these poor expectations created low levels of confidence in the court's ability to reach fair and just decisions. People's experiences were interpreted in light of these negative images of courts. Successful outcomes were attributed to luck and personal perseverance; negative outcomes were considered the norm and blamed on the lack of litigants' social status, the corruption of the courts or on other parties' personal connections with the judge. The lack of trust in the impartiality of Russian courts is reinforced by the direct accessibility of the judges during pre-trial sessions, even though these sessions served multiple purposes.

Russian people do not go to court with high expectations of legal remedies; in fact, they go with a pessimistic outlook on the possible outcome. While people's personal evaluations of the Justices of the Peace can be positive after a successful outcome, they do not affect their overall evaluation of Russian courts – they see them as bureaucratic institutions serving the interests of the state, and individual judges as persons who are influenced by social status, money and connections. The Russian procedural element of pre-trial hearings allows people to establish informal relationships with the judges which, in effect, reinforces existing perceptions of courts being biased and corrupt.

Litigants' satisfaction with individual case outcomes did not improve existing attitudes towards local courts or the system of justice in general. Negative outcomes seemed merely to reinforce already existing negative attitudes. My observations and interviews suggest that, even following a positive outcome, Russians are more likely to characterise this as a lucky exception to the general situation of injustice in courts, which would seem to indicate that a successful outcome does not necessarily improve pre-existing negative attitudes towards courts. Russian people tend to describe outcomes in court as something they managed to achieve despite the limitations of the system and its imperfect organisation.

This suggests that evaluations of individual case outcomes build upon existing attitudes towards legal institutions. This fact points to a particularly persistent failing in Russian attitudes towards legal institutions, where existing attitudes are negative and remain so despite people's satisfaction with the individual outcome of their case (Kurkchiyan 2012). These expectations are deeply rooted in Russian socio-cultural and historical tradition and tend to be reinforced due to the specifics of the procedural model of the Russian lower court.

CONCLUSION

What can these seemingly 'trivial' experiences of ordinary people in lower courts tell us about Russian legal culture? In light of the original purpose of re-establishing Justice of the Peace courts, we can see that their everyday operation has the broad aim of bringing justice closer to the people, of conciliation, of the negotiation of justice and of providing a legal education for ordinary citizens. However, these institutional objectives are challenged by the ever-increasing case loads of the Russian lower courts and the realistic need for the judges themselves to assume responsibility for the everyday operation of the courts.

My research showed that the procedural specificity of Russian lower courts puts the emphasis on the pre-trial stage of case resolution, which shapes the ways in which people perceive their relationships with the judges and the very process of justice in legal institutions. My analysis of people's time in court offers an insight into how litigants interpret their experiences, as well as how they evaluate and reflect upon their more stable attitudes to law and justice in Russia.

My analysis of personal interviews and observations in Russian lower courts allows me to conclude that these courts operate in similar ways to other bureaucratic state institutions in Russia. This means that ordinary citizens prepare for any dealings with these courts in the same, traditionally accepted ways in which they would deal with other bureaucratic state institutions, i.e., by turning to informal interactions. This informal approach is made possible by the institutional organisation of Justice of the Peace courts, and particularly the importance of the pre-trial sessions, which allow a specific degree of direct and unchecked communication between judges and court users. This structural informality of the Russian lower courts, together with the procedural focus on the pre-trial stage of case resolution, contributes to making the final public hearings appear as a pure formality and reinforces people's existing images of state institutions.

References

Bogdanova, E., Ezhova, L. and Olympyeva, I. (2008) *Chto Nuzhno Znat o Mirovih Sudyah*. St Petersburg: Aleteiia.

Chechina, N. A. (1999) 'Miroviye Sudy v Rossiyskoy Federatsii (Sudebnaya reforma i novoye zamonodatelstvo)', *Pravovedeniye*, 4: 229–237.

Hendley, K. (2012b) 'Assessing the role of the Justice-of-the-Peace courts in the Russian judicial system', *Review of Central and East European Law*, 37(4): 377–93.

—— (2012a) 'The unsung heroes of the Russian judicial system: the Justice-of-the-Peace courts', *The Journal of Eurasian Law*, 5(3): 337–366.

—— (2011) 'Varieties of legal dualism: making sense of the role of ;aw in contemporary Russia', *Wisconsin International Law Journal*, 29(2): 233–62.

Kurkchiyan, M. (2012) 'Perceptions of law and social order: a cross-national comparison of collective legal consciousness', *Wisconsin International Law Journal*, 29(2): 366–93.

Ledeneva, A. (1998) *Russia's Economy of Favours: Blat, Networking and Informal Exchange*. Cambridge: Cambridge University Press.

Lind, A. E., MacCoun, R. J., Ebener, P. A., Felstiner, W. L. F., Hensler, D. R., Resnick, J. and Tyler, T. R. (1989) *The Perception of Justice: Tort Litigants' Views of Trial, Court-Annexed Arbitration, and Judicial Settlement Conferences*. Santa Monica, CA: RAND Corporation Report R-3708-ICJ.

Rimskiy, V. L. (2009) *Obzor Sotciologicheskih Issledovaniy Sudebnoy Sistemi Rossii, Vipolnennyh v Period s Kontsa 1991 Goda po Nastoyashiy Moment*. Moscow: Fond INDEM.

Shaposhnikov, V. (2006) 'Miroviye Sudy Rabotayut v "Shagovoy" Dostupnosti ot Moskvichey', interview in *Moskovskiy Komsomolets*, 04 August 2006, accessed 26 November 2016, at http://ums.mos.ru/presscenter/mass-media/.).

Solomon, P. H. Jr (2008) 'Assessing the courts in Russia: parameters of progress under Putin', *International Journal for Court Administration*, 1(2): 26–32.

—— (2002) 'Putin's Judicial Reform', *East European Constitutional Review*, 11: 117–24.

—— (1997) *Reforming Justice in Russia, 1864–1996: Power, Culture, and the Limits of Legal Order*. Armonk and London: M.E. Sharpe.

Tyler, T. R. (2008) 'Procedural justice and the courts', *Court Review*, 44(1/2): 26–31.

CHAPTER FIVE

IN SEARCH OF JUSTICE

Migrants' Experiences of Appeal in the Moscow City Court

Agnieszka Kubal

This chapter moves up a level in the Russian justice system hierarchy and focuses on the district and regional courts of general jurisdiction which pronounce on immigration law cases. It is primarily based on the observations of what are the most typical immigration law cases – offences against Articles 18.8 and 18.10 of the Code of Administrative Offences (CAO). The said offences concern not having a valid residence registration (18.8 CAO Part 3) or working without a work permit (18.10 CAO Part 2). Based on long-term ethnographic observations in courts and on interviews with the different parties to the process, this chapter discerns the most common trends in the adjudication of these immigration cases. This examination serves to open up a broader question: What do immigrant experiences tell us about the Russian justice system? Through the prism of the immigration law cases, this chapter particularly studies the mechanisms of decision-making in Russian courts and investigates the potential new role for Russian judges – as immigration law enforcers.

The main idea behind this chapter is to understand and shed light on immigration cases in Russia beyond the standard arguments of, 'This is how the law does not work in Russia.' It develops an alternative understanding of the everyday processes of immigration law cases, migrants' experiences of the court and the role of judges as immigration law enforcers. This alternative understanding is based on two different and competing logics that unfold in the courtroom: the case file logic and the humanitarian logic. The former refers to a very heavy, if not exclusive, reliance on written submissions in rendering judgments – what could be termed 'a trial by paper'. Here I refer to the scrupulous attention given by the judge to the written evidence contained in the case file – protocols from the immigration and workplace raids, reports by immigration law enforcement agencies, affidavits signed by migrant defendants – often at the cost of human interaction in the courtroom or examining the witnesses. I argue that case file logic is employed by the judge as a way for him or her to cope with, but also often to circumvent, the messy, empirical reality of immigration rules and regulations that are open to interpretation (cf. Kubal 2016a). Case file logic also allows a judge to sidestep the question of how this paper evidence has been gathered by the Federal Migration Service (FMS) – a state agency responsible for enforcing immigration law and hence a party to the proceedings.[1]

Case file logic by far determines the great majority of immigration law cases. In other words, almost all the decisions rendered by appeal judges in the 18.8 and 18.10 CAO cases before Russian domestic courts were file-driven. In certain exceptional circumstances, however, humanitarian logic could be applied to understand the infrequent deviations from how a majority of immigration law cases are adjudicated. Here the judge does not strictly follow the case file, but focuses more on the attenuating circumstances derived from the international human rights obligations to which Russia is a party (e.g., the European Convention on Human Rights, ECHR). This occurs particularly in situations where the right to family life and family reunification (as derived from Article 8, ECHR), the prohibition of torture and degrading treatment (Article 3 ECHR) or humanitarian considerations (medical treatment) are involved. As one direct consequence of the majority of judgments in immigration cases is deportation (expulsion), the humanitarian logic provides a limited opportunity to soften these arguably unduly harsh sentences.

Taking a step back, and looking analytically at the two logics asymmetrically unfolding in the courtroom, begs the question of whether the *prima facie* 'paper cases' (resulting from the application of

---

[1] It is important to mention that the Federal Migration Service (FMS) was disbanded by Presidential Decree No. 156 of 5 April 2016. The functions of the FMS have been transferred to the Main Directorate for Migration Affairs of the Russian Federation, Ministry of Internal Affairs (GUVM, MVD). This major institutional change does not significantly affect the argument or the conclusions of this chapter, as MVD officials now perform the functions of the FMS officials.

case file logic) more resemble 'trouble cases', as conceptualised by Austin Sarat et al. (1998) in the introductory chapter in their edited volume, *Everyday Practices and Trouble Cases*. Using Blumberg's (1967) definition, they see trouble cases as ostensibly resting on impeccable legal rationale yet providing a lens through which to interrogate more pertinent questions relating to the wider legal system. The trouble cases metaphor helps to observe how the law shapes experiences, interpretations and understandings of social life, and how legal rules are used, re-enacted and remade to colonise everyday life and give it substance, to 'capture it and hold it in its grasp, to attach itself to the solidity of the everyday and, in doing so, to further solidify it' (Sarat et al. 1998: 3). As Yngvesson (1993) notes, trouble cases can become 'a vehicle for extended or situational analysis rather than a means for deriving a corpus of legal rules' (Yngvesson 1993: 8). Trouble cases may be the starting point in the study of legal consciousness, language, ideology and legal pluralism, but they also enable reflection upon the instrumental power of law – to serve a particular purpose and interest.

This chapter proceeds in three parts. Firstly, it provides the legal background to the immigration law cases under study and explains the recently observable surge in these cases, particularly in Moscow and St Petersburg, based on empirical statistical data. Secondly, on the basis of a number of case studies from the courtroom, the chapter discerns the two logics according to which the decisions in these cases are rendered. It concludes with a discussion on the potential relationship between the 'paper cases' and the 'trouble cases'.

METHODOLOGY

My investigation of the Russian justice system, leading to the development of an interpretative framework of a case file and a humanitarian logic (which follows in the later part of this chapter), was empirically informed by a qualitative and ethnographic inquiry into the Russian courts and how the legal process intersects with migrants' livelihoods. I spent over five months in Russia in 2014 collecting empirical data in a variety of settings.

The empirical material presented in this chapter primarily comes from a three-month ethnographic study of a sample of low-level courts in Moscow (District Courts, Moscow City Court, and Moscow Oblast Court). I entered the court building as a researcher and observed the cases once I had received permission from the judge hearing the cases.

I usually sat at the back of the room facing the judge, on the benches reserved for the audience. Normally I would be the only person not involved in the proceedings who would be occupying this place, as immigration cases are not particularly spectacular or known to attract a public audience. The immigration cases in the Moscow City Court are organised so that the court's president allocates them to a selected number of judges who, with time, specialise in immigration questions. When I was observing cases in the Moscow City Court there were two or three judges who, throughout the morning or afternoon sessions of the court's working day, would be hearing solely immigration law cases. Each judge would be allocated approximately five to seven of the 18.8 and 18.10 CAO cases per session. He or she usually heard the cases alone; there were no clerks or assistants present in the courtroom. As a result the proceedings had to run swiftly, with about five to ten minutes being spent per case. What was initially peculiar for me to observe was that sometimes, for one time slot, there were two or three cases allocated. The judge explained that this happens as sometimes the parties do not show up in court, so these additional allocations help to reduce the judge's waiting time. However, the other side of the coin was that, when all the parties did actually show up, these overbookings led to delays in cases being heard, and inspired derisive comments about the (dis)order of justice in Russia among the parties waiting in the corridors of the courts of justice.

The courtroom proceedings were organised as follows. An usher normally called the party – consisting of the defendant, with or without legal representative – to enter the room. He showed them to their place in front of the court's bench, facing each other. When required, this place would also be occupied by an interpreter – either ordered by the court or brought in by the defendant. Shortly afterwards, the usher ordered the parties to stand and the judge (dressed in a black robe) entered the courtroom from the adjacent office and sat on a raised platform behind the bench. In this appeal stage, the Federal Migration Service was absent. The FMS was present only in the District Court – the first level of the immigration proceedings – to provide evidence from the investigation (i.e., that the migrant was working without a work permit, or had no residence registration). The defendant or his/her legal representation usually kept silent until requested to speak by the judge. It was evidently the judge who was in charge of the room.

Every case hearing would follow a similar script. First the judge would check all the documents submitted by the FMS, the decision of the lower court and the appeal, as contained in the case file, including the power of attorney (*doverennost'*) for the defence lawyer. S/he would inspect the passports of the defendant and his or her legal representative to confirm their identity. The judge then opened the proceedings by introducing him or herself and asking the defendant if s/he trusted the judge to hear the case. Upon an affirmative response, the judge quickly read out the procedural rights of the defendant under an administrative process (including the right to an interpreter), which the defendant would be requested to acknowledge in writing. Only after seeing to these formal procedures would the judge move on to the facts of the case, hear the arguments of the defence and finally render a judgment.

These ethnographic observations in the courtroom were informative about the nature of cases when migrants or their representatives mobilised the law – either by challenging the alleged immigration law violations resulting in deportation or expulsion orders, or appealing against the decisions of the Federal Migration Service. Observation of the interactions in the courtroom gave me first-hand information on the type and volume of immigration law cases, on how the migrants were treated in court and about their ability to defend themselves. Through informal conversations with judges and the opposing parties (FMS legal representatives) I learnt how the justice system views migrant litigants and how it responds to their grievances.

In addition to the court observations, I gathered empirical material for this chapter through participatory observation in a number of Russian non-governmental organisations (NGOs), legal aid clinics and migrant organisations that help immigrants in Russia with problems of legal status, residence and access to the labour market. The lawyers and members of these organisations also often represent migrants in courts, especially in the aforementioned 18.8 and 18.10 CAO cases and in disputes with employers or with state immigration agencies like the Federal Migration Service. Over several months, I volunteered in these organisations in a variety of roles. I sometimes accompanied the clients during their reluctant visits to state immigration agencies like the FMS, either to attend an interview or to clarify questions regarding their residence permits. I also shadowed the lawyers when they represented clients in domestic courts and assisted with writing submissions to the European Court of Human Rights in more serious cases.

THE BACKGROUND TO IMMIGRATION LAW CASES IN RUSSIA

The great majority of the immigration cases that take place in Russian courts are, respectively, offences against Articles 18.8 (Part 3) and 18.10 (Part 2) of the Code of Administrative Offences (CAO) – the lack of residence registration (legacy of the Soviet *propiska* system) – and working without a work permit. Until relatively recently (2013), the sanction for both these offences, according to the CAO, was a fine of up to 5,000 roubles (approximately £70), together with a discretionary expulsion order. These terms of sentencing prevail in the majority of jurisdictions (subjects) of the Russian Federation; however, following amendments to the CAO in 2013 (No. 207-FZ of 23.07.2013) in Moscow, Moscow Oblast, St Petersburg and Leningrad Oblast, the expulsion (deportation) now follows automatically and the removal order is included in the 'minimum' sentence.

Making the administration of deportation non-discretionary in the places of greatest concentration of immigrants, like Moscow or St Petersburg, suggests that the judges and courts have been called upon to be important enforcers of Russian immigration law because of their special role in the immigration management and control system.

The court statistics demonstrate that, as a result of this new legislation, the number of immigration administrative cases increased by 100 per cent between 2012 and 2013. The record year thus far was 2014 with 249, 303 Article 18.8 and 18.10 CAO cases. This translates into nearly 250,000 foreigners brought to trial, with potential expulsion orders issued against their names (see Figure 5.1). The sheer volume of the 18.8 and 18.10 CAO cases puts a lot of pressure on judges to resolve these cases in the courts of first instance – the District Courts – quickly and unequivocally.

In these first-level courts, immigrants generally lose the majority of the proceedings, as the evidence presented to the judge is mainly based on reports and protocols from the immigration raids prepared by a party to the proceedings – the office of the Federal Migration Service. This strategy, however, encourages all-too-frequent procedural irregularities – human mistakes in assessing the evidence – and opens up loopholes in the facts of the case. For example, practice has it that migrants caught in the raid by the FMS are often taken straight to the District Courts after a night at a police station. Due to pressure to process these cases 'quickly and effectively', the migrants are often

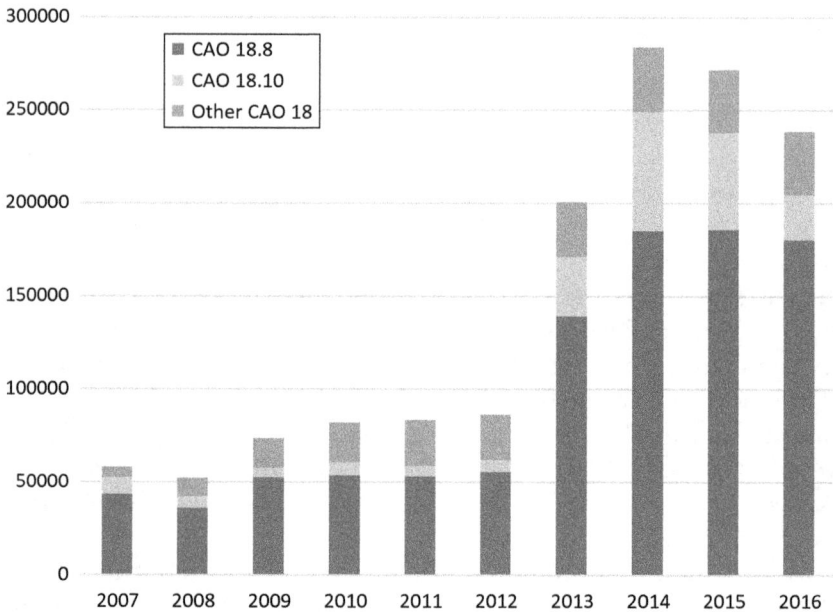

Figure 5.1 Immigration law cases in District Courts in Russia, 2007–2016.
Source: Judicial Department of the Supreme Court of RF Statistics source for courts' activity in RF: www.cdep.ru/index.php?id=79.

asked to sign a document declining their right to legal counsel, which many of them do (some under duress). As many of the younger immigrants from Central Asia do not speak good Russian, and if the court lacks an interpreter *in situ*, one of the accused who seems to speak the language is called upon to interpret for the others. These procedural irregularities have been contained in many court monitoring reports, recently by an NGO, Civic Assistance Committee (Troiskiy 2016).

The project of court monitoring conducted by the Civic Assistance Committee in 2014–15 investigated the different dynamics behind the sentencing in immigration law cases in the domestic courts of the Russian Federation. According to the statistics of the Judicial Department of the Supreme Court of the Russian Federation, the decisions in these administrative cases in 2014 were different in St Petersburg and in Moscow – in the latter, the District Courts reviewed 68,200 cases and imposed a penalty in 65,817 cases (96 per cent), whereas, in the same year in St Petersburg, 13,898 cases were considered and penalties were imposed in 9,618 cases (69 per cent).

What sort of administrative penalties were issued? In Moscow, 87 per cent of all decisions resulted in expulsion. In St Petersburg, the judges relied on a more diversified array of administrative penalties. In the same period only 46 per cent of decisions resulted in expulsion, 18 per cent of defendants were sent on remand and 13 per cent dismissed.

Immigrants, however, have a right of appeal against the decision of the District Court in a court of the second instance – the Regional Court – such as Moscow City Court or a specific Oblast Court. According to the Code of Administrative Offences (CAO), the appellate level reviews the case in full, in relation to both the facts and the law. In other words, the court conducts a review of the evidence, examines case materials and may look at the lawfulness of the decision of the court of first instance in relation to substantive or procedural law. Here, the ratio between cases won and cases lost is more complex, as the defendants, especially if supported by a legal professional, can demonstrate that their papers were in order or that a particular immigration law enforcement agent or low-level judge incompetently or too hastily assessed the evidence before them.

The following sections present the empirical material that supports and illustrates my thesis on the two logics of decision-making in immigration law cases before the Russian courts of appeal in Moscow: the case file and the humanitarian logic. These two logics – albeit used in an asymmetrical manner – hold the key to a broader understanding of the everyday life of immigration cases in Russia.

CASE FILE LOGIC

Some of the typical cases that I observed – relating to Article 18.8 of the CAO (the lack of residence registration) – resulted from raids by the Federal Migration Service on premises occupied by migrants. The charges put forward by the state agency were that migrants lived in those places and at addresses without valid residence registration. In other words, they lived there in contravention of the immigration law that requires a person to be registered (*propisan*) in the place of actual abode. From an observer's perspective, these types of cases could potentially be very difficult to adjudicate: how does one prove, without long evidence gathering and cross-examination of witnesses (e.g., neighbours), that the person actually lived in one place, rather than just 'visited' (when the FMS raid happened) or 'stayed a couple of nights'? In order for the appeals court to process the large case load relating to immigration offences of this nature, the judge could not allow the launch of a new, full investigation into the facts of the case. The judge was not expected to call on, question or examine witnesses. To arrive at a decision, the judge instead turned to evidence contained in the case file and to the facts already established by the lower court. The judge, during the course of the case before the Moscow City Court, resorted to strict reliance on existing documentary materials; the result of the appeal would, therefore, rarely go against the evidence already included in the case file as established by the court of lower instance. In other words, the result of the appeal would rarely overturn the decision of the lower court, which would be the basic operation of case file logic.

Nevertheless, a number of questions remain: How to establish that a person actually lived at one address and was not merely visiting? What documents were usually contained in the case file for the judge to rely on as evidence? How was this evidence approached and potentially challenged by the defence?

The Federal Migration Service would supply the lower court with (1) protocols from the immigration raids, each accompanied by (2) a collection of photographs taken on site and (3) elaborate affidavits, signed by migrants, confirming that they actually lived at the raided addresses. This type of evidence was then debated and reviewed by the appeals court.

For instance, in the case of M., an Uzbek national facing charges against Article 18.8 of the CAO, the defence lawyer's strategy in the appeals court was based on the fact that a photograph is not evidence of actual abode. The lawyer went on to explain that the place raided by the FMS was not in a suitable condition to be lived in *usloviya prozhivaniya*. The lawyer presented a believable story: the man was found at this address during the raid by an unlucky accident – he actually went there to discuss work opportunities. The lawyer presented his client as a law-abiding person: M. had a patent (a type of work permit), he was clear of any offences and was not doing anything illegal in visiting a place that happened to be raided by the FMS. The lawyer then moved on to present the personal situation of his client: he had two small children and a wife back in Uzbekistan. If he were to be deported, he could not support them financially; he needed to stay in Russia and work to provide for his family.

In considering the appeal, the judge immediately turned to the written evidence contained in the case file and asked the defence about the protocol from the raid, where M. was listed as indeed 'living at the address':

> Any comments on the Federal Migration Service's protocol? M. had signed it and confirmed its validity with his signature.

The lawyer replied:

> Yes, your honour, I am familiar with the materials of the case. My client did not fully understand what document he was signing and the questions the FMS asked of him, as he doesn't speak Russian very well. Now, during the appeal trial, he also requires an interpreter and his friend here is able to help.

This argument by the defence regarding the procedures of evidence gathering would have potentially left any judge with a number of questions. In order to process this case within the limited time frame, the judge could not allow herself to cast any doubt on the legality of the pre-trial procedures of evidence collection (already affirmed by the lower court), otherwise it would have meant reopening the case and a potentially long and protracted process of assessing the particular FMS officers' actions and professionalism in the field. The judge, when delivering her judgment, could not allow herself to be diverted by the fact that the arguments of the appeal went against the evidence already included in the case file. She upheld the decision of the lower court, arguing:

> The defendant, M., confirmed with his signature that he understood the FMS protocol from the raid, where he admitted that he indeed lived at the raided address. That leaves me with no choice but to sentence M. to a fine of 5,000 roubles and expulsion (deportation) from the Russian Federation. This is the minimum sentence that I can order in these circumstances.

The case above is a direct example of the application of case file logic. When faced with the messy empirical reality of potentially unenforceable laws of residence registration and multiple possible scenarios about what really happened on the day of the raid at the said address (including the style of evidence gathering by FMS), the written documents contained in the case file and signed by the accused were the only 'stable and solid' pieces of evidence, according to which the judge seemed able to manage the reality and adjudicate the case. With complex legal rules and their haphazard enforceability by the FMS, the judge had to make a choice according to which s/he could take control over the volume of cases that still awaited decisions.

This observation is consistent with previous research on formalism as an inseparable trait of Russian legal culture. Bryan Garth (1982) defines legal formalism with reference to Weber's ideal type of formal legal rationality: law legitimated by reference to criteria intrinsic to a refined legal system, where 'facts which are neither stipulated nor alleged and proved, and facts which remain undisclosed by the *recognised* methods of proof (...) do not exist as far as the judge is concerned' (Weber 1954: 61–64, 227, quoted in Garth 1982: 184, my emphasis). In Russia, the recognised methods of proof are limited to formal paper evidence. The extreme rigidity of literal formalistic preference encourages a mainstream thinking that 'there can be no legitimate requirement for negotiation, flexibility or adjustment when the time comes to implement the law' (Kurkchiyan 2009: 355). What follows is the conclusion that any discretion in the kind of evidence that is admitted – beyond documentary evidence – must be regarded either as a 'violation of the law or, at best, a manipulation' (Kurkchiyan 2009: 355).

In the second type of case, I observed the defence attempting to challenge more fiercely the whole process of evidence gathering by the FMS, even going so far as to allege that the evidence was fabricated. Take this case of another Uzbek migrant worker, B., charged with offences against Article 18.10 of the CAO – working without a permit. He did not come to the trial, but his lawyer was there to represent him. The appeal was based on the fact that there was no substantive proof that the defendant was actually working on the construction site that was raided by the FMS; the defendant did not speak Russian and must have signed the protocol under duress. The defence challenged the evidence as fictitious – the FMS officers made the defendant pose for photographs which merely showed him holding different construction tools and materials, rather than actually reflecting his genuine work on the site:

> Your Honour, look at the evidence. Take this picture, for example. Look at the defendant's face – he is imitating work. There is no other CCTV material except for this one doubtful picture – no proofs of contract, no

payment and no witnesses. I am saying that he [my client] went there to ask for work, and that he had not actually been working there.

The judge seemed genuinely puzzled by this open and bold statement by the defence. She pondered for a minute on the need to interrogate the actual labour relationship. However, with the grey sphere of employment being part of the legal environment not only for migrants but also for Russian citizens, and with a number of cases still to be adjudicated that same day, the judge decided to again resort to the formal written evidence contained in the case file. On delivering the judgment of upholding the lower court's decision and dismissing the appeal, the judge turned to the lawyer and said:

> Look, in the protocols from the FMS raid, it says black on white that B. was working there. There is his signature. And there is another signature that he understands Russian. He himself, according to the protocol, explained that he was working there based on an oral contract. He has been in Moscow since 2009 – should he not know by now what one goes to a construction site for? In the lower court, B. pleaded guilty to the offence. It would not be prudent to go against this evidence.

These cases have to be understood in their systemic context, defined by regular violations of residence registration requirements by migrants and Russian citizens alike. Similarly, the general labour conditions in large part rely on informal arrangements: people (again – migrants and Russian citizens alike) are used to working without contracts or formal payslips or with contracts that cover only part of their duties. In this type of environment it is difficult for the FMS to obtain conventional evidence like copies of employment contracts or salary slips. The FMS therefore resorts to a different type of evidence – photographs, together with ready-prepared affidavits, which the migrant workers are then made to sign. This constitutes the bulk of the case file, based on which the decision is made. These written pieces of evidence, with all the correct stamps and signatures, give an impression of formality in an otherwise largely informal environment that defines working and living conditions in migrant Moscow (Reeves 2013, 2015). Shortly before concluding these cases and rendering judgments according to case file logic, the judge would often turn to the defendant with a series of cautionary statements such as, 'Look, this is your testimony. You signed it. It is printed out but you signed it. How come you are now not agreeing with it?'

Subsequently, in the majority of 18.8 and 18.10 CAO cases, the affidavits signed by the accused – whether printed or handwritten – served as the primary evidence. The court of appeal did not enquire into how they were composed, whether the defendant was made to sign them under duress or even whether the defendant really understood what was written there. The affidavits were examples of defendants' submissions to FMS allegations in light of the lack of stronger substantive evidence. Formally they were, however, deemed sufficient by the court to deliver the sentence.

The third type of cases I observed were therefore the legally ambiguous or factually problematic cases in which the court decision had been rendered mainly (or solely) on the basis of affidavits signed by the defendants at the pre-trial stage. These affidavits often simply worked as self-incriminating evidence. They were prepared in order to push the case through the courts, even though, in the course of the proceedings, multiple questions about the facts of the case could (and would) emerge.

The importance of written affidavits as primary evidence was stressed by yet another case following allegations of working without a permit. A., a migrant worker from Tajikistan, was found guilty of offences against Article 18.10 of the CAO by the lower court on the basis of a photograph provided by the FMS in which he was sitting in a car behind the steering wheel, and an elaborate affidavit where he confirmed that he had been working as a driver. He attempted to clarify this evidence before the appeals court saying that he *was* sitting in the car but he was waiting for a friend, who he also took with him to testify in court. The judge did not seem to give much credibility to this explanation and again brought everyone's attention to the signed affidavit already contained in the case file:

JUDGE: But I have an affidavit signed by you, saying you were hired to work by company X., you were supposed to drive and deliver a package from this place to this place, it was an oral contract and you were to be paid 4,000 roubles per day...

A: [interrupting] But I have never earned that much, anywhere in Moscow. This is not a day's going rate of pay, it is far too high!

The man was not trying to be disrespectful to the judge – he, indeed, interrupted the judge but actually made an important observation about the artificiality of the affidavit-only-based evidence. He was genuinely astonished by the figure quoted in the testimony. He was attempting to challenge the affidavit for what it was: a piece of paper with all the correct signatures and official stamps to make it look like formal evidence, but which was in no way connected to the reality of the situation. It did not account for what had happened on that particular day, nor was it true in general when it described the context of going wages for migrant workers in Moscow. The judge responded, 'But you have signed it. This is your signature. I have to expel you, as this is the minimum penalty.'

In these ambiguous and borderline cases, the judges all seemed eventually to turn to the case file, as they saw no reason to go against the written evidence that had already been scrutinised and legitimised by a decision of the lower court. When faced with the empirical reality of shadow work performed to an equal degree by migrants and Russian citizens, the appeal judges had to adhere to the formal written evidence, otherwise they ran the risk of opening a Pandora's box and having to actually scrutinise the abstruse and often confusing facts of the case.

The judges therefore followed case file logic as the most effective way of processing the appeals and managing the case load in front of them. The collateral effect – particularly vocal in the corridors of justice immediately after the trial – was that the appeals court was often blamed for the procedural injustices of the pre-trial stage and that all the different (arguably autonomous) elements in the law enforcement hierarchy were conflated into one big, oppressive and unjust institution. As one legal expert told me:

> The structure of the process makes it impossible to win the case. There is no FMS representative present at the appeal stage. Only the defendant's legal representation is present, if at all. The result? Due to this imbalance, the court is often compelled to assume the double function of an arbiter and a prosecutor [for the FMS].

'It is all one and the same ... we are just simple people, we only work and get punished', concluded one migrant defendant.

This is not to say, however, that case file logic meant that no decisions of the lower court could ever be overturned by the Moscow City Court. Case file logic has also been successfully relied on by the defence in challenging lower court decisions and in casting doubt on the evidence gathered by state law enforcement agencies.

Take the case of P., a migrant worker from Tajikistan, as an example of a successful appeal. One day P. was stopped by the police near the metro entrance in Moscow and accused of possessing false residence registration papers. The police brought charges against him in the lower court on the basis of Article 18.8 of the CAO. The court agreed with the police charges and sentenced P. to a 5,000 rouble fine and expulsion (deportation) from Russia.

However, the police, whilst gathering the evidence, failed to check – or to check diligently enough – the status of P.'s residence registration on the Federal Migration Service database, the main state agency responsible for the enforcement of immigration law. Whilst preparing the appeal, P. sought help from a *pro-bono* immigration lawyer, who advised him to go to the local field office of the FMS and ask for a printout from their database on the exact status of his residence registration. P. waited in a long queue but finally received the information he was after. The FMS officer confirmed that his registration *had* been put onto the database, and that it was valid and legitimate. The FMS officer himself expressed concerns over the lower court's decision in a private chat with P. and provided the Tajik migrant with a printout from their database confirming the validity of his registration with a stamp certifying its legality. Based on this evidence, P.'s lawyer prepared an appeal which she then filed with the Moscow City Court.

In the Moscow City Court the judge, upon checking the formal documents and reading out excerpts from the lower-court decision where the facts of the case had been established, proceeded to familiarise herself with the appeal and the defendant's reasons for contesting the court's decision. She then asked the defendant, 'So the FMS did not have your registration in their database?' He responded, 'They had. I have a copy of it with me here, and you also have a copy attached to my [case] file. It was the police['s mistake]. They did not provide any proof that my registration was invalid.' 'Understood', replied the judge and ruled a verdict in the Tajik migrant's favour, acquitting him and annulling his removal order. The case lasted no longer than seven to ten minutes. The judge struggled to balance the overwhelming evidence added to the case file by the defence lawyer (documents from the FMS certifying P.'s rightful residence) with the at first sight formal but not actually accurate documents provided by the police on the basis of which the lower court had rendered its judgment. The judge, following case file logic, could make no other decision.

IN SEARCH OF JUSTICE: MIGRANTS' EXPERIENCES OF APPEAL

Formal, written (paper) evidence is therefore highly scrutinised and relied on by both parties to a case. 'Everything is in the case file' (*vse v materialakh dela*), one lawyer told me as a way to explain this logic. An FMS lawyer representative rather jovially recalled the following anecdote to reiterate the importance of written case materials:

FMS OFFICER:	It is not really about the trial. The case mostly depends on what is in the case file. The quality and type of documents; if they are strong – no worries, the case will be won.
AK:	Who gives strong documents?
FMS OFFICER:	It is as if Manchester United played a local football team from Kaluga... The FMS being Man United, to be exact. We hardly ever give decisions that are not confirmed in documents that are not based on legal ones. Surely, sometimes, there are mistakes. We put that someone is a male rather than a female, but these are printing, trivial mistakes. If you issue a hundred decisions a day, you can make such a mistake. In the great majority of cases, our decisions are legal (*zakonnyye*); the lawyers cannot disprove these during the trial.

The idea behind the presentation of this empirical material was not to justify why the judge nearly always agrees with the lower-court judgment or fails to agree with the appeal. Case file logic, as an analytical instrument, is helpful in understanding how and on the basis of what evidence the judge arrives at the given ruling and decides the outcome of the case. Given the unequal power relations between state law-enforcement agencies and migrant workers, in the majority of cases it is the evidence provided by the former that plays the most crucial role in deciding their outcome. This is not to say, however, that migrants have absolutely no chance of obtaining formal evidence to counter that provided by state agencies. The routes for obtaining such evidence are, of course, limited and necessitate considerably more effort, given the administrative backlogs and delays in, and understaffing of, the FMS offices. But in principle, they are available.

HUMANITARIAN LOGIC

Case file logic is particularly difficult to understand and reconcile with the principles of proportionality, justice and equity if one approaches immigration law cases from a human rights' perspective. The arguably harsh penalty – deportation – meant disrupted livelihoods, severed family ties and on many occasions, a contribution to a growing undocumented migrant population in Moscow. Not in all cases, however, was the court impervious to human rights arguments.

Humanitarian logic was primarily extended to asylum seekers in Russia who could not be expelled to their home countries for committing offences against immigration law, as that would mean returning them to places of grave conflict where their lives could be at risk. So why did the asylum seekers even find themselves in court on charges of administrative offences? Due to backlogs and administrative delays in the processing of their asylum applications (Burtina *et al.* 2015), many asylum seekers would try to work to support themselves and their families. Until relatively recently, the question of access to the labour market for asylum applicants in Russia was not explicitly regulated. In practice, the authorities had actually been known, on many occasions, to 'turn a blind eye' to asylum seekers engaged in paid labour who could prove they were subject to a status determination procedure (either waiting for a decision or appealing a refusal of refugee status (Kubal 2016b: 275). However, following legislative change No. 127-FZ of 5 May 2014, their access to the labour market has been explicitly forbidden in the Federal Law 'On the Legal Status of Foreign Citizens in the Russian Federation'. As a result, the Federal Migration Service could take them to District Courts as casual immigration law offenders and charge them with working without a permit or patent (Article 18.10 CAO).

In such cases, appeal judges would usually uphold the decision of the lower court but exclude the deportation from the administrative penalty, leaving only the fine to be paid. In the written decisions, the judges argued that the expulsion would have contravened Russian humanitarian obligations with regard to Articles 2 and 3 (the right to life and the prohibition of inhumane and degrading treatment) of the European Convention of Human Rights and Decision No. 4 of the Constitutional Court of the Russian Federation of 14 February 2014, which urged judges to apply the principles of justice and humanity in issuing penalties for administrative offences. This operation of humanitarian logic was particularly observable in the courts of appeal located in the two main Russian cities of Moscow and St Petersburg,[2] in cases

---

[2] This, however, could not be said for the courts operating in the different regions of Russia; see Kubal (2016b) and the analysis of the *LM and Others* v. *Russia* case, ECtHR 2017, demonstrating that the Russian legal environment is geographically not only vast but also patchy and inconsistent.

against Syrian asylum seekers who had arrived in Russia after fleeing the Syrian civil war (2011–) and against citizens of Eastern Ukraine who were escaping armed conflict (2014–).

There was, however, a significant imbalance in how these two logics – case file and humanitarian – operated and were relied on by judges in the decision-making process. As already indicated in the introduction to this chapter, not only was humanitarian logic used in exceptional and very limited circumstances, but it was also quite often deemed subservient to case file logic, demonstrating that paper ruled supreme in Russian courts even when humanitarian arguments were involved.

As an illustration, we can take the case of K., who was apprehended by the FMS during a raid on an apartment and charged with offences against Article 18.8 of the CAO for not being formally registered at the said address. His appeal was based on the fact that he had never actually lived at that address but went there to seek advice from his family on the medical condition of his son and discuss his treatment in Russian hospitals:

> I came to this address as my family members live there; I came to consult with them about the medical treatment of my son, as I don't know this town very well. My son has heart failure; he is often short of breath.

The judge initially did not give much consideration to these arguments, instead raising a formal point that K.'s migration card[3] stated that he came to Russia to seek employment and not medical treatment. However, K. continued his complaint:

> As I was taken by the police and spent a night at the police station I missed my son's medical appointment. When I finally arrived in the hospital with him, the doctor said that I had missed my appointment but gave me some medication and told me to monitor my son's condition. But I will treat my son here as I do not believe the doctors in my country.

The judge seemed compelled as the man weighed in with an important humanitarian argument: the urgent medical treatment of a minor. She decided to adjourn K.'s appeal hearing in order to enable him to collect more formal evidence from the hospital both confirming that he had

---

[3] The migration card is a form of landing card filled in by all foreign citizens arriving in Russia. It states the reason for their travel.

missed his appointment and providing more information about his son's condition. At the same time, the judge was firm and official:

> I am adjourning the hearing for four days, to give you the chance to bring more evidence [spravki] that your son is being treated here. But I am warning you: if you do not come or bring any written evidence, the case will be heard without you.

Whilst I was not able to wait until the conclusion of this case, this particular hearing illustrates that the judges, in more complex cases involving humanitarian arguments (beyond those of asylum seekers from the regions currently affected by armed conflict or civil war), would give due consideration to such arguments only in tandem with the strict application of case file logic. Ultimately, we do not know whether the man's expulsion or deportation order was cancelled or whether he was allowed to stay in Russia to continue his son's medical treatment, but the very fact of adjourning the hearing revealed that the judge was willing to do just that, once given the opportunity to examine more formal, written evidence.

The type of case where I was able to observe the application of humanitarian logic the most clearly, pertained to the presence of Ukrainian citizens from the areas affected by armed conflict in the Lugansk and Donetsk oblasts. My fieldwork in Moscow coincided with the arrival of Eastern Ukrainian asylum seekers following the aftermath of the Euromaidan revolution in Ukraine (2013). Whilst the barriers to access to refugee or temporary asylum status for Eastern Ukrainians were on a par with the experiences of asylum seekers from other countries in Russia (Burtina et al. 2015), the situation of Eastern Ukrainians was more complex. It resulted from an existing multifaceted relationship between Eastern Ukraine and Russia embodied in long-established migration patterns and family ties with Russian citizens (Malynovska 2004, 2007). Many Ukrainians, when faced with the bureaucratic barriers to the obtention of asylum, would therefore seek different ways of regularising their stay in Russia. Many would avail themselves of the routes accessible to regular migrant workers from the CIS republics,[4] and apply for work permits or special out-of-quota

---

[4] The Commonwealth of Independent States (CIS) formed when the former Soviet Union (now called Russia) dissolved in 1991. At its conception it consisted of ten former Soviet Republics: Armenia, Belarus, Kazakhstan, Kyrgyzstan, Moldova, Russia, Tajikistan, Turkmenistan, Ukraine and Uzbekistan.

work permits – patents (Davé 2014; Kubal 2016c). Some would slip through the procedural net and often – through no fault of their own – become undocumented or have a precarious semi-legal status (Kubal 2016c; Reeves 2013). At the same time, the Federal Migration Service – during raids on apartments or workplaces – would apply the immigration law in an indiscriminate fashion towards all foreign workers, regardless of their nationality. As a result many Eastern Ukrainians – *de facto* refugees but *de iure* migrant workers – found themselves before the Russian courts, facing charges of contravening Russian immigration law.

For example, two Ukrainian women were charged with offences against Article 18.10 of the CAO – working without a permit. They both arrived from areas of Eastern Ukraine affected by armed conflict. They went to the appeals court without legal representation, spoke for themselves and were very respectful to the judge, who heard their cases individually though both of them were present in the courtroom. In their appeal, they asked for the expulsion order to be withdrawn from the administrative penalty. The first woman explained that she and her sister had come to the shop that had been inspected by FMS officers to ask for work. As she and her sister looked very similar, the shop manager put ID badges on them, so as to be able to distinguish them whilst he was interviewing them. This is when the FMS raid took place. The FMS officers wrongly understood the two sisters to be working in the shop, due to their ID badges. The two women also supported their appeal with the fact that both were married to Russian citizens and included their marriage certificates (*svidetel'stvo o brake*) in the appeal documentation.

The judge accepted their appeal and overturned the decision of the lower court by excluding the expulsion order from the penalty. In announcing the sentence, the judge relied directly on Article 8 of the European Convention of Human Rights – the right to private and family life. The women had close family ties with Russian citizens which they had formally proven by appending their marriage certificates to the case file. Their removal to Eastern Ukraine would have been disproportionate to the offence with which they had been charged and would have been in contravention of international human rights obligations.

This case seemed a clear example of the application of humanitarian logic. In a private conversation with me after the trial, however, the judge added: 'You see, the shop manager put ID badges on them because they looked so alike. The FMS mistook them for workers. Things like that happen, it's easy for a misunderstanding to occur.'

I was positively surprised by the judge's comment, which seemed reasonable and based on common sense. It departed from her somewhat formalistic style of rendering decisions which I had become used to whilst observing her previous cases and style of reasoning. The judge's comment after the case made me realise that she was, indeed, aware that 'there was a mess out there' when it came to immigration law enforcement on the ground and evidence gathering by FMS officers. It was an implicit recognition that FMS officers can and do get things wrong, even if the documents they submit to the lower courts (photographs, protocols and affidavits confirming their version of events) would appear to make the cases clear and simple to adjudicate.

In the case of the two Ukrainian women, the removal of deportation from their sentence and the reversal of the lower court's judgment were based on international legal obligations to which Russia was a party, as both women had close family ties to Russian citizens. This is ultimately what the written judgment overturning the decision of the lower court had said. However, the judge's personal comment about the case in a private conversation afterwards made me realise that my initial impression of judges as being locked in some sort of ivory tower and being unaware of the empirical reality of everyday life law enforcement was actually misguided. The judges knew perfectly well what was going on – after all, when they removed their robes and left the court, they were also part of this broader legal environment. By rendering extremely formalistic decisions and making the whole process dependant on formal documents, they were adopting a strategy for coping with the messy empirical reality and for managing their case load.

PAPER CASES OR TROUBLE CASES?

This staggering asymmetry between the application of quite simple case file logic and the limited recourse to humanitarian logic in deciding immigration law cases in Russia presents itself as potentially problematic due to the consequences involved – non-discretionary expulsion (in Moscow and St Petersburg and their respective oblasts) with a five-year entry ban (*zapret na v'ezd*). These harsh repercussions result in the disruption of livelihoods for many individual migrants, who do not have at their disposal even limited human rights' grounds of appeal but who have, nevertheless, established lives and families in Russia. Often, due to no fault of their own, they simply fall through the cracks of the complex and ever-changing immigration laws. When migrants do not comply with the judgment and do not physically leave the country after the judgment enters legal force, their subsequent presence in Russia becomes illegal. They are prevented from renewing their immigration documents – either residence or work permits – and live the precarious lives of irregular migrants. The human face of these immigration cases therefore involves acute personal loss and disrupted livelihoods that are barely visible from under the stack of case file evidence.

Due to the harsh and detrimental consequences for human lives of an unsuccessful appeal, my chapter actually queries whether *prima facie* 'paper cases' actually bare a close resemblance to 'trouble cases', in the way that they have been conceptualised by Sarat *et al.* (1998). Following Blumberg (1967: 16) these authors define trouble cases within the contextual realities of social structure, where: 'a particular decision may rest upon a legally impeccable rationale; at the same time, it may be rendered nugatory or self-defeating by contingencies imposed by aspects of social reality of which the lawmakers are themselves unaware'. This conceptualisation of trouble cases goes beyond dispute resolution. These cases are conceived around a broad range of law and society scholarship concerned with normative violations, deviance, conflict and challenges to accepted practices and routines (Sarat *et al.* 1998): 4). The everyday life, intuitive interpretations of trouble cases focus on their potential non-conclusiveness, on difficulties with interpretation of the facts or on the specific challenges that they pose to the law or established legal practices.

The metaphor of 'trouble cases' attaches itself to the crucial question of how the case file is actually put together in the pre-trial stage in Russia. Whilst, at a distant appeal level, the decision might indeed rest upon a 'legally impeccable rationale', it exacerbates the power of the paper in creating an alternative reality. This approach confounds and confuses the different procedural irregularities that may and often do take place at the pre-trial stage. The irregularities range from the FMS creatively interpreting reality in the statement of facts contained in their protocols to making immigrants sign self-incriminating affidavits under duress. This takes place whilst law enforcement officers try to discern – from the messy legal environment of shadow working and the general disregard for residence registration – convincing evidence enabling them to secure a strong case against the defendants and eventually an administrative conviction.[5]

A comparative look at the role of documentary evidence under different jurisdictions demonstrates that the case files are treated by some courts with more caution and criticism. A study by Max Travers on British immigration courts stressed adjudicators' own evaluation of the evidential value of reports produced by different immigration law enforcement agents – in other words, the Home Office (Travers 1999: 124). Whilst the immigration courts studied by Travers dealt with appeals following the rejection of asylum claims – therefore different in substance from the immigration law cases I observed in Russia – I draw on them because the repercussions under both jurisdictions were of a grave nature, meaning deportations, disrupted livelihoods and often the broken lives of the defendants.

Adjudicators interviewed by Travers critically approached the documentary evidence presented before them by the Home Office; some went as far as to express the view that the 'Home Office often presented a rosy view of political problems in particular countries' and stressed that it was necessary to be discriminating when reading reports, including those submitted by the defendant (Travers 1999: 124). The critical evaluation of the documentary evidence was considered by the adjudicators as an intellectual exercise – a metaphor I struggled to find in the reasoning of Russian judges.

In the cases that I observed in Russia, the attitude to paper evidence went beyond the general idea that the written word reflects the reality in a more-or-less accurate manner. The relationship between the protocols produced by the FMS and the reality was not a matter of opinion for Russian courts. The accuracy of the reports was not questioned by the judges, giving the impression that they were an exact representation of the facts and reality. In fact, however, these reports or protocols actively constructed 'reality', an alternative reality that put a seemingly orderly structure on the complexity of everyday life. In the most extreme cases, they falsified the reality. The courts, in not critically scrutinising the paper evidence, became inherently part of a wider societal phenomenon: the lack of a system of checks and balances on 'paper production' in Russia.

---

[5] For more discussion on the various specificities of the pre-trial stage in Russia, see the chapters by Solomon and by McCarthy in this volume.

CONCLUSION

Immigration law cases in Russia are experienced in everyday life by migrants, lawyers and immigration judges alike, through a number of core characteristics. These include the very high volume of such cases, the high sentencing rate, the quick processing times and the strict adherence to the formal legality of how the cases are adjudicated. The decisions in these cases are made on the basis of formal documents, protocols from immigration raids, printouts from FMS databases and affidavits signed by the accused. However, what really matters is the quality of the written, formal evidence produced by the Federal Migration Service or other law enforcement bodies.

The main conclusion from this chapter is therefore that the majority of these cases are adjudicated according to case file logic. The role of the judge in these immigration administrative cases does not seem to be to establish the facts of the case by examining both parties to the trial. The facts appear to be already agreed and contained in the written documents – the case file. The trial itself is not too important, colloquially speaking – it is hardly likely that the trial will be a 'game changer'. Unless the defendant submits a new written piece of formal evidence that disproves the documentary evidence presented by the FMS, the way in which the case can develop during the trial is somewhat limited.

At the appellate level, the 'life' of these cases gets more complex. From my observations and my interviews with immigration lawyers I determined that there are certain, though limited, grounds for appeal that are admitted by the judge, and these are primarily derived from the human rights obligations to which Russia is a party. Aside from Article 8 of the ECHR in certain exceptional circumstances, Articles 2 and 3 have been successfully called upon to reverse the expulsion of asylum seekers, particularly those from Syria and Eastern Ukraine, who were found working without documents in Russia or who lived in Moscow without valid residence registration.

From a legal point of view, the immigration law cases are therefore very straightforward. The law is simple, there is enough evidence in the case file and therefore the decision can easily be made on the basis of the written material. The volume of these CAO cases is quite high; hence there was enough practice for patterns of judgments to be established.

From the wider, societal point of view, however, the matter appears much more complex. It remains an open question whether these 'paper cases', adjudicated according to case file logic, are actually more like 'trouble cases'; this could inspire more research into the role, production and evaluation of documentary evidence in the Russian justice system.

References

Blumberg, A. (1967) 'The practice of law as a confidence game', *Law and Society Review*, 1(2): 15–40.

Burtina, E., Korosteleva, E. and Simonov, V. (2015) *Russia as a Country of Asylum: Report on the Implementation of the 1951 Convention Relating to the Status of Refugees by the Russian Federation*. Moscow: Civic Assistance Committee.

Davé, B. (2014) 'Becoming "legal" through "illegal" procedures: the precarious status of migrant workers in Russia', *Russian Analytical Digest*, 159: 2–6.

Garth, B. (1982) 'The movement toward procedural informalism in North America and Western Europe: a critical survey', in Abel, R.L. (ed.) *The Politics of Informal Justice*, Vol. 2. New York: Academic Press, 183–214.

Kubal, A. (2016a) 'Spiral effect of the law: migrants' experiences of the state law in Russia – a comparative perspective', *International Journal of Law in Context*, 12(4): 453–468.

(2016b) 'Refugees or migrant workers? A case study of undocumented Syrians in Russia – *LM and Others v. Russia* (ECtHR 14 March 2016)', *Journal of Immigration Asylum and Nationality Law*, 30(4): 265–282.

(2016c) 'Entry ban or surreptitious deportation? Analysing *zapret na v"yezd* in Russia from a comparative perspective', *Law and Social Inquiry*, DOI: 10.1111/lsi.12232.

Kurkchiyan, M. (2009) 'Russian legal culture: an analysis of adaptive response to an institutional transplant', *Law and Social Inquiry*, 34(2): 337–364.

Malynovska, O. (2004) *International Migration in Contemporary Ukraine: Trends and Policy*. Geneva: Global Commission on International Migration.

(2007) 'Migration in Ukraine: challenge or chance?' *European View*, 5: 71–78.

Reeves, M. (2013) 'Clean fake: authenticating documents and persons in migrant Moscow', *American Ethnologist*, 40(3): 508–524.

(2015) 'Living from the nerves: deportability, indeterminacy, and the "feel of law" in migrant Moscow', *Social Analysis*, 59(4): 119–136.

Sarat, A., Constable, M., Engel, D., Hans, V. and Lawrence, S. (1998) 'Ideas of the "everyday" and the "trouble case" in law and society scholarship: an introduction', in Sarat, A., Constable, M., Engel, D., Hans, V. and Lawrence, S. (eds.) *Everyday Practices and Trouble Cases: Fundamental Issues in Law and Society*. Evanston, IL: Northwestern University Press, 1–13.

Travers, M. (1999) *British Immigration Courts: A Study of Law and Politics*. Bristol: The Policy Press.

Troiskiy, K. (2016) *Administrative Expulsion from Russia: Court Proceedings or Mass Expulsion?* Moscow: Civic Assistance Committee, 1–48, http://refugee.ru/wp-content/uploads/2016/05/Doklad-o-vydvoreniyakh_pechat.pdf.

Weber, M. (1954) *Max Weber on Law and Economy in Society*. Cambridge, MA: Harvard University Press.

Yngvesson, B. (1993) *Virtuous Citizens, Disruptive Subjects: Order and Complaint in a New England Court*. New York: Routledge.

CHAPTER SIX

WHEN BUSINESS GOES TO COURT
Arbitrazh Courts in Russia

Timur Bocharov and Kirill Titaev

This chapter explores how the relatively unique and autonomous structure of Russian commercial courts – known as Arbitrazh courts – operates. The main role of these courts is to resolve disputes in the sphere of economic transactions, over cases that involve economic interests and where parties are legally registered entities (business establishments, individual entrepreneurs or state institutions). This chapter takes a close look at the types of dispute decided on by Arbitrazh courts, how they process their case load and the experiences of the different users of this institution of justice in Russia. It is a shared view among scholars and experts on 'law in action' in Russia that Arbitrazh is one of the most autonomous, independent and progressive elements in the Russian legal system.[1] This makes it particularly interesting to examine how this substructure was created, what makes it stand out from the rest of the justice system in Russia and what the broader impact is of this specific separation of commercial courts' jurisdiction on the overall Russian judicial system.

To address these questions, an extensive empirical study – using a variety of techniques of data collection – was conducted by the research team at the Institute for the Rule of Law at the European University of St Petersburg. We analysed 10,000 decisions reached by Arbitrazh courts

---

[1] For example, the ECHR supports this evaluation in '*Kovaleva and others* v. *Russia*' and in '*LLC "Link Oil Spb"* v. *Russia*'. An analogous view of this issue is shared by Hendley (2013) and by Granville (2012).

from 2007–2011.[2] In order to nuance our interpretation of the decisions, a set of more than thirty interviews was conducted with claimants, judges and court administration. It should also be noted that one of the authors of this article has the extensive first-hand experience of working as a legal representative in Arbitrazh courts. Putting together inferences from these varied data sources allowed us to create a realistic image of the day-to-day operation of Arbitrazh courts in Russia.

The structure of this chapter is as follows. We start by presenting an overview of the institutional organisation and operation of the Arbitrazh courts. This is followed by a discussion on how these courts operate in practice, with an emphasis on the types of dispute, the speed of their resolution, the typical case load and the court's day-to-day operation. Our main conclusion is that the popular images of these courts widely held in Russian society frequently do not match the reality of their everyday operation.

THE ORIGIN AND THE STRUCTURE OF ARBITRAZH COURTS

The initiative of creating this system of specialised courts for resolving economic disputes was finally realised at the beginning of the 1990s. In fact, prior to this, the State Arbitrazh System ('Gosarbitrazh') – an official institution with the power to resolve economic disputes between different state enterprises during the Soviet period – had existed for a number of years. Despite the fact that Gosarbitrazh did not necessarily conform to an international image of an institution of justice, from the procedural point of view it was a well-established and highly competent court (Kleandrov 2006). It functioned in accordance with predefined rules strictly adhered to by professional arbiters.

When the new Arbitrazh court was introduced in 1992, it consisted of two levels: Arbitrazh courts for the subjects of the Russian Federation (as courts of first instance) and the Supreme Arbitrazh Court, with its supervisory role in overseeing the operation of the lower courts. However, responding to the demands of an emerging and growing market economy, this structure started to change and was progressively transformed, always staying a few steps ahead of the courts of general jurisdiction. Thus, in the middle of the 1990s, the second and third

---

[2] For a description of the project methodology, see Titaev (2011); the main findings are presented in Dzmitryieva et al. (2012, 2014, 2016).

Presidium of the Supreme Court of the Russian Federation
(supervisory agency for criminal, civil and economic disputes)

Chamber for Economic Disputes at the Supreme Court of the Russian Federation
(2nd cassation instance)

District (*Okrug*) Arbitrazh courts
(1st cassation instance)

Appellate Arbitrazh courts
(appellate instance)

Arbitrazh courts of the Subjects of the Russian Federation
(1st instance)

Figure 6.1 The current structure of Arbitrazh courts in Russia.

levels of Arbitrazh courts were created: the appellate and cassation levels. The former was charged with the subsequent review of evidence, and the latter with the review of decisions reached in relation to violations of substantive or procedural law. The Supreme Arbitrazh Court assumed this supervisory role to overturn lower court decisions only if they violated the uniformity of legal practice or fundamental rights in the area of economic transactions.

Further developments took place in August 2014, when the Supreme Arbitrazh Court was transformed into the Chamber for Economic Disputes at the Supreme Court of the Russian Federation (often informally referred to as "Economic Chamber"). The transition was accompanied by a different selection process for the judiciary, which resulted in only eight judges of the former Supreme Arbitrazh Court being appointed to the newly formed Economic Chamber. The current structure of the commercial courts consists of five hierarchically positioned levels (see Figure 6.1) designed to decide disputes between business entities and, in so doing, to ensure the stability, reliability and predictability of economic life in Russia.

The most important characteristic of the current structure is the placement of cassation and appellate courts outside the administrative boundaries of the Subjects of the Russian Federation. To determine the geographical frontiers of their jurisdiction, ten new, larger, territorial entities were created for cassation courts and twenty for appellate courts. This geographic placement of appellate and first cassation courts outside of the existing administrative territorial structure was intended to minimise the risk of political pressure from local government institutions in local subjects (Yakovlev 2013) and take away any potential influence by still actively practiced networking in Russia and the so-called 'telephone law' on decision-making (for a review of this problem see Hendley 2009; Ledeneva 2008).

Other advantage of the Arbitrazh courts, in comparison to courts of general jurisdiction, is the relatively high level of their financial and administrative independence. Each Arbitrazh court, regardless of its level, is an independent legal institution in charge of its own budget. Courts of general jurisdiction, on the other hand, do not have such autonomy; decisions concerning their financial needs and the allocation of resources are made centrally by the Judicial Department of the Supreme Court of the Russian Federation. In addition, the different levels of Arbitrazh courts are linked by a procedural hierarchy, rather than by the administrative supremacy of one level over another. For instance, the head of a cassation court does not have the authority to influence administrative decisions made by the lower Arbitrazh courts. In contrast, this administrative and financial autonomy is not present in the structure of courts of general jurisdiction.

The financial independence of Arbitrazh courts has allowed them to introduce certain innovations without the fear of being shut down or supressed by the higher courts.[3] For instance, a North-Western District Arbitrazh court initiated a trial of extensive use of computer technology in the court procedure, labelled as an electronic system of justice. This work was later taken up and developed by the Supreme Arbitrazh Court of the Russian Federation. It was assumed that information about a case would be stored electronically and most of the legal steps related to a claim could be accomplished by distant communication in front of a personal computer. This electronic database would have allowed the participants of a process to access not only the final decisions but also the case materials.[4] In addition, video conferencing became a way for claimants separated from the court by a long distance to participate in Arbitrazh hearings. Taking into consideration the vast distances between cities in Russia, this technical innovation has been of considerable practical value.

The presence of an effective electronic system of justice and the resulting openness of the system, with all cases being published on

---

[3] Interview with a male attorney, St Petersburg, 19 July 2009.
[4] This practice of 'electronic case files' was successfully implemented in the United States in the late 1990s as part of the PACER (Public Access to Court Electronic Records) initiative.

courts' websites,[5] is one of the most important features of the current Arbitrazh courts. It is considered to be an impressive achievement by the Supreme Arbitrazh Court of the Russian Federation, which encouraged this practice to be introduced into the whole system of commercial courts. The level of development of information technology in Russian Arbitrazh courts meant that they began not only catching up with their Western counterparts but also, in fact, superseding them. A number of helpful features of this system have quickly entered into wide use among businessmen and legal professionals. As one advocate commented: 'The system has changed considerably, it has become transparent. Now, we have one database of practically all court decisions on the website of the Supreme Arbitrazh Court. I am referring only to the system of commercial courts, because it is very specific.'

In this regard, Russian courts of general jurisdiction have fallen considerably behind Arbitrazh courts. Although the procedural innovation of teleconferencing was introduced in the courts of general jurisdiction in 2013 (Civil Processual Code RF, Art.155.1),[6] the technical requirements for the implementation of this innovation have not yet been put in place. In addition, courts of general jurisdiction do not have a unified database of cases and decisions are published irregularly, with long delays.

To sum up, Russian Arbitrazh courts have very specific jurisdiction with four institutional levels linked to the highest level of justice in Russia, the Presidium of the Supreme Court. The responsibilities of the Supreme Arbitrazh Court are now performed by the Chamber for Economic Disputes at the Supreme Court of the Russian Federation. These courts are considered to be effective and 'advanced' from a formal institutional perspective. So how do they operate in practice?

CASE LOAD AND OPERATIONAL PRACTICES IN ARBITRAZH COURTS

Although it is unquestionably true that Arbitrazh courts have jurisdiction primarily over cases that involve economic interests, there is

---

[5] This development allowed for a number of independent investigations into the practice of Arbitrazh courts in a variety of areas (see Novikov 2015).

[6] Grazhdanskii protsessual'nyi kodeks Rossiiskoi Federatsii, No. 138-FZ, 14 November 2002 [GPK RF].

no clear definition of an 'economic dispute' in Russian legislation. Therefore, it is quite often left to the discretion of a judge to decide whether a claim involves a sufficient economic element to allow it to proceed or whether it should be dismissed because this element is lacking. The second reason that would allow a case to fall under the jurisdiction of the Arbitrazh courts is the legal status of the claimants: private businesses (a company or an individual entrepreneur) and state institutions.

It should be noted that the state could appear in two substantially different contexts. It can be a party in an economic dispute related to ownership rights or contractual performance, in which case, as a litigant, it does not differ from the other legal parties and would be involved just like any business entity initiating a claim against an opponent or defending itself from a business or an entrepreneur. The most common type of conflict in this category involves a breach of contractual obligations. However, the state can also appear as a regulator and law enforcement agency – for example, in cases related to the collection of taxes and other administrative violations. Despite the varied (private and public), nature of these two types of disputes, they both fall under the jurisdiction of the Arbitrazh courts, although they would be processed by different procedural rules.

Some cases, although they do not fall into either of the two categories described, would still be processed by the Arbitrazh courts. Examples are cases of bankruptcy, reviews of business registration rejections or disputes related to internal company management. Some of these cases involve private citizens, whose claims, strictly speaking, do not stem from their economic activity – for example, employees of a bankrupt company claiming their unpaid salaries.

In practice, these different types of cases are represented very unevenly in the overall workload of Arbitrazh courts.[7] To convey a more realistic picture of what the work routine of the courts looks like, we should closely examine what these cases are actually about and how often they are filed.

---

[7] The total number of cases heard by Arbitrazh courts in 2014 was 1.43 million while 1.16 million cases were closed with a decision on merit. Other cases were frequently terminated by the court due to the withdrawal of one of the claimants or a settlement between the parties. The case load of Arbitrage courts has been growing consistently but quite slowly. Since 2009, these courts have delivered more than a million decisions on merit annually.

As a starting point, it is helpful to separately scrutinise disputes between private businesses and those where the state is involved.

Contractual Petty Disputes
The largest category of disputes heard in Arbitrazh courts is breach of contract. In 2014 there were about 820,000 cases, while an average claim in this category was for about 3.08 million roubles (about $90,000 in 2014 prices). At first glance this looks to be in line with what would be expected in the business environment of a market economy. However, close examination of the data for the period between 2007 and 2014 (see Dzmitryieva et al. 2012, 2014, 2016) suggests that this relatively high figure arises in the generalised statistical data due to a rather modest number of excessively big cases involving milliards of roubles. In practice, a majority of cases are about negligibly small claims. If the average claim during that period was close to 2 million roubles ($60,000 in 2014), the median cost amounted to only 150,000 roubles ($4,500). The implication is that more than half of the cases dealt with disputes over very small sums of money. Furthermore, the main bulk of cases involved claims that were for less than the cost of bringing those claims to courts. If we also consider that more than half of all claimants were companies located outside regional centres, where the courts were located, then the behaviour of the entrepreneurs might seem irrational and difficult to explain. Why would businesses bother to spend money going to court in order to recover small debts or arrears without any expectation of tangible gain? Our statistical analysis and interviews with participants provided some explanations for this conundrum.

Firstly, the largest number of cases, up to 20 per cent, might look like genuine disputes between two different types of business from a formal point of view, yet this category requires some sociological deconstruction. These cases are filed by state entities, such as federal and municipal enterprises and organisations.[8] Organisations of this type are set up by the Russian state mostly for utilities such as electricity and water companies and almost all the social service providers such as nurseries,

---

[8] The Russian Code of Civil Procedure defines state entities as non-commercial organisations. As a result, it is impossible to formally call them business structures. However, in practice they are engaged in a wide range of economic activities. The status of 'organisation' makes it obligatory to distribute all revenue according to the established goals.

hospitals, schools, etc. There are also a large number of companies that are formally considered to be non-state entities but which, in practice, function very much as state institutions. This category includes Russian railroads (officially an open public company) as well as most defence companies, etc. Interviews with employees of these companies and research on web forums dedicated to professional matters have shown that decisions to file a case in court are made not on the basis of economic reasoning and interests, but of bureaucratic needs and routine procedure. For example, according to the employees of one company that we studied, it had established a practice of turning to the courts in all cases of legal dispute without exception. Other companies established qualifying criteria, such as arrears in excess of a certain amount. However, the qualifying amount is usually very low (in two cases known to us it was in the range of 10,000 roubles [$300]). It seems that initiating a court procedure and obtaining a judgment are motivated by recording purposes rather than the desire to resolve a dispute.

Another factor that explains the practice of using the Arbitrazh courts when evidently there is no economic incentive to do so was that, for many companies, filing cases in court was an important performance indicator of internal legal departments. Consequently, lower-ranking company employees are motivated to send all cases to court regardless of their value.

Furthermore, businesses tend to file cases in court even if there is no disagreement between parties. In this context, a court judgment is obtained as insurance that the business partner will eventually pay back any monies owed. This behaviour pattern accumulates cases where there is no dispute to be resolved by law – i.e., the party accepts its liabilities and an agreement of repayment is in place. Yet, the claimant prefers to obtain an enforceable court order as an assurance that the liabilities will be paid. Thus, 5 per cent of all cases in 2011 that looked like contractual disagreements were, in fact, heard in court with the full consent of both parties.

Finally, there is a considerable number of cases in Arbitrazh courts where the disputed sum is so trivial that parties for the defence simply ignore the legal process altogether and resolve cases with no objections. For an assessment of the insignificant cases in the overall workload of the courts, the number of cases that proceed to the appellate level is telling. In 2014 only 101,000 cases – or one in eight cases related to contractual obligations – were brought to the appellate courts. In other words, the judgment of the lower court has been disputed in only one in eight cases. Yet, it is well acknowledged by experts that, in every relatively serious case, the losing party always appeals – i.e., takes their case at least to the cassation courts.

Therefore, when closely scrutinised, a new image of the Arbitrazh courts regulating contractual relationships is emerging. About half of the cases in this category are either ones in which the economic interests are questionable or are not actually about real disputes. They arise either due to the specifics of internal bureaucratic productivity evaluation of the state in state-related businesses, or in situations where the court acts as an instrument in the creation of additional enforcement guarantees for the claimant to prevent future disputes. A particularly simple system of filing a claim, a wide use of information technology and low state fees have created a situation in which Arbitrazh courts are widely used by businesses, albeit in ways which are unusual and unintended by the court.

Disputes with the State

The second significant group of cases heard by Arbitrazh courts are those that stem from relationships between businesses and institutions of executive power. As our data suggest, their number reached more than 405,000 in 2014. Taken together with the type of cases described earlier, this would account for 87.6 per cent of all cases heard in Arbitrazh courts.[9] Therefore it is reasonable to argue that these types of cases define the main operation of the Arbitrazh and its role in regulating business environments in Russia.

Cases arising out of interactions between businesses and executive agencies are substantively different from those related to contractual obligations. It is considerably more difficult to determine the average financial value involved in these cases as they often do not involve a monetary element or its equivalent. However, some of their characteristics could still be deduced from the statistics of the Judicial Department for 2014. Thus, an average dispute involving a tax authority (95,600 cases) requires a sum of 385,000 roubles (approximately $12,000), which leads to an average award in favour of a business claimant of 180,000 roubles ($6,000 in 2014). Cases involving the Pension Fund (88,600 cases) included an average claim of 123,300 roubles ($4,000) with an average award being 72,000 roubles ($2,500).

---

[9] The remaining 11.4 per cent of cases are spread over a wide range of categories which is beyond the scope of our analysis.

Cases of administrative violation were decided, with the average award being 14,500 roubles ($480). In terms of the outcomes in this category, 43.7 per cent were decided in favour of the claimant according to the data from 2014. However, this might lead to a distorted conclusion, as the way in which statistics are collected does not allow identification of the initiator of the claim – it could have been the tax authority, another state institution or a private business.

In order to create a more comprehensive picture of the outcomes of litigations between the state and private businesses it is more revealing to scrutinise a detailed data set from 2007–2010 (see Dzmitryieva et al. 2014, 2016). Close scrutiny of the cases showed that most of them were pseudo-claims filed by the state when state officials were clearly not motivated by economic reasoning. Thus, the median value of a claim initiated by state institutions in 2012 was just over 3,000 roubles (less than $100 at that time). This covered more than half of all cases initiated by the state, and up to 20 per cent of all cases in Arbitrazh courts. In such cases, business owners simply ignore the claim against them and are not represented in the proceedings nor do they show up in court.

Our interviews with business representatives and lawyers help to explain such an attitude. Our interviewees told us that the sums are so small that it is easier and more economical to wait for a court decision and then to implement it rather than invest any effort in taking part in the legal process. Another reasoning behind this passive tactic was that many cases are decided in a summary proceeding, in which cases are heard without parties present and solely on the basis of the original documents submitted with the claim. For instance, in 2014 the number of such cases was over half a million. This procedure is used in cases when the value of the claim is insignificant and, in fact, has become widespread as a result of the use of electronic databases in Arbitrazh courts. Parties can upload their documents and evidence into their 'electronic case' and familiarise themselves with the materials of the other party by using an identification key. A majority of cases – valued at less than 100,000 roubles (about $3,000) – that are resolved in summary proceedings are related to a lack of funds in the state pension fund or to unpaid taxes.

To give a flavour of these mundane (or what we called pseudo-) cases, which comprise the bulk of the workload in Arbitrazh courts, we randomly picked one for illustration. In this case a pension fund issued a claim against a private business in the Stavropol region. The initial request was for the payment of a fee of 4,541.49 roubles (about $75 in 2015) for the business not submitting payroll information about its employees.[10] A claim was filed in the Arbitrazh court of Stavropol region on 20 May 2015. Within three days, the judge scheduled a summary hearing. Interested parties were sent identification keys allowing them to access the case file online and upload scanned versions of written statements (to the pension fund) together with any objections to the claim (from the company). The hearing was held on 23 May 2015 as a summary proceeding without the parties present. Because the company ignored the hearing and did not present any objections to the pension fund's claim, the judge ruled in favour of the latter, for the full amount of the claim. Interestingly, the fee for the court proceedings itself, expected to be repaid by the the losing party, was significantly reduced, bringing it down from 2,000 roubles ($40 in 2015) to 500 ($10 in 2015). The judge found it unreasonable to impose a penalty on the defendant that would have been half of the value of the claim itself.[11]

One of the key questions about the operation of the courts of all jurisdictions in Russia is the level of their independence from state influence – in other words, if judgments are bias towards the state in substantial disputes between the state and private businesses. As the data indicate, there is a trend of favouring the state in administrative cases. However, the outcome of cases is far from predetermined. Table 6.1 presents the outcome of disputes in the Arbitrazh courts from 2007–2011.

Regression analysis provides a better understanding of the factors contributing to judgments of the courts (see Dzmitryieva et al. 2014, 2016). It tells us that the more active the parties are during the process, the more balanced the hearing and the outcome of the case. If only one party is present at the hearing, it is very likely that the case will be decided in his or her favour. Evidently, this refers to cases which were filed by the claimant, who was not intending to defend his or her position, or whose position changed before the hearing but did not result in a withdrawal of the case. On the other hand, if both the claimant and the defendant actively participate in the hearing, the

---

[10] Case No. A63–2925/2015.
[11] There are cases that involve substantive legal matters yet involve very small sums of money. However, according to our data, the number of such cases is negligible and they will therefore not be examined here.

TABLE 6.1 The outcome of administrative cases in the Arbitrazh courts (%) from 2007–2011

Claimant / Respondent	Case lost	Claim partially satisfied	Claim satisfied	Other outcome	Total
Private business / Private business	17.4	12.4	41.3	28.9	100
Private business / State agency	24.4	9.5	39.4	26.7	100
State agency / Private business	13.2	4.4	61.4	21.0	100
State agency / State agency	17.9	7.7	34.7	39.7	100
All Cases	17.1	6.4	52.6	24.9	100

court is more likely to rule in favour of the claimant. An important predictor of the outcome of the hearing is the complexity of the case expressed in the total length of time it is open: the longer the case is open, the lower the chances of the claimant.

To sum up the issue of the impartiality and independence of the Arbitrazh courts, we can conclude that there is a trend towards a more preferential decision when the state is a party in the litigation. However, these tendencies are not significant and arise mostly in cases that do not involve the interests of a private business owner. Overall, the courts act quite effectively in defending private businesses from the state.

Substantive Cases in Arbitrazh Courts
As demonstrated in the previous section, half of all cases that enter the Arbitrazh courts are pseudo-claims, where the courts are used for reasons other than resolving commercial conflicts. However, the remaining cases are substantive, where private businesses have their own interests at stake and are prepared to defend them at multiple levels of the courts. It is in these cases, as research suggests, that Arbitrazh courts have proved to be an effective institution in which to settle disputes by negotiating conflicting interests with the aspiration of finding a balanced resolution. This image stands in sharp contrast with other courts in the Russian system of justice (Bogdanova et al. 2007; Hendley 2012; Volkov 2015). But what makes their everyday

practice so considerably different from the work of courts of general jurisdiction when it comes to substantive disputes? How can we explain the success of a single structure within the overall compromised legal space of the Russian institution of justice?

One explanation is the high professional level of the actors involved in the process. As a rule, parties are represented by qualified lawyers who are knowledgeable and skilled in building legal arguments and presenting cases. They are well informed about the technicalities of legal procedures. This generates an environment in which the judge and the legal representatives collaborate in a collegial professional discussion. This also makes it possible to run the court in an adversarial style when parties present arguments and the judge resumes the role of a neutral, uninvolved adjudicator. The judges we interviewed pointed out that most legal representative are highly qualified professionals, which allows them to act as an arbiter between two well-defined and articulated legal positions. The quality of legal representation and the pattern of professional communication in Arbitrazh courts are in sharp contrast with the courts of general jurisdiction. Here, in many cases, there is often no representation at all or the lawyers are so poorly qualified that the judges have do their job for them, running the case and bringing it to a reasonable conclusion.

Most lawyers involved in litigation also spoke of the smooth and professional interaction between lawyers and judges. For instance, they told us that they put significant effort into developing their position and passing a written statement to the court that is sufficient for the judge to use by simply copying the text into the final decision. To simplify the judge's work of writing up the decision, an electronic version of the lawyer's statement is also provided.

There was an attempt at the beginning of the 2000s to further raise the benchmark of legal professionalism when the Arbitrazh Code was amended with provisions requiring mandatory membership of the Advocacy Bar for legal representatives if they were not employed by one of the litigants.[12] However, this provision only lasted for a couple of years. The Constitutional Court of the Russian Federation found this requirement unconstitutional because the mandatory presence of qualified legal representatives in Arbitrazh courts violated the principle of

---

[12] In Russia, professional legal representatives (advocates) are required only in criminal cases; their required presence in other courts has been under discussion recently.

equality with respect to courts of general jurisdiction (Resolution of the Constitutional Court of Russian Federation from 16.07.2004, N. 15-P).

The second explanation for the efficiency of the Arbitrazh courts is linked to the very nature of the economic activity that presupposes a large proportion of 'written' evidence in these hearings. Practically all evidence (as accepted by the court) consists of a variety of documents related to business cases – such as contracts, invoices and similar documents supporting certain business activities. Witness and expert testimony, audio statements and other evidence involved in the proceedings are admitted but, in reality, are used extremely rarely.

Thirdly, Arbitrazh courts are staffed with sufficiently competent members of the court administration. Although the salary of the administrative staff is no different to that of their counterparts in other Russian courts (on average about 15,000 roubles or $250) and the gap between their salaries and those of judges is huge (average salary is about 90,000 roubles, $1,500), employment in the Arbitrazh courts is highly prestigious and considered a good career prospect. As a result, the court enjoys strong administrative support. For instance, judicial assistants carry out all the preparatory work and draft the final decisions. Our data suggest that, as a result, judges in Arbitrazh courts have considerably more time to review documents, familiarise themselves with the developments in the field, etc. This is far from the reality of the understaffed courts of general jurisdiction, where judges have to do almost all the administration themselves.

Finally, the judicial practice of Arbitrazh courts is highly specialised. As a rule, every judge considers only one quite narrow category of cases. During our study we met and talked with judges who specialised in areas such as retail contracts, credit agreements, insurance matters, etc. This narrow specialisation ensures the high competence of judges in Arbitrazh courts.

The contrast between Russian commercial courts and courts of general jurisdiction is not limited to legal matters concerning how cases are handled and the law is implemented. The disparities between institutions are also apparent in the way in which users of the courts are treated in the social microclimate in the courts, and even in the experience of physical space. Arbitrazh courts are usually located in large, recently built multistorey buildings with modern ambiance. They are well equipped with electronic screens that provide a variety of information – regularly updated – and, most importantly, which list both the flow of scheduled cases and those in progress in the courtroom.

The list of cases is also available online and is accessible by any legal professional on his or her smartphone. Meanwhile courts of general jurisdiction often work in old buildings – with narrow, tacky corridors – which have been in dire need of renovation since Soviet times.[13] A printed list of scheduled cases is displayed on the door of the courtroom and could be as much as a day old if a judicial assistant was not on the ball. While hearings can be delayed in both Arbitrazh courts and courts of general jurisdiction, litigants in the former are able to follow the schedule of cases and organise their time appropriately while, in the latter, litigants have to spend hours sitting outside the courtroom waiting for their case to be called.

The culture and practices in the courtrooms are also significantly different. In commercial courts the language of communication is professional; legal terminology is comfortably used and understood by all participants and procedural rules are strictly observed. Because actors involved in the trial have a clear understanding of their roles, hearings tend to unfold in a routine and quick manner. In contrast to this, due to the absence or low quality of professional representation in courts of general jurisdiction, cases tend to be heard with partial disregard for procedural requirements and often become emotional. Judges are frequently compelled to switch to using colloquial language in order to make sure that the parties understand what is happening in the courtroom. To a degree this happens because, in courts of general jurisdiction, there is no audio recording of cases, therefore judges are not worried about the risk that their statements could be reviewed by senior authorities. In contrast, in Arbitrazh courts audio recording is a strict requirement. Judges of general jurisdiction sometimes forego official procedural rules – for example, they can enter the courtroom not wearing the judge's robe, which would rarely happen in an Arbitrazh court.

The formalistic approach to hearings in Arbitrazh courts is not always positively viewed by legal professionals, who work in both jurisdictions, and who argue that, to reach a just decision, it is often necessary for the judge to immerse him- or herself into real life and the personal situation of the people before them. As one lawyer put it:

---

[13] It should be noted that the condition of the buildings housing courts of general jurisdiction, more often appellate and cassation courts, has slowly started to improve.

There are judges who try to resolve everything in an informal ('domestic') setting. Justices of the Peace[14] in Tumen' are one example. They work out a fair solution in the proceedings by talking to both the claimant and the defendant. They make sense of what and how things have happened and reach a just verdict. This is what we call the village way. When we take cases to the appellate Arbitrazh court, everything is done in a more respectable way. They have a new building; their tribunes are higher, desks bigger, but common sense – lower.[15]

ASSESSING CORRUPTION IN THE ARBITRAZH COURTS

Arbitrazh courts, along with all other courts of the Russian institution of justice, are often accused of being corrupt. Although corruption is often talked about in judicial circles, the extent of it and its forms and practice of giving bribes are difficult to verify and assess. The problem is that the narrative of corruption is often used to justify lost cases – i.e., a client losing a case is often told by his or her legal representation that the opposite side 'carried something in' (offered a bribe) and the unfavourable outcome cannot be blamed on the attorney. Besides, narratives of corruption are sometimes used by lawyers to present themselves as players with insider knowledge or 'know-how' and an understanding of how the courts 'really operate'. It is believed that such an image would strengthen the confidence the clients would have in them when relying on lawyers to secure a desirable outcome. In all these cases, narratives of corruption are used strategically by attorneys, one extreme example of which is very close to the criminal offense of extortion – receiving money from a client with an apparent goal of bribing the court, while the money is actually kept by the attorney (or an intermediary). It is assumed that there is always a likelihood of winning, even without resorting to bribery. If there is an unfavourable decision, the money is 'professionally' and 'honestly' returned, suggesting the incorruptibility of the judge or an excuse for why, in this particular case, 'it did not work'. However, there is no way for the

---

[14] Justices of the Peace is the lowest level of courts of general jurisdiction. They hear small criminal cases (with a maximum sentence of not more than three years), administrative and some civil cases (i.e., divorce or property disputes involving claims of up to 50,000 roubles – $ 1,000 in 2016).
[15] Interview with an attorney in St Petersburg, previously practicing in Tumen', 2014.

client to check whether the money was, in fact, used for the purpose of getting a favourable court outcome.

In our interviews, the legal professionals explained that corruption is possible but, because there is no hierarchical dependency between the different levels within the Arbitrazh court structure, a bribe might 'buy the outcome' only at one particular level. Therefore, the reach of the bribe is somewhat limited. Because the percentage of reversals on appeal in Arbitrazh courts is reasonably high (about 20 per cent in appellate courts and 10 per cent in cassation courts), a client has to re-establish a channel to the new level of courts or come to terms with losing a 'prepaid' case. As we discussed earlier, Arbitrazh courts of varying levels are spread around and often located in distant regions. This structure creates numerous obstacles to corruption because finding intermediaries in courts often at considerable distance from each other is problematic.

Another corruption prevention measure in the Arbitrazh courts was the prohibition of the 'no win, no fee' principle in Russian legal practice, introduced by the Supreme Arbitrazh Court in 1999, and later reinforced by a decision of the Constitutional Court in 2007.[16] Although the courts offered a formal legal reasoning for their position (a judicial decision cannot be the subject of a deal in legal practice), it was commonly understood that the real consideration behind the policy decision was an attempt to eliminate the stimulus behind the corruption prevalent among legal professionals wanting get an outcome by any means.

The random distribution of cases in the Arbitrazh courts also proves to be an effective barrier to corruption. The implementation of the electronic system of justice in Arbitrazh courts has made it much more difficult to steer the case towards the 'preferred' judge.[17] Prior to this, cases were assigned to judges by the chairman of the

---

[16] Informational Circular VAS RF 29 September 1999 No. 48, Resolution of the Constitutional Court, 23 January 2007 No. 1-P.

[17] For example, in the dispute between the general prosecutor of the Ukraine, Gennadiy Vasilyev, and a prominent patron of the Orthodox Church, Viktor Nusenkis, a former judge of the Arbitrazh court of Kemerovo Region – according to a member of her staff – made her change the category of this case so that it was assigned to a particular judge. As a result, the former judge was removed from her position for tampering with the automated electronic system, although corruption was not established. For more detail see Merkulova (2013).

court, making a chain of corruption much easier. This is still a widespread practice in courts of general jurisdiction.

When explaining the relatively low level of corruption in Arbitrazh courts, it is also helpful to remember that the average value of claims heard on the daily basis is not high. As already stated, more than 50 per cent of disputes involve sums of money that do not exceed a monthly judicial salary. The job of a Russian judge is difficult, intense and often leads to exhaustion. As a result a secure retirement is a very valued and anticipated prospect, as sociological studies among the judiciary tell us (Volkov 2015). Retired Russian judges receive a lifelong pension equal to the average salary of an acting judge of the same rank. Consequently, participation in corrupt deals which could lead to judicial removal would make sense for them only if the deals were to involve substantially large enough sums of money to justify the risk. Our research indicates that the amount that would tempt an Arbitrazh judge to engage in corruption deals must be comparable to their average annual salary, which is more than one million roubles (slightly more than $20,000). It would be reasonable to assume that the overall amount of the claim must be considerably higher than this amount in order to motivate a litigant to resolve the dispute through corrupt practice. The number of such big cases is in practice, negligible. We have also been told that it is still too risky and therefore irrational to take a bribe in simple and straightforward cases, even if the money at stake is significant. The involvement of corruption would seem reasonable only if the case were able, in principle, to be resolved in favour of one or other of the parties. Following this logic, we tried to roughly estimate possible corruption levels based on the length of the proceedings and other characteristics of a case. We ended up with an assessment showing that negotiations for a corrupt deal would make sense in approximately 3–5 per cent of cases, although this is not to say that corruption actually occurred.

To sum up, we can safely say that corruption probably does take place in Arbitrazh courts, but it is clearly not part of their everyday practice and deals are the exception rather than the rule.

Concluding Remarks: The Duality of Justice in Russia and Current Trends

The Arbitrazh courts are the most telling example of a paradoxical duality of the Russian institution of justice. After the end of the Soviet era in 1991, state institutions have developed along two parallel paths.

Some of them directly stemmed from and followed in the footsteps of preceding Soviet institutions, such as the police authorities and the criminal court system. Others, in effect, were created from scratch to serve the newly emerging needs of the transitional society. Not surprisingly, the greatest need for the creation of these completely new structures, with very little or no reliance on existing Soviet structures, appeared to be in the area of the regulation of commerce, such as the tax authorities, antimonopoly services and the Arbitrazh courts. These market-orientated institutions had the advantage of being relatively free from any Soviet legacy, and therefore developed a friendly appearance and an internal culture that stood out against the backdrop of institutions whose evolution was still based on the recent Soviet past. While we are far from idealising these institutions, they do appear to be considerably more progressive in comparison to other branches of power in Russia.

More importantly, these two parallel institutional streams have developed virtually opposing ideologies. Thus, whilst the tendency to criminalise commercial activity in Russia is still strongly apparent in the courts of general jurisdiction, it is completely incomprehensible in Arbitrazh courts and for the tax authorities. Consequently, two systems of justice have formed in Russia: one which could be labelled 'for business' and the other 'for private citizens'. When these two legal ideologies intersect they create conflict and misunderstanding. For example, for the last ten years there has been a debate over the protection of business owners during criminal investigations. Business representatives continue to argue for a special status for 'business crime' and special rights for business owners. The argument of the business community is that a law that might work for civil citizens could not be applied to business practices without consideration of the specifics of the market environment. Practice shows that, as a rule, the 'citizens' approach tends to dominate, yet the relative autonomy of the 'business' legal order is maintained. The Arbitrazh courts continue to provide direction for business regulation. They also create core standards which are expected to be followed by state agencies engaging in business transactions with private companies. This was achieved through the everyday routine work of the courts which, over time, have become more and more predictable and reliable. To court-users, interaction with the Arbitrazh courts is assessed as relatively comfortable.

The Arbitrazh courts also influence the business environment by introducing precedents. The Russian legal system does not operate on principles of precedence and the uniform applicability of the Supreme Arbitrazh Court (SAC) decisions is not set out in the law. Yet, in the procedural law of the Arbitrazh courts the plenary decisions of the SAC and the clarifications carried by these decisions are presented as binding and mandatory for application in the lower courts.[18] This provision has remained in force despite the dismantling of the SAC in 2014, and its principles continue to be applied in the lower courts.[19] With this in mind, we tend to agree with the argument that the decisions of the higher courts can be called precedents – and are a form of judicial lawmaking that fills in any missing or incomplete provisions in the law. As one of our interviewees put it:

> It is without question that judges in Arbitrazh courts first of all focused on clarifying the position of the Supreme Arbitrazh Court and rarely on stepping aside from their explanations and recommendations. It is therefore reasonable that, if the Supreme Arbitrazh Court produces certain clarifications on a number of issues, the judges, above all, gravitate towards them. These clarifications may be even more important for the judges than the actual law involved and set out in the legislative act.[20]

Because these acts of judicial lawmaking substantively changed the rules of the game in economic interactions, the discussions of the plenary decisions of the SAC have attracted the intense interest of the main stakeholders. The draft legislative projects (bills) were usually first published on the official website, which allowed all interested parties to send in their comments and suggestions. This was followed by an open public discussion in the Presidium with representatives of business associations and the relevant state institutions. Furthermore, the members of legal academia were consulted, setting a pattern of routine consultations with a stable pool of experts. Overall, among legal professionals and private entrepreneurs the SAC was generally perceived as an effective institution capable of developing high-quality legal positions and filling existing gaps in the legislature.

---

[18] Art. 31, Federal Constitutional Law of 28 April 1995 No. 1-FKZ, 'About Arbitrazh Courts'.
[19] As to the legal nature of the decisions of plenary meetings and their status as sources of law, there has been no consensus in the Russian legal community (see Budilin 2012).
[20] Interview with a male attorney, Tomsk, 2014.

However, other socio-political forces came into play and the purposeful development of the initiative to use precedent was thwarted by its ideological proponent. In 2013 the president of the Russian Federation announced an unexpected decision about dismantling the SAC and its incorporation into the highest court for civil and criminal cases – the Supreme Court. The reform was very quickly implemented, leading to the final undoing of the SAC in August 2014. The official explanation for these changes was the need to end the incongruity of the coexistence of two Supreme Courts – the Supreme Court (the highest incidence of review of civil and criminal cases in the Russian Federation) and the Arbitrazh Supreme Court – and to avoid any legal uncertainty that might occur if two separate branches of the judicial power should express conflicting views.

This reasoning was taken with a pinch of salt by sceptics. There were, in fact, very few areas of intersection between the two structures. There was also a mechanism in place to negotiate disagreements by inviting a joint plenary meeting to come up with an agreed position. The view that prevailed among experts about the real reasons behind the reform was the SAC's prolific activity in lawmaking and its initiative in filling any legislative gaps, an activity that was unwelcome at the highest level of political power. The fact that the SAC usually sided with private businesses in disputes that involved state institutions, especially in the area of taxation, was probably also a contributing factor.

Under the new arrangement since 2014, it is the Presidium of the unified Supreme Court which in the last instance has the final say in all types of cases: criminal, civil (non-commercial) and now commercial disputes as well. In practice, the number of commercial cases is proportionally negligible and does not attract much attention at the highest level. It is left to the Chamber for Economic Disputes at the Supreme Court to perform the task of bringing uniformity to the judgments of the Arbitrazh courts. It is a shared view among observers that this institutional transformation has had a negative effect on the quality of decision-making due to the reduced pool of expertise in the Economic Chamber and also due to its lower institutional position in the unified structure, compared to the dismantled SAC.

To sum up, in the current development of Russian institutions of justice, the tendency is to subsume the 'justice for business' model under the 'justice for citizens' model, rather than the other way around. Or, to put it differently, it is a downward move, rather than the raising up of institutions that are lagging behind. However, it should be acknowledged that the Arbitrazh courts still remain the lead provider of the new rules of the game for businesses and a guide for how business relationships should be regulated. They do this through a sufficiently consistent application of the relevant laws and by clarifying and correcting the far-from-perfect legislation. The high professionalism which has accumulated in the Arbitrazh courts and the self-correction mechanism which has developed as part of their structure have visibly improved the quality of the justice delivered. The use of modern technology has made the courts more open and their decisions more accessible for monitoring. The creation of a strong procedural hierarchy on the basis of precedent has enhanced certainty and legal clarity, which has made the outcome of legal disputes more predictable for parties and reduced the likelihood of corruption influencing the outcomes. Yet, it remains to be seen how the Arbitrazh courts will develop in future; the battle between 'justice for citizens' and 'justice for businesses' is ongoing.

ACKNOWLEDGEMENTS

This work could not have been produced without the help of our colleagues at the Institute for the Rule of Law: Aryna Dzmitryieva, Irina Chetverikova, Mikhail Pozdnyakov, Ella Paneyah and Vadim Volkov. We are grateful to Kathryn Hendley, Peter Solomon and Marianna Muravyeva for their comments and suggestions. This research would also have been impossible without the support of the Catherine and John MacArthur Foundation and Grant No. 14–18–02219 of the Russian Science Foundation.

References

Bogdanova, E., Ezhova, L., Karchavets, K. and Olimpieva, I. (2007) 'Mirovoi sud: dostupnost' i effektivnost'', in *O sostoianii i perspektivakh razvitiia mirovogo suda v sovremennoi Rossii na primere Sankt-Peterburga*. St Petersburg: Citizen Watch, 32–75.

Budilin, S. L. (2012) 'Chto tvorit sud? Pravotvorchestvo sudov i sudebnyi pretsedent v Rossii', *Zakon*, 10.

Dzmitryieva, A., Titaev, K. and Chetverikova, I. (2012) *Issledovanie raboty rossiiskikh arbitrazhnykh sudov metodami statisticheskogo analiza*. St Petersburg: Institut problem pravoprimeneniia pri Evropeiskom universitete v Sankt-Peterburge.

(2014) 'Gosudarstvo i biznes v arbitrazhnom protsesse', *Voprosy ekonomiki*, 6: 40–62.

(2016) 'The state and business at Arbitrazh courts', *Russian Politics & Law*, 54(2–3): 281–311.

Granville, C. (2012) 'Russia's commercial courts: a bright spot', in Granville, C., Hanson, P. and Ledeneva, A. (eds.) *Three Views on Modernisation and the Rule of Law in Russia*. London: Centre for European Reform, 29–43.

Hendley, K. (2009) 'Telephone law and the rule of law: the Russian case', *Hague Journal for the Rule of Law*, 1(2): 241–264.

(2012) 'The unsung heroes of the Russian Judicial system: the justice-of-the-peace courts', *Journal of Eurasian Law*, 5(3): 337–366.

(2013) 'Too much of a good thing? Assessing access to civil justice in Russia', *Slavic Review*, 72(4): 802–827.

Kleandrov, M. E. (2006) *Ekonomicheskoe pravosudie v Rossii: proshloe, nastoiashchee i budushchee*. Moscow: Wolters Kluwer Russia.

Ledeneva, A. (2008) 'Telephone justice in Russia', *Post-Soviet Affairs*, 24(4): 324–350.

Merkulova, C. (2013) 'Sud'e ne dali perelozhit' vinu na sotrudnika apparata', *PravoRu*, 29 July 2013, 13:57, http://pravo.ru/court_report/view/87188/

Novikov, V. (2015) *Biulleten' antimonopol'noi statistiki. Ezhegodnyi doklad po itogam 2014 goda*. Moscow.

Titaev, K. (2011) 'Kak sudy prinimaiut resheniia: issledovanie vliianiia vnepravovykh faktorov na rossiiskie sudy', *Ekonomicheskaia sotsiologiia*, 12(4): 122–125.

Volkov, V. (ed.) (2015) *Rossiiskie sud'i. Sotsiologicheskoe issledovanie professii*. Moscow: Norma.

Yakovlev, V. F. (2013) *Izbrannye trudy. T. 3. Arbitrazhnye sudy: stanovlenie i razvitie*. Moscow: Statut.

CHAPTER SEVEN

JOURNALISTS, JUDGES AND STATE OFFICIALS
How Russian Courts Adjudicate Defamation Lawsuits against the Media

Maria Popova

Defamation, which is defined as civil or criminal litigation provoked by the dissemination of false or insulting information that denigrates a plaintiff's dignity and reputation, has deep roots both in common law and in civil law systems. At its best, it is an effective tool for guaranteeing personality rights by protecting a person's good name from unfair damage. At its worst, it is a tool for governments that have access to dependent courts to suppress unwanted speech and indirectly censor the media. The global rise of the human rights agenda during the twentieth century shaped defamation litigation profoundly as courts were called upon to balance the right to an untarnished reputation against the right to free speech. Partly as a result of this rights trade-off, defamation case volume differs dramatically across states. A high volume of cases signals the prioritisation of a person's right to a good name over the right to free speech. A low volume of cases suggests that free speech is privileged over personality rights. Russia is among the states with the highest number of defamation cases *per capita* in the world. Throughout the 1990s and 2000s, Russian courts heard between 10,000 and 15,000 defamation cases per year, which means that there was one per approximately 14,500 Russians. By comparison, in the UK, often dubbed a 'defamation tourism' destination for its supposedly high volume of defamation cases, courts hear only about 250 cases per year, for a *per capita* rate of one in 1.5 million. In other words, Russia's *per capita* defamation lawsuit rate is 100 times greater than the UK's!

Why do Russians generate so many defamation cases? Who sues to protect their dignity and reputation the most often? What are some common triggers of defamation lawsuits? How do Russian judges decide defamation disputes? Who wins and who loses? Who gets a moral damage award and what determines its size? Does the political affiliation of the plaintiff affect their chances in court? The answers to these questions reveal part of the civil justice experience in Russia and illuminate the influence of Russian legal culture over judicial outcomes. They also carry important implications for the state of Russia's media landscape and the independence of the courts from political interference. To address these questions, this chapter delves into the legislative basis for defamation disputes and the jurisprudence of Russia's top court on the subject. It also analyses an original dataset that I compiled based on information collected by the Glasnost Defence Foundation (GDF). The dataset contains extensive information on close to 2,000 civil defamation complaints against media outlets, adjudicated by ordinary Russian courts from the majority of Russian federal regions, between 1997 and 2011.

Analysis of the legislation and jurisprudence on defamation suggests that the law's routine implementation, more than its content – in combination with the low professional standards of the Russian media – explain the high volume of defamation suits against media outlets. The outcomes of defamation cases are far from predetermined. The win rate has decreased from over 70 per cent to under 50 per cent as both plaintiffs and defendants have learned how to mount good cases. The GDF dataset analysis shows that the largest share of defamation lawsuits is filed by plaintiffs who hold state office and thus often have access to administrative resources. It also reveals potential court bias in favour of such plaintiffs. Regional and federal officials, as well as members of law enforcement agencies – known as *siloviki* – appear to have an advantage in court; they win more often and they receive larger moral compensation awards than ordinary citizens, even including rich private business actors who probably have access to the best legal representation that money can buy.

These findings contribute to the already nuanced picture of Russian civil justice. Russia's highly formalist legal culture is on full display in defamation cases. Judges regularly rely on formulaic expert testimony from linguists, rather than on lawyers' argumentation or their own reasoning, to decide whether a certain phrase is denigrating or not. In addition, the analysis bolsters previous research that argues that the Russian judiciary functions within a politically bounded space. There is no strong indication that political actors orchestrate the outcomes of defamation cases outside of the judicial decision-making process. However, the systematic advantage that administratively endowed plaintiffs enjoy in defamation cases points to the lack of clear separation between the judiciary and the political branches of government.

LEGISLATIVE BASIS AND JURISPRUDENCE ON DEFAMATION

This chapter focuses on civil defamation. Civil defamation suits are known in Russian as 'claims for the protection of honour, dignity and business reputation' (*iski o zashchite chesti, dostoinstva i biznes reputatsii*). They are filed by civil plaintiffs (either individuals or organisations) under civil code provisions. By filing a defamation suit, the plaintiff claims that her/his honour, dignity and/or business reputation have been damaged as a result of the dissemination of denigrating (*porochayashchaya*) and false information about her or him by the defendant. If the plaintiff is successful, s/he can demand the retraction of the disseminated information by the defendant. The plaintiff could also ask the court to order the defendant to pay civil damages to compensate for the emotional suffering brought on by the defamation. By contrast, criminal defamation cases (*kleveta*) are brought by the prosecution and litigated under the criminal code. These charges carry the possibility of a fine and custodial and non-custodial sentences.

The Russian courts have been hearing thousands of civil defamation lawsuits per year since the mid-1990s (see Figure 7.1). These numbers are great in comparative terms, as most countries around the world log fewer than 100 defamation cases per year.[1] In relative terms, the data show that the number of claims against individuals and organisations has fluctuated, but the number of lawsuits against media outlets has been steadily dropping since Putin came to power. Media-related cases decreased more than fivefold from a high of 5,437 in 2000 to 844 in 2015. How can we explain these trends?

The civil code provisions and Supreme Court decrees that delineate the justiciability rules in defamation suits reveal a major reason why Russians file so many cases: it is easy! A natural motivator for

---

[1] See research on civil defamation caseloads conducted by Article 19, an international NGO that tracks freedom of information trends around the world: www.article19.org/data/files/pdfs/publications/civil-defamation.pdf.

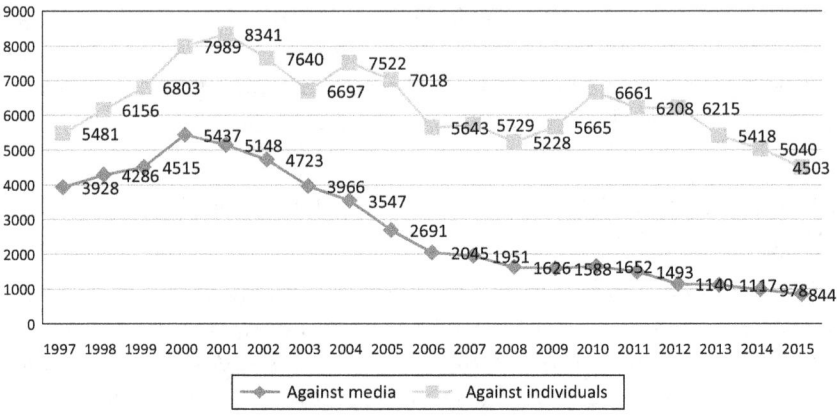

Figure 7.1 Number of civil defamation cases in Russia, 1997–2015.

defamation litigation is the location of the burden of proof – it rests with the defendant rather than with the plaintiff. Article 152, paragraph 1 stipulates that the plaintiff's claim succeeds unless the defendant can prove to the court that the disseminated information actually corresponds to reality. Put in comparative context, Russia's placement of the burden of proof is not unique. Like Russia, all common-law countries have traditionally placed the burden of proof in defamation cases with the defendant. Only the United States has decisively diverged from this norm since the seminal 1964 *New York Times* v. *Sullivan* decision, in which the US Supreme Court ruled that, even if the defendant had disseminated false information, in order for a defamation claim to be successful, the plaintiff would have to prove that the defendant disseminated the false information with 'actual malice', i.e., in full awareness that the information is false and with the intent to hurt the plaintiff through the dissemination. Thus, the United States shifted the main burden of proof in defamation cases on to the plaintiff – the truthfulness or falseness of the disseminated information becomes moot if the plaintiff has trouble proving malice (Kenyon 2016).

So, with the burden of proof on the defendant, Russian plaintiffs have to prove two things to the court in order to win: 1) that the allegedly false information was, indeed, disseminated by the defendant; and 2) that the allegedly false information discredits (*porochit*) the plaintiff. The first task is straightforward in claims against the media and only requires attaching a copy of the article or a video or audio recording of the programme that disseminated the information. Two 1990s' decrees by the plenary of the Supreme Court[2] further clarify the conditions under which a piece of information can be considered to have been disseminated for the purposes of Article 152. The Supreme Court casts a very wide net with the justiciability rules. According to the decrees, information can be disseminated via workplace issued letters, public pronouncements or letters to official organs and by oral communication with one or more persons. In other words, virtually any mode of communicating information can trigger a defamation claim.

The second task, namely proving that the information is discrediting (*porochashchaya*), is a bit more complicated but still casts a wide net for potential defamation cases. The inclusion of the *porochashchaya* qualifier distinguishes defamation from simple factual inaccuracy. For example, the plaintiff's age, place of residence, height, etc. may be misidentified but these mistakes are not automatically justiciable. According to the previously mentioned 1995 decree of the Supreme Court Plenum, to be justiciable, the information needs to diminish the plaintiff's honour, dignity or reputation in the eyes of other individuals or society. Thus, it is sufficient if only a few people think less of the plaintiff as a result of the disseminated information. Without additional limits, any information deemed denigrating by the plaintiff would have to be accepted by the court, since all the plaintiff would have to do is produce a couple of witnesses who assert their perception of the information as denigrating. The decree, however, does contain a weak limit on the definition of *porochashchaya*. It stipulates that the information has to point to a specific characteristic of the plaintiff, rather than a general description (such as 'talentless painter') and assert (*soderzhit utverzhdenie*) that the plaintiff has violated 'existing laws' or 'moral tenets'.

When the *porochashchaya informatsiya* are assertions of any illegal activity, the defendant's duty to show that the disseminated information corresponds to the truth puts journalists in a particularly vulnerable position. If they report on any evidence of illicit behaviour, they have to provide proof that this behaviour indeed took place in order to defend themselves successfully in a defamation case. According to jurisprudential analysis, the only type of evidence that the court can accept as proof that the information corresponds to the truth is a court

---

[2] Supreme Court Plenum, Decree #11, 21 December 1993 and Supreme Court Plenum, Decree #6, 25 April 1995, cited in Anisimov (2004: 32).

decision in a criminal or administrative case, which incriminates the plaintiff.[3] However, the media outlet cannot have such proof, by definition; if a court had already convicted the plaintiff, the media would not be investigating and writing about the case in the first place! It is not clear whether including qualifiers such as 'allegedly' would protect the media outlet from litigation.

A 2004 case from Volgograd illustrates this catch-22 situation, which results both from the strict evidence rules and from the Russian media's general disregard for the difference between allegations and established facts. The newspaper *Inter* wrote an article about a fire that had ravaged the constituency office of the speaker of the Volgograd Oblast Duma, Roman Grebeninnikov. Grebeninnikov's preferred narrative about the fire was that it was a politically motivated act of arson. *Inter*'s journalist, Yuliya Kurganova, on the other hand, attributed the cause of the fire to an out-of-control, alcohol-infused party, which may have involved prostitutes, since the investigators of the fire reported finding 'rubbers' at the scene. Grebeninnikov was not mentioned as a participant in the party. In fact, his name was mentioned only in the description of the location of the fire – his constituency office. Kurganova's article was based exclusively on official sources from the Ministry of the Interior and presented the information supplied from these sources as findings of fact, rather than allegations. However, the investigation of the fire was not complete at the time the article was written and, when completed, it did not end in any criminal or administrative case against any perpetrator. When Grebeninnikov filed a defamation lawsuit against Kurganova and *Inter*, they could not produce any court decision backing up the facts reported in the article. As a result, the court accepted Grebeninnikov's claim that the defendants had not proved that the facts corresponded to the truth and ruled in the plaintiff's favour.

The Russian media's professional journalistic standards tend to be quite low (Lipman 2009; Voltmer 2000). Many articles contain few

---

[3] Although, jurisprudential analysis states that 'different forms of proof' can be given by the defendant to establish the veracity of the information, the only examples given are different types of court decisions. Moreover, if the behaviour alleged in the disseminated information is criminal, a criminal conviction becomes the only admissible proof in the context of a defamation case (see 'Так, в подтверждение действительности распространенных сведений, что гражданин совершил преступное деяние, должен быть представлен только приговор суда или его копия', Reshetnikova 2005).

facts and rely mainly on subjective manipulation and innuendo to make the point that the journalist aims to convey. It is possible, or even probable, that articles such as Kurganova's might also have triggered a defamation lawsuit had they been published in other countries. However, had the case been tried in a British, Australian or US court, Kurganova's lawyers would have had the opportunity to bring up at least two lines of defence that were not available to their Russian counterparts. Defence lawyers could have invoked a 'fair report privilege' defence, which allows journalists to report defamatory statements if they come from official sources or public proceedings (for a discussion of fair report privilege in common-law countries, see Kenyon 2016). In other words, Kurganova could have claimed that, even though the allegations did not stand up in court, because she took them from official sources, she should not be liable for disseminating them. Defence lawyers in common-law countries could also have reached for the 'public interest privilege', which allows journalists to publish defamatory statements if a reasonable argument can be made that the allegations were in the public interest. In other words, whether the allegations against Grebenninikov turned out to be true or false would ultimately be irrelevant to the defamation case if the newspaper's lawyers made a convincing case that writing about out-of-control parties and a fire in the constituency office of a top regional elected official is in the public interest.

Russian plaintiffs usually prove the discrediting character of the disseminated information via expert testimony by a linguist and/or a psychologist. The linguist is called upon to analyse the text of the article that offended the plaintiff and has to tell the court whether the phrasing is neutral or denigrating and whether a statement is an assertion (*utverzhdenie*) or an opinion. For example, in a 2004 defamation lawsuit filed by Serpukhovo mayor, Pavel Zhdanov, against the MIG newspaper, both the plaintiff and the defendant presented expert opinions by linguists to debate whether eighteen different phrases were denigrating false assertions or not – *inter alia*: '[Zhdanov] is a person who says one thing, thinks another, and does a third', 'he cruelly, like a tank, drives over people, crushes them and does away with those who think differently from him' and 'he has superbly mastered the art of lying'. On the basis of the competing expert testimonies, the court accepted eight out of eighteen phrases as denigrating assertions and ruled that they defamed the mayor.

The frequent use of linguists and psychologists as expert witnesses probably flows from the high degree of formalism that permeates Russia's jurisprudence. In taking decisions, Russian judges prefer to rely on written documentation produced by other state actors rather than on their own interpretation and judgement. They do not use their professional knowledge of jurisprudential norms, nor even common sense, to interpret whether a given phrase qualifies as incriminating or to attempt to identify distinctions between assertion and opinion. Instead they opt to delegate this task to linguists, even though the latter will probably not have intricate knowledge of the legal provisions. By using a linguistic expert, both the lawyers and the judge effectively outsource the legal reasoning task – arguing and deciding whether the words and phrases in a concrete text constitute an assertion or an argument and whether they are denigrating or neutral. As a result, the potential for arbitrary decisions with weak legal reasoning, and even sometimes non-credible logical reasoning, increases. For example, in a case from 2011, a plaintiff brought a case in a Moscow court for having been called a 'trained poodle'. The linguistic expertise concluded that phrase was negative but neither obscene, nor insulting (*oskorbitel'naya*), so it did not meet the criteria for discrediting (*porochashchaya*) information (Mikhalevich 2013: 62). While it seems that anybody would take offence at being called a 'trained poodle', the judge dismissed the plaintiff's case on the basis of this linguistic expert testimony.

Another potential problem with the use of linguistic experts is that they are usually lecturers at local universities and academic freedom is far from guaranteed in Russia. When called upon to testify in cases involving plaintiffs with significant administrative resources (the governor, the mayor, members of the regional Duma, federal ministers, etc.), university lecturers are vulnerable to pressure. Universities in Russia are public and their finances are disbursed by regional authorities. During electoral campaigns, regional officials can and routinely do, lean on universities to turn out the vote for the incumbent by subtly communicating to high-level university administrators that failure to help out may result in financial consequences for the university. Since university lecturers are low in the hierarchical chain of university administration and do not enjoy significant academic freedom protection, they are likely to be highly deferential to powerful state officials who appear as plaintiffs in defamation cases. Defence lawyers sometimes invoke this potential conflict of interest, but judges rarely accept this argument. For example, defence lawyers for the independent TV station *TVK* sought to disqualify the expert witness testimony of linguistics professors from Lipetsk University in a 2004 defamation case brought by Governor Oleg Korolev, but the judge rejected their motion (Glasnost Defence Foundation – *GDF Monitor* 02 April 2002). In another case, defence lawyers for a Kostroma regional newspaper sued by Governor Shershunov reported that professors from several philology faculties at local universities refused their request for an independent linguistic expertise, citing their fear that the regional administration or even the governor personally would retaliate against the university (GDF 10 November 2005).

In comparative terms, the linguistic expert tool is very unusual. For example, in the United States, linguists are very rarely called upon to testify in defamation trials. The only comprehensive research on the topic (Shuy 2010) estimates that, in the thirty-five years covered by the study, only around a dozen defamation cases involved expert testimony by a linguist. Linguistic experts are simply rarely called to the stand. In another estimation of the use of linguists as expert witnesses, Tiersma and Solan (2002) found that, in 1998, out of 6,000 published court opinions, only eleven referred to a linguist as an expert witness. They found that even if lawyers attempted to use the testimony of a linguist in building their case, judges often balked at accepting the testimony, arguing either that it is intrinsically unreliable due to its subjectivity or unnecessary since juries and judges could interpret text themselves. This attitude among US judges contrasts fundamentally with the view of their Russian counterparts. In a rare exception, a judge in Saransk made a similar argument and rejected a defence motion for a linguistic expert by ruling that 'one does not need any special knowledge to know whether a text is offensive'. The defence appealed the outcome of the case precisely because of this decision by the judge and argued that the latter had violated a core jurisprudential norm – set by the Supreme Court – in defamation cases (*GDF Monitor*, May 2004).

The final component of a defamation claim is the moral damage award for non-material damages, which victorious plaintiffs are entitled to under Article 151 of the Civil Code of the Russian Federation. Moral damage is the 'physical and emotional suffering' that the plaintiff incurs as a result of the 'unfavourable consequences' stemming from the dissemination of false discrediting information. In addition to the Civil Code provision, a 1994 decree of the Plenum of the Supreme Court provides judges with guidance on how to interpret these categories.[4] Examples of unfavourable consequences are provided in a template defamation claim published in a defamation law jurisprudence collection and include things such as: 1) the divulgence of personal or family secrets; 2) the inability to find a spouse; 3) the forced change of place of residence or work; and 4) the inability to find work or continue a professional activity (Tikhomirov 2000). The damage could be aggravation (*nravstvennye perezhivaniya*) or physical illness. If the plaintiff decides to ask for moral compensation, s/he has to estimate the value of the non-material damage and demonstrate a link between the disseminated information and the physical or moral damage. It would seem like a big hurdle to establish a causal link between the dissemination of information – as hurtful and denigrating as it may be – and a consequence, such as a physical ailment or the inability to find a spouse. However, plaintiffs in defamation lawsuits regularly provide the court with medical notes that attribute physical ailments to emotional suffering caused by the denigrating false information. For example, in a suit against the Krasnodar newspapers *Mir Kubani* and *Rossiiskaya Gazeta*, Krasnodar Governor Dyakonov alleged that defamation led to 'higher blood pressure, constant headaches, loss of appetite and sleep deterioration' and estimated that this suffering amounted to 1 million rubles in moral damages (*GDF Monitor*, 28 June 2004).

The permissive justiciability rules go a long way towards explaining why, comparatively, Russians file more defamation lawsuits *per capita*. However, why have the number of lawsuits against media outlets decreased five times in the last fifteen years, while the number of lawsuits against individuals has remained fairly steady? One possibility is a significant jurisprudential change. In February 2005, the Supreme Court issued an explanation that offers additional instructions to lower court judges on how they should adjudicate defamation cases. The 2005 Explanation narrowed the rules of justiciability and thus made important strides towards less arbitrary court practice in defamation cases (Krug 2006). First, the 2005 Explanation distinguishes between fact and opinion in printed communication and instructs judges that only facts can be classified as 'dissemination of information'. Identifying the exact disseminated information which is to be the subject of

---

[4] Decree #10 of the Plenum of the Supreme Court of the Russian Federation: 'Nekotorye voprosy primeneniya zakonodatel'stva o kompensatsii moral'nogo vreda', 20 December 1994.

litigation is the first element that a defamation complainant has to establish in court. In other words, if the plaintiff cannot convince the court that the offending passage is a 'dissemination', the complaint is not even justiciable and is dismissed without further consideration. Second, the 2005 Explanation reminds judges that the Russian Constitution guarantees both a person's right to his/her reputation and dignity and the right to freedom of expression; it explicitly recognises that judges adjudicating defamation disputes have to balance the two rights against each other. Consequently, the Supreme Court instructs judges to pass judgements that do not 'unduly threaten' and circumscribe freedom of speech for the sake of the right to a good name and reputation. While the explanation does not attempt to define whether 100,000 or 10 million rubles would surpass the threshold for an undue threat to the media outlet, it is clearly urging judges to recognise that the trade-off is a step in the direction of bolstering freedom of speech. Third, the 2005 Explanation states that individuals who hold public office should be aware that their position makes them a natural subject of public scrutiny. The courts should be especially careful not to allow public officials to use complaints about defamation to intimidate media outlets and thereby avoid or minimise proper scrutiny. Finally, the 2005 Explanation introduces European Court of Human Rights (ECHR) jurisprudence on defamation into Russian law and urges Russian lower court judges to 'take into account' previous ECHR decisions. Again, the Supreme Court does not explain in sufficient detail what exactly would constitute 'taking into account' ECHR jurisprudence, but clearly the Explanation opens an important door for the defence counsel of media outlets (Krug 2006).

The 2005 Supreme Court Explanation seems substantively important but does not provide concrete steps – either about how lawyers could distinguish between fact and opinion, or about how they could build an argument that the lawsuit 'unduly threatens' their client's freedom of speech – that defendant legal counsel could use in building a defence. In contrast, in many common-law countries such as the United States, the UK, Australia, Canada and New Zealand, defendants' lawyers can use several concrete defences: fair report privilege, fair comment privilege and public interest privilege, all of which allow defendants to avoid liability even if they have disseminated false information about the plaintiff. In the first case – fair report privilege – the defence argues that the defendants based their communication on official sources of information (courts, the police or other government agencies) that they could trust to provide true facts to the best of their knowledge. The second defence – fair comment privilege – is similar to the fact–opinion distinction laid out in the 2005 Explanation by the Russian Supreme Court – reasonable expressions of opinion are exempt from defamation claims. However, the common-law countries' case law contains a body of judicial decisions in concrete cases that hammer out the details of how judges distinguish between fact and opinion. The Russian Explanation contains only general and somewhat vague guidelines. The third defence – public interest privilege – allows defendants to escape liability for having distributed false information, if they can prove that the communication they made was in the public interest. In other words, the public interest in knowing about a certain event supersedes the requirement to be 100 per cent accurate in reporting the facts. Defendants only have to prove that they acted responsibly in collecting the information they disseminated and in reporting the facts they believed in good faith to be accurate. The public interest defence is available not only in common-law countries, which are also well-established democracies, but also in new and unconsolidated democracies like South Korea.[5]

Not only does the 2005 Supreme Court Explanation seem to provide insufficient detail to act as a meaningful tool for defendants' legal counsel in defamation trials, but the defamation trend data also suggest that the Explanation has failed to produce jurisprudential change. The year 2005 does not mark a turning point in the overall volume of cases. Rather, the trend points to 2000 as the critical juncture. The number of cases filed against individuals increased in the late 2000s, before decreasing again after Putin's return to the presidency in 2012. The 2005 directive to balance freedom of the press against personality rights, as well as to avoid threatening the livelihood of media outlets through defamation cases may seem to explain the steep drop in the number of cases against the media. However, the early 2000s posted a steeper decline in the volume of lawsuits against the media than in the decade after 2005.

A second, and more plausible, explanation of the downward trend in the number of cases against media outlets points to the gradual and significant decline in political competition during the Putin era. Media

---

[5] For a discussion of the public interest defence in the United States, the UK, Australia, Canada and New Zealand, see Kenyon (2016); for a discussion of the same defence in South Korea, see Youm (1994).

competition decreased over the 2000s, as key oligarchs with media holdings (Berezovsky, Gusinsky and Khodorkovsky) were politically marginalised and either jailed or driven into exile. Both national and regional media markets were slowly consolidated under the control of the Kremlin (Lipman 2009; Vartanova 2012). The print media's public reach and relative importance declined significantly, while the reach and influence of Kremlin-controlled television grew (Pietiläinen 2008). The few independent media outlets that have survived often practice auto-censorship (Lipman 2009), as a result of which the number of controversial articles that could potentially trigger a defamation case have declined. In addition, as electoral competition in the regions ground to a halt, the benefit of smearing a political opponent in the media also declined. The fading of the journalistic practice of publishing politically motivated compromising articles full of made-up stories (*zakazukha*) also reduced the number of potential defamation cases. In short, it seems more likely that the trend of defamation cases declining in volume is not produced by the court but stems from the response to changes in the electoral and media landscape.

WHO SUES FOR DEFAMATION AND WHY?

The aggregate statistics on defamation cases discussed thus far cannot tell us who the typical plaintiff is and what triggers her/his claim. To answer these questions, we need detailed information about the identities of the litigants and the content of the communicated information that is litigated in court. Official court statistics collect these data not on a case-by-case basis but cumulatively. *Sudebnaya praktika* publications, which are usually the best source for court statistics, contain success rates for different courts and some socio-economic information about the plaintiffs, but not on a case-by-case basis. The best available data source for the systematic analysis of defamation case trends is the *Glasnost Defence Foundation (GDF) Monitor*, a monthly publication, which tracks media-related disputes and journalist rights violations in Russia and the other CIS states.[6] The GDF is a Moscow-based non-governmental, non-profit organisation with ten regional centres that serve as hubs for collecting and sorting information about media disputes.

---

[6] Sluzhba Monitoringa, Fond Zashchity Glasnosti, information accessed from: www.gdf.ru/monitor/index.shtml.

TABLE 7.1 Regions represented in the sample by percentage and number of cases

Over 10% of the sample			5–10% of the sample		
Region	Cases	%	Region	Cases	%
Moscow	300	18.4	Primor'e	90	5.5
Volgograd	186	11.4			
2–5% of the sample			**1–2% of the sample**		
Region	Cases	%	Region	Cases	%
Sverdlovsk	53	3.3	Pskov	31	1.9
Voronezh	52	3.2	Krasnoyarsk	29	1.8
Rostov	47	2.9	Perm', Bryansk	28	1.7
Kirov	39	2.4	Chelyabinsk	27	1.7
St Petersburg	38	2.3	Tatarstan, Kursk	24	1.5
Krasnodar, Karelia	37	2.3	Samara	23	1.4
Arkhangelsk	36	2.2	Vladimir, Nizhnyi Novgorod	22	1.4
			Omsk, Saratov	19	1.2
			Lipetsk, Moscow Oblast, Yaroslavl	16–18	1.1

Total: 1,886 cases from all regions of the Russian Federation, except the Republic of Ingushetiya and Chukotskii Autonomous Okrug

GDF researchers use three information-gathering channels to collect information for the *GDF Monitor*: references to defamation cases in the regional press, direct accounts of trials sent to a GDF centre by trial participants (usually the defendant) and accounts of trials provided by lawyers involved in defamation disputes. The data contain information from all Russian federal units, except Ingushetiya and the remote and sparsely populated Chukotskii Autonomous Okrug (see Table 7.1 for data breakdown by region).

On the basis of the information gathered by the GDF, I compiled a dataset with information on 1,886 defamation cases adjudicated by the courts of first instance between June 1997 and August 2011. For each case I recorded the following characteristics:

- the federation unit where the case took place;
- the identity of the defendant;
- the identity of the plaintiff;

JOURNALISTS, JUDGES, STATE OFFICIALS: ADJUDICATE DEFAMATION

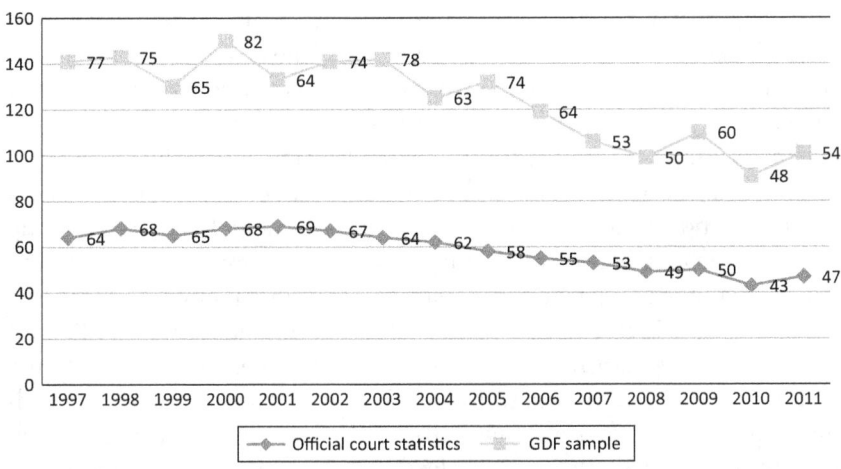

Figure 7.2 Plaintiff success rate, 1997–2011 (in %).

- the month and year in which the complaint was filed;
- the plaintiff's estimate of the moral damage that s/he suffered as a result of the dissemination of false information;
- the court where the case was heard;
- the court's decision;
- the size of the compensation that the ruling delivered.

This dataset is not a random sample of all defamation disputes heard in the Russian courts and is therefore potentially biased. It is possible that GDF researchers received more information about cases in which the media outlet was expected to lose the defamation trial and thus sought help either by raising awareness in other media outlets or by approaching the GDF in the hope of receiving legal aid. The result would be a skewing of the GDF sample towards a higher plaintiff win rate. To check whether the GDF sample is biased, I compared its annual plaintiff win rate to the corresponding figures in annual official court statistics collected by the Court Department at the Supreme Court. Figure 7.2 shows that, effectively, the GDF sample's plaintiff win rate is a bit higher than those officially reported. Like the official statistics, however, the GDF sample displays a declining plaintiff win rate over time, from between 65 and 75 per cent in the late 1990s to around 50 per cent in the early 2010s. The comparison suggests that the GDF sample captures overtime trends well enough to justify making some cautious inferences.

To verify who brings defamation lawsuits against the media most often, I used the GDF narrative about each case to categorise plaintiffs according to their potential access to administrative resources. In the category of 'federal officials' I included federal ministers, heads of federal agencies, Duma deputies and Federation Council deputies. In the category of 'regional officials' I included governors, regional Duma deputies and regional ministers. The 'municipal officials' group included mayors, members of municipal councils and heads of municipal government departments. '*Siloviki*' contained employees of the FSB, the MVD, the armed forces, prosecutors and judges. I did not code specific allegations or information about any of these plaintiffs' use of administrative resources to influence their defamation case proceedings, but assumed that all have either direct or indirect access to such resources. Regional officials and *siloviki* are the most endowed with such resources as courts are directly financed from the regional budget. Finally, I created a category of plaintiffs whom I assume are the least likely to have access to administrative resources – ordinary citizens, typically teachers, doctors and pensioners. I refer to them as *byudzhetniki*, as they are all on the state's payroll.

The GDF dataset suggests that the majority (70–80 per cent) of defamation cases against the media are filed by plaintiffs with potential access to different types of administrative resource. Municipal officials and regional officials were the most active plaintiffs. Each group filed between 10 and 30 per cent of cases over the years (see Figures 7.3 and 7.4). Federal officials and *siloviki* each filed between 10 and 15 per cent of cases (Figures 7.5 and 7.6), and the remainder – about 30 per cent – were filed by *byudzhetniki* such as doctors, teachers and pensioners (Figure 7.7).

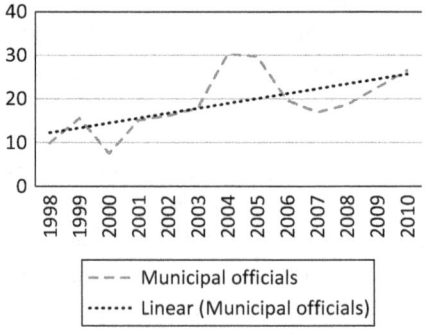

Figure 7.3 Share of municipal officials among plaintiffs (in %).

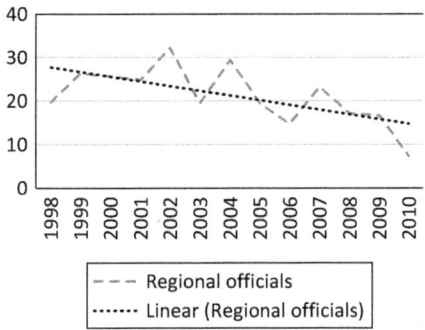

Figure 7.4 Share of regional officials among plaintiffs (in %).

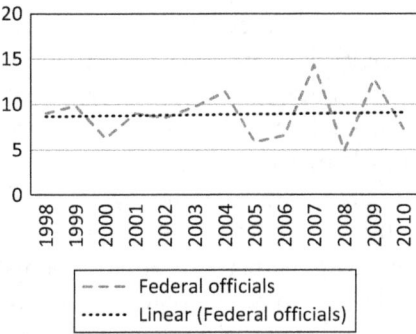

Figure 7.5 Share of federal officials among plaintiffs (in %).

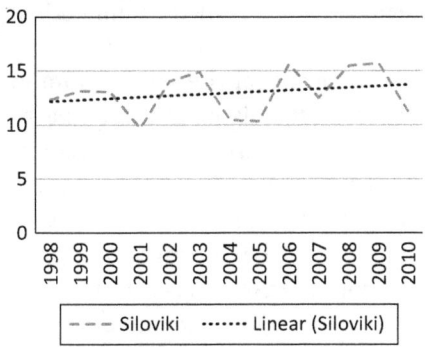

Figure 7.6 Share of *siloviki* among plaintiffs (in %).

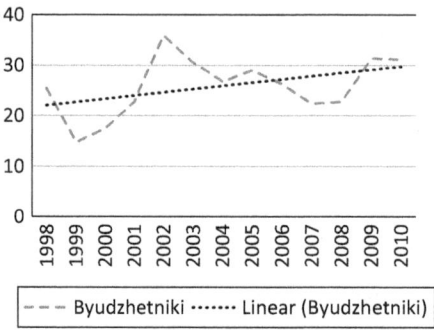

Figure 7.7 Share of *byudzhetniki* among plaintiffs (in %).

More interesting than the absolute share of the cases filed by each group is the trend over time. The GDF data suggest that cases by municipal officials and *byudzhetniki* have increased, those by regional officials have decreased and cases by federal officials and *siloviki* have remained stable over time. The contrast between an increasing volume of cases by municipal officials and a decreasing volume by regional officials probably reflects the loss of political competition in the regions. The move from gubernatorial elections to gubernatorial appointments in 2005 meant that the media was no longer an active player in highly contested electoral campaigns, and regional political figures had fewer reasons to guard their good name and reputation through the courts. As the last bastions of political competition, municipal elections probably account for the increasing share of defamation cases filed by municipal officials.

The case descriptions in the *GDF Monitor* reveal the most common defamation case triggers. Elected and state officials most often sue to retract articles that contain allegations of corruption, malfeasance, embezzlement and abuse of office. The proliferation of such cases puts investigative journalism on a very shaky footing as journalists cannot safely write about any malfeasance that has not been proven in court, even if they have incontrovertible evidence that the plaintiff had engaged in certain actions. In fact, even a court decision does not provide full protection from a defamation claim. In July 2003, the newspaper *Chelyabinsk Rabochii* was sued by a local bailiff's office for publishing an article about a bailiff who had been arrested for dealing drugs in the courthouse. Even though the article referred only to information that came out during the criminal prosecution of the bailiff and the plaintiff could not dispute the facts, the claim argued that the defamation came from the tone of the article, which discredited the plaintiff's name and caused moral damage (*GDF Monitor*, 27 July 2003).

Many defamation cases also result from vague editorialising about the incompetence or bad judgement of elected officials. Duma deputy and former Vladivostok mayor Viktor Cherepkov sued the newspaper *Primorskie Vesti* for stating that he 'had ruined the city and would ruin the region' if he were to become governor (*GDF Monitor*, 06 March 2002). Clearly, such assertions cannot be proven with a court decision. The jurisprudential practice of favouring written documentation over legal argumentation by the litigants in the context of the trial puts a significant muzzle on editorialising.

Siloviki often sue after articles allege that they have connections to underworld figures whom they are supposed to be investigating and prosecuting. Another trigger are allegations of participation in intrigues and behind-the-scenes political deals. Teachers, doctors and other *byudzhetniki* usually sue for articles that present them as incompetent, allege that they abuse alcohol on the job or claim that they sought bribes from students and patients. There are also many cases that stem from descriptions of conflict between neighbours. In 2009, a pensioner who was featured in an article in *Komsomol'skaya Pravda* sued for being referred to as *skandalistka*. She won the case and was awarded 15,000 rubles in moral damages (*GDF Monitor*, 03 April 2009).

Finally, plaintiffs do not always dispute the veracity of the disseminated information but argue that the information is communicated in a way that denigrates their honour and dignity. A pensioner in Nizhnevartovsk sued a TV station for airing an interview with her without her consent. Even though none of the information in the interview was false as the plaintiff was herself the respondent, she felt that it was denigrating to her honour and dignity. The court not only sided with the plaintiff but also awarded her 30,000 rubles in moral damage compensation (*GDF Monitor*, 20 October 2006).

WHO WINS AND HOW MUCH?

Moral damage award data are not included in official court statistics. Those from the GDF sample suggest that an increasing proportion of victorious plaintiffs received no compensation for their bruised egos and tarnished reputations. The median award dropped from 5,000 rubles in the late 1990s and early 2000s to 0 in every year after 2005 (Figure 7.8).

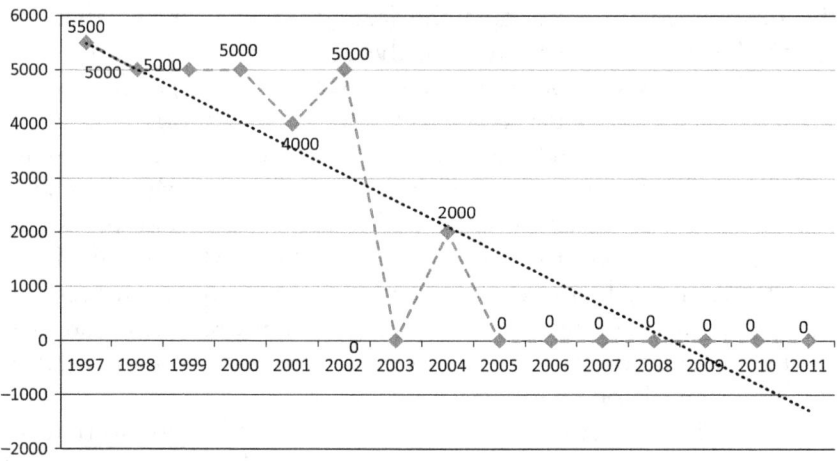

Figure 7.8 Median Compensation Award (in rubles), 1997–2011.

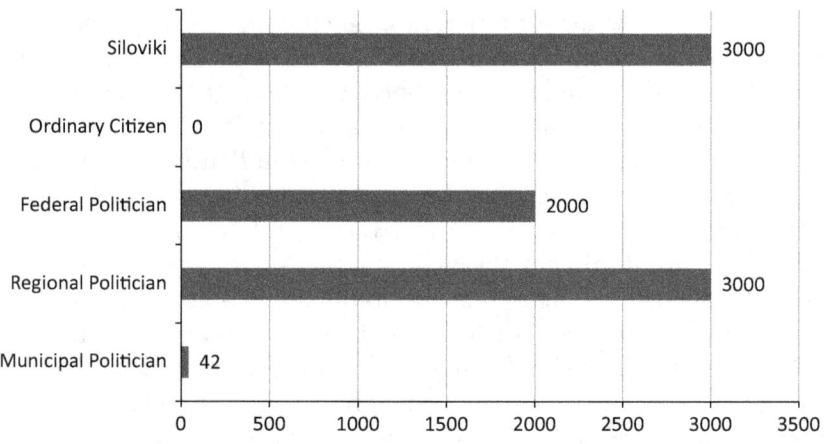

Figure 7.9 Median Moral Compensation Award (in rubles).

A breakdown of compensation awards across the socio-political groups of plaintiffs suggests that regional and federal officials as well as *siloviki* received substantially higher moral compensation awards than *byudzhetniki* and municipal politicians. More than half of ordinary citizens received no moral compensation award at all. Municipal politicians received a median compensation award of only 42 rubles compared to federal officials, who received a median compensation award of 2,000 rubles, and regional officials and *siloviki*, who received 3,000 (see Figure 7.9).

TABLE 7.2 Moral compensation awards by plaintiff group

Plaintiff group	Size of compensation award in rubles			
	Largest	2nd largest	3rd largest	4th largest
Siloviki	30,000,000	3,000,000	2,500,000	1,000,000
Byudzhetniki	1,000,000	610,000	374,000	200,000
Politicians				
Municipal	1,500,000	1,000,000	1,000,000	1,000,000
Regional	80,000,000	1,500,000	1,000,000	1,000,000
Federal	30,000	4,000,000	1,500,000	1,500,000

These are by no means great sums of money, but they do suggest that state officials are more likely than administrative-resource-poor plaintiffs to not only win their case in court but also to win some compensation. For ordinary plaintiffs, on the other hand, a victory in a defamation case is just symbolic more than half of the time.

Some may argue that reputation is a more important commodity to a public official than to a private citizen and therefore any damages from defamation to the former are larger than those to the latter. However, the Civil Code provisions on the calculation of damages stipulate that the size of the damage award should be proportional to the suffering (emotional or physical) rather than to the relative importance of a person's reputation to her/his professional activity. In other words, if a pensioner can show that a defamatory article is behind a near-fatal heart attack, s/he should be entitled to higher compensation than should a governor who was irked by a defamatory article about her/him. Moreover, as already mentioned, in 2005 the Supreme Court explicitly urged lower courts to set a higher bar for public figures who are supposed to be more open to public scrutiny by the press.

A look at the four largest awards to different administrative resource groups underscores and amplifies the point that ordinary citizens generally receive lower compensation awards than other plaintiffs (see Table 7.2). The highest compensation award received by an ordinary citizen is 1 million rubles, whereas politicians have received up to 80 million rubles. In contrast, regional and federal politicians have received many awards over 1 million rubles. Later in the chapter, I use regression analysis to move beyond these few outlier cases and to test whether, effectively, a plaintiff's access to administrative resources significantly alters the predicted size of her/his moral compensation award.

IS THERE BIAS IN DEFAMATION CASES?

I use the GDF dataset to analyse both the outcomes of defamation cases and the size of the moral compensation awards that courts sometimes grant to victorious plaintiffs. The main goal of the trial outcome analysis is to determine whether some of the individual characteristics of the plaintiff are a significant predictor of her or his predicted probability of winning in court. More specifically, I am trying to find out whether the access to administrative resources that comes with holding elected office is significantly and positively correlated with court victory. If, for example, governors are more likely to win a defamation case in court than the average plaintiff, we have indirect and suggestive evidence showing that courts are vulnerable to political pressure. If, however, we detect no differences in the predicted probabilities of success in court, we can conclude that, even if politicisation mars many high-profile cases, it does not significantly affect judicial output more broadly.

To estimate the probability of success in court for different groups of plaintiffs, I use a logit estimator with the two court decision categories (plaintiff complaint granted=1; plaintiff complaint dismissed=0) as the outcome variable and the plaintiff group dummies as the explanatory variables. An important control is the quality of legal representation used by each plaintiff, as we can expect that it will affect the plaintiff's probability of victory in court. Put simply, plaintiffs with better lawyers will win more often, all else being equal. I do not have sufficient systematic information about the quality of legal representation available to each plaintiff. However, the GDF information allows me to create a group of plaintiffs who are major private business owners. I then assume that these rich plaintiffs have access to better legal representation than the average plaintiff, just like powerful state officials are likely to have access to better legal representation. This variable allows me to begin to parse out the differences between the relative importance of administrative resources and legal resources and the outcomes of defamation cases. If quality of legal representation matters to the outcome of the case, rich plaintiffs should have a higher probability of victory in a defamation case than the average plaintiff.

In addition, dummy variables for each year represented in the sample are used as control variables. The rationale for using year controls is that, even in civil-law countries, precedent plays some role and there may be trends in court rulings over time, i.e., the decisions which courts reach in

TABLE 7.3 Logit coefficients for the probability of success in court by plaintiff group, 1998–2011

Administrative resource group	Coefficient		Std error
Siloviki (police, tax police, FSB, procuracy, judiciary	.38	*	(.19)
Ordinary citizens	–.16		(.15)
Municipal politicians	.17		(.16)
Regional politicians	.69	**	(.16)
Federal politicians	.55	*	(.23)
Rich plaintiffs	.29		(.21)
Controls			
Capital	–.09		(.15)
1998 dummy	.17		(.57)
1999 dummy	–.45		(.56)
2000 dummy	.55		(.57)
2001 dummy	.04		(.56)
2002 dummy	.41		(.57)
2003 dummy	–.33		(.55)
2004 dummy	–.17		(.57)
2005 dummy	–.55		(.56)
2006 dummy	–.40		(.57)
2007 dummy	–.98	*	(.56)
2008 dummy	–.94	*	(.56)
2009 dummy	–.74		(.57)
2010 dummy	–1.01	*	(.56)
2011 dummy	–.81		(.61)
Constant	.78		(.53)
$N=1613; \chi^2=133.21$; Pseudo $R^2=.06$			

year n are not entirely unrelated and independent from the decisions they reached in year $n-1$. Finally, the model includes a dummy for decisions reached by Moscow courts. Not only is the capital over-represented in the sample, but it is possible that judges in the capital behave differently to provincial judges. We can hypothesise that they may either be under more severe political pressure or have more opportunity to withstand political pressure due to greater scrutiny by the local and international public. The results of the logit model are listed in Table 7.3.

The results show that regional and federal officials and *siloviki* all have a higher-than-average probability of winning a defamation case, and that cases adjudicated in 2007, 2008 and 2010 are less likely than

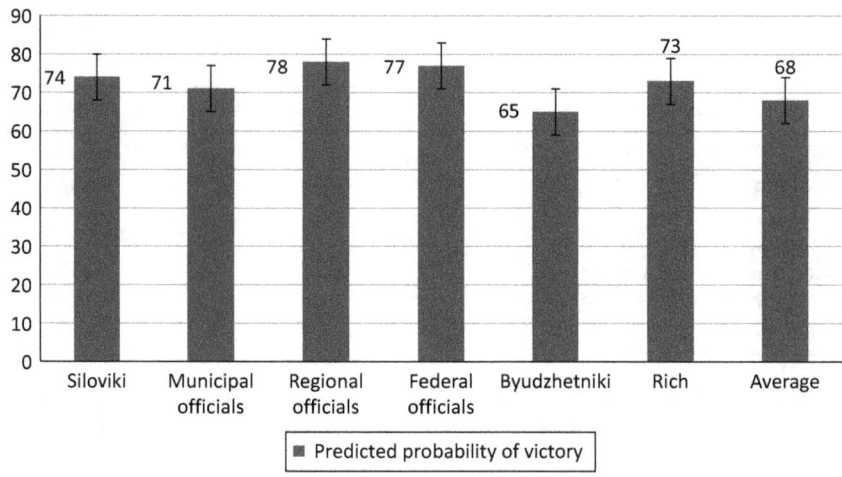

Figure 7.10 Predicted probability of victory in court by plaintiff group (%).

average to end up with a victory for the plaintiff. Rich plaintiffs do not have a significantly different victory rate than the average plaintiff. This is an important non-result, because it suggests that quality of legal representation does not play much of a role in determining a plaintiff's probability of winning in court. We can assume that major private business owners will care deeply about the outcome of their defamation claims and will have the money to hire good lawyers. The fact that their money does not translate into a better-than-average win rate in court suggests that the advantage enjoyed by regional and federal officials and *siloviki* is more likely to flow from their access to administrative resources than from their access to good lawyers.

To understand just how much of an advantage state officials enjoy in court in comparison with the average plaintiff, I calculated the predicted probabilities of a victory in court for each plaintiff group (see Figure 7.10). The model shows that *siloviki*, regional and federal officials have between a 9 and a 13 per cent greater probability of winning their defamation case in court than byudzhetniki. These differences indicate that plaintiffs with administrative resources have a better chance of succeeding in court, but they are far from guaranteed a victory. The advantage is there, but it is small in size. In other words, the political resources of the plaintiff are only one of the factors that courts consider when adjudicating defamation cases – the politicisation of justice may be present, but it does not dictate the outcome.

These results, however, raise an additional question. Do regional and federal officials win more often because of their administrative status or because of their political affiliation? Distinguishing between these two scenarios is important. If the higher win rate comes from administrative status, then either the courts are deferential to state officials or state officials have access to better legal representation. However, if state officials win more often because they are political incumbents, then the judicial decision-making process is subject to political manipulation.

To disentangle these possibilities empirically, I added two variables to the model. For each plaintiff, I coded pro-Kremlin affiliation as United Russia membership. I also identified whether plaintiffs were political allies of the regional governor by scouring regional media sources for information about each of the former's political leanings. The results are reported in Table 7.4.

The coefficients of both political affiliation variables are positive but not significant, suggesting that being a political ally of the incumbent governor or belonging to United Russia do not translate into an advantage in court in defamation cases. Regional and federal officials (as well as *siloviki*) still have higher-than-average win rates. In fact, the size of the coefficients does not change much. Rich plaintiffs also continue to have average success in court. In other words, administrative status brings the biggest advantage for defamation plaintiffs. It seems that courts are deferential to regional and federal officials neither because of their superior legal representation nor because of their political affiliation but, rather, because of their access to the leverage of public office.

A cross-sectional time series generalised least-squares regression of the determinants of the size of the moral compensation award reinforces these findings. Ordinary citizens receive lower-than-average moral compensation awards, while federal and regional politicians receive higher-than-average ones, even when we control for their political affiliation. The results are presented in Table 7.5.

WHAT DO DEFAMATION CASES REVEAL ABOUT RUSSIAN JUSTICE?

Analysis of the adjudication of defamation cases provides additional evidence of the rich literature on legal formalism in Russia (Kashanin

TABLE 7.4 Logit coefficients for the probability of success in court by plaintiff group, 1998–2011

Administrative resource group	Coefficient		Std error
Siloviki (police, tax police, FSB, procuracy, judiciary	.38	*	(.19)
Ordinary citizens	−.11		(.16)
Municipal politicians	.14		(.16)
Regional politicians	.61	***	(.17)
Federal politicians	.51	*	(.23)
Rich plaintiff	.28		(.22)
Kremlin ally	.26		(.19)
Governor ally	.05		(.18)
Controls			
Capital	−.12		(.16)
1998 dummy	.19		(.57)
1999 dummy	−.42		(.56)
2000 dummy	.57		(.57)
2001 dummy	.07		(.56)
2002 dummy	.41		(.57)
2003 dummy	−.34		(.56)
2004 dummy	−.19		(.57)
2005 dummy	−.59		(.56)
2006 dummy	−.53		(.57)
2007 dummy	−1.04	*	(.56)
2008 dummy	−1.00	*	(.56)
2009 dummy	−.80		(.57)
2010 dummy	−1.07	*	(.56)
2011 dummy	−.89		(.61)
Constant	.75		(.53)
N=1613; χ^2=136.63; Pseudo R^2=.07			

2010; Kurkchiyan 2009, *inter alia*). A typical defamation case in Russia revolves around the collection of written documents that can be used to prove the absolute veracity of the disseminated information and its degrading nature, or the objective damage sustained by the defamatory statements – court documents, linguistic expert reports, medical opinions and psychologist expert reports. There are very few concrete defences that the lawyers representing the media could use in order to protect their clients from liability. There are no exceptions that would allow a media outlet to distribute inaccurate information without penalty – neither applying reasonable due diligence, nor using only

TABLE 7.5 FGLS coefficients for size of moral compensation award by plaintiff group, 1996–2011

Administrative resource group	Coefficient		Std error
Media/journalists			
Siloviki (police, tax police, FSB, procuracy, judiciary	.50		(.38)
Ordinary citizens	–.94	**	(.41)
Municipal politicians	–.21		(.36)
Regional politicians	.90	**	(.38)
Federal politicians	1.01	**	(.50)
Political affiliation groups			
Governor allies	.36		(.44)
Regional opposition	–.26		(.50)
Kremlin allies	.28		(.45)
Kremlin opposition	–.24		(.49)
1998 dummy	–.26		(1.41)
1999 dummy	–2.02		(1.42)
2000 dummy	–.19		(1.40)
2001 dummy	–.73		(1.56)
2002 dummy	–.14		(1.41)
2003 dummy	–1.69		(1.41)
2004 dummy	–.98		(1.43)
2005 dummy	–1.52		(1.43)
2006 dummy	–1.74		(1.43)
2007 dummy	–2.33		(1.43)
2008 dummy	–2.48	*	(1.43)
2009 dummy	–2.35		(1.44)
2010 dummy	–2.19		(1.42)
2011 dummy	–2.72	*	(1.50)
Constant	6.07	***	(1.36)
N=1573; Wald χ^2=81.07			

official sources of information or appeals to serving the public interest by pursuing the story. Overall, there is very little room for legal reasoning and the interpretation of evidence or statutory text, either to be done by the legal counsel or by the judge.

At the same time, defamation case outcomes underscore that Russian courts operate in a political environment where they have to weigh the preferences of both regional and federal political incumbents. The weak separation of power between the branches means that judges have to be deferential to plaintiffs with administrative resources in order to avoid potential problems. This deference translates into slightly higher win rates and higher moral damage compensation awards for regional and federal officials. In comparative perspective, this finding sets Russia apart from other jurisdictions. The existence of a public interest privilege defence in many other countries (in, for example, the UK, Australia, Canada and South Korea) raises the bar much higher for public officials who are plaintiffs than for private citizens. Because state officials' behaviour is in the public interest *par excellence*, the media has some leeway to distribute inaccurate information as long as it can make a credible case in court that they adhered to professional journalistic standards of due diligence. Even if the Russian media's professional standards are generally lower and many stories would not qualify for the public interest privilege in other jurisdictions, this is a moot point, because the privilege does not explicitly exist in Russia. In other words, the Russian media often lose in defamation cases brought by public officials, not because of sloppy reporting but because only statements that are 100 per cent provably truthful are exempt from defamation claims.

Legal formalism and low judicial independence from politicians are closely intertwined. Scholars have argued in other post-Communist contexts that excessive formalism means that judges cannot effectively constrain politicians (Bobek 2008). Judges perceive themselves to be docile interpreters of the will of the legislator and therefore stick to legal formalism. There is a chicken and egg problem, though, with this argument. On the one hand, it is possible that a legal formalist culture prevents judges from stepping out of their comfort zone to challenge incumbent politicians. On the other hand, it is also possible that judges who are acutely aware that they lack independence both from their superiors within the judiciary and from powerful extra-judicial actors, use legal formalism in their decisions as a shield. If they minimise legal interpretation, it would be harder for anyone to accuse them of using the wrong interpretation. This analysis of defamation cases does not allow me to disentangle this causal relationship, but it does emphasise that, in Russia, both legal formalism and judicial deference to politically powerful litigants are widespread.

References
Anisimov, A. L. (2004) *Chest', Dostoinstvo, Delovaya Reputatsiya pod Zashchitoi Zakona*. Moscow: Norma.
Bobek, M. (2008) 'Fortress of judicial independence and the mental transitions of the Central European judiciaries', *European Public Law*, 14(1): 99–123.

Kashanin, A. (2010) 'Vliianie gospodstvuiushchego pravoponimaniia na sostoianie I prestizh iuridicheskoi professii', in Mishina, E. A. (ed.) *Kakova eto – byt iuristom?* Moscow: Fond Liberal'naia Missiya, 24–57.

Kenyon, A. T. (ed.) (2016) *Comparative Defamation and Privacy Law*. Vol. 32. Cambridge: Cambridge University Press

Krug, P. (2006) 'Internalizing European Court of Human Rights interpretations: Russia's courts of general jurisdiction and new directions in civil defamation law', *Brooklyn Journal of International Law*, 32(1): 1–65.

Kurkchiyan, M. (2009) 'Russian legal culture: an analysis of adaptive response to an institutional transplant', *Law and Social Enquiry*, 34(2): 337–364.

Lipman, M. (2009) *Media Manipulation and Political Control in Russia*. London: Chatham House.

Mikhalevich, E. (2013) 'Rol' lingvisticheskoi ekspertizy po delam o zashchite chesti, dostoijstva i delovoi reputatsii', *Monitoring Pravoprimeneniya*, 2: 62. http://cyberleninka.ru/article/n/rol-lingvisticheskoy-ekspertizy-po-delam-o-zaschite-chesti-dostoinstva-i-delovoy-reputatsii (last accessed 11 October 2016).

Pietiläinen, J. (2008) 'Media use in Putin's Russia', *Journal of Communist Studies and Transition Politics*, 24(3): 365–385.

Reshetnikova, I. V. (2005) *Spravochnik po dokazyvaniyu v grazhdanskom sudoproizvodstve*. Moscow: Norma.

Shuy, R. W. (2010) *The Language of Defamation Cases*. Oxford: Oxford University Press.

Tiersma, P. and Solan, L. M. (2002) 'The linguist on the witness stand: forensic linguistics in American courts', *Language*, 78(2): 221–239.

Tikhomirov, M. Yu. (2000) *Sudebnaya i Sudebno-Arbitrazhnaya Praktika. Spory o zashchite chesti, dostoinstva I delovoi reputatsii: Sbornik Dokumentov.* Moscow: Yurinformtsentr.

Vartanova, E. (2012) 'The Russian media model in the context of post-Soviet dynamics', in Hallin, D. C. and Mancini, P. (eds.) *Comparing Media Systems Beyond the Western World*. Cambridge: Cambridge University Press, 119–142.

Voltmer, K. (2000) 'Constructing political reality in Russia *Izvestiya*: between old and new journalistic practices', *European Journal of Communication*, 15(4): 469–500.

Youm, K. H. (1994) 'Libel law and the press: US and South Korea compared', *UCLA Pacific Basin Law Journal*, 13(2): 231–264.

CHAPTER EIGHT

ACCUSATORIAL BIAS IN RUSSIAN CRIMINAL JUSTICE

Peter H. Solomon, Jr

Observers of criminal justice in Russia in the new millennium have expressed concern about the extraordinarily low rate of acquittal in their country (well under 1 per cent) and many have concluded that it is a symptom of 'accusatorial bias' (*obvinitel'nyi uklon*) – a feature of late Soviet justice that seems to have persisted in the post-Soviet era (Churilov 2010a, 2010b; Mikhailovskaia 2010; Paneiakh *et al.* 2010; Petrukhin 2009, 2011). This diagnosis is reminiscent of the era of *glasnost* (in the mid and late 1980s), when open discussion of the problems of acquittal and bias in Soviet criminal justice first occurred (Solomon 1990).[1]

The purpose of this chapter is to determine whether the low rate of acquittal in post-Soviet Russia does, indeed, signify bias against the accused. The experience of other countries suggests that the connection between acquittals and accusatorial bias is not a simple one. As we shall see, there are countries with both inquisitorial and adversarial procedures where rates of acquittal are low and there is little or no perception of bias.[2] In fact, high rates of acquittal for criminal cases

---

[1] In 1986 alone, the low level of acquittals was discussed in a dozen newspaper articles. One of the first was an interview by Iuryi Feofanov with Supreme Court Judge E. Smolentsev (Feofanov 1986). Especially revealing was Arkadii Vaksberg's (1986) account of a Supreme Court Plenum late in the year, which discussed the issue at length.

[2] In theory, rates of acquittal at trial should be lower in inquisitorial than in adversarial systems and perhaps this was so in the distant past. However, I see no signs of such a difference in practice for most of the twentieth century. While, to my knowledge,

overall are a thing of the past, at least in Western countries (for example, both France in the 1920s and 1930s and Russia from 1905 to 1930 had acquittal rates over 20 per cent). What countries with high rates of acquittal had in common were the absence of significant pre-trial screening on the part of police and prosecutors and the readiness of officials to send weak cases to court because they lacked either the power to dismiss them or the capacity – human and/or intellectual – to review them (Donovan 2010: 58, 60; Zelitch 1931: 353–54).[3]

In the late twentieth and the twenty-first centuries, typical rates of acquittal in European countries stood in the 3 to 5 per cent range, regardless of the type of criminal procedure. Most of these countries also had significant systems of pre-trial filtering of cases, often involving prosecutors reviewing cases and, in the view of some observers, acting like judges. Plea arrangements and reconciliation procedures were also a major part of the story in some countries. Thus, in England and Wales in the 1970s and early 1980s, acquittals in contested cases at both crown and magistrates' courts occurred in more than 40 per cent of trials but, with more than 90 per cent of cases featuring guilty pleas, the overall rate of acquittal was close to 4 per cent (Baldwin and McConville 1978; McConville and Baldwin 1981). I contend that the various kinds of pre-trial filtering have a profound effect on not only the rate of acquittal at trial but also its meaning. This applies to Japan – where the low rate of acquittal (1 per cent) has aroused controversy among scholars – as well as to Western countries (Johnson 2012; Ramseyer and Rasmusen 2001).

The paper out of which this chapter grew was prepared for a spring 2013 conference in St Petersburg that was devoted to the problem of acquittals and accusatorial bias in post-Soviet states, most of which

---

there has been no scholarship on this issue, one can surmise that, in adversarial systems, guilty plea arrangements and the practice of diversion curtailed formerly high rates of acquittal, while pressures to improve the protection of the accused affected acquittal rates in inquisitorial countries, leading to a convergence. Generalisations of this kind may not hold water, however, because the intervening variables such as bureaucratisation and the degree of pre-trial screening highlighted here are so influential.

[3] The acquittal rate in Russia's district (*okrug*) courts in 1904 was 36.9 per cent (Svod 1907). See (1907). The rate of acquittals in Soviet peoples' courts stood at 26.2 per cent in 1925, 25.4 per cent (1926) and 25.6 per cent (1927) and in provincial and circuit courts (higher levels) at 21.9 per cent in 1925 and 26.2 per cent in 1927 (Zelitch, 1931).

have acquittal rates similar to those of Russia. To this audience, the fact of and reasons for the low acquittal rate in Russia (including the system of evaluating judges and law enforcement officials) were well known, but the relevant experience of Western countries was not. For this reason, I chose to devote a major part of the paper to the patterns of pre-trial screening displayed in a group of Western countries, including the role of prosecutors in diverting cases – both weak and strong – from consideration by courts. For this, I relied in part on recent empirical studies of prosecutors and their exercise of discretion in the pre-trial phase – literature unknown to most Russian jurists and legal scholars and probably also to some specialists on Russian law in the West. I maintained this emphasis in a journal article published for English-speaking readers but, in the version presented here, I reduce the coverage of Western comparators.[4]

This chapter begins with a short discussion of the problem of acquittals in Soviet and post-Soviet Russia, including its emergence as a policy issue. It proceeds to an analysis of case dispositions and pre-trial screening in Canada (a country with adversarial procedure and a low rate of acquittal) and Germany (the prototypical modern neo-inquisitorial system). There follows a discussion of the recent Western phenomenon of prosecutors acting as judges and an inquiry into the nature and extent of pre-trial screening by investigators and procurators in Russia. Finally, the chapter explores the feasibility and potential impact of the proposed introduction of pre-trial conditional disposals into Russian criminal law and procedure.

ACQUITTALS AND ACCUSATORIAL BIAS IN THE USSR AND RUSSIA

By the 1970s, judges in the Soviet Union gave acquittals in fewer than 1 per cent of criminal trials (down from 10 per cent in 1946), and this practice continued in post-Soviet Russia and most other post-Soviet states. This low rate of acquittal was accompanied by the use of substitutes for acquittals in cases where the evidence at trial turned out to be weak, including returns to supplementary investigation at the end of a trial (a unique Soviet institution that lasted in Russian law

---

[4] For a full discussion of the pre-trial filtering of criminal cases (and the coverage of France and the Netherlands), see Solomon (2015a). For the paper as presented in Russia, see Solomon (2015b).

until 1999) and 'compromise decisions' – that is, convictions to lesser charges with lenient punishments (Solomon 1987, 1996).[5]

The decline of acquittals in the USSR began in the late 1940s when, as part of a campaign for perfection in the administration of justice, acquittals were stigmatised as the failures of investigators and procurators, and judges were discouraged from giving them. The drop in the rates of acquittal continued in the post-Stalin period, moving from 5.3 per cent in 1956 to 2.5 per cent in 1966, partly as the result of a shift of many cases of personal accusation from regular courts to the comrades' courts (Petrukhin 2011; Solomon 1987, 1996). By 1970, judges risked not only censure but even the loss of their job if they gave more than the occasional acquittal. A large share of acquittals was overturned by higher courts and hurt the judge's record on stability of sentence, a key criterion in their formal performance evaluation. This decline of acquittals in the USSR and the role of judicial evaluation in producing it were the subject of an article I published (Solomon 1987) based mainly on interviews with émigré jurists, and later in an archive-based study of Soviet criminal justice under Stalin (Solomon 1996). The topic also received detailed examination by two Soviet legal scholars, Igor Petrukhin and Tamara Morshchakova, in a brilliant two-volume study of judicial mistakes published in 1975 (Kudriavtsev 1975), for which Petrukhin gained access to archives that included secret statistics on the work of courts. However, CPSU Central Committee censors deemed this work too sensitive for open publication (even though it reported data only in percentages) and limited access by assigning to the book the classification mark (*grif*) 'For service use only' (*dlia sluzhebnogo pol'zovaniia*), the only book ever published by the Institute of State and Law of the Academy of Sciences to receive this. At end of his life, in a monograph on acquittals published posthumously, Petrukhin (2011) produced data and analysis from the 1975 study.

---

[5] The Soviet pattern of low (or exceptionally low) rates of acquittal continued not only in Russia but also in other post-Soviet countries and former socialist countries of East Central Europe. Thus, the rate of acquittal in 2010 in Ukraine stood at 0.2 per cent (down from 0.78 per cent in 1992), in Belarus at 0.36 per cent, in Kazakhstan at 1.25 per cent and in Georgia, 0.1 per cent; in Moldova (the anomaly) it stood at 3.4 per cent in 2009. In Bulgaria in 2009, 2.1 per cent of those accused were acquitted and, in Poland in 2008, 2.3 per cent (Trochev 2014).

The low rate of acquittals became public knowledge in the USSR during the *glasnost* period, and it was then that the connection with an accusatory or prosecutorial bias (*obvinitelnyi uklon*) was made by observers, specialist and journalistic alike (Feofanov 1986; Sobolev and Potapenko 1989; Solomon 1990; Vaksberg 1986). For legal scholars specialising in criminal procedure, this bias could be overcome only if judges had the independence and power to act impartially and to hold investigators and procurators to account. The Conception of Judicial Reform of 1991 even treated judicial and prosecutorial power as a zero-sum game. The same white paper also called for the development of adversarial trials, which the authors assumed would empower judges. Through life appointments and removal only for cause, the judicial reforms of the 1990s were meant to give judges the protection needed (Solomon and Foglesong 2000). In addition, the 2001 Criminal Procedure Code (hereafter CPC) was supposed to correct the balance between the sides, at least at trial (for example, by requiring a procurator to establish evidence orally and detaching the judge from any search for objective truth). However, none of these steps had a lasting effect on the rate of acquittal, even with the loss of the option of returning cases to supplementary investigation at the end of trials. The reasons were clear. On the one hand, the system of evaluating the work of judges remained unchanged. On the other hand, judges continued to defer to procurators – out of professional solidarity rather than party discipline (Paneiakh *et al.* 2010; Pozdniakov 2012; Solomon 2005).

During the period of implementation of the new CPC, it also became public knowledge that the real rate of acquittal was lower than previously recognised. It turned out that no fewer than two-thirds of the small number of acquittals happened in cases of personal accusation, where the state – in the person of a procurator – was not involved. Many of these were cases where one neighbour accused another of personal insult. Once one subtracted out these minor conflicts, then the rate of acquittal in cases prosecuted by the state was, in most years of the post-Soviet period, 0.2 per cent, and was never higher than 0.4 per cent (Churilov 2010b; Paneiakh *et al.* 2010). Moreover, defenders of Russian criminal justice have claimed (with justification) that cases stopped for rehabilitative reasons (such as a determination that no crime happened or that the accused did not participate in it) were the functional equivalent of acquittals. If their number reached 1.9 per cent in 2008 and they were added to the rate of acquittals of 0.7, then the total would be a respectable 2.6 rate of acquittal. However, it turned out that a large portion of the cases stopped for rehabilitative reasons were also cases of personal accusation! (Paneiakh 2012; Paneiakh et al. 2010). As a result, even if one counts this case disposition as an acquittal, the rate of acquittal in cases prosecuted by the state (in 2008) is still only 0.7 per cent (0.2 per cent acquittals and 0.5 per cent stopped for rehabilitative reasons).

While the CPC of 2001 turned out to have little effect on acquittals, it did affect the rate of conviction by enhancing the possibility of ending criminal cases with reconciliation between the victim and the accused, leading to the judge's stopping of the case for non-rehabilitative reasons. In 2008, after omitting cases of personal accusation, 18 per cent of criminal cases ended with reconciliation of the sides, and the actual rate of conviction attained 80 per cent (Paneiakh et al. 2010).[6] To Supreme Court Chairman Lebedev this meant that there could not be an accusatory bias, since nearly a quarter of persons facing criminal charges in court avoided conviction.[7] There was also another major change affecting the criminal process – the introduction of a kind of plea arrangement, the so-called 'special procedure' which, by 2011, was used in more than two-thirds of criminal cases. I will discuss what this meant in practice and its relationship to pre-trial screening later in the chapter.

Starting with the presidency of Dmitry Medvedev, the issues of acquittals and accusatory bias once again became part of public discussion, if not also part of the policy agenda. This happened in part because of the accidental publication of a number of academic studies of the criminal process by such scholars as Igor Petrukhin, Iuryi Churilov and the talented group of young social scientists at the Institute of the Rule of Law in St Petersburg, including Ella Paneiakh, Mikhail Pozdniakov, Kirill Titaev, Maria Shkliaruk and Vadim Volkov. At the same time, Dmitry Medvedev's repeated criticism of the courts and commitment to their reform helped to

---

[6] Another 1.5 per cent of cases were stopped for a different non-rehabilitative reason – namely the demonstration by the accused of sincere repentance. If one includes cases of personal accusation, 23 per cent were stopped for non-rehabilitative reasons and nearly 2 per cent for rehabilitative ones; the rate of conviction was 74 per cent.
[7] For two of his statements, see Lebedev (2010, 2011).

stimulate commentary by journalists and specialists in the press and to provide answers to their criticism from official sources, such as Supreme Court Chairman Lebedev and his press spokesman Pavel Odintsev.[8] The discussions revealed disagreement and confusion about not only the meaning of Russian statistical data but also the frequency of acquittals in Western countries, where some observers imagined acquittal rates of 20 per cent (Pozdniakov 2012).[9] As recently as 2013, Prime Minister Medvedev (a former law professor) stated that Russia had a disturbingly low rate of acquittal of 3–5 per cent, for him a sign of accusatory bias. In fact, as we have seen, Russia's acquittal rate was actually well below 1 per cent, and a rate of 3–5 per cent was the respectable norm for countries in Western Europe (Shkliaruk 2013). As we shall see, however, this rate was accompanied by levels of pre-trial screening of weak cases and alternative judicial dispositions that gave those numbers extra meaning.

Moreover, as low rates of acquittal returned to the public agenda in Russia, some high-ranking Russian judges (e.g., the Chairs of the Arkhangelsk regional court and Kirov city court) expressed their belief that the trial courts in Russia encountered very few cases meriting acquittal because of their significant filtering out during the preliminary investigation (Pozdniakov 2012: 92; Shkliaruk 2014). We will see whether they were correct.

The pre-trial screening of cases became common in many Western countries during the last decades of the twentieth century. It is time to examine the patterns of case disposition, both at and before trial and in both Canada and Germany, in order to provide a baseline for interpreting and assessing the situation in the Russian Federation. Both countries featured the widespread stopping of cases by prosecutors, often with conditions attached, some of which did not have enough evidence to support conviction.

---

[8] A list of many of these contributions is found in Pozdniakov (2012), among them Odintsev (2011) and Morshchakova (2011). Already, in 2009, President Medvedev expressed shock at hearing that the rate of acquittal was less than 1 per cent. He told reporters that he would check with Chair of the Supreme Court Lebedev, http://dolboed.livejournal.com/1712289.html.

[9] Examples of mistaken views of acquittals rates in Europe or the West include Trunov (2009), Gutsenko et al. (2002) and Poluyan (2009).

PRE-TRIAL DISPOSITIONS IN CANADA

Canada, a common-law country with an adversarial system, has a high level of guilty pleas, comprising 95% of convictions. At the same time many charges are withdrawn, and cases stayed at the request of the prosecutor before the start of trial.[10] 'Cases stayed' is an especially large category in English Canada (all the provinces and territories other than Quebec), accounting for the bulk of cases where convictions are not entered. Official data on case outcomes from 2008/9 distinguish four outcomes and include breakdowns by province. For the country as a whole, 66.3 per cent of cases resulted in a conviction, 29.3 per cent were withdrawn, 3.2 per cent ended in acquittals and 1.2 per cent had other endings (including mistrials and findings that the accused was not criminally responsible or fit to stand trial). The acquittal rates varied from a high of 13.1 per cent in the province of Quebec (which had only 9.6 per cent withdrawals) to a low in the province of Ontario, where only 0.6 per cent of cases overall ended in acquittal (or 23.6 per cent of contested trials, if one assumes that they constituted 5 per cent of the total number) and 38.4 per cent ended in the withdrawal or staying of charges before trial (Thomas 2008/9).[11]

The withdrawal of charges in Canada, an action that ends the case and leaves no criminal record, can be based on a number of legal, rational and practical considerations. One is that, in the judgment of the prosecutor, the evidence is not strong enough for a conviction, so that a trial would lead to acquittal. According to the law (Criminal

---

[10] This figure is conventional wisdom and confirmed by crown prosecutors with whom I have spoken. However, it is not official, for there are no statistics kept on the frequency of guilty pleas, nor are there separate data on trials where charges were contested.

[11] See also, Dauvergne (2012). Since 1999, Canada has maintained national statistics on criminal courts (missing data from municipal courts in Quebec and superior courts in two provinces); these data show little change from year to year in rates of acquittal or withdrawal. Before 1999, there were no such data compiled and only the occasional, irregular airing of data from particular provinces. In the early 1970s, Statistics Canada published detailed national data, with some gaps, on the handing of indictable offences only – that is, the most serious crimes. While the acquittal rate came in at 9 per cent for Ontario, this supplies no basis for comparison with the global data from the past decade. For 1998 through to 2002, see PBC (2003). For national data on indictable offenses only, see Information Canada (1973). See also, Kari's (2010) press report.

Code of Canada S579), a prosecutor (known as a crown attorney or simply crown) is required to withdraw a charge if he or she believes that there is no reasonable prospect of conviction. This judgment is made on the basis of experience with contested trials, where weak cases routinely end in acquittals. The rate of acquittal in contested cases is not known, but informed estimates for the province of Ontario indicate that acquittals at such trials happen between a quarter and a third of the time, if not more.[12] Moreover, while recording individual acquittals is not problematic for a prosecutor, coming up with a large number of them suggests that the prosecutor is not making good judgments about the strength of the evidence (no one counts the prosecutor's wins and losses, but individual crown attorneys develop reputations). In short, the rules and the organisational culture, combined with the practice of independent judges applying tough evidential standards, provide strong incentives for prosecutors to withdraw charges and not proceed to trial when they conclude that the evidence might be insufficient for conviction.[13]

Secondly, the prosecutor or crown attorney may also withdraw or drop charges and close a case when he or she determines that it would not be in the public interest to continue (even when there is enough evidence to convict). Using this legal category, he can seek a peace bond (through which the accused promises to follow particular conditions) or require the accused to make a donation to charity or perform some community service. The latter can be done informally or as part of a formal diversion programme, of which Ontario, for example, has

---

[12] The Ontario acquittal estimates are based, in turn, on an estimate of the percentage of contested trials. If 5 per cent of cases were contested (a high estimate), then the acquittal rate at trial would be 20 per cent; with 4 per cent of cases contested, 25 per cent; and with 3 per cent of cases contested, 33 per cent. Note that, in the view of at least one crown prosecutor in Toronto, the chances of acquittal at trial were actually higher, but his perception could reflect regional variation within the province. Also note that, in England and Wales in 2011, the rate of acquittals in contested cases at crown courts stood at 62 per cent, but with 30 per cent of cases there contested (the rest had guilty pleas), the effective rate was 19 per cent. Since crown courts heard only 2 per cent of criminal cases overall, the contribution of these acquittals to the overall data was 0.4 per cent. No national data are gathered on the work of the magistrates' courts, which hear most criminal cases, so there is no way to determine the aggregate rate of acquittal in the UK (see Ministry of Justice 2012).

[13] Interview with a crown attorney (prosecutor) in Toronto, 31 January 2013; correspondence with criminal justice expert, January 2013.

many. Some of these programmes are funded by the government itself under its 'direct accountability' legislation of 2006.[14]

Decisions relating to withdrawals are usually made by the crown attorney who is handling the case although, in the most serious cases (e.g., murder), he would be expected to get approval from the chief crown attorney himself. However, it is clear that many cases, especially those with less serious charges, are handled by individual prosecutors without trial or formal punishment. As a rule, the police rather than the prosecutor lay the original charges (although, in the province of New Brunswick, an interview with a crown attorney revealed that prosecutors screen charges before they are laid).

One should add another category to this portrait of case outcomes short of full conviction – discharges, absolute and conditional. Technically, these are considered to be sanctions, and the cases where they apply are counted as convictions. Nevertheless, in practice, they are clearly less than that. An absolute discharge means that, despite the finding of guilt, the accused has been forgiven and there is no punishment and no criminal record. A conditional discharge, often combined with probation and conditions that may include reporting requirements, repaying the victim or receiving counselling, also leads to the cancellation of a criminal record in three years. Discharges are often the sanction of choice in minor drug offences and, while not the same as acquittals, are less than full convictions. There do not seem to be data on the use of discharges in the public record.

While there has been a proliferation of diversion-related programmes in the province of Ontario in the past decade, the overall pattern of dispositions is not new. Data from 1998–99 indicate a 55.3 per cent rate of conviction and a 40.1 per cent rate of withdrawals. It is also clear from older legal literature that prosecutors in Canada have long had the discretion to withdraw cases at any stage in the criminal process. They have had no obligation to continue a charge, nor do their decisions to withdraw or drop call for judicial consent in practice. In fact, in Canada, discretion has been the hallmark of the prosecutor's official mandate for many decades, and a classic study of Toronto prosecutors from 1969 highlights this feature (Grosman 1969; see also, McGlynn Ganney 1976). At the same time, despite the crown's adversarial role at trial, the prosecutorial ethos in Canada stresses not the achievement of convictions at any

---

[14] See www.attorneygeneral.jus.gov.on.ca/englishjot.jot_in_action.asp. Also, google 'Ontario direct accountability' for information on the various programmes.

cost but a balanced approach that produces a fair and efficient result. The crown attorney is said to occupy a dual role as a minister of justice and advocate, and public interest requires him to exercise judgement and discretion in a balanced way. 'Fairness, moderation and dignity should characterize the conduct of crown attorneys during criminal litigation', says a handbook for prosecutors or crowns (ODPP 2007) in one Canadian province (Newfoundland). In short, prosecutors in Canada have 'a duty to be fair', which takes precedence over their adversarial role. This understanding of the role of the crown is both traditional and laid out in a series of court decisions. Thus, in 1954 the Supreme Court of Canada in R. v. *Boucher* wrote, 'Crown counsel's duty is not to obtain a conviction', but 'to lay before a jury what the Crown considers to be credible evidence relevant to what is alleged to be a crime'. While the crown should press fully and firmly every legitimate argument tending to establish guilt, he must at the same time be 'accurate, fair and dispassionate' (Province of Ontario 2005).[15]

CASE PROCESSING IN GERMANY (AND ITS NEIGHBOURS)

The hallmark of the European approach to case disposition in the twenty-first century was the large role of prosecutors and the resolution of many criminal cases without trials. There were many mechanisms involved, including penal orders, conditional dismissals, punishment without conviction and outright dismissals. Each country had its own rules and repertoire, and the space left to the courts varied as well. However, the process of filtering was often, if not typically, so rigorous that weak cases did not reach the courts, let alone have trials.[16] All the same, as we shall see, rates of acquittal

---

[15] See the 'Duties and Responsibilities of Crown Attorneys' section of a guidebook for crown attorneys, Province of Newfoundland (ODPP 2007). See also, Gorman (2000–2001); Rosenberg (2009). The latter refers to the 'quasi-judicial status' of Canadian crown prosecutors. Note that the quasi-judicial portrait of the prosecutor's responsibilities found in Canada is much less developed in the United States where, for the most part, district attorneys represent one side in the adversarial contest. While they are supposed to charge accurately, they do not usually have the obligation to seek evidence that exonerates or discloses (see Brown 2012).

[16] For details on the tools that prosecutors use to dispose of cases before trial in European countries, see Jehle and Wade (2006), Luna and Wade (2010, 2012a).

were not negligible (3 per cent in Germany, 5 per cent in France and an estimate in the Netherlands of 3.2 per cent).

The prosecutor in Germany has extremely broad discretion and many options for the handling of cases, both on his own and with the judge's consent. Using data from 2006, one can report that nearly half of the cases that come to the prosecutor's office are either dropped due to insufficient evidence or sent to another authority. This unusually high level of cases being dropped reflected the fact that the police were not allowed to stop cases and were obliged to send incomplete ones (e.g., where there was no suspect) to the prosecutor. All the same, the dropped cases included some with suspects where a judge might have acquitted. Of the rest of the cases handled by prosecutors in Germany, a substantial share (40 per cent) ended in an unconditional dismissal (the prosecutor simply closes cases of lesser crimes committed by adults); one-tenth had a conditional dismissal (e.g., the accused must pay to a charity but gets no conviction); and one-fifth received a prosecutor-initiated penal order (a proposal to accept conviction and penalty). Only 20 per cent of cases where prosecutors do a substantive review (11.5 per cent of their total load) resulted in a public charge and transfer to a court![17] This contrasts with France, where prosecutors sent 47 per cent of their cases to court (in 2004), and England and Wales, Hungary and Finland, where prosecutors bring more than two-thirds of their cases to court. There are also major regional variations within Germany, with higher rates of prosecutorial disposal of cases in northern states than in southern ones (Boyne 2012).[18]

As if this were not enough, of the criminal cases that reach the courts in Germany, only 47.2 per cent had a full trial with verdict. Some cases were combined with others, sent to other courts or stopped for insufficient evidence (all grouped under 'other conclusion' in the official statistics). Other cases experienced conditional termination (more contributions to charity or treatment for narcotic use) and 10 per cent involved unconditional discharges (the most common with juveniles). Of the cases that were actually adjudicated, the rate of conviction was 81 per cent (80 per cent had been the norm for thirty years).

---

[17] The principal source for the German statistical data is Jehle (2009). A research assistant has also consulted the official data on the web.

[18] For insight into how German prosecutors understand their responsibilities, including for pre-trial diversion, see Boyne (2014).

The other 19 per cent included not only what were called acquittals (around 3 per cent overall; higher for crimes of violence, lower for property crimes), but also new penal orders (3 per cent), discharges after trial began and decisions to dispense with punishment, some of which were the functional equivalent of acquittals (Elsner and Peters 2006; Jehle 2009).[19]

In sum, German criminal justice included many mechanisms through which criminal cases, weak and strong, could be filtered out of the stream and never attract a court verdict or sentence. All the same, 20 per cent of trials did not produce convictions and, of these, acquittals and functional equivalents figured prominently.

The German practice of the pre-trial filtering of criminal cases was not unusual in a European context. In the Netherlands, prosecutors played at least as great a role in case disposition. For forty years, prosecutors have settled at least half (if not more) of all criminal cases that were recorded and resolved, and have done so through the outright dismissal of cases, through the conclusion of a form of conditional disposal known as a 'transaction' (involving an admission of guilt and a sanction) or, most recently, through a penal order (Blom and Smit 2006; Tak 2012; van der Bunt and van Gelder 2012). Even in this context the rate of acquittal was no less than 3 per cent (see Solomon 2015a). In France, prosecutors also had many options. They could drop cases, lower charges to reduce punishments, send cases to mediation or from 2001, apply a form of conditional disposal known as *composition penale*. The accused must admit guilt and agree to a condition (a fine, community service, compensation to the victim and/or drug rehabilitation) in exchange for the dropping of the charge (Hodgson 2012). Overall, prosecutors in France screened out fewer cases than their counterparts in Germany (though still a substantial share), but the rate of acquittal was correspondingly higher, with an aggregate rate in 2004 of over 5 per cent[20] (Chauseebourg and Lumbroso 2008; Solomon 2015a).

---

[19] This variety of court disposition has produced a higher acquittal rate of 7.7 per cent for 2004 in a report from the European Commission for the Efficiency of Justice (ECEJ 2006). Data for each country were provided by a national correspondent and checked by the editors, but the report does not allow for checking on their origins.

[20] Annuaire Statistique (n.d.) available at www.justice.gouv.fr/statistiques.html. Data supplied by Fabrice Leturq, statistics division of the French Ministry of Justice.

PROSECUTORS AS JUDGES, PROSECUTORS AND JUDGES

Only in the past decade have scholars systematically compared the work of prosecutors in the developed world, but this study has led to an important argument, namely that prosecutors in Europe and North America alike increasingly perform the function of adjudication or, to put it simply, act as judges. The theme of 'prosecutor as judge' appeared first in the literature on plea bargaining in the United States, where the shift to determinate sentencing in the 1980s gave prosecutors control of punishment as well as charging (Lynch 1998; Stuntz 2001). However, it was later also adopted by students of European development, who saw many parallels (Luna and Wade 2010; Wade 2008). Our brief accounts of case disposition in Germany and in Canada support this view. In both countries (and others too) prosecutors drop or withdraw a major share of potential cases because of assessments of the evidence or the seriousness of the offence and, at the same time, provide resolutions of many other cases (not only minor ones) that pre-empt the need for a trial (sometimes also avoiding a criminal record). Most commentators assume that this trend reflects the practical difficulties of holding trials in many cases, whether or not there are guilty pleas or the equivalent.[21]

The reality of prosecutorial adjudication cuts across traditional distinctions in criminal procedure. It is equally developed in adversarial and inquisitorial systems and, within the latter, a country's traditional attachment to the legality principle has not limited the growth of prosecutorial power.[22] These distinctions may influence important details. In some inquisitorial systems, the prosecutor replaced the *juge d'instruction* as the key figure in the pre-trial phase only within the past fifty years, whereas, for the most part, prosecutors have a longer history in the adversarial world. Likewise, only in the inquisitorial systems do judges have access to case files that alert them to potential deficiencies in evidence to which they may react before or at the start of trial; in adversarial systems, such problems may emerge from oral testimony at preliminary hearings. Countries with strong attachments to the legality principle (like Germany) may be more inclined than others to try to

---

[21] The mechanisms used by prosecutors to drop or resolve cases without trial overlap with what Thaman has called 'consensual procedures' or the functional equivalents of plea bargaining; for descriptions of these mechanisms see Thaman (2010).

[22] On these distinctions and their potential effects, see Tonry (2012).

regulate decisions about case disposition through internal guidelines, in the hope of standardising outcomes for similar persons and situations. Nevertheless, the evidence shows that such guidelines do not constrain prosecutorial discretion (Tonry 2012; Wade 2006).

There is considerable debate about the implications of prosecutorial adjudication for the traditional guarantees of fairness in criminal procedure, and about the need for more mechanisms to hold prosecutors accountable.[23] It is also clear that the meaning of prosecutors as judges will vary from one country to another. There are, in my view, two contextual factors that have a major impact upon the fairness of the exercise of discretion by prosecutors before trial – the cultural expectations surrounding the role of prosecutors and the role and power of judges *vis-à-vis* prosecutors.

Within Europe and North America alike, there are traditional conceptions of the prosecutor as a neutral figure obliged to seek all kinds of evidence and to act in a balanced way. This view is stronger or less diluted in Europe, where it is derived from the inquisitorial understanding of the criminal process as a search for the objective truth, and prosecutors are meant to display the same detachment as the *juge d'instruction* before them. Moreover, in some European countries, prosecutors are formally part of the judiciary and may even move back and forth between the roles of prosecutor and judge. For the most part (e.g., in Germany) the success of prosecutors is not measured by the rate of convictions nor are acquittals regarded as failures. Even within some adversarial systems, prosecutors are meant to serve the public interest and reach fair conclusions to cases that are consistent with the evidence. This is true in Canada and increasingly so in Britain (Luna and Wade 2012). In the United States, where district attorneys are elected officials, ambitious prosecutors do feel pressure to gain convictions, especially in publicised cases, and some of them become overly aggressive.

The role and power exercised by actual trial judges is equally, if not more important, for the performance of prosecutors as judges. If prosecutors know that judges act objectively and have the power to decide cases and assign punishments, they in turn will understand which cases to drop for insufficient evidence and how to use conditional disposals effectively. But if judges are weak or dependent, there will be no

---

[23] For an overview of the debate, see Wright and Miller (2010). For a brilliant analysis of the issue from an earlier time, see Vorenberg (1981).

external constraints on prosecutorial discretion. In the United States (some states and the federal realm), the combination of plea bargaining and determinate sentencing effectively removed judges from the process of sentencing, and with state district attorneys facing elections, the latter were under pressure to act more aggressively than a balanced approach would allow (Stith and Cabranes 1998; see also Stuntz 2011, especially chapter 9).

THE RUSSIAN STORY: PRE-TRIAL SCREENING, ACQUITTALS AND OTHER DISPOSITIONS

Our analysis of the German and Canadian practice of criminal justice revealed that, while rates of acquittal fell in the low single digits, there was significant screening or filtering of cases at the pre-trial stage, typically by prosecutors, including cases where the evidence was not strong. At the same time, judges acted autonomously and impartially so that prosecutors were held accountable for their quasi-judicial practices. The question now is what sort of pre-trial filtering takes place in Russia and what is the role of procurators and investigators in it? This examination relies, in part, upon the innovative research and analysis of data from the MVD and other investigative agencies performed by a team of scholars at the Institute for the Rule of Law at European University in St Petersburg (Amara *et al.* 2014; Shkliaruk 2014, 2015).[24] In a nutshell, we will find that, in practice, there is minimal screening of cases with suspects or the accused during the pre-trial phase *and* that most cases no longer include a trial of the evidence, once guilty plea proceedings and reconciliation with the victim are taken into account. Even so, the rate of acquittal remains very low when compared to those found in Western countries.[25]

---

[24] For a versions of the findings aimed at a public audience see Shkliaruk (2013); Shkliaruk and Paneiakh (2013). Both are reprinted in www.enforce.supb.ru/publi katsii-sotrudnikov.

[25] The pre-trial filtering of cases through dismissals was commonplace in the USSR in the 1920s and 1930s, averaging 20 per cent of cases at the very time when acquittal rates at trial stood at a similar level. To be sure, until 1933, the stopping of a case by an investigator for lack of evidence required the approval of the court, but courts routinely approved the requests of investigators. The decline in the number of cases being stopped by investigators started in 1940 and continued from 15 per cent in 1945 to 9.3 per cent in 1947 (data from the City of Moscow). At this point, the data

As in other countries, in Russia the bulk of crimes reported to the police (over 80 per cent) do not lead to the opening of criminal cases or even, usually, to their registration. Absent a suspect who can be accused of a crime, police do not in practice open cases unless there is a clear victim or vocal complainant. The reason is that, the rules notwithstanding, the police cannot risk the censure or worse that can result from a low rate of clearance – or of solving crimes (Shkliaruk 2014: 18).

The data from 2011 indicate that, of the cases that were formally opened (*vozbuzhdeno*) by the MVD, 40 per cent had their inquiry or investigation 'suspended', as per chapter 28 of the CPC (*priostanovleno*), but this is not really a part of the filtering process. Of these cases, 97 per cent were suspended because no suspect or accused had been identified within the legal time period, so there was, in effect, no case. The other 3 per cent consisted of situations where it turned out that no crime was committed or that the suspect was not involved; most of these cases were eventually stopped.[26]

During the course of the investigation, MVD investigators themselves stopped 2.2 per cent of cases that they had started (as per chapter 29 of the CPC), but nearly two-thirds of these were for non-rehabilitative reasons and not connected to the existence of a crime or the guilt of the accused. The reasons included the death of the accused, the impact of the statute of limitations, amnesties and occasional early reconciliation. The stopping of cases for rehabilitative reasons – such as the absence of a crime or evidence of participation of the accused – happened in a fraction of 1 per cent of cases under investigation (Amara et al. 2014; Shkliaruk 2014: 18–21).[27] Before cases were sent to court, they could be

are no longer available, but the competition for 'best investigator' in 1951 gave high marks to investigators who managed to send all their cases to court, and particular regions claimed overall rates in low single digits. It turns out that the decline in acquittals from 1947 until the 1950s was matched by a decline in cases stopped in the pre-trial phase, but there was no change in the level of cases returned to supplementary investigation. To be sure, there was a temporary increase in the share of cases stopped by judges, but the tendency from the 1960s on was to discourage slippage at all stages of the criminal process (Golunskii 1955: 265–66, 489–90, 543; Sheinin and Albitskii 1933: 3–9).

[26] Shkliaruk (2014: 9–11). Note that the MVD handled investigations and inquiries in 88 per cent of cases, the Investigatory Committee in 6 per cent, and the Federal Narcotics Agency 3 in per cent (2014: 18).

[27] In cases handled by the Investigatory Committee (which included business crimes) over 5 per cent were stopped during the investigation, mostly also for non-rehabilitative reasons.

reviewed by a procurator (as per CPC article 221). Procurators returned for further investigation nearly 5 per cent of cases handled by the MVD and 4 per cent of those by the Investigatory Committee. Most of these cases did get to court eventually, and only a tiny share of them were stopped – well under 1 per cent of the total (Shkliaruk 2014: 21). Neither investigators nor procurators had the legal option of applying a punishment directly, of requiring the accused to have treatment or of diverting a case to social services (as was the case in the Western countries we examined).

There was one further stage of filtering that took place once cases reached the court but before an actual trial. These were cases where the judge concluded – after examining the file and discussing it at a preliminary hearing – that a case had evidentiary problems requiring repair before a conviction could be achieved at trial and therefore should be returned to the procuracy. The option to return to the procuracy was included in the 2001 CPC (Article 237) as a way of dealing with small obvious mistakes by investigators (e.g., failing to indicate the value of stolen goods). While the short time period for this procedure was usually violated, 85 per cent of cases did come back to the court eventually (Shkliaruk 2014: 17). Return to the procuracy replaced the former practice of 'return to supplementary investigation', a part of Soviet criminal procedure from the 1930s (added to the CPC only in 1961) and a common substitute for acquittals at the end of trials, which was declared unconstitutional in 1999 by the Constitutional Court of the RF (Solomom 2005). Of cases returned to the procuracy in 2011, about 6 per cent were stopped; however, in that year, returns to procuracy consisted of 1.5 per cent of cases heard by judges. So the practice of returns to the procuracy led to their substitute for acquittal in 0.1 per cent of cases (Shkliaruk 2014: 17). Note that the practice of returns to the procuracy declined from a high of 4 per cent of criminal cases handled by judges in 2004 to a mere 1.1 per cent in 2013. It was during this very period that the stopping of cases because of reconciliation and the use of plea arrangements became the norm for at least 80 per cent of cases. One can infer that the use of returns to the procuracy continued to comprise around 4 per cent of cases where judges had to seriously review the evidence.[28]

---

[28] 'Osnovnye statististicheskie pokazateli sostoianiia sudimosti v Rossii za 2003–2007 gody i 2008–2013 gody', *Sudebnaia statistika*, http://www.cdep.ru.

To make sense of the continuation of an extremely low rate of acquittals in Russia, one needs to take into account not only the minimal screening of cases before trial but also the drastic reduction in the number and share of cases where judges had to test the evidence, a result of two changes in the new CPC. The Criminal Procedure Code of 2001, best known for making trials more adversarial, changed the landscape of the criminal process in Russia by enabling greater use of reconciliation between accused and victim and by introducing a form of plea negotiation known as 'special procedure'.

Reconciliation between the accused and the victim entered Russian criminal justice in 1996, when an amendment to the CPC allowed its use and the consequent stopping of a criminal case for the least serious offences. The 2001 CPC (Article 25) expanded the use of reconciliation to the second of the four categories of offences set out in the 1996 Criminal Code – crimes of moderate gravity – which included many property offences. This change accompanied the creation of Justices of the Peace – a new layer of the court system – which was encouraged to resolve cases through mediation (in civil cases) and reconciliation (in criminal cases). As of 2008, 20 per cent of all criminal cases were stopped as a result of reconciliation, often with restitution, the bulk of these among the 40 per cent of criminal cases now heard by Justices of the Peace (Hendley 2012; Paneiakh et al. 2010).

The truly dramatic change in Russian criminal justice came with the establishment of plea agreements in the 2001 CPC (chapter 40). In exchange for accepting guilt, agreeing to a shortened trial and waiving the right to appeal, the accused is guaranteed a sentence outside the upper third of the sentencing range. The accused consults a lawyer, sometimes one provided by the investigator, and signs the agreement after seeing the case file. This 'special procedure' was proposed by high-ranking judges, who feared that new adversarial trials would take longer than their inquisitorial predecessors. The model adopted was the Italian version of plea bargaining, in which there are no explicit deals for particular accused. At first, this option was available only for less-serious crimes (maximum punishment of five years), but, in 2003, eligibility was extended to serious crimes – those with a maximum punishment of ten years (Solomon 2012; see also Titaev et al. 2012).

The new simplified procedure proved popular. By 2008 it was used in 50 per cent of criminal cases; in 2010, the figure reached 63.6 per cent (70 per cent of theft cases). It was clear that avoidance of the upper third of the sentencing range was not the only incentive for the accused. In practice, some judges deducted a third from the sentence that they would have given (usually not in the upper third), offenders were glad to leave primitive pre-trial detention facilities for the better conditions in penal colonies and, sometimes, informal negotiations led to significant reductions in punishment, including suspended sentences in place of real time. Suspended sentences became the norm for first-time offenders not held in detention when they agreed to special procedure (Volkov et al. 2014).

Whatever the dynamics in practice, the plea process in Russia simplifies the role of judges. They are obliged to check that the file contains supporting evidence, but do not have to test it in public or deal with new evidence offered by the defence. As a result, conviction is based only on the case file, along with admission of guilt. To critics, this represented the return of Soviet-style inquisitorialism, a paradoxical result of a measure embedded in a Code meant to promote adversarialism. There was also the danger (common to plea bargaining everywhere) that the accused would be pressured into confessing by investigators or defence counsel, especially when the latter was appointed by the investigators.

With nearly two-thirds of criminal cases handled through special procedure, and other accused (often not eligible for that option) also pleading guilty, it turned out that, in 2010, only 8 per cent of accused persons insisted on their innocence and challenged the charges. While the general rate of acquittal in cases prosecuted by the state in 2010 was under 0.2 per cent, for those accused who actually challenged the indictment the figure stood at 3.56 per cent (Paneiakh 2015; Volkov and Titaev 2013). This rate resembles that found in Japan (around 5 per cent), though not that in Canada (20–30 per cent). In comparison with practice in countries of Western Europe, a rate of 3.5 per cent acquittals in contested cases seems very low. Recall that the rate of acquittal for *all* court cases in France was 5 per cent and in Germany nearly the same – or more if one included court-ordered dismissals – and these were both countries where many cases involving clear guilt were handled by penal orders or conditional discharges before trial. A European country with less pre-trial disposition of cases (but still some) was Sweden, and its overall rate of 'dismissal' in court (the equivalent of acquittals and cases stopped for rehabilitative reasons) was 15 per cent![29]

Higher rates of acquittal are often associated with trial by jury, as opposed to trials by judges. This has proven to be the case in post-Soviet Russia, which began experimenting with juries in 1994. In 2002, the Russian government made jury trials an option for all cases heard at regional courts (with jurisdiction for about 1 per cent of criminal cases), which included murder, rape and political offences. Russian juries gave out acquittals to at least 15 per cent of accused persons (as high as 40 per cent in one region) – that is, twenty times more often than did judges sitting alone – but a third of these acquittals did not survive appellate review. While reformers such as Sergei Pashin called for the expansion of the jury option in some cases at district courts, the authorities pursued the opposite course of narrowing the availability of the jury option – first, in late 2008, by eliminating it for given political offences (including terrorism, spying and treason) and then, in summer 2013, by moving major crimes of violence, such as most kinds of murder and rape, to the jurisdiction of district courts where the jury option was unavailable (Federal'nyi Zakon 2013; O'Malley 2006; Solomon 2013a).[30] Early in 2015, President Putin ordered top legal officials to expand eligibility for jury trials, but the response of Supreme Court Chair Lebedev was to propose small mixed panels (laypersons and judges) for some cases now heard at district courts. The proposal aroused intense criticism (Latukhiina 2015).

In short, the combination of an extremely low rate of acquittal and the minimal screening of cases during the investigatory stage indicates that Russian criminal justice does have an accusatorial bias. For, simply put, once a case with serious charges has been started, it is extremely difficult for an accused to avoid conviction. It is worth reflecting further on the sources of this bias and on the adjustments made by the players in Russian criminal justice.

---

[29] 'Courts statistics 2011', *Official Statistics of Sweden*, Table 1.6. www.domstol.se/Publikationer/Statistik/court_statistics_2011.pdf.

[30] Note that Kazakhstan and Ukraine were starting to organise jury trials in 2013, but their juries were actually mixed panels of judges and laypersons (less likely to acquit than real juries) and the jurisdiction was even narrower than that in Russia after the changes of 2013. For details on the use of laypersons in adjudication in the post-Soviet space, see Kovalev (2010).

THE DYNAMICS OF RUSSIAN CRIMINAL JUSTICE: SOURCES OF ACCUSATORIAL BIAS AND ADJUSTMENTS TO IT

What are the sources of accusatorial bias in Russia? While informed observers have identified a list of proximate factors, such as the practice of evaluating legal officials and the inadequate tools available to defence counsel, there is one major underlying cause – the imbalance of power within Russian criminal justice (Churilov 2010a, 2010b; Pozdniakov 2012).

As I have explained in detail elsewhere, the post-Soviet criminal process (like its predecessor) features strong investigators and weak judges – a situation reinforced by incentives associated with evaluation (Solomon 2015c). The investigators who create criminal cases are not judges on rotation, as in traditional neo-inquisitorial systems, but officials of law enforcement agencies. To be sure, they do not open cases without clear suspects (so that their rates of solution will not be harmed). But once they open a case, as we have seen, they avoid stopping them and, when a case is sent back by procurator or judge, this reflects badly on them. This renders the position of judges all the more important in holding investigators and procurators to account and countering investigatory decisions. Nevertheless, it is difficult for judges to fulfil this mandate, for they are also expected to co-operate with law enforcement, and this limits their readiness to critically scrutinise its work. With co-operation treated as a value and a virtue, judges come under fire for rendering acquittals, both after their awarding and, later, when a sizeable portion of them are overturned by higher courts (procurators tend to appeal almost all of them). Achieving a low rate of reversal (or stability of sentence) is a must for judges who want to stay in office (a few acquittals in a year can lead to disciplinary measures and firing), let alone promotion to a higher court or administrative position.

This portrait describes not only late Soviet and early post-Soviet practice, but also the situation over the past fifteen years, since the new Criminal Procedure Code of 2001 came into operation. The authors of the Code wanted to eliminate accusatorial bias and did what they could to reduce the imbalance of sides in procedural law. The trial itself became officially adversarial and procurators were, for the first time, required to introduce evidence orally instead of relying on the file from the preliminary investigation. Defence counsel gained new rights in the pre-trial phase, including access to the dossier and to their clients. Crucially, the concept of the criminal process as a search for objective truth was discarded and replaced by the notion of a contest. As a result, judges were no longer officially part of a concerted fight against crime. However, with the same system of assessing their work, and their traditional ties to law enforcement (where many worked before becoming judges), the change had only minimal impact on accusatorial bias in practice (Solomon 2005). Moreover, in a decade and a half of implementation of the new CPC, a series of amendments weakened the position of defence counsel, further aggravating the power asymmetry between the sides (Burnham and Kahn 2008; Solomon 2015c).

The difficulty associated with judges awarding acquittals or the related disposition of 'stopping a case for rehabilitative reasons' (which would constitute acquittals in many countries) did not mean that judges lacked the discretion to distinguish between offenders and to find alternative ways of recognising weak evidence and different degrees of guilt. To begin, they could adjust the charges either by lowering the most serious charge or convicting only particular ones. However, they could do more. Judges could and did encourage persons accused of crimes in the two lower categories (minor and average gravity) to enter into reconciliation with their accusers, leading to the case being stopped for non-rehabilitative reasons (the result in some 20 per cent of criminal cases). Under such circumstances the accused might have to restore property to or pay the victim, but the former would have no criminal record. Moreover, with more serious crimes, judges often recognised the weakness of evidence or lesser degree of responsibility in a case by giving a suspended custodial sentence rather than actual time in confinement. Judges might also turn to suspended sentences to recognise admission of guilt (and use of special procedures) and/or the inducements, proper or improper, supplied by advocates. All of these patterns were established or confirmed in research, conducted by scholars at the Institute for the Rule of Law in St Petersburg, which included both statistical analysis and interviews with judges (Paneiakh 2012; Paneyakh 2016).

For their part, advocates found ways to advance the interests of the accused. To be sure, like judges, they faced a conflictual situation. They, too, were faced with pressure to contribute to state interests, especially if they worked on assignment (*po naznacheniiu*) and were paid by investigative agencies or courts. However, like their Soviet predecessors, many defence counsel did find ways to help their clients, accusatorial bias notwithstanding. Research by another team of scholars at the Institute for the Rule of Law, including Ekaterina Khodzhaeva and Iuliia Rabovski (Shesterina), revealed that the best defence counsel had strong informal ties with investigators and were able to enter cases early, gaining access to evidence and opportunities to deal with investigators before cases were formally opened. Another common tactic was for counsel to carefully monitor cases in search of procedural errors. While the exposure of errors could be accomplished at the trial and used in appeals, a better approach used by some counsel was to confront investigators and procurators and use a promise to ignore errors in exchange for a lesser sentence (such as a non-custodial one) or a reduction in the number of episodes, or sometimes to avoid pre-trial detention. Lawyers also used inconsistencies in evidence for the same purposes. It was also possible, as I argued elsewhere (Solomon 2012), to use agreements by the accused to admit guilt and follow special procedures to obtain lesser punishments, especially suspended sentences. In short, advocates in Russia fashioned for themselves 'weapons of the weak' as a way to work within the context of power imbalance and accusatorial bias, so Khodzhaeva and Rabovski (2015) contend.

PRE-TRIAL SCREENING AS A REFORM OPTION FOR RUSSIA

We have seen that, in Russia, once criminal cases have been opened against an accused, the stopping of the case by an investigator or procurator happens rarely. This is not because the officials lack the legal power to so do but because not moving a case to the next stage is treated as a sign of failure for the official concerned and hurts the assessment of his performance (Paneiakh and Titaev 2011; Shkliaruk 2014). If the case is given a preliminary hearing in court, the judge may recognise evidentiary issues and return the case to the procuracy, but this does not happen often (only in about 3 per cent of cases that reach court).

At the same time, as of 2015, neither procurators nor investigators in Russia had the legal power to dispose of cases through forms of diversion or informal dispositions other than reconciliation. The introduction of the pre-trial disposition of cases into Russian criminal procedure would require grappling with the fact that, in Russia, investigators assemble and assess the evidence (gathered mainly by police) and decide on the opening of cases and sending them to court – functions now performed by prosecutors in most of Europe. From a comparative point of view, the investigator in Russia is a peculiar figure. Originating in Tsarist times as the Russian version of the *juge d'instruction*, he moved to the exclusive domain of the procuracy in the late 1920s and then also to that of the MVD (police) in the 1950s. While meant to be legal officials, some investigators lack higher legal education, and their placement in or near police and prosecution makes them far from neutral. Moreover, whereas in Soviet times the work of investigators was supervised by procurators (the prosecutors in the Soviet and post-Soviet worlds), in Russia, in 2007, procurators lost the right to approve the opening of cases and, with this loss, much of their power to supervise investigations. This measure was partially reversed in 2014 (Aleksandrov and Kukhta 2009; Ozerova 2014; Shtykina 2014).

In mid-summer 2015, the Russian Supreme Court through its chairman, Viacheslav Lebedev, proposed giving these very investigators (along with police officials or *doznavateli*) who do the paperwork for some minor crimes, the power to give a pre-trial disposition to persons accused of crimes of small and average gravity (the lower two categories of crimes in the Russian criminal code). Through the proposed new institution of 'release from criminal responsibility with the application of other measures of a criminal character', investigators themselves could assign fines, corrective work, obligatory work or loss of the right to hold a particular post, as long as the accused made restitution for the losses his actions caused. No conviction would be recorded and there would be no criminal record.

This change – part of a larger package of reforms in the processing of minor crimes that was to include decriminalising some offences and allowing investigators to do reconciliation with the victim – could apply to a lot of offenders, in theory up to the 46 per cent of offenders now convicted of crimes of small and average gravity. Many of these persons had already pursued the option of plea bargaining and received non-custodial sanctions but were stuck with a record of conviction that got in the way of finding jobs. The new form of pre-trial disposition would mean that fewer offenders would end up with criminal records and the number of cases handled by courts would be reduced. However, there is no indication that it would help any accused person against whom the evidence was weak (Kornia 2015a, 2015b). Moreover, the new conditional disposal would not come into play for serious and very serious crimes, where almost no cases were stopped for non-rehabilitative reasons and the conviction rate was over 99 per cent.

It is important to stress that the draft law containing this measure has not yet been formally introduced in the state *Duma*, apparently because it has failed thus far to gain approval by the government's Commission on Legislative Activity. The public endorsement of this draft law by President Putin, in his annual address to the Federal Assembly on 2 December 2015, will probably force the government to take action on the bill, but not necessarily to approve all of its contents, including the proposal of conditional disposal.

As some experts in Russia have noted, the introduction of conditional disposals into Russia may be ill-advised if it is not accompanied by two deeper reforms – the full revival of the supervision of the pre-trial phase by procurators and the encouragement of judges to hold both investigators and procurators to account. Investigators should not be able to impose punitive measures on their own without supervision because, unlike prosecutors in Germany or Canada, they lack the neutrality to assure fairness – or at least the appearance of it. Either procurators should review and approve conditional disposals, or they should be made responsible for granting them. Such an approach would be consistent with the existing practice in Russia of prosecutorial approval of the use of special procedures in court hearings, or 'plea bargaining Russian style' (Paneyakh 2014; Solomon 2012). Some might object to empowering procurators who, in the late Soviet period, struck reformers as too powerful. However, changes in the law and practice of criminal procedure in two post-Soviet decades have made investigators, rather than procurators, the most powerful figures in the criminal process, and the investigators face far too little accountability (Aleksandrov *et al.* 2013; Solomon 2015c).

However, even this step would not be enough, because procurators also did not face sufficient accountability. In my view, giving procurators in Russia new powers to dispose of cases would be premature and misguided, as long as judges were not sufficiently autonomous and powerful enough to hold these procurators to account. In the Western countries we examined, the accountability of prosecutors to judges encouraged the former to handle their quasi-judicial functions in a fair and impartial way. In Russia, judges handling criminal cases faced strong incentives to cooperate with the prosecution, through avoiding acquittals – many of which were reversed on appeal and spoiled the record of the stability of sentences for the judge and the court, the most important criterion of performance – and by playing their traditional part in the fight against crime, notwithstanding the neutrality that the new CPC mandated (Pozdniakov 2014a, 2014b).[31] As if this were not enough, starting in 2013, officials on the Investigatory Committee (the former investigatory department of the procuracy) pressed for the return of the concept of 'objective truth' into the CPC, as an orienting goal for judges and law enforcement alike (Solomon 2013ab. For a strong defence of the return of objective truth by a high official of the Investigative Committee, see Kozlova 2014). Such a step would move Russia back, in theory as well as in practice, to the criminal justice of the Soviet period, where judges were officially part of the fight against crime and expected to co-operate with law enforcement. Fortunately, both the Supreme Court and the government have opposed the relevant draft legislation so that, as of the summer of 2015, this initiative seems to have stopped (Churakova 2015). Its revival, however, remains a threat to the autonomy and power of judges.

CONCLUSION

This chapter has demonstrated that, as of 2015, Russian criminal justice has continued to have an accusatorial bias. On the one hand, the rate of acquittal in Russia has remained unusually low – in cases prosecuted by the state, down to 0.1 per cent in 2014, in contrast to rates in the 1.5–5.0 per cent range in Western countries (Paneiakh 2015). On the other hand, unlike those Western countries, Russia failed to do the extensive screening of cases (including weak ones) in the pre-trial phase, instead sending almost all of them to trial. While trials for less-serious charges could end in judge-organised reconciliation, trials of serious ones almost always resulted in convictions.

The underlying problem was a power imbalance in the criminal process, in which investigators had too much strength and judges too little to serve as an adequate counterweight. While this was due, in part, to the legal definition of their roles, the imbalance was aggravated,

---

[31] While the stability of sentences was a universal criterion in the evaluation of the performance of judges throughout Russia, the regulations did not provide a uniform definition. In some regions decisions that were overruled and changed were treated as one indicator, in others they were separated. In some regions changes to the substance of a decision were distinguished from procedural errors.

in practice, by the incentives that resulted from formal evaluations (on the evaluation of judges, see Solomon 2013b).

ACKNOWLEDGEMENTS

The original version of this chapter was prepared for the conference 'Obvinenie i opravdane v postsovetskoi kriminalnoi iustitsii' (Accusation and Acquittal in Post-Soviet Criminal Justice) held on 17–18 May 2013 at the Institut problem pravoprimeneniia, European University in St Petersburg. The author is grateful for the help and advice of Anthony Doob, Gilles Favarel-Garriques, Fabrice Leturcq, Todd Foglesong, Matthew Light, Alexei Trochev and Vadim Volkov, and the research assistance of Ben Noble and Milosz Zak. He also acknowledges the thoughtful critiques and suggestions provided by reviewers of this volume.

References

Aleksandrov, A. S., Lapatnikov, M. V. and Terekhin, V. V. (2013) 'Ot polusostizatelnosti k polnoi inkvizitsii: traektoriia razvitiia sovremennogo russkogo ugolovno-protsessualnogo prava', unpublished paper.

Aleksandrov, A. S. and Kukhta, A. A. (2009) 'Vlast sledstvennaia i vlast obvinitel'naia: kvadrtury kurga', *Pravovedenie*, 4: 22–8.

Amara, M. N., Shkliaruk, M. S. and Begtin, I. V. (2014) *Kriminal'naia statistika i otkrytost' Politsii: analiticheskie obzor*. Moscow: Institut problem, http://www.enforce.spb.ru/issledovaniia.

Baldwin, J. and McConville, M. (1978) 'The new Home Office figures on pleas and acquittals: what sense do they make?' *The Criminal Law Review*, (April 1978): 196–201.

Blom, M. and Smit, P. (2006) 'The prosecution service function within the Dutch criminal justice system', in Jehle, J. -M. and Wade, M. (eds.) *Coping with Overloaded Criminal Justice Systems: The Rise of Prosecutorial Power across Europe*. Berlin: Springer, 237–56.

Boyne, S. (2012) 'Is the journey from the in-box to the out-box a straight line? The drive for efficiency and the prosecution of low-level criminality in Germany', in Luna, E. and Wade, M. (eds.) *The Prosecutor in Transnational Perspective*. Oxford: Oxford University Press, 3–53.

Boyne, S. M. (2014) *The German Prosecution Service: Guardians of the Law?* Heidelberg: Springer.

Brown, D. K. (2012) 'American prosecutors: powers and obligations in the era of plea bargaining', in Luna, E. and Wade, M. (eds.) *The Prosecutor in Transnational Perspective*. Oxford: Oxford University Press, 200–13.

Burnham, W. and Kahn, J. (2008) 'Russia's Criminal Procedure Code five years out', *Review of Central and East European Law*, 33(1): 1–94.

Chauseebourg, L. and Lumbroso, S. (2008) 'L'appel des décisions des cours d'assizes: conséquences sur la declaration de culpabilité', *Infostat Justice*, 100.

Churakova, O. (2015) 'Pravitelstvo ne podderzhibaet ob'ektivnuiu istinu kak tsel ugolovnogo protsessa: ocherednaia inisiativa Sledstvennogo komiteta povisla v vozdukhe', *Vedomosti*, 3 August.

Churilov, I. (2010a) 'Statistika opravdanii: fakty i vymysel', www.gazeta-yurist.ru/prnarticle.php?i=1054.

Churilov, I. (2010b) *Aktual'nye problemy postanovleniia opravdael'nogo prigovora v rossiskom ugolovnom sudoproizvodstve*. Moscow: Volters Kluwer.

Dauvergne, M. (2012) *Adult Criminal Court Statistics in Canada, 2010/2011*. Ottawa: Juristat.

Donovan, J. (2010) *Juries and the Transformation of Criminal Justice in France in the Nineteenth and Twentieth Centuries*. Chapel Hill: University of North Carolina Press.

ECEJ (2006) *European Judicial Systems*. Brussels: Council of Europe.

Elsner, B. and Peters, J. (2006) 'The prosecution service function within the German criminal justice system', in Jehle, J. -M. and Wade, M. (eds.) *Coping with Overloaded Criminal Justice Systems: The Rise of Prosecutorial Power across Europe*. Berlin: Springer, 207–36.

Federal'nyi Zakon (2013) No. 217 ot 23 iiulia 2013 'O vnesenii izmenenii v Ugolovno-protsessualnyi kodeks RF i stati 1 i 3 Federalnogo zakon "O vnesenii izmenenii v Ugolovno-protsessualnyi kodeks RF i priznanii utrativshimi silu otdelnykh zakonodatelnykh aktov (polozhenie zakono-datelnykh aktov) Rossiiskoi Federatsii'po voprosam sovershenstvovaniia protsedury appelliatsionnogo proizvodstvo"', *Rossiiskaia gazeta*, 26 July 2013, www.rg.ru/2013/07/26/prozess-dok.html.

Feofanov, I. (1986) 'Mera otvetstvennosti', *Izvestiia*, 14 March, 3.

Golunskii, S. A. (ed.) (1955) *Istoriia zakonodatel'stva SSSR i RSFSR po ugo-lovnomu protsessu i organizatsii suda i prokuratury, 1917—1954 gg. Sbornik dokumentov*. Moscow: Gosiurizdat.

Gorman, W. (2000 –2001) 'Prosecutorial discretion in a charter-dominated trial process', *Criminal Law Quarterly*, 44(1): 15–33.

Grosman, B. (1969) *The Prosecutor: An Inquiry into the Exercise of Discretion*. Toronto: University of Toronto Press.

Gutsenko, K. F., Golovko, L. V. and Filimonov, B. A. (2002) *Ugolovnyi protsesse zapadnykh gosudarstv*. Moscow: Zertsalo.

Hendley, K. (2012) 'The unsung heroes of the Russian judicial system: the Justice-of-the-Peace courts', *Journal of Eurasian Law*, 5(3): 337–66.

Hodgson, J. (2012) 'Guilty pleas and the changing role of the prosecutor in French criminal justice', in Luna, E. and Wade, M. (eds.) *The Prosecutor in Transnational Perspective*. Oxford: Oxford University Press, 116–34.

Information Canada (1973) *Statistics of Criminal and Other Offenses for the Period January 1, 1970 to December 31, 1970*. Ottawa: Information Canada.

Jehle, J. -M. (2009) *Criminal Justice in Germany: Facts and Figures*. Berlin: Federal Ministry of Justice.

Jehle, J. -M. and Wade, M. (eds.) (2006) *Coping with Overloaded Criminal Justice Systems: The Rise of Prosecutorial Power across Europe*. Berlin: Springer.

Johnson, D. T. (2012) 'Japan's prosecution system', in Tonry, M. (ed.) *Prosecutors and Politics: A Comparative Perspective*. Chicago: University of Chicago Press, 35–74.

Kari, S. (2010) 'Just 3 per cent of criminal cases end in acquittal: data', *The National Post*, 2 August.

Khodzhaeva, E. and Rabovski, I. (Shesterina) (2015) 'Stretegii i taktiki advokatov v usloviiakh obvinitelnogo uklona v Rossii', *Sotsiologiia vlasti*, 27(2): 135–67.

Kornia, A. (2015a) 'Verkhovvnyi sud izbavliaetsia o melochevki: neznachitelnye khishcheniia stanut administrativym pravonarusheniem, a za melkie provinnosti smogut nakazyvat bez suda i sledstviia', *Vedomosti*, 31 July.

(2015b) 'Za netiazhnkie prestupleniia budut nakazyvat bez sudimosti', *Vedomosti*, 2 August.

Kovalev, N. (2010) *Criminal Justice Reform in Russia, Ukraine, and the Former Republics of the Soviet Union: Trial by Jury and Mixed Courts*. London: Edward Mellen Press.

Kozlova, N. (2014) 'Obvinitelnyi uklon: zakonoproekt ob ob'ektivnoi istine stal odnim iz samykh obsuzhdaemukh iuristami dokumentov', *Rossiiskaia gazeta*, 3 February, www.rg.ru/2014/02/03/istina.html.

Kudriavtsev, V. N. (ed.) (1975) *Effektivnost pravosudiia i ustraneniie sudebnykh oshibok*. Moscow: IGPAN.

Latukhiina, K. (2015) 'Prisiazhnykh stanet bolshe: Vladimir Putin poruchil podgotovki predlozheniia po sudebnoi sistem', *Rossiiskaia gazeta*, 22 January, www.rg.ru/2015/01/22/prisyajnie-site.html.

Lebedev, V. (2010) 'Glava VS Lebedev: Rossiiskie sud'i opravdyvaiut kazhdogo chetvertogo', *Pravo.ru*, 11 November, http://pravo.ru/news/view/41897.

(2011) 'V tselom Rossiiskaia sudebnaia sistem effektivna' (Interviu s Viacheslav Lebedev), 27 May, www.vsrf/print_page.php?id-7241&lang=ru.

Luna, E. and Wade, M. (2010) 'Prosecutors as judges', *Washington and Lee Law Review*, 67(4): 1413–532.

(eds.) (2012a) *The Prosecutor in Transnational Perspective*. Oxford: Oxford University Press.

(2012b) 'Adversarial and inquisitorial systems: distinctive aspects and convergent trends', in Luna, E. and Wade, M. (eds.) *The Prosecutor in Transnational Perspective*. Oxford and New York: Oxford University Press, 177–87.

Lynch, G. (1998) 'Our administrative system of criminal justice', *Fordham Law Review*, 66: 2117–52.
McConville, M. and Baldwin, J. (1981) *Courts, Prosecution and Conviction*. Oxford: Clarendon Press.
McGlynn Ganney, E. (1976) *Prosecutorial Discretion in England and Canada*. Ottawa: Law Reform Commission of Canada.
Mikhailovskaia, I. (2010) 'Problema kriterii otsenki sudebnoi deiatelnosti', *Sravnitelnoe konstitutsionnoe obozrenie*, 5: 116–128.
Ministry of Justice (2012) *Judicial and Court Statistics 2011*. London: Ministry of Justice.
Morshchakova, T. (2014) 'Zakon ob 'ob'ektivnoi istine' unichtozhit opraveatelnye prigovory', www.pravo.ru, 16 March.
O'Malley, K. (2006) 'Not guilty until the Supreme Court finds you guilty: a reflection on jury trials in Russia', *Demokratizatsiya*, 14(1): 42–58.
Odintsev, P. (2011) 'Predely transparentnost', *RAPSI*, 17 February.
ODPP (2007) 'Duties and responsibilities of crown attorneys', in *Guide Book of Policies and Procedures for the Conduct of Criminal Prosecutions in Newfoundland and Labrador*. St John's: Office of the Director of Public Prosecutions, available at www.justice.gov.nl.ca/just/prosect/guidebook/006.PDF
Ozerova, M. (2014) 'Sledstvennyi komitet stanet podnadzornym: Gosduma daet Genprokurature pravo proveriat SK', *Moskovskii komsomolets*, 21 October, www.mk.ru/politics/2014/10/21/sledstvennyy-komitet-stanet-podnadzornym.html.
Paneiakh, E. (2015) 'Evoliutsiia rossiiskoi sudebnoi sistemy v 2014 godu', *Kontrpunkt*, 1.
(2012) 'Prakticheskaia logika priniatiia sudebnykh reshenii: diskretsiia pod' davleniem i kompromissy za schet podsudimogo', in Volkov, V. V. (ed.) *Kak sud'i prinimaiut resheniia: empiricheskie issledovannia prava*. Moscow: Statut, 107–29.
Paneiakh, E. and Titaev, K. (2011) 'Ot militsii k politsii: reforma sistemy otsenki deiatelnosti organov vnutrennikh del'. St Petersburg: Institut problem pravoprimeneniia, March 2011, www.enforce.spb.ru/analitiches kie-zapiski/5047-2011-mart.
Paneiakh, E. L., Titaev, K. D., Volkov, V. V. and Primakov, D. Ia. (2010) 'Obvinitelnyi uklon v ugolovnom protsesse: faktor prokurora', *Analiticheskaia zapiska Instituta prava i pravoprimeneniia*, 8 March.
Paneyakh, E. (2014) 'Faking performance together: systems of performance evaluation in Russian enforcement agencies and production of bias and privilege', *Post-Soviet Affairs*, 30(2): 1–22.
(2016) 'The practical logic of judicial decision making: discretion under pressure and compromises at the expense of the defendant', *Russian Politics and Law*, 54(2–3): 138–63.

PBC (2003) *Criminal Court Rates and Trends*. Ottawa: Parole Board of Canada, http://pbc-clcc.gc.ca/rprts/pdf/pfop.
Petrukhin, I. (2009) 'Opravdatel'nyi prigovor', *Gosudarstvo i pravo*, 2(1): 30–36.
(2011) *Opravdatel'nyi prigovor i pravo na reabilitatsiiu*. Moscow: Prospekt.
Poluyan, P. (2009) 'Obvinitelnyi uklon v sudakh RF', http://poluyan.livejournal.com/1744/html.
Pozdniakov, M. (2012) 'Smysl' i dvukhsmyslennost' obvinitel'nogo uklona', in Volkov, V. V. (ed.) *Kak sud'i prinimaiut resheniia: empiricheskie issledovannia prava*. Moscow: Statut, 54–106.
(2014a) 'Sud i pravookhranitel'naia sistema: politika otmeny opravdatel'nykh prigovorov', Preprint. St Petersburg: Institut problem pravoprimeneniia, http://enforce.spb.ru/images/Issledovanya/2014/IRL_Preprint_2014_03_M.Pozdnyakov_Sud-i-pravoohranitelnaya-sistema.pdf.
(2014b) 'Kriterii otsenki kachestva raboty sudei i distsiplinarnaia otvetstvennost', www.enforce.spb.ru/images/Issledovanya/2014/2014.03_Mihail-Pozdnyakov_Voprosy-disciplinarnoy-otvetstvennosti.pdf.
Province of Ontario (2005) *Role of the Crown: Preamble to Crown Policy Manual*. Toronto: Province of Ontario, available at http://attorneygeneral.jus.gov.on.ca/english/crim/cpm/2005/CPMpreamble.pdf.
Ramseyer, J. M. and Rasmusen, E. (2001) 'Why is the Japanese conviction rate so high?' *Journal of Legal Studies*, 30(1): 53–88.
Rosenberg, M. (2009) 'The attorney-general and the prosecution function in the twenty-first century', *Queen's Law Journal*, 43(2): 813–62.
Sheinin, G. and Albitskii, P. (1933) 'K voprosu o zadachakh sledstvennogo apparata na sovremennom etape', in *Voprosy sovetskoi kriminalistiki*. Leningrad: 3–9.
(1951) *Rabota luchshikh sledovatelei. Materialy uchebno-metodicheskoi konferentsii luchshikh sledstvennykh rabotnikov organov Prokuratury* (sbornik 1). Moscow: Prokuratura SSSR.
(1940) 'Respublikanskoe soveshchanie sledstvennykh otdelov', *Sotsialisticheskaia zakonnost*, 7(1): 22–44
State Archive of the Russian Federation (1957) 'Tablitsy sravnitel'nykh statisticheskikh dannykh o dvizhenii i rezul'tatakh rassmotreniiu sudami ugolovnykh del po SSSR i soiuznym respublikam za 1937–1956 gg', GARF, f.9492, op.6S, d.15, ll.6–21, state archive.
(1948) 'Osnovnye pokazateli raboty Prokuratury goroda Moskvy za 1945–1947 gg', GARF, f.8131, op.24, d.34, 22–25, state archive.
Shkliaruk, M. (2013) 'Nevernyi diagnoz', *Polit.ru*, 4 February, http://polit.ru.
(2015) 'Rossiiskii ugolovnyi protsess kak sistema fil'trov: dosudebnye traektorii i otbor ugolovnykh del na primere MVD', in Volkov, V. V. (ed.) *Obvinenie i opravdanie v post-Sovetskoi ugolovnoi iustitsii*. Moscow: Statut, 154–82.

(2014) 'Traektoriia ugolovnogo dela v ofitsial'noi statistike na primere oboshchennykh dannykh pravookhranitel'nykh organov', Institut problem Pravoprimeneniia. St Petersburg.

Shkliaruk, M. and Paneiakh, E. (2013) 'Extra jus: sistema ne filtruet. Skol'ko ugolovnykh del otseivaetsia na rannykh stadiiakh', *Vedomosti*, 25 April.

Shtykina, A. (2014) 'Putin vernet Genprokurture obshchei nadzor nad Sledstvennym komitetom', *RBK*, 26 September, http://top.rbc.ru/politics/26/09/2014/951553.shtml.

Sobolev, V. and Potapenko, S. (1989) '"Boiazn" vyneseniia opravdatel'nykh prigovorov: ee korni', *Sovetskaia iustitsiia*, 10, 8.

Solomon, P. H. Jr (2013b) 'The accountability of judges in post-communist states: from bureaucratic to professional accountability', in Seibert-Fohr, A. (ed.) *Judicial Independence in Transition*. Heidelberg: Springer, 909–36.

(1987) 'The case of the vanishing acquittal: informal norms and the practice of Soviet criminal justice', *Soviet Studies*, 39(4): 531–55.

(2013a) 'Courts, law, and policing under Medvedev: many reforms, modest change, new voices', in Black, J. L. and Johns, M. (eds.) *Russia After 2012: From Putin to Medvedev to Putin – Continuity, Change or Revolution*. London: Routledge, 19–41.

(2005) 'The Criminal Procedure Code of 2001: will it make Russian justice more fair?' in Pridemore, W. (ed.) *Ruling Russia: Law, Crime, and Justice in a Changing Society*. Lanham: Rowan and Littlefield, 77–100.

(2015b) 'Dosudebnoe prekrashchenie del i prokurorskoe usmotrenie v razlichnykh pravovykh sistemakh', in Volkov, V. (ed.) *Obvinenie i opravdanie v postsovetskoi ugolovnoi iustitsiia*. Moscow: Norma, 131–53.

(1990) 'Gorbachev's legal revolution', *Canadian Business Law Journal*, 17 (2): 184–94.

(2012) 'Plea bargaining Russian style', *Demokratizatsiya*, 20(3): 282–299.

(2015c) 'Post-Soviet criminal justice: the persistence of distorted neoinquisitorialism', *Theoretical Criminology*, 19(2): 159–78.

(1996) *Soviet Criminal Justice under Stalin*. Cambridge: Cambridge University Press.

(2015a) 'Understanding Russia's low rate of acquittals: pretrial screening and the problem of accusatorial bias', *Review of Central and East European Law*, 40(1): 1–30.

Solomon, P. H. Jr and Foglesong, T. S. (2000) *Courts and Transition: The Challenge of Judicial Reform*. Boulder: Westview Press.

Stith, K. and Cabranes, J. (1998) *Fear of Judging: Sentencing Guidelines in Federal Courts*. Chicago: University of Chicago Press.

Stuntz, W. J. (2011) *The Collapse of American Criminal Justice*. Cambridge, MA: Harvard University Press.

(2001) 'The pathological politics of criminal law', *University of Michigan Law Review*, 100: 505–600.

Svod statisticheskikh svedeniia po delam ugolovnym proizvodivshimsia v 1904 godu v sudebnykh uchrezdeniiakh (1907) [Corpus of statistical information on criminal cases in 1904 in judicial institutions] St Petersburg: Publication of the Ministry of Justice, 15.

Tak, P. (2012) 'The Dutch prosecutor: a prosecuting and sentencing officer', in Luna, E. and Wade, M. (eds.) *The Prosecutor in Transnational Perspective*. Oxford: Oxford University Press, 35–155.

Thaman, S. (ed.) (2010) *World Plea Bargaining: Consensual Procedures and the Avoidance of the Full Criminal Trial*. Durham: Carolina Academic Press.

Thomas, J. (2008/2009) *Adult Criminal Court Statistics, 2008/2009*, www.statcan.gc.ca/pub/.

Titaev, K. D. and Pozdniakov, M. P. (2012) 'Poriadok osobyi – prigovor obychnyi: praktika primeneniia osobogo poriadka sudebnogo razbiratelstva (Glava 40 UPK RF) v rossiiskikh sudakh', *Analiticheskaia zapiska Instituta prava i pravoprimeneniia*, March, www.enforce.spb.ru/analitiches kie-zapiski/5683-2012-mart.

Tonry, M. (2012) 'Prosecutors and politics in comparative perspective', in Tonry, M. (ed.) *Prosecutors and Politics: A Comparative Perspective*. Chicago: University of Chicago Press, 1–34.

Trochev, A. (2014) 'How judges arrest and acquit: Soviet legacies in postcommunist criminal justice', in Beissinger, M. R. and Kotkin, S. (eds.) *Historical Legacies of Communism in Russia and Eastern Europe*. Cambridge: Cambridge University Press, 152–78.

Trunov, A. V. (2009) www.trunov.com/content/php?act=showcont&id= 5755.

Vaksberg, A. (1986) 'Pravde v glaza', *Literaturnaia gazeta*, 17 December, 13.

Van de Bunt, H. and van Gelder, J. -L. (2012) 'The Dutch prosecution service', in Tonry, M. (ed.) *Prosecutors and Politics: A Comparative Perspective*. Chicago: University of Chicago Press, 117–40.

Volkov, V. and Titaev, K. (2013) 'Extra Jus: Zavedomo vinovnye', *Vedomosti*, 28 February, www.enforce.spb.ru/publikatsii-sotrudnikov/mi-v-smi/5887-v-volkov-k-titaev-extra-jus-zavedomo-vinovnye-lish-8-obvinyaemykh-gotovy-borotsya-za-svoe-dobroe-imya.

Volkov, V. V., Dmitreva, A. and Skugarevskii, D. (2014) *Ugolovnaia iustitsiia v Rossii v 2009: kompleksnyi analiz sudebnoi statistiki*. Moscow: Statut, 44–9, www.enforce.spb.ru/images/Issledovanya/2014/IRL_2014.06_Ugo lovnaya-Justicia-Rossii-v-2009-g.pdf.

Vorenberg, J. (1981) 'Decent restraint of prosecutorial power', *Harvard Law Review*, 94(2): 1521–73.

Wade, M. (2008) 'The januses of justice: how prosecutors define the kind of justice done across Europe', *European Journal of Crime, Criminal Law and Criminal Justice*, 16(4): 433–55.

(2006) 'The power to decide: prosecutorial control, diversion, and punishment in European criminal justice systems today', in Jehle, J. -M. and Wade, M. (eds.) *Coping with Overloaded Criminal Justice Systems: The Rise of Prosecutorial Power Across Europe*. Berlin: Springer, 27–126.

Wright, R. F. and Miller, M. L. (2010) 'The worldwide accountability deficit for prosecutors', *Washington and Lee Law Review*, 67(4): 1587–620.

Zelitch, J. (1931) *Soviet Administration of Criminal Law*. Philadelphia: University of Pennsylvania Press.

CHAPTER NINE

DECISION-MAKING IN THE RUSSIAN CRIMINAL JUSTICE SYSTEM
Investigators, Procurators, Judges and Human Trafficking Cases

Lauren A. McCarthy

The decision-making that occurs in the Russian criminal justice system is often obscured, when talking to its participants, by a strict emphasis on legal positivism. The decision concerning which crime to charge an offender with, in particular, is painted as a cut-and-dried formula: if the evidence matches the elements of the crime as defined in the code, the charge should be clear. However, in legal systems in Russia, as in many other countries, investigators and procurators have a significant amount of discretion in their charging decisions. Unlike in more 'standard' cases where the charging decision is fairly straightforward and hard to observe, in cases where laws have vague or uncertain parameters or introduce new legal concepts, we can see how procurators and courts try to determine the meaning of these laws and how to apply them.

This chapter uses the case study of human trafficking laws to discuss key features of the Russian criminal justice system, including its conservative nature and its general lack of openness to new legal claims. Human trafficking laws, introduced into the Russian Criminal Code in 2003,[1] provided Russian law enforcement with the legal basis for dealing with a phenomenon they had been seeing but did not have any way of prosecuting. Initially, it seemed that these laws would serve to cover a wide variety of activities that could be defined as human trafficking. A number of procurators made novel legal arguments that pushed for a more expansive understanding of the human trafficking

---

[1] *Ugolovnyi Kodeks Rossiiskoi Federatsii* of 13 June 1996, No. 63-FZ. SZ RF, 1996, No. 25, item 2954 [Criminal Code of the Russian Federation].

law's provisions. However, over time, they moved away from this approach, recognising that broader interpretations are not particularly well received by judges and therefore have the potential to lead to acquittals. Judges – out of concern that their decisions will be reversed on appeal – have also been wary of using their discretion to widen applications of the trafficking laws.

Ultimately, while new laws like those on human trafficking can offer an opportunity for discretion and for legal interpretations that are novel and expansive, the pressure to have a clean record where the accuracy of their legal judgments cannot be called into question pushes ordinary procurators and judges away from making bold arguments. Though these pressures exist throughout the criminal justice system, for the purposes of this chapter, I will concentrate on the final stage – that of the interplay between procurators who approve the final charging decision, courtroom procurators (*gosobvinitel'*) who take the case to court on the state's behalf and judges who hear the cases. These parties are all concerned about potential harm to their career prospects, should they step too far outside the box and produce legal outcomes that may be contested.

There is one important exception to this argument – politically motivated laws and cases. In the latter, law enforcement personnel and judges experience strong pressure from above to produce results (see Jeffrey Kahn's chapter in this volume). Laws such as those criminalising extremism, insulting the religious feelings of others, defaming the Soviet Union's role in World War II or forcing foreign-funded non-government organisations to register as foreign agents are outside the scope of this chapter. Instead I focus here on a type of case that is both ordinary – in that it is processed largely at the local level by ordinary law enforcement personnel – yet unusual, in that it is rare enough that most law enforcement personnel, upon encountering a trafficking case, will have to interact with this law for the first time. This combination enables us to peer inside the day-to-day operations of the Russian criminal justice system and to see what drives the decision-making of its personnel.

This research is based on a larger project which uses a unique dataset of publicly available Russian-language news media articles (e.g., television transcripts, newspapers, online reporting), court documents and information from court websites in order to follow cases of human trafficking through the Russian criminal justice system over a ten-year period from December 2003 to December 2013 (for a more detailed methodology, see McCarthy 2015). The sources were coded for details about the offence, the offender, the victims and the crime's progress through the criminal justice system, including a detailed narrative of each case.[2] The result was 279 cases which, at some point, had a human trafficking charge attached to them, though not all defendants were ultimately convicted of human trafficking. The court documents used in this chapter include forty-five convictions in which all victim testimonies and court proceedings are written up in detail, and eighty-seven appeals to regional high courts and the Supreme Court of the Russian Federation in which the procurators and defendants have the ability to outline what they view as the legal shortcomings of the case. Additional information comes from interviews conducted with over 150 law enforcement professionals, activists and experts in Russia between 2007 and 2012.

HUMAN TRAFFICKING IN RUSSIA AND ITS CRIMINALISATION

Human trafficking has become a particularly salient problem since the fall of the Soviet Union. In the 1990s, the sex trafficking of women for prostitution to areas in Europe, Asia, the Middle East and North America was the predominant form of trafficking in Russia (Erokhina and Buryak 2003; Granville 2004; Hughes 2000; Orlova 2004). However, over the following two decades, the trade diversified (McCarthy 2015). Along with Russia's economic boom in the 2000s came an increased demand for labour, some of which was satisfied by the trafficking of victims in the construction, factory and agriculture industries. Labour trafficking victims, though often migrant workers, were also Russians who were down on their luck, homeless, alcoholic or otherwise marginalised. Additionally, the geography of sex trafficking changed. While women were still taken abroad and forced into prostitution, some were also trafficked for sexual exploitation into and within Russia, from smaller towns and villages to larger regional centres. Cases of parents selling their children for illegal adoption also became a well-publicized issue (McCarthy 2016).

---

[2] Basic information on all cases is located on the author's website: http://people.umass.edu/laurenmc/traffickingjustice.

In 2003, after signing the UN Transnational Organized Crime Convention and its associated protocol on human trafficking, the Russian legislature passed an amendment criminalising human trafficking in Criminal Code Article 127.1 (Table 9.1). Though there was significant international pressure on Russia to pass these laws and implement them, domestic actors, including law enforcement agents, also pushed hard to criminalise a phenomenon which they had encountered frequently, but felt that they could not adequately prosecute under existing law (McCarthy 2015).

The numerous actions that seemingly qualify a case as human trafficking caused confusion for, and varying interpretation among, law enforcement, procurators and judges. Did all the actions have to be included in order to qualify as human trafficking or was one sufficient? Could a person voluntarily accepting a job that turned into exploitation be considered a trafficking victim? Did the buying and selling of people as if they were objects have to be for the purpose of exploitation or was it sufficient to constitute trafficking in its own right? While the last question was resolved in 2008 with an amendment to the law, confusion persisted.[3] Even four years after the passage of the laws, when I conducted interviews in 2007 and 2008, agents in multiple areas of the country gave various definitions of what constituted trafficking and emphasised different parts of the law. The human trafficking statute was joined by Article 127.2 which prohibited the use of slave labour. It was written in an equally vague and broad language, requiring on-the-ground interpretation in its use (Table 9.2). Together, these two Criminal Code statutes make up the legislative response to human trafficking in Russia.

Not unlike other criminal cases, human trafficking cases proceed through the criminal justice system in a fairly typical manner. Evidence of a trafficking case usually first comes to the attention of an on-the-ground operative (*operativnik*) whose job is to develop relationships with informants, uncover crimes, conduct preliminary investigative activities and find and detain criminals. Once the evidence is gathered by the operatives, the information is passed to an investigator

---

[3] The basic definition of human trafficking now reads, 'Buying/selling a person, any transaction involving a person and likewise the recruitment, transportation, transfer, harboring or receiving of a person for the purpose of their exploitation.' Additionally, the amended law added two aggravating factors – trafficking a woman known to be pregnant and trafficking a person known to be in a state of helplessness.

TABLE 9.1 Human trafficking (Article 127.1) definition as of 2003

Basic definition	First-level aggravating factors	Second-level aggravating factors
The buying and/or selling, recruitment, transportation, transfer, harbouring or receiving of a person for the purpose of their exploitation **Punishment:** up to 5 years' imprisonment	• two or more people; • known minor; • using official status; • crossing Russian borders or illegally holding someone abroad; • use of false documents or the taking, hiding or destruction of ID documents; • violence or the threat of violence; • goal of removing organs or skin **Punishment:** 3 to 9 years' imprisonment	• leading to accidental death or severe consequences to health or other severe consequences; • done in a way that endangers the life and health of many people; • done by organised criminal group **Punishment:** 8 to 15 years' imprisonment

Source: Russian Criminal Code.

TABLE 9.2 The use of slave labour (Article 127.2)

Basic definition	First-level aggravating factors	Second-level aggravating factors
Using the labour of a person over whom one has authority akin to ownership, and in which a person cannot refuse to perform labour (services) for reasons unrelated to him- or herself **Punishment**: up to 5 years' imprisonment	• two or more people; • known minor; • using official status; • through blackmail, violence or the threat of violence; • the taking, hiding or destruction of ID documents **Punishment**: 3 to 9 years' imprisonment	• leading to accidental death or severe consequences to health or other severe consequences; • done by organised criminal group **Punishment**: 8 to 15 years' imprisonment

Source: Russian Criminal Code.

(*sledovatel'*) who puts the case together in a way that complies with the requirements of the Criminal Procedure Code and makes a charging decision. All of this is written up in an indictment document (*obvinitel'noe zakliuchenie*). Trafficking cases differ from many other types of crimes, nevertheless, in the fact that investigative jurisdiction, as assigned by the Criminal Procedure Code, is split between two agencies, depending on the severity of the offence. While most trafficking cases are handled by the Investigative Committee, trafficking with no aggravating factors is handled by investigators in the police (MVD), although it is rare to see trafficking cases of this type.[4] While it is the investigator's job to make the final charging decision, the procuracy's role of general supervision (*nadzor*) over the criminal justice process and over individual cases making their way through that process gives it the final say in signing off on the indictment document. This marks, at the very least, the procuracy's tacit approval of the charges, and more often, its active involvement in selecting the charges. Once the case is ready for trial, it is passed to a courtroom procurator (*gosobvinitel'*), who will present the state's case at trial. While there is nothing preventing the roles of oversight and courtroom activity from being fulfilled by the same person, procurators usually specialise in one or the other (Paneyakh et al. 2012). At that time, the case is mostly ready to go, but the courtroom procurator does have an important moment of discretion. He/she may choose not to support one or all of the charges or any individual part of the charges as outlined in the indictment document. The case is then decided by a judge.

REJECTING NOVEL INTERPRETATION

Laws are written by the legislature but their real meanings are constructed by their use in practice. With a new law, where the waters are untested and the meaning of the statute not yet clear, the participants in the criminal justice system must sometimes make guesses about what the formal criteria of the law require and how they will be interpreted by others. This creates an opening for resourceful and ambitious

---

[4] Before 2007, investigators were located in the procurator's office but, since a 2007 reform, they have been located in a stand-alone investigative agency – the Investigative Committee. For its first four years, the Investigative Committee was a stand-alone unit under the purview of the Procuracy but, in 2011, it was separated entirely and now answers only to the president.

investigators and procurators to propose their own interpretations of the law through their charging decisions and the justifications for them as written up in the indictment. When the wording of the law is vague and the parameters unclear, judges also have the power to apply the law with broader understandings of its meaning. With no clear guidance from above on what the trafficking law means and how it should be interpreted via a resolution (*postanovlenie*) from the Plenum of the Supreme Court they, too, have the opportunity to take a more expansive view of the types of crime that fall under the statute.

During the first few years that the trafficking laws were on the books, innovative interpretations were attempted by a number of procurators. However, it soon became clear that judges were not particularly open to these types of claim and procurators quickly returned to doing what was safe, which often involved avoiding human trafficking charges altogether.[5] Looking at documents from human trafficking cases prosecuted between 2003 and 2013, this section outlines the various attempts to expand legal understandings of human trafficking and demonstrates how these interpretations were almost always rejected by the court.

In the early years after the trafficking law was passed, procurators seemed to have a more flexible understanding of human trafficking. Though there was considerable confusion over exactly what the law required, there was an attempt to get it to cover a broad variety of situations. For example, in a 2004 case where women were trafficked from the city of Saratov to Germany, the women were willing participants in the trafficking process and said in statements to the police that they had no complaints about the defendant's behaviour. Even though not a single one of the victims testified against the defendant, the case was prosecuted anyway, because the defendant had engaged in sending them abroad for prostitution using false documents. In fact, many of them returned to him repeatedly – after being deported from Europe – for help in obtaining new false travel documents so they could return under different names. This type of case would be much less likely today. The investigators and procurators whom I interviewed expressed their reluctance to push cases

---

[5] Though this chapter focuses on cases that had a trafficking charge at some point (279 in total), there were an almost equal number of cases that came up under search terms for human trafficking (111 sex and 121 labour) that were not charged as trafficking, despite having all of the required elements (McCarthy 2015).

forward in which the victims seem complicit or unwilling to testify against or attribute blame to their traffickers.

In 2004, Rostov law enforcement was quite aggressive in pursuing a trafficking case where women were sent abroad. In this case, the defendant recruited women to send to her daughter's brothel in Malta, getting them tourist visas and promising to find them jobs as waitresses. Once there, they were offered a choice – either prostitute themselves to pay back the debt or ask their parents to send the money. The defendant was arrested – as the parents of a recent victim paid her the money – and was charged and convicted of attempted trafficking. The new Criminal Code article being used this aggressively to prosecute an *attempt* at trafficking when they could have charged the defendant with something easier and more familiar, such as extortion, is another example of the expansive interpretations of the law by procurators in the early days.

Procurators also tried to use the UN Protocol on trafficking to which Russia is a signatory to argue for a wider variety of situations to fall under the ambit of the trafficking law. In 2008, procurators did this in two separate cases. In the first case, which took place in the Krasnodar region, the defendants forced homeless men to work at a rubbish dump collecting recyclable materials that would then be sold to a processing factory for profit. The men were held there against their will (bars on the windows, locks on the doors), were not paid, had their passports taken away and experienced violence – both psychological and physical. If they refused to work or tried to escape they were beaten and locked up. After getting into a disagreement with another local businessman, the traffickers gave two men to the businessman without the men's consent as reparation for the harm caused in the fight. The defendants were charged with human trafficking for having traded the victims, not for buying or selling them. This interpretation did not fit easily into Russian law which, at the time, specified that a victim had to be bought or sold, not traded,[6] although this reasoning did have a basis in the UN Protocol's definition of trafficking. This case was paired with a forced labour charge, so that the indictment had a more solid footing and a better chance of being successful. However, the group was also convicted of human trafficking using the reasoning drawn from the UN Protocol.

---

[6] This was changed in an amendment passed in November 2008 which specified that 'any transaction involving a person' counted as human trafficking.

In the second case, involving international sex trafficking in the city of Yoshkar Ola, the procurator actively used the UN Protocol to make the argument that recruitment, when combined with exploitation, is sufficient to prove trafficking and was able to convince the judge of this reasoning. In this same case, the defence tried to argue that, because the victims had not themselves written a complaint against the defendants, they should not be considered victims. The procurator used the UN Protocol to show the judge that the international definition of trafficking considers the women to be victims even if they consented to the exploitation against them – even though Russian law does not make this distinction.

In the early years, procurators were also more aggressive in appealing cases when their interpretation of the law's wording conflicted with the judge's decision. For example, in a 2005 case in the Kurgan region, the procurator asked for a new trial on appeal, alleging that the court groundlessly dismissed the human trafficking charges. In the appeal, the procurator argued that, because all the women victims were already in prostitution and were not planning to leave, the recruitment into prostitution charge, which the defendants were convicted of, did not make sense. Human trafficking charges were a better fit for the situation, considering that the women had been moved to a different city and held against their will in an apartment for the first few weeks that they were there, under constant supervision and unable to leave on their own. The courtroom procurator in the case, Andrei Banshchikov, noted in a media interview: 'In the Urals region this is the first case like this. We tried to find a similar experience in other regions in Russia, but we couldn't find anything. So we can say, this is the first precedent in the country' (Efimov 2006). With all this fanfare, it is perhaps unsurprising that the procurator appealed when the court rejected the charge, but his eagerness to be the first is also indicative of the occasional flashes of original and expansive thinking when it comes to having the opportunity to shape interpretation of the law. In later years, appeals were more focused on technical issues and sentencing rather than on interpreting the meaning of the statute itself.

Another discretionary decision that investigators and procurators can make is to specify which aggravating factors apply to a crime. The trafficking law sets out two levels of aggravating factor, each outlining elements of the crime that would move it beyond 'ordinary' human trafficking. Of course, there must be evidence to prove the presence of each aggravating factor, but using them can signal a higher degree of severity and, by extension, make the defendant susceptible to a more substantial punishment. In the human trafficking statute, the highest aggravating factor category includes, among other things, the charge of human trafficking committed by an organised group and specifies a punishment of between eight and fifteen years in prison (see Table 9.1).

Most trafficking crimes are, indeed, committed by organised groups. Whether they are small local groups that traffic locals or larger groups that traffic across international borders, most have more than one person and some delineation of roles between the participants. Of the 279 cases charged as trafficking that I examined, 190 had multiple defendants. In domestic sex trafficking cases the average number of traffickers was between four and five, and in international sex trafficking cases between three and four. In labour trafficking cases the average group size was two to three members. The only form of trafficking where single perpetrators was the norm was child trafficking for illegal adoption, in which desperate parents sold their babies for money. Thus, including the aggravating factor of trafficking by an organised group – the literal interpretation of the law – ought to have been the default for procurators. Indeed, during the first year that the laws were on the books, over half (56 per cent) of the cases with multiple defendants were charged in this way. Over time, however, the court's chilly reception to using this aggravating factor has meant that most trafficking cases are now prosecuted using mid-level aggravating factors, resulting in lower sentences but greater success. In only two other years in the 10-year study period – 2010 and 2011 – did the number of eligible cases that used the highest aggravating factor top even 35 per cent. Why?

A careful reading of case documents reveals that judges have made it very difficult to meet the standards of proving trafficking committed by an organised group. In order to determine whether a group was organised, the court relied on the definition in Criminal Code Article 210 (participation in an organised crime group). This statute requires that the group has a clear (*chetkoe*) delineation of roles, has created durable contacts between the members of the group (*ustoichivost'*) and has the intent to commit grave or especially grave crimes as a group.[7] Using this

---

[7] Grave crimes (*tyazhkoe prestuplenie*) have a maximum punishment of ten years in prison and especially grave crimes (*osobo tyazhkoe prestuplenie*) are punishable by between ten years and life in prison (Criminal Code Article 15).

definition, procurators focused their cases on outlining who served what role and showing that the roles had been clearly and specifically delineated in the trafficking operation.

Judges rarely accepted these arguments. The most common recurring problem was showing the durability of the criminal contacts over time. For example, in a 2006 case in Saransk, the charge was lowered from trafficking as an organised group to the most basic level of trafficking because the judge said that the procurators needed to show more constant contact between the members of the group and a clearer organisational structure. The prosecution had tried to prove durability and intent by showing that the accused had a clear plan to conceal their crime – registering the sauna at which the prostitution took place under someone else's name. However, according to the judge, this one-time act was not enough to establish the durability of their contacts even though the rest of the court record showed a clear and ongoing relationship between the defendants. The most successful way to prove durability seemed to be through phone records and recorded phone conversations taking place over several months, which was the situation in a case from the Marii El region where the trafficking conviction was under the most serious aggravating factor, trafficking committed by an organised group.[8]

Unlike procurators, who occasionally attempted expansive interpretation of the human trafficking law's provisions and tried to secure higher prison sentences through the use of aggravating factors, judges were almost universally averse to interpreting the human trafficking laws broadly. Much like their technically correct but very narrow understanding of what constitutes an organised criminal group in the trafficking cases described earlier, court documents reveal that conservative interpretations are the norm for judges, who fear having to issue an acquittal or having their decisions overturned on appeal. In fact, when presented with cases that involve human trafficking statutes, judges have assiduously tried to avoid using them. They do this by saying that human trafficking was incorrectly charged or, in a few cases, acquitting the defendants on the human trafficking charge but

---

[8] It is worth nothing that this type of investigation requires extensive resources, including wiretaps, which were available in this case because it was investigated by the Federal Security Service (FSB). These sorts of resource are not usually available to ordinary police and investigators.

convicting them on the other charges. This has happened in both sex and labour trafficking cases, as the following examples demonstrate.

In one sex trafficking case in Izhevsk, the judge decided that the transportation of the women for prostitution fell under the organising prostitution charge and therefore that this piece of evidence could not be used to support the trafficking charge. In this same case, the accused were found to have created a specific group to organise and recruit women into prostitution but not to traffic them. The defendants were ultimately acquitted of trafficking but were convicted of the other crimes. Likewise, in a case in Primorskii Krai, the judge said that the buying-selling of the victim was intended to fulfil the goal of organising prostitution, not human trafficking, even though the trafficking statute clearly states that buying-selling for the purpose of exploitation in prostitution constitutes human trafficking.

This cautious reasoning also extended to labour trafficking. In one case in the Republic of Karelia, the head of a state psychiatric hospital forced disabled patients to work on his private garden plot. The man was originally convicted of using slave labour, but the decision was overturned on appeal because the appellate judge said that the victims were unable to refuse to work (a key part of proving slave labour) because they were mentally ill, not because the accused had put them in a situation of slavery. The judge also said that the criminal activities committed by the defendant were already covered by the abuse of authority charge of which he was ultimately convicted and that the slave labour charge was therefore superfluous. Another case of labour trafficking from the Irkutsk region saw a defendant acquitted of a use of slave labour charge because the judge found that there was no intent to use the victim as a slave or to exercise powers of ownership over him, he just wanted the victim to pay back his debts. Despite witness testimony to the contrary, the court found that the victim was not threatened or physically harmed. The fact that he was able to report the exploitation to the police was also used as evidence that his freedom of movement was not restricted and therefore he was not held. Unfortunately, the stereotype that a victim must be held and be unable to escape is common amongst legal professionals, even though it is not required under the legal definition of labour trafficking.

In a final example from a labour trafficking case from the Primorskii region, the judge hewed so closely to the letter of the law and its technicalities as to border on absurdity. Here, the defendants were accused of recruiting three men with promises of well-paid work picking nuts in a local forest. Once there, the victims were beaten and threatened with violence if they did not work well, with one eventually being beaten to death. The judge found the defendants not guilty of using slave labour because the men had been beaten so badly that they could not work. Even though they were supposed to be being used as slave labour, the fact that they were not working meant the crime had not been committed, according to the judge. In this case, the defendants were punished harshly for the murder, notwithstanding the acquittal on charges of slave labour. Though this is probably the most extreme example, the tendency towards conservative interpretations of the trafficking laws is a pattern reflected time and again in court documents in such cases.

Conservatism is so entrenched in the judicial culture in Russia that judges are reluctant to engage with trafficking laws even when they are largely insulated from the possibility of having to issue an acquittal. Of the 279 cases I examined, 65 per cent of labour trafficking cases and 77 per cent of sex trafficking cases were brought with additional charges (McCarthy 2015: 177). This means that, no matter what happens with the human trafficking charge, the defendants are almost guaranteed to be convicted of something. Yet, as described earlier, judges still tried to avoid dealing with the trafficking charges in any way. In only two cases did a judge take a more expansive view of human trafficking than that which he was given by the procurator in the indictment. In a case in the Tiumen region, the trial court judge folded the charge of false imprisonment into the trafficking charge, saying that false imprisonment was a part of harbouring, as defined by the trafficking statute. The Russian Supreme Court had a similar interpretation in the appeal of a case from the Komi region. There, the court suggested that the exploitation of a person, as defined in the human trafficking statute, by nature included false imprisonment, so an additional charge of it was unnecessary.

Of course, one could interpret these conservative judicial decisions as another way of avoiding acquittals by convicting defendants of a lesser charge when the evidence of trafficking is weak (Solomon 2015). However, having read through the evidence presented in court documents from these cases, the judge could have arguably found support for convicting the accused of trafficking in all of them. Likewise, in many other cases where there was evidence of the elements of a trafficking crime, procurators avoided bringing trafficking charges, refused to support them in court or tended towards risk aversion and narrow interpretations. That this tendency is so universal in the Russian criminal justice system raises important questions about why its personnel are so averse to new claims and expansive understandings of new laws, even in a situation like human trafficking, where law enforcement itself had been an important driving force behind advocating for the new laws. The next section explores how the incentive structures of the criminal justice system push its personnel away from creativity and towards conservatism.

PROCURATORS, JUDGES AND THE CRIMINAL JUSTICE EVALUATION SYSTEM

Explaining the reticence of the criminal justice system to engage with human trafficking laws requires an examination of the incentives facing investigators, procurators and judges. Here I focus on the quantitative assessment system, which demonstrates who is doing a 'good job' by agency standards and who is not. For procurators, this system creates significant pressure to convict, not because they are personally fixated on convictions but because doing a 'good job' by their agency's standards requires them to focus on that particular metric. As one former procurator noted, 'An acquittal is like a falling star – very rare' (Solopov 2016). Judges, on the other hand, are very concerned with having their decisions and sentences upheld on appeal and so remain reluctant to engage in expansive interpretations of the law that may later be questioned.

It is important to note that, by the time a case has made it to the trial stage, it has probably gone through several rounds of negotiations and pre-clearance between operatives, investigators and procurators, so it is unsurprising that most of the cases (163 out of 279) that do make it to trial using human trafficking statutes end up with convictions under those statutes. Five more were closed by procurators at the indictment stage and, in seven other cases, courtroom procurators refused to support the trafficking charges.[9] At that point, all participants in the criminal justice system except the judge (although sometimes he, too, is involved) have come to an agreement that the case has enough merit

---

[9] For two more cases, it was unclear what statutes the defendants were ultimately convicted under and, for fifty-eight cases, the outcome was unclear. In another thirty cases, they were convicted but not of human trafficking. Sixteen cases were still ongoing as at the end of 2014.

and strong enough evidence that it will most probably result in a conviction under the chosen charge. In fact, of the 279 cases charged as trafficking, only three saw the defendants acquitted of all charges and released from custody.

All participants in the criminal justice system are judged by a set of quantitatively oriented performance indicators (*palochnaya sistema*) that measure how many activities they have completed and in what time frame, and how these numbers compare to the previous year's statistics. Because the statistical performance indicators are aggregated up from the individual to the department to the regional level, there is always pressure from above for them to look good. The system is also heavily paperwork-oriented. Detailed records are kept of each stage of the process, creating both a system of accountability and a system that enables blame to be apportioned when a case is not cleared or a conviction is not secured. This paperwork is not only onerous but also often duplicative, as individual departments have to report to multiple superiors.

Each participant in the criminal justice system has an eye toward a successful resolution of the case according to his/her agency's standards. For the operatives and the investigators, success means a cleared case – one where a suspect has been identified and charged with a crime. For procurators, success means a conviction. For judges, success means not having the case reversed on appeal. Cases that make it easy to accomplish these goals have several characteristics in common – the charges are straightforward and it is clear both what evidence needs to be collected and that it can be collected in a timely manner (Paneyakh 2014). The criminal justice system as a whole, then, prefers cases with charges that are familiar and are seen with some regularity.[10] Trafficking cases rarely meet these criteria. As one non-government organisation manager who trained law enforcement agents on how to deal with human trafficking noted, the law enforcement agents who were willing to push ahead with human trafficking cases were generally those who were older, well established and did not have to worry about making their careers or reputations. The younger agents, she said, were much more hesitant to do anything outside the box.

---

[10] Although this is common across jurisdictions in the Western world as well, in the Russian context it has a stronger effect in that it narrows the field of investigation.

The incentives facing procurators push them towards case clearance and conviction.[11] Their two functions, oversight and in-court prosecution, means that they are on the hook not only for supervising individual cases and ensuring convictions but also for the smooth operation of the entire legal system. For the procurators who perform oversight on individual cases, the most important statistical marker is the number of cases sent to court – in other words, the number of indictments they sign off on. As is common in the rest of the system, more is always better, leading to a less-critical eye on the cases that come across their desks, especially if their yearly tallies are running low.[12] The procurator who signs off on the indictment for any individual case also has a personal interest in seeing that case result in a conviction and will often consult informally with operatives and investigators beforehand to do a pre-clearance. Once the procurator receives the indictment, he can, according to the Criminal Procedure Code, send it back to the investigator for more work; however, this would imply that the procurator had not done an effective oversight job of the criminal process and thus would weaken his or her record in addition to the investigator's.

As guardians of the entire legal system, procurators are also assessed by markers that indicate the success of crime-fighting in their regions – cases cleared and crimes registered. This means they have an interest, just like the police and investigators, in clearing cases and preventing difficult ones from being registered in the first place. Finally, procurators are also assessed on the number of cases opened in priority areas – narcotics, economic crimes and organised crime – so they have a particular interest in making sure that these cases are successful.

The final role which procurators play in the criminal justice system is as courtroom prosecutors (*gosobvinitel'*), which they must perform without ever having seen the case or having been involved in the approval of the indictment, and regardless of their belief in the quality of the

---

[11] For an excellent description of life as an ordinary procurator, see Solopov (2016), a retired procurator from St Petersburg who explains the incentives facing procurators and other participants in the criminal justice system in their day-to-day working environment.

[12] They are also assessed on a number of other indicators such as how many citizen complaints they have reviewed, how many violations of operative activity they have uncovered, how many disciplinary actions they have issued and the number of multiple other procedural issues they must decide on. However, these are less critical for overall statistical assessment than cases sent to court and therefore given less attention by procurators (Paneyakh et al. 2012).

evidence. Though detailed knowledge of the case may be somewhat less important given the centrality of the case file in Russian courtroom processes, the system is technically adversarial and so the courtroom procurator must still do an oral presentation of the evidence. Securing a conviction is the primary statistical marker of the courtroom procurator's work. This gives them, of all the participants in the criminal justice system, the most to lose if the case results in an acquittal or a closure based on rehabilitative reasons (no crime happened or the accused did not participate). The latter happens very rarely but is a significant black mark on the procurator's record, indicating that a 'bad' case has slipped through due to his or her oversight. Failing to obtain a conviction is an indicator of bad work and can lead to increased oversight by superiors and possibly dismissal. Procurators are reviewed every five years and, if they have any outstanding disciplinary actions on their records, they will be unlikely to make it through the review process unscathed; they may also lose out on the opportunity for promotion or be reassigned to a lower role (Solopov 2016). The courtroom procurator is also judged on how many cases she or he handles per year and it is important to make sure that the numbers stay relatively steady from year to year, which can be difficult because of the ebbs and flows of the criminal justice process.

For courtroom procurators, the fact that they have largely been left out of the pre-trial informal discussions about charging means that it is sometimes a wise choice for them to refuse to support a trafficking charge once it gets to them. This was the situation in two selected cases. In one case in the Primorskii region, the defendants insisted that the transaction that formed the basis of the human trafficking charge was not for the woman herself, but to pay back a debt that she owed to her previous pimps after she had voluntarily left to go to work at another brothel. To this courtroom procurator, it was probably clear that with the witnesses differing drastically on the purpose for which the money was exchanged, it would be too difficult to prove that the sale was conducted for the purpose of exploitation. He thus refused to support the trafficking charge. Nevertheless, the defendants were convicted to a substantial prison term for recruitment into prostitution. In a slave labour case in the Murmansk region, six homeless men were forced to pick berries and scavenge for nuts in the woods. They were given quotas and beaten if they did not fulfil them and one was eventually forced to dig his own grave, after which he was killed. They had little shelter and were barely fed. As the procurator noted in a media interview, 'This is the first time in our city that we have had to work this kind of complex and atypical case. In all our procurators' previous work, we have never seen the elements of this crime – the use of slave labor with violence or threat of violence' (Iarotskaya and Glodeva 2007). However, the courtroom procurator ultimately did not support the trafficking charge, probably because of a fear of acquittal given the complexity of the case. In both of these cases, the courtroom procurator made a safe decision to not use the trafficking statute and, instead, to go with what was familiar – in the first case, recruitment into prostitution charges and, in the second, murder. Interestingly, these cases also demonstrate that it may not be necessary to engage with trafficking charges when other charges are an option.

The pressure to do good work according to agency standards does not only apply to procurators. Judges are also assessed by quantitative indicators, including the number of reversals that their decisions lead to and the timeliness and efficiency of their court proceedings. Every court's chairperson examines these statistical indicators for each individual judge and has significant power to issue disciplinary sanctions (Paneyakh *et al.* 2012; Solomon 2007). Not meeting the expected statistical markers can cause embarrassment for the court or unwanted attention from the judicial bureaucracy.

The incentive to avoid a case reversal by the appellate court is a powerful motivator. Maintaining the 'stability of sentences' is a primary goal of the legal system and is considered to be a key indicator of the professionalism and competence of individual judges, though there is no objective measure of stability and no statute of limitations dictating how long a reversal can count against a judge (Paneyakh *et al.* 2012). Despite the fact that up to a third of reversals are not due to judicial mistakes but are, instead, a result of changed circumstances, this differentiation is not reflected in their yearly assessments, making it appear that they have made significantly more errors than they actually have (Pozdnyakov 2014). Too many reversals may harm a judge's potential for career advancement or, at the very least, may draw unwanted attention to their courtrooms. With laws that are vague or uncertain – often the case with new laws – this possibility increases. Appellate judges could have legitimately different understandings of the law or could be convinced by a compelling defence argument that the law has been interpreted incorrectly. In the case of the human trafficking law, this uncertainty appears to have led judges to take the more conservative option.

Ultimately, incentives push court personnel to process cases quickly while minimising the risk of acquittal. Procurators and judges must figure out how to balance these pressures when implementing a new law such as that on human trafficking. Consequently, in trafficking cases, investigators and procurators select charges that are more familiar to courtroom procurators and judges and encompass part of the human trafficking crime (i.e., recruitment into prostitution for the recruitment stage, false imprisonment for the harbouring stage), rather than using the human trafficking statute which covers all stages of the crime in one charge. This is made easier by the fact that many of these crimes have actually been committed in the process of human trafficking. In other words, an investigator or procurator would not be wrong to charge a case of sex trafficking as recruitment into prostitution or a case of labour trafficking as organising illegal entry or false imprisonment. As these laws have been on the books for so long, it is easier for procurators to default to them. Familiarity with the evidence required and the definitions of the crimes make cases brought under these alternative statutes easier to clear (for investigators) and to convict under (for procurators) because all the actors in the criminal justice system are mostly on the same page about what they mean.[13]

RUSSIA IN COMPARISON

How does Russia compare to other countries? In many ways the challenges which we see in Russia are quite similar to those in other countries around the world, particularly on the issue of human trafficking. Research from other countries on implementing human trafficking laws suggests that the problems which procurators and judges face in Russia are not unique. In countries around the world, law enforcement professionals use their discretion about whether, when and how to investigate trafficking cases cautiously, often defaulting to other, easier statutes that have the same ultimate effect – convicting and sentencing human traffickers (Farrell et al. 2014; McDonald 2014; Wade 2011). More broadly, cautious approaches to new cases and new laws are often the norm in law enforcement, as is the tendency for prosecutors to avoid engaging in cases that they do not think they can win.

---

[13] In addition, in the case of sex trafficking, this practice was enabled by a strengthening of the laws against organising and recruitment into prostitution in amendments passed at the same time as the trafficking laws (McCarthy 2015).

For example, research in the United States' context has shown the difficulties of getting law enforcement agents and prosecutors to implement new laws on a variety of topics, including hate crimes (Boyd et al. 1996; Jenness 2007; Jenness and Grattet 2005; Jenness and McPhail 2005/6), domestic violence (Robinson 2000; Spears and Spohn 1996; Spohn et al. 2001) and harsher laws against drunk-driving (Mastrofski and Ritti 1992; Meyers et al. 1987, 1989). This reticence is often attributed to institutional culture and pre-existing norms and practices, much like in Russia.

Russia is also not unique in its use of quantitative indicators to measure police, prosecutorial and judicial performance. This tendency has been the most pronounced in the police, where law enforcement agencies – from the United States to France to the UK and South Africa – have instituted systems of quantitative indicators, also known as 'performance-based management systems', both to evaluate crime trends and to manage and assess personnel performance (Eterno and Silverman 2012). Research on these systems is increasingly revealing their perils; the falsification and manipulation of statistics, resulting in inaccurate data on the true incidence of crime, criminal justice personnel who are too afraid to innovate for fear of ruining their statistics, an increase in pressure from above and bullying as superiors gain significant leverage over their subordinates and a breakdown in community–police relations, as fulfilling quotas takes the place of engaged policing (Eterno and Silverman 2012; Faull 2016).

For prosecutors, statistical assessment is generally not formalised to the same degree as for the police; nevertheless, in many systems, prosecutors remain acutely attuned to bureaucratic concerns, including the prospects of successful prosecution for each individual case. Research from the United States, where prosecutors have tremendous discretionary power, suggests that prosecutors consider the likelihood of winning a conviction when making their decisions to charge, including assessing any characteristics of the victim or perpetrator that may be more likely to lead to conviction (Albonetti 1987; Spohn 2014). Research in other civil law systems, where victories are not the primary marker of success, suggests that, as in Russia, prosecutors are also sensitive to concerns of expediency in case processing. Consequently, they often use their discretion to reduce court backlogs and to divert cases out of the system that may be difficult to conclude successfully (Boyne 2010, 2014; Ma 2002). Much like in the Russian case, research shows that prosecutors in both common and civil law systems also try to anticipate how other actors in the criminal justice system will interpret the case and mould their decisions in order to ensure the greatest likelihood of a successful prosecution (Boyne 2014; Frohmann 1991).

CONCLUSION

What does an examination of human trafficking cases tell us about the Russian criminal justice system? First and foremost, it demonstrates a strong institutional resistance to absorbing new laws because of the fear of uncertainty that their use brings. New laws present new opportunities for novel legal interpretations but they also present risk. As demonstrated throughout this chapter, when procurators had opportunities to invoke more expansive interpretations of the human trafficking laws through their charging decisions and legal arguments, they were almost always shut down in their attempts by judges who were nervous about their decisions being reversed on appeal. Eventually this led investigators and procurators to take the safer bet and avoid the human trafficking laws altogether or to double up with other charges to ensure that they were successful in obtaining a conviction for at least one crime.

A second lesson when studying the Russian criminal justice system is the importance of understanding the underlying incentive structures that drive behaviour. Here, the quantitative assessment system places pressure on the early stages of the investigation, primarily on operatives and investigators, in order to filter cases out of the system that are unlikely to result in a conviction by not opening them, or to create a body of evidence that, no matter its veracity, will lead to a conviction (Shklyaruk 2016). This concern about meeting agency standards and keeping a clean record then continues up the criminal justice chain to procurators, who end up focusing primarily on conviction rates. As Solopov noted in describing their work, 'Procurators fight for their cases not because they want to imprison people – they're fighting for their careers. It's nothing personal' (2016). Thus, even when individual agents and judges are willing to be innovative, over time the system tends to push decision-making in the direction of conservatism, formalism and risk aversion so as not to harm their career prospects.

This does not mean that the decisions that are made in this system have no legal basis – they almost always do. An important cause for optimism is evidence that law enforcement personnel do sometimes try to use the skilful application of existing laws to respond to new realities.

In the case of human trafficking, they have defaulted to more familiar criminal laws to prosecute such crimes – including, *inter alia*, recruitment into prostitution and false imprisonment – rather than use the new laws which create too much uncertainty (McCarthy 2015).

What are the consequences of the excessive bureaucratisation of the criminal justice system through its focus on quantitative indicators? Several come to mind. The first consequence is for those caught up in it. This is a system that does not admit mistakes easily or stop cases from moving forward if there is a suspect who can be charged, even if it is not the correct suspect (Paneyakh et al. 2012). All pressures point to convicting whoever is in the dock, for whatever crime it is that they have been charged with. The driving need to move cases quickly through the system means that there are very few incentives for judges or procurators to question the quality or veracity of the evidence gathered in the investigation. The low rates of acquittal system-wide are testament to this fact (see Peter H. Solomon, Jr in this volume), as are qualitative analyses of the mentality of judges, procurators and investigators (McCarthy 2015; Paneyakh et al. 2012; Shklyaruk 2016). Thus, for those who are wrongly arrested, wrongly imprisoned, wrongly charged or wrongly convicted, there is little recourse.

A second and longer-term consequence has to do with popular perceptions of the efficacy of the criminal justice system. For those citizens, in particular, who report crimes that are difficult to solve (the theft of a wallet or mobile phone, for example), law enforcement's first instinct is not to help but to avoid. This, in turn, makes citizens avoid law enforcement, choosing to accept their losses rather than to report minor crimes that they believe law enforcement will not even bother to register, much less solve. For more serious crimes like human trafficking, agents' and judges' fear of not meeting their statistical markers may lead them to downplay the severity of these crimes by registering them as something else. While that may make their lives easier and result in criminals being imprisoned, it means that there is little accurate information about the true incidence of crimes in Russia, including human trafficking.

Finally, cautionary approaches to new laws are so ingrained in the mentality of criminal justice professionals that it is difficult to spur policy innovation and implementation without clear signals from above. Law enforcement agents end up participating in a 'race to the bottom', settling on doing the bare minimum to move the case forward and check the necessary boxes, rather than a 'race to the top' where they strive to find ways to innovate and implement new policies well' (McCarthy 2015: 13). Ironically, these features also mean that, when given the proper signals and prioritisation, the criminal justice system can be turned on at the drop of a hat, as it has been in many recent politicised cases. The informal relations that permeate the Russian system mean that straightforward policy fixes like streamlining and improving assessment systems may not have much of an effect. The Russian criminal justice system would do well to consider ways of incorporating meaningful qualitative elements into the assessment system for its personnel, but would have find a way to do so without these changes creating yet another stimulus for cautionary and risk-averse behaviour – a task easier said than done.

References

Albonetti, C. A. (1987) 'Prosecutorial discretion: the effects of uncertainty', *Law and Society Review*, 21(2): 291–313.

Boyd, E. A., Berk, R. A. and Hamner, K. M. (1996) 'Motivated by hatred or prejudice: categorization of hate-motivated crimes in two police divisions', *Law and Society Review*, 30(4): 819–850.

Boyne, S. (2014) *The German Prosecution Service: Guardians of the Law?* New York: Springer.

(2010) 'Uncertainty and the search for truth at trial: defining prosecutorial 'objectivity' in German sexual assault cases', *Washington and Lee Law Review*, 67(4): 1287–1360.

Efimov, V. (2006) 'U sosedei devki slashche?', *Kur'er Belomor'ia*, 11 July. www.arhpress.ru/kurbel/2006/7/11/15.shtml.

Erokhina, L. and Buryak, M. (2003) *Torgovlya Zhenshchinami i Detmi v Sotsialnoi i Kriminologicheskoi Perspektive*. Moscow: Profobrazovanie.

Eterno, J. A. and Silverman, E. B. (2012) *The Crime Numbers Game: Management by Manipulation*. New York: CRC Press.

Farrell, A., Owens, C. and McDevitt, J. (2014) 'New laws but few cases: understanding the challenges to the investigation and prosecution of human trafficking cases', *Crime, Law and Social Change*, 61(2): 139–168.

Faull, A. (2016) 'Measured governance? Policing and performance management in South Africa', *Public Administration and Development*, 36(2): 157–168.

Frohmann, L. (1991) 'Discrediting victims' allegations of sexual assault: prosecutorial accounts of case rejections', *Social Problems*, 38(2): 213–226.

Granville, J. (2004) 'From Russia without love: the "fourth wave" of human trafficking', *Demokratizatsiya*, 12(1): 147–155.

Hughes, D. (2000) 'The Natasha trade: the transnational shadow market of trafficking in women', *Journal of International Affairs*, 53(2): 625–651.

Iarotskaya, Z. and Glodeva, A. (2007) 'Dvukh Kirovchan Obviniaiut v Ubiistvakh, Ispol'zovanii Rabskogo Truda i Vymogatel'stve', *Dvazhdy Dva*, 11 April.

Jenness, V. (2007) 'The emergence, content, and institutionalization of hate crime law: how a diverse policy community produced a modern legal fact', *Annual Review of Law and Social Science*, 3: 141–160.

Jenness, V. and Grattet, R. (2005) 'The law-in-between: the effects of organizational perviousness on the policing of hate crime', *Social Problems*, 52(2): 337–359.

Jenness, V. and McPhail, B. (2005/6) 'To charge or not to charge? That is the question: the pursuit of strategic advantage in prosecutorial decision-making surrounding hate crime', *Journal of Hate Studies*, 4(1): 89–119.

Ma, Y. (2002) 'Prosecutorial discretion and plea bargaining in the United States, France, Germany and Italy: a comparative perspective', *International Criminal Justice Review*, 12(1): 22–52.

Mastrofski, S. D. and Ritti, R. R. (1992) 'You can lead a horse to water ... : a case study of a police department's response to stricter drunk-driving laws', *Justice Quarterly*, 9(3): 465–491.

McCarthy, L. A. (2015) *Trafficking Justice: How Russian Police Enforce New Laws, from Crime to Courtroom*. Ithaca, NY: Cornell University Press.

(2016) 'Transaction costs: prosecuting child trafficking for illegal adoption in Russia', *Anti-Trafficking Review*, 6: 31–47.

McDonald, W. F. (2014) 'Explaining the under-performance of the anti-human-trafficking campaign: experience from the United States and Europe', *Crime, Law and Social Change*, 61(2): 125–138.

Meyers, A. R., Heeren, T. and Hingson, R. (1987) 'Cops and drivers: police discretion and the enforcement of Maine's 1981 OUI law', *Journal of Criminal Justice*, 15(5): 361–368.

(1989) 'Discretionary leniency in police enforcement of laws against drinking and driving: two examples from the state of Maine, USA', *Journal of Criminal Justice*,17(3): 179–186.

Orlova, A. V. (2004) 'From social dislocation to human trafficking: the Russian case', *Problems of Post-Communism*, 51(6): 14–22.

Paneyakh, E. (2014) 'Faking performance together: systems of performance evaluation in Russian enforcement agencies and production of bias and privilege', *Post-Soviet Affairs*, 30(2–3): 115–136.

Paneyakh, E., Pozdnyakov, M., Titaev, K., Chetverikova, I. and Shklyaruk, M. (2012) *Pravookhranitel'naia deiatel'nost' v Rossii: Struktura, Funktsionirovanie, Puti Reformirovaniia, Part I: Diagnostika Raboty pravookhranitel'nikh Organov RF i Vypolneniya Imi Politseiskoi Funktsii*. St Petersburg: Research Institute for the Rule of Law.

Pozdnyakov, M. (2014) *Kriterii Otsenki Kachestva Raboty Sudei i Distsiplinarnaia Otvetstvennost'*. St Petersburg: Institut problem pravoprimeneniia pri Evropeiskom universitete v Sankt-Peterburg.

Robinson, A. (2000) 'The effect of a domestic violence policy change on police officers' schemata', *Criminal Justice and Behavior*, 27(5): 600–624.

Shklyaruk, M. (2016) 'Extra Jus: Zakaz Ot Sistemy', *Vedomosti*, 3 March.

Solomon, P. Jr (2007) 'Informal practices in Russian justice: probing the limits of post-Soviet reform', in Feldbrugge, F. (ed.) *Russia, Europe and the Rule of Law*. Leiden: Koninklijke Brill NV, 79–92.

(2015) 'Post-Soviet criminal justice: the persistence of distorted neo-inquisitorialism', *Theoretical Criminology*, 19(2): 159–178.

Solopov, M. (2016) 'Opravdatel'nyi Prigovor–Eto Kak Padaiushchaia Zvezda', *Mediazona*, 10 May.

Spears, J. and Spohn, C. (1996) 'The genuine victim and prosecutors' charging decisions in sexual assault cases', *American Journal of Criminal Justice*, 20(2): 183–205.

Spohn, C. (2014) 'The non-prosecution of human trafficking cases: an illustration of the challenges of implementing legal reform', *Crime, Law and Social Change*, 61(2): 169–178.

Spohn, C., Beichner, D. and Davis-Frenzel, E. (2001) 'Prosecutorial justifications for sexual assault case rejection: guarding the gateway to justice', *Social Problems*, 48(2): 206–235.

Wade, M. (2011) 'Prosecution of trafficking in human beings cases', in Winterdyk, J., Perrin, B. and Reichel, P. (eds.) *Human Trafficking: Exploring the International Nature, Concerns, and Complexities*. Boca Raton, FL: CRC Press, 153–180.

CHAPTER TEN

THE RICHELIEU EFFECT

The Khodorkovsky Case and Political Interference with Justice

Jeffrey Kahn

Cardinal Richelieu allegedly said, 'If you give me six lines written by the hand of the most honest of men, I will find something in them that will hang him.'[1] How does this claim relate to the administration of justice in Russia today? The story of Mikhail Khodorkovsky, whose rise to post-Soviet riches was followed by a decade in prison after seriatim criminal convictions, is not the story of 'the most honest of men'. However, Richelieu's boast purports to be generalisable beyond any one case and presents a universal danger for the honest and dishonest alike.

That is the *Richelieu Effect*: the Cardinal's corruption of the institutions he controlled and his ability to weaken institutions meant to constrain him. Quashing a conspiracy in 1642, Richelieu could not separate Cinq-Mars and de Thou from their heads without the verdict of a court of law (Price 1912). However, this would-be autonomous state institution was too weak to withstand the will of the king's chief minister. The defendants' treason trials were not models of judicial procedure. In the words of an early account, 'the Will of the Cardinal was Paramount to Rules', the lead judge in the case 'had sold his Conscience to Cardinal Richlieu [sic]' and, leaving nothing to chance, Richelieu himself 'closeted the Judges one after another; recommending to them to do Justice, that is, in the Cardinal's sense of the Word, to

---

[1] 'Qu'on me donne six lignes écrites de la main du plus honnête homme, j'y trouverai de quoi le faire pendre'. Attribution is disputed, see Fournier (1882: 255). It is sufficient for my purposes that Richelieu might have said it.

condemn the Accused' (Anon. 1744: 60–61, 65–66). By false promises of leniency, and perhaps the threat and 'dread of infamous Suffering' (i.e., torture), testimony by the most guilty in the case was acquired to condemn the one least involved in the affair (Anon. 1744: 67).

Cinq-Mars may have been a scoundrel, but de Thou was the most decent of men. Their differing degrees of honesty did not matter. Both lost their lives to Richelieu's perversion of justice. On the other hand, on the honesty of Richelieu and the judges he suborned, *everything* depended. The operation of a judicial system requires a baseline of integrity by the state's agents (police and investigators, prosecutors and judges) and those private persons who are, for a time, either officers of the court (attorneys) or obliged by oath to true performance of their duties (witnesses or jurors). Modern criminal justice systems today buttress these promises with checks and balances of various kinds.

What might be called 'internal' checks and balances seek to promote the judicial enterprise from within the institutions of justice. The state criminalises the sort of dishonesty that could undermine the system: perjury, bribe-taking, the falsification of evidence and other crimes that weaken these essential public institutions and corrupt office-holders.[2] The necessity of multiple actors working together, subject to appellate review, in a public forum constantly surveilled by journalists and interested parties, are additional checks. Constitutionally protected speech and press freedoms both promote individual liberty and provide what might be called external checks on state institutions.

Such approaches, of course, swim against the tide of Russian history; the preference was for combining institutional authorities, not separating them. The antipathy of the Soviet period to the concept of checks and balances emerged from different origins than centralised imperial rule, but was just as fundamental a feature of institutional construction.[3] There is a textual commitment to the

---

[2] Chapter 31 of the RF Criminal Code ('Crimes Against Justice') identifies twenty-four enumerated crimes, including Obstruction of Effectuation of Justice and Proceedings of Preliminary Investigation (Art. 294) that, ironically, formed the basis of a criminal investigation of the Human Rights Council's experts tasked to report on the second Khodorkovsky case.

[3] Art. 6 of the 1977 Soviet Constitution embedded the Communist Party of the Soviet Union as the 'guiding and directing force of Soviet society, the core of its political system and of state and social organizations'. In his memoirs, Mikhail Gorbachev refers to 'this accursed Article 6', noting that the ruling elite 'very quickly acquires a taste for power and is ready to do anything so as not to part with it'. Gorbachev wryly

concept in Russia's current constitution, though it has been eroded in practice since its adoption in 1993.[4]

What happens when the separation of powers is insufficient or absent? What happens when the state chooses *not* to police good faith, but to pressure the parties in the system (the state's agents or others) to achieve a preordained, politically desirable result?

This chapter analyses how the Richelieu Effect corroded the judicial opinion that convicted Mikhail Khodorkovsky in 2010. It also examines the post-trial reprisals against academic experts invited to examine its merits. I was directly involved in that second part of the story as one of nine individuals selected in April 2011 to submit a report to the Council of the President of the Russian Federation on Development of Civil Society and Human Rights in October of that same year. This chapter also consolidates excerpts from my report for the Council and subsequent writing on the topic (see Kahn 2011, 2013a, 2013b).

THE TRIALS OF MIKHAIL KHODORKOVSKY

A Brief Case History

The story of Mikhail Khodorkovsky's rise and fall is well reported (see, for example, Hoffman 2011; Sakwa 2014). Only the bare facts of his investigation, arrest, trials and conviction, and the seizure and dismemberment of Yukos Oil, need be recalled here.[5]

---

notes the problem's transcendence: 'In its time the nobility probably felt the same way' (Gorbachev 1996: 314–315).

[4] The 1993 Constitution declares the 'autonomy' ['самостоятельны'] and 'separation ['разделения'] of the legislative, executive and judicial' state power to be 'fundamentals of the constitutional system' alterable only by adoption of a new constitution drafted by a specially convened Constitutional Assembly (see Arts. 10, 16 and 135).

[5] The facts are drawn primarily from the verdict of 27 December 2010 by Judge V. N. Danilkin, presiding judge of the Khamovnichesky District Court of the City of Moscow; the judgments of the European Court of Human Rights arising out of applications by Mikhail Khodorkovsky (App. No. 5829/04 decided 31 May 2011), Platon Lebedev (App. No. 4493/04 decided 25 October 2007), Vasilii Aleksanyan (App. No. 46468/06 decided 8 December 2008) and OAO Neftyanaya Kompaniya Yukos (App. No. 14902/04 decided 20 September 2011); and the admissibility decision of the European Court of Human Rights arising out of the application by Platon Lebedev (App. No. 13772/05 declared partly admissible 27 May 2010).

Yukos Oil Company

Following various inspections beginning in November 2002, the Tax Ministry of the Russian Federation concluded that the Yukos oil company had avoided payment of a variety of taxes. The Ministry concluded that this was accomplished using various subsidiary, trading and holding companies that, although controlled and owned by Yukos, obscured the company's real business activity. The Ministry also found that the trading companies served as intermediaries between oil production companies and oil processing and storage companies, all belonging to Yukos.

On 15 April 2004, the Tax Ministry ordered payment of over €2.8 billion in tax arrears, default interest and penalty payments, all due the next day. By a decision of the Moscow City Commercial Court rendered on the same day that Yukos was served with a copy of the Tax Ministry's decision, judicial proceedings began against Yukos to obtain this amount. The company was enjoined from disposing of certain assets in anticipation of a judgment.

On 4 August 2006, the Moscow commercial court declared Yukos bankrupt and, with the consent of the leading creditor, Rosneft – a state-owned oil company – appointed a trustee to manage Yukos. This decision was upheld by the 9th Commercial Court of Appeal. On 12 November 2007, bankruptcy proceedings concluded and Yukos ceased to have corporate existence.

The First Trial

On 20 June 2003, the first criminal investigation was opened concerning the Yukos oil company and its top management. It concluded on 20 August, having compiled a case file consisting of 162 volumes. The case began with a suspicion of fraud during the 1994 privatisation of Apatit, a mining company. Arrests followed on suspicion of a 'large-scale fraud and embezzlement of the shares of several Siberian oil refineries, including *Tomskneft PLC* '.[6] Yukos' CEO, Mikhail Khodorkovsky, was arrested in Novosibirsk on 25 October and sent to Moscow.

---

[6] *Aleksanyan v Russia*, App. No. 46468/06 (22 Dec. 2008), at para. 8. Platon Leonidovich Lebedev, a close business associate of Khodorkovsky, was arrested on 2 July while in hospital and sent to a pre-trial detention centre. The next day, he was remanded to a detention facility by a court order made without the participation of Lebedev's lawyers.

On 8 January 2004, a separate criminal investigation was opened on suspicion of fraud, embezzlement and misappropriation of the shares of several oil companies, including Tomskneft, by Yukos executives (the investigation ended on 12 December 2006; the case file contained 113 volumes).

On 16 July 2004, the criminal trial of Khodorkovsky and Platon Lebedev, a close business associate, began in the Meshchanskiy District Court of the City of Moscow. In May 2005, both were convicted of fraud (Article 147 of the RSFSR Criminal Code and Article 159 of the RF Criminal Code), causing property damage by deceit or breach of trust (Article 165 CC RF), and tax evasion (Article 198 and Article 199 CC RF). They were sentenced to nine years in prison. The verdict was upheld on cassational appeal but the sentences were reduced to eight years in prison.

The Second Trial

On 5 February 2007, a second indictment was announced alleging embezzlement (Article 160 CC RF) and money laundering (Articles 174 and 174.1 CC RF) by both Khodorkovsky and Lebedev (*BBC News* 2007).[7] The final version of the indictment lodged with the court and dated 14 February 2009 comprises fourteen volumes (3,460 pages). The crimes alleged in the indictment span roughly the same time period as those for which the defendants were arrested in 2003 and convicted in 2005. Both sets of crimes concern the defendants' conduct as executives of the Yukos oil company.

The second trial of Khodorkovsky and Lebedev began on 31 March 2009. A verdict was expected on 15 December 2010 (see, for example, *RIA-Novosti* 2010). Without explanation, the announcement of the verdict was postponed on that date until 27 December 2010, when the verdict – 689 pages long – was read out. Judge Viktor Danilkin took four days to read it aloud (as he was required to do by law). Khodorkovsky and Lebedev were found guilty of embezzlement and money laundering and sentenced to fourteen years' imprisonment. On 24 May 2011, the defendants' appeal was heard and decided. The Khamovnichesky court's verdict was upheld with a modest reduction in the original sentence.

---

[7] The indictment ('обвинительное заключение') is dated 14 February 2009. The discrepancy may reflect the final version of the indictment filed with the court pursuant to Art. 215 of the Criminal Procedure Code.

Khodorkovsky and Lebedev were expected to remain in prison until 2016. In an unexpected development, President Putin pardoned Khodorkovsky and he was released from state custody on 20 December 2013. Platon Lebedev was released a month later. Vasily Aleksanyan, the top lawyer at Yukos, had died in custody in 2011.

THE RICHELIEU EFFECT ON THE RIGHT TO A REASONED JUDGMENT

The Khodorkovsky case was the *ne plus ultra* political trial of the tandem presidencies of Vladimir Putin and Dmitry Medvedev. The arrest, detention and conditions of confinement of the accused were the subject of numerous trial motions (unsuccessful) in the Russian court and petitions (successful) to the European Court of Human Rights. Similarly, numerous aspects of the trial itself – delays in the proceedings, the independence and impartiality of the tribunal, respect for the presumption of innocence and equality of arms, etc. – were the subject of critical commentary and litigation. Limited space prevents their analysis here (but see Kahn 2011 for more detail).

This section illustrates the Richelieu Effect by describing one particularly salient violation of the separation of powers in the second trial: the right to a reasoned judgment. The RF Code of Criminal Procedure (Статья 297 УПК РФ) requires that '[t]he judgment of the court must be lawful, well-founded and fair'. The Code then provides detailed requirements for the composition of the judgment and prohibitions against speculation beyond what the evidence confirms. The Code also expressly requires that the *court itself* shall write the judgment.

Beyond this domestic law, Russia has agreed to be bound by the European Convention on Human Rights. Article 6 § 1 of the Convention requires that, 'In the determination ... of any criminal charge against him, everyone is entitled to a fair and public hearing ... by an independent and impartial tribunal'. This provision is understood to require that courts give reasons for their judgments.[8] In particular, courts must 'indicate with sufficient clarity the grounds on which they based their decision'.[9] The court is 'under a duty to conduct a proper examination of the submissions, arguments and evidence adduced by

---

[8] See *Van de Hurk* v. *The Netherlands*, App. No. 16034/90 (19 April 1994) at para. 61.
[9] *Hadjianastassiou* v. *Greece*, App. No. 12945/87 (16 December 1992) at para. 33.

the parties, without prejudice to its assessment of whether they are relevant to its decision'.[10] The Court determines a violation of the right to a reasoned judgment on a case-by-case basis, with a margin of appreciation accorded to national law and practice.

Professor Stefan Trechsel elaborated on the importance of this requirement from the perspective of legal theory:

> The only possibility to verify a hypothesis in law lies in the reasons given. They must be complete and logical. Without reasons, a decision cannot claim to have legal character, let alone to be correct. Thus, without reasoning it would not be possible to distinguish a correct judgment from an arbitrary one. In other words, a judgment which does not give reasons may not be, but certainly appears to be arbitrary.
> (2005: 103–104)

In addition, the requirement of reasoned judgments has numerous 'instrumental and intrinsic virtues' for the pursuit of justice in a democratic society that have been widely recognised, including the value that inheres in the guarantee that a person is 'being treated with dignity as a person, a sovereign agent, and not merely as an object who can be manipulated at the will of the authorities' (Roberts 2011).

At first glance, it may seem counter-intuitive to suggest that the December 2010 verdict of 689 pages may violate the right to a reasoned judgment. The verdict's volume, however, should not be confused with its mass. The verdict is indeed voluminous. Its concentration of legal reasoning, however, is slight.

The narrative rationale part of the verdict, required by Article 303 of the Code of Criminal Procedure, begins on page 3 under the heading 'Established' ('Установил'). The court appears to have complied with the Code's requirements in the most hyper-literal fashion. On pages 3–130, the court presents its 'description of the criminal act which the court determined was proven', as required by Article 307(1). On pages 130–132, the court summarises the defendants' separate arguments and testimony in their defence. On pages 133–615, the court presents 'the evidence on which the court's findings regarding the defendant[s] are based and the reasons the court rejected other evidence', as required by Article 307(2).

With regard to pages 3–130 of the narrative rationale part of the verdict, these cannot be understood to have 'established' anything at

---

[10] *Kraska v. Switzerland*, App. No. 13942/88 (19 April 1993) at para. 30.

all, because no evidence is cited from any source. The assertions and conclusions in this section might be described as a summary of the court's findings if this section was not so long (especially as compared to the summary of the defendants' responses to these charges on pages 130–132, a tiny fraction of this amount). No particular assertion of fact is linked to any piece of evidence in the record. Neither is there any evaluation (or acknowledgment) of conflicting evidence, nor legal analysis that would apply evidence to law. Thus, this section reads more like a prosecutor's indictment than a court's reasoned judgment. Indeed, as noted shortly, that appears to be its provenance. It cannot be described as a reasoned evaluation of the evidence.

The artificial division of the court's conclusions from the evidentiary basis for them obscures instances where the court fails to provide any reason, based in law or evidence, for its verdict. For example, the court concludes on page 4:

> The given contract was wrongful and contradicted the fundamental principles of civil law under Art. 1 of the RF Civil Code, since OAO NK Yukos as a legal entity was placed from the outset in such conditions under which it exercised its civil rights not by its own will, but by the will of a group of its core shareholders – which by this time had become M. B. Khodorkovsky, P. L. Lebedev and the members of the organised group acting jointly with them – and not in its own interests, but in the interests of the given organised group.

However, neither in this section nor later in the verdict are the 'fundamental principles of civil law' identified; nor is an explanation given as to how the contract was 'wrongful' or how it 'contradicted' them.

Additional evidence of the lack of reasoning in this section of the verdict manifests itself in its drafting. Multiple pages and paragraphs are duplicated, as if cut and pasted from one part of this section to another. For example, seventy-six lines of text on pages 7 to 9 are identical to text on pages 75 to 77, with the exception of seven lines of text added to page 8 and a few other very minor differences. Likewise, the last two paragraphs on page 12 are, with the exception of the last ten words, identical to the last two paragraphs on page 13. On pages 18 and 19, twenty-two lines are virtually identical (save for one new sentence, one name and assorted typographical errors) to lines found on pages 104 and 105. Again, between pages 20 and 22, 114 lines are virtually identical to lines found on pages 105 through 107. The last two paragraphs on page 30, amounting to seventeen lines of text, are identical to the first two paragraphs on page 31. The fifty-six lines on pages 74 and 75 are virtually identical to lines found on pages 105 and 106.[11]

Perhaps the most revealing aspect of the verdict's composition in this regard is its extensive duplication of the indictment ('Обвинительное заключение по уголовному делу №18/432766–07'). The indictment, of course, is composed by a criminal investigator pursuant to Article 220 and approved and forwarded to the court by the prosecutor pursuant to Article 221(1)(1) of the Criminal Procedure Code. Both the investigator and the prosecutor, of course, are participants in the criminal proceedings on the prosecution side, as indicated in Articles 37 and 38 of the Criminal Procedure Code. By law, the indictment must indicate, *inter alia*,

> the nature of the charges, the place and the time of the commission of the crime, how it was committed, the motives, goals and consequences involved and other circumstances that are relevant to the criminal case; a statement of the charges brought, citing the Point, Paragraph and Article of the Criminal Code of the Russian Federation that specifies liability for the crime; a list of the evidence supporting the charges made; [and] a list of the evidence relied on by the defense.
> (Статья 220(1)(3)-(6), (УПК РФ))

In this case, the indictment consists of fourteen volumes containing 3,460 pages. Astonishingly, the first 130 pages of the verdict (and, quite possibly, many more) are a near-exact copy of it. An annotated copy of those pages, indicating all differences and identifying the source of the material in the indictment, was attached to my report to the Human Rights Council as an appendix. The vast majority of differences between the two documents are not substantive. Thus, the indictment frequently identifies by name, individuals to whom the verdict refers in general terms as 'members of the organized group' or 'other persons'. Similarly, the verdict tends to include the initials of Khodorkovsky's first name and patronymic (omitted from the indictment) and often adds Lebedev's name alongside that of Khodorkovsky. Abbreviations may be spelled out, spaces added or symbols changed into words. Occasionally, the name of a company listed alongside others in the indictment is omitted from the verdict, although this is rare. Otherwise, the texts are identical.

---

[11] The differences referenced earlier are detailed in the report itself but generally range from minor variances in prepositions and proper names to the occasional inversion of word order or one paragraph with another.

Such brazen copying is compelling circumstantial evidence that the court has not engaged in its own process of reasoned decision-making to reach its judgment. It is also persuasive support for a finding that the court has violated other rights held by the accused, including the right to an independent and impartial tribunal and to equality of arms.

Even if this cutting and pasting between indictment and verdict were to be disregarded as insufficient proof, *eo ipso*, that the court failed to engage in reasoned decision-making, the manner in which the remainder of the verdict relates the evidence to the charges draws the court's reasoning process into serious question. In short, the court frequently *identifies* evidence but rarely *reasons* from it to a legal conclusion. In this way, the verdict mimics what was observed at trial by a rapporteur of the Parliamentary Assembly of the Council of Europe:

> The trial itself, so far, consists in reading out, apparently at random, short passages of corporate and other documents without any discussion of their significance, even from the point of view of the accusation. The demand of Mr. Lebedev "that the prosecutors explain which evidence corresponded to which episode and charge" seems reasonable to me, as does the insistence of the defence lawyers that "the documents should be not only read out but also examined". To me, this should go without saying in any trial.
>
> (Leutheusser-Schnarrenberger 2009: 29 [fn. omitted])

The verdict makes its first citation to any piece of evidence in the record on page 133. From there to page 615, the court provides lists of evidence from identified portions of the record. Each list is headed by a paragraph (sometimes) set in boldface type. The boldface paragraph is written in a standard form that states a conclusion and then provides a list of evidence (with citation to the case file or trial record) as support for that conclusion. This section appears to be organised to conform with the literal requirement of Article 307(2) of the Criminal Procedure Code to 'contain ... the evidence on which the court's findings regarding the defendant are based'.

However, the mere *listing* of documents under a conclusory heading is not equivalent to *reasoning* from this evidence to reach the conclusion that the elements of the charged offences have been proven. For example, the court's first boldface heading appears at page 140:

> The court links building of a vertically-integrated structure of management of OAO NK Yukos with the [criminal] intent of the defendants aimed at creating conditions for oil theft. Creation with the

involvement of M. B. Khodorkovsky and P. L. Lebedev of the executive bodies for the oil producing companies represented by ZAO Yukos EP turned out to be one of such conditions.

The verdict then states that, 'This circumstance is corroborated by:' and follows this phrase with a list of nine pieces of evidence from the case file, including five sets of minutes of shareholder meetings, three contracts and a corporate order, all of which are described as concerning the transfer of powers between different companies. No part of any document is quoted to support its conclusory description by the court. No analysis of this evidence is provided nor any explanation offered to support the conclusion asserted in the boldface heading. Nor is the concept of establishing a 'link' between the Yukos corporate structure and the defendants' criminal intent explicated in terms of Russian law.

As another example, the boldface heading on page 143 states: 'The guilt of the defendants in building of the vertically-integrated structure of management as of [sic] mechanism of management of the process of theft and realization of the stolen oil by means of establishing ZAO Yukos RM and transfer to it of the required powers is corroborated by the following documents:'.

Twenty-four items of evidence are then listed with brief summaries of their contents: the testimony of two witnesses, eight sets or extracts of corporate minutes, a corporate charter, seven contracts, three corporate orders, a power of attorney, an extract from a share registry and an 'information statement'. No analysis is conducted. Nor is any interpretation of these materials – on their faces, ordinary business documents – provided to explain how the court concluded from them that they indicate any form of 'guilt' or intent to organise these entities for the 'management of the process of theft and realization of the stolen oil'. Indeed, Khodorkovsky is mentioned in only two of these documents, extracts of minutes from general shareholder meetings at which he appeared as Chairman of the Board of ZAO Yukos RM.

Sometimes the court claims to have established facts and legal positions that, in fact, have not been established. On page 147, the court asserts that '[i]t has been established' that the corporate structure it has described in the preceding pages 'was an abuse of right'. However, no such legal analysis was attempted in the preceding section of the verdict, nor was the particular right that the court states to have been abused even identified in Russian law. The court continues by saying that these structures 'entailed violation of equality of its participants since, as legal entities, the oil producing companies were intentionally put at a disadvantage when they were unable to exercise their rights at their own will and to achieve the major goal of their activity – generating profit'. But no evidence appears in the preceding section concerning any profit at all. Finally, the court continues: 'The management of the oil producing enterprises was performed exclusively in the interests of the group of the main shareholders which, by that time, already included M. B. Khodorkovsky and P. L. Lebedev, as well as other members of the organized group acting together with them'. On the contrary, no evidence concerning the 'interests' of anyone is presented. The minutes, charters and other corporate documents merely describe the basic organisational structures of these companies and their relationships with other companies.

Another example of a conclusory heading unsubstantiated by the evidence listed in support of it is found on pages 155–157. In this section, the court states that 'the following pieces of evidence' established the defendants' 'purpose of facilitating and concealment of the commitment of the theft of oil from the oil producing companies'. The documents that follow are the 1996 charters for Yuganskneftegas, Samaraneftegas and Tomskneft VNK, contracts establishing terms for the future conclusion of oil purchase and sale contracts, an amendment to one of those contracts and an undated document that the court asserts was approved by Khodorkovsky and that states,

> responsibility of officers and Board members to shareholders for decisions that should have definitely lead [sic] to losses for the entity (trading transactions are unequivocally such since they formally lead to understatement of the plant's profit) provided for by the law is also a factor that would be desirable to be avoided.

Other than the bare description of these items, nothing more is said. There is no legal analysis applying the relevant Russian law to these documents or explaining how they demonstrate the intent of anyone to steal oil, which, on the face of it, they do not. This technique continues up to page 615 of the verdict.

In other parts of the verdict, the court reaches conclusions about the defendants' intent that are not only unsupported by the evidence it references, but contradicted by it. On page 157, the verdict presents one of its boldface conclusions:

> The guilt of the defendants in the arrangement of conditions for stealing of the oil under the guise of concluding of [sic] the economically

unfounded general agreements is also corroborated by the pieces of evidence examined by the court in the course of the trial.

There then follows one piece of evidence entitled 'Draft decisions of the Board of Directors of OAO Tomskneft VNK of 22 January 1999, including the following records'. On the basis of this document, the verdict states that:

> The court presumes that this document corroborates the intent of the defendants to embezzle the oil produced at the price of RUB 250 per tonne, while they were aware of the fact that its market price was RUB 1,665.61 [per tonne] which also corroborates their intent to embezzle someone else's property by means of clearly nonequivalent payment of its value.

On the contrary, the document as described in the verdict does nothing more than indicate that two different markets were in operation – a domestic market and a foreign market for oil. The document indicates the relative values at which the oil traded in both markets. However, the verdict, while identifying two prices, refers to only one market. By eliding this fact of two separate markets, the court creates the false impression that only one market was in operation with only one price set for the sale of oil.

The very next piece of evidence cited in the verdict, on pages 159–160, in fact confirms the very opposite of this assertion. The court cites the minutes of a shareholder meeting for OAO Tomskneft of 16–29 March 1999 at which the oil purchases referenced in the previous document are approved. This document, as described in the verdict, makes clear that sales will occur at the different prices determined by the relevant markets:

> As a result of the voting, the majority made the following decision: since the production and the sale of oil produced has for a long time been regular business activities of OAO Tomskneft VNK, to declare the production and the sale of oil to be the core activities of OAO Tomskneft VNK in future as well, and, to this end, to conduct transactions on purchase and sale of the oil and/or oil-well fluid on behalf of OAO Tomskneft VNK in compliance with the following set conditions: sale of the oil produced by OAO Tomskneft VNK, to the following companies: OAO NK Yukos, OAO VNK, Total International Limited, Behles Petroleum S.A., ROSCO S.A. in the amount of 50 million tonnes over the period of 3 years at the current market price of RUB 250.08 per tonne in the domestic market and RUB 1,665.61 per tonne in the foreign market of the RF.

Although the verdict states that this document corroborates its statement that the defendants intended to embezzle oil by using a lower price than 'its market price', the evidence that the court cites in fact reveals two markets, not one, and for sales to both domestic and foreign companies.

Unsurprising, then, that Judge Danilkin read 'his' opinion with breathless speed, never once looking up and retiring to his chambers as soon as he had finished.

POST-TRIAL: REPORTS AND REPRISALS

The Putin aftermath of the Medvedev-sanctioned investigation by the Kremlin's Human Rights Council further illustrates these separation of powers problems.[12] This Council has no power other than to investigate and report; its existence depends on presidential decree.[13] Its strength lay not in its legal powers but in the opportunities for persuasion and publicity that its access to the president provided (Nemtsova 2010).[14]

The Council spent a year studying the second trial. It obtained the assistance of nine experts: six Russian scholars, two Europeans and me – the one American. An April 2011 invitation from the Council's Chairman, Mikhail Fedotov, and one of its leading members (and a distinguished former Constitutional Court justice), Tamara Morshchakova, offered participation 'in an independent public expert analysis of official documents and proceedings' with the aim 'to inform civil society about judicial practice in particular cases'.[15]

---

[12] It is unclear whether the Council or President Medvedev initiated the idea of examining the case, although the Council takes the latter view (see Press Release, 21 December 2011, http://president-sovet.ru/structure/group_6/materials/ukos_2.php).

[13] Указ Президента Российской Федерации от 6 ноября 2004 г. № 1417 'О Совете при Президенте Российской Федерации по содействию развитию институтов гражданского общества и правам человека'.

[14] At the time, its membership included some of the leading lights of the Russian human rights movement, including, *inter alia*, Lyudmila Alexeeva, Valentin Gefter, Tamara Morshchakova and Elena Pamfilova. Указ Президента Российской Федерации от 1 февраля 2011 г. № 120 'О Совете при Президенте Российской Федерации по развитию гражданского общества и правам человека'.

[15] Letter from Fedotov and Morshchakova to the author (2 April 2011), reproduced in Kahn (2013a: 26). The letter noted: 'The list of experts involved and the content of their opinions shall be made public only after they have been submitted to the Council.'

This would be conducted 'on a voluntary basis and on the condition of confidentiality', meaning work would be conducted *pro bono publico* and without knowing the other experts selected by the Council.[16] These measures aimed to protect the autonomy and integrity of the process.

The experts' reports analysed Russian criminal law and procedure, contract law and tax law – both in general and as applied to the Yukos case – as well as the general economics, organisation and practices of the oil extraction industry. All the reports were collected, along with the Council's own observations and recommendations, in a 427-page, three-volume hardbound set that was physically delivered to President Medvedev on 27 December 2011. The picture of its transfer made news.[17]

The Council's primary recommendation was that the Procurator General should begin the process of supervisory review (надзор) of the verdict with a view to its repeal and that the Investigative Committee should initiate proceedings for reconsideration (пересмотр) on the basis of newly discovered circumstances (namely the findings of fundamental errors and violations of law during the trial).[18] The Council also recommended several systemic legal reforms:

- expand the use of juries for white-collar crimes; elaborate the bases for the exclusion of judges due to conflicts of interest, including the

---

[16] The authors of the Khodorkovsky reports were announced on 21 December 2011: Sergei M. Guriev, Rector of the New Economic School; Otto Luchterhandt, Law Professor, University of Hamburg; Anatolii V. Naumov, Professor, Academy of the General Procurator's Office; Oksana M. Oleinik, Chair, Department of Entrepreneurial Law, National Research University Higher School of Economics; Alexei D. Proshliakov, Chair, Department of Criminal Procedure, Urals State Law Academy, Ekaterinburg; Mikhail A. Subbotin, IMEMO, Russian Academy of Sciences; Astamur A. Tedeev, National Research University Higher School of Economics; Ferdinand Feldbrugge, Law Professor, University of Leiden (see note 12and statement issued by the working group on the experts' subjects of analysis: http://president-sovet.ru/structure/group_6/materials/izlozenie_tem.php).

[17] Photograph and transcript of meeting between President Medvedev and Chairman Fedotov available at: http://news.kremlin.ru/news/14153. This meeting occurred near the height of demonstrations in Moscow that followed accusations of fraud in the parliamentary elections held on 4 December 2011.

[18] Рекомендации по итогам проведения общественной научной экспертизы по уголовному делу М.Б. Ходорковского и П.Л. Лебедева, 21 December 2011.

appearance of influence on the judge by officials connected with the court, prosecutors, or law enforcement; provide greater rights to confront witnesses and present evidence in open court;
- amend the criminal code to prevent its interpretation so broadly as to deprive the accused of the constitutional protection against prosecution for an act not regarded as criminal at the time that it was committed;
- expand limitations on the prosecution of certain property crimes in the absence of a victim's request;
- limit the use of pre-trial detention in white-collar crimes;
- reform of requirements for parole;
- reform of requirements for pardon, and commutation of sentences; and, finally, a recommendation of broad amnesty for individuals convicted of certain economic crimes.

On 5 March 2012, one day after the Russian presidential election that reinstalled Vladimir Putin in the Kremlin, the now lame-duck President Medvedev ordered the Procurator General to verify the legality of the convictions of Khodorkovsky, Lebedev and thirty other individuals (Gridasov and Petelin 2012; Schwirtz 2012). The following day, Putin himself conceded the propriety of a full investigation into the legality of that verdict by his own Ministry of Justice, though his words were not exactly a ringing endorsement of the work of the Council: 'I think this is correct. The Kremlin commission for human rights is involved here. Since these people have doubts[,] the president demonstrated due respect for them and issued instructions' (*Interfax* 2012a).

The first signs of mounting trouble for the participants in the Human Rights Council's report were evident just weeks later. A source later identified as Investigative Committee spokesman Vladimir Markin smeared the Council's participants, linking several to organisations that had received funding from Yukos almost a decade earlier (*Interfax* 2012b). Mikhail Fedotov vigorously rejected the attempt to compromise the integrity of the report (*Interfax* 2012c; *RIA-Novosti* 2012); however, worse was yet to come.

Once the presidential transition was complete, the report and its authors were subjected to increasing criticism by state officials and in state-controlled media outlets. Over the summer and early autumn of 2012, as many as four of the six Russian experts found themselves in the sights of Russian investigators. They were subjected to search warrants, their property seized and their homes and places of work searched. Four of them – Guriev, Oleinik, Tedeev and Subbotin – were brought before investigators and subjected to lengthy questioning as witnesses (Balmforth 2013).

Witnesses to what? According to Tamara Morshchakova, the search warrants that were issued carried the same reference number as the first case brought against Khodorkovsky in 2003 (Balmforth 2013). The criminal matter under investigation? Possible violation of Article 294 of the RF Criminal Code: obstruction of justice (Zheleznova 2013). The status of the witness (which under Russian law does not trigger the right to counsel or the right against self-incrimination)? This seemed a harbinger of things to come. Morshchakova noted: 'They have not brought formal allegations against the experts. They are witnesses by status. But the measures being implemented here are not used against just witnesses. You don't confiscate materials from a witness' (Zheleznova 2013).

The theory behind the investigation seemed to be that the experts' reports had been funded by Khodorkovsky and thus were not only lacking impartiality but had also attempted to influence the judicial action in his case. This was beyond strange. Great effort had been made by Morshchakova, who organised the experts, to delay the start of their work until the final appeal in Khodorkovsky's case had run its course. 'This is all incomprehensible to me', Mikhail Fedotov told the *Wall Street Journal*, 'All this expert work was conducted on the instructions of the head of state' (White 2013).

In early June 2013, Sergei Guriev, the Rector of the New Economic School and one of the most prominent Russian experts, announced his self-imposed exile in Paris for 'any foreseeable future ... The truth was that I could not come back to Russia because I feared losing my freedom' (Guriev 2013). In an interview with *Der Spiegel* (2013a), Guriev noted that he observed the same typographical errors on both the investigator's materials and the court order that authorised the search of his e-mail correspondence since 2008. 'In other words', Guriev concluded, 'the court in question simply copied the investigators' documents' (Guriev 2013). This claim is not hard to believe, given the extraordinary copying between indictment and judgment that was referenced earlier.

Guriev's description of the treatment that led him to leave his country resonates with the experience of others:

As for me, interrogations started in February 2013. After that, I heard that in February, a colleague of Mr. Putin had talked to him about my situation, and the president had reassured the colleague that I had nothing to worry about. This did not stop the investigation — I was interrogated twice and received demands for all sorts of documents and personal information. Moreover, the investigators introduced 'operative measures' — the police euphemism for surveillance. Whenever I or my wife (who has nothing to do with the case) crossed the Russian border, we were subjected to special attention. Interestingly, during the interrogations the investigators asked me to produce 'alibis', though they did not explain for what, and insisted that I was a 'witness', not a 'suspect'. Then, on 25 April, the investigators scheduled an interrogation but, instead, came to my office with a court warrant to seize my e-mails going back five years.

In Russia, e-mails are treated as correspondence and therefore are protected by the constitution. To seize them, the investigators need a court order. The warrant gave no specific reasons why my e-mails had to be seized, yet concluded they had to be seized. When I complained to the investigators, one of them said that I was better off than Andrei Sakharov, the Soviet dissident who was sent to internal exile in Gorky. They also hinted that they had a warrant to search my home.

This demonstrated that the investigators can produce any search warrant they want without any respect for my rights, and that they can do it without warning. I concluded that my next meeting with them could result in the loss of my freedom. I bought a one-way ticket from Russia and will not return to my country.

(Guriev 2013)

In late June, Russian news media reported that the Investigative Committee would call former Constitutional Court Justice Tamara Morshchakova in for questioning, too, notwithstanding the immunity from prosecution that this status gave her (*Sputnik News* 2013).

On 5 May 2015, *Interfax* quoted an unnamed source 'familiar with the situation' claiming that the investigation of the experts had closed with no charges filed: 'The investigation found no *corpus delicti* in the actions of the scientists who participated in the examination of the "second Yukos case", and advocated a liberalization of the Criminal Code of the Russian Federation.'

In the investigative process, however, lives had been drastically changed.[19] Guriev was in self-imposed exile. Subbotin's professional

---

[19] The non-Russian experts appear to have gotten off lightly, although Otto Luchterhandt seemed to have some travel difficulties (*Der Spiegel* 2013b).

work had been seized and his institute 'paralysed' as a result: 'I asked them to at least give me a chance to copy my materials. I have my whole archive on the flash disks. I gather information and correspondence with people. Everything is there and I have been unable to work for half a year' (Balmforth 2013). Even those peripheral to the experts – such as Elena Novikova, head of research at Subbotin's NGO, the Center for Legal and Economic Research – were in the crosshairs: Novikova had her home and *dacha* searched and her foreign passport seized (Balmforth 2013).

This served a broader, political purpose beyond any particular criminal investigation, as I noted in an op-ed in the *New York Times*: 'Punishing the leaders to quiet the herd is an old practice for authoritarian regimes, and this message was intended for news editors, television reporters, bloggers and others who would speak their minds to the public' (Kahn 2013b). This view was shared by Nils Muižnieks, the Council of Europe's Commissioner for Human Rights. Recounting the reprisals, he observed: 'Any pressure applied on experts because of the opinions they voice or conclusions they reach may have a "chilling effect" on all other persons participating in the debate, making them increasingly reluctant to share their knowledge and experience' (Muižnieks 2013: 177–178).

Perhaps the most succinct summary, however, was provided by Mikhail Subbotin, who suffered one of the first bouts of search, seizure and interrogation:

> What expert extends himself with his independent thoughts, having our experience before his eyes? … That is because participation in the presidential expert examination just yesterday seemed an honorable, prestigious thing, but today it is a criminal matter.
>
> (Subbotin 2013)

A concrete example may bring the point home and perhaps reduce the likelihood that readers of the next section may find analogies to Soviet practices hyperbolic. Subbotin, was shocked when a senior investigator searching his home referenced the trials and purges of Soviet Russia in the 1930s:

> I hadn't had breakfast so I asked if I was allowed to go to the kitchen. He said, 'Of course, it's not 1937, after all.' I said, 'It may not be 1937 yet, but it certainly seems like 1930 already.' That was the year they grabbed all the major Russian economists.
>
> (White 2013)

POLITICAL INTERFERENCE WITH JUSTICE: CONTEXTS

There are many ways for legal institutions to become servants of political power. Indeed, Marxist legal theory was premised on the notion that law could not be in the service of anything but the prevailing political forces in a society; the doctrine of separation of powers was 'a bourgeois fiction' (Henderson 2011: 88). This sentiment paved the way for the worst abuses of justice in Soviet and similar systems. Although political scientists and Russian studies specialists often implicitly adopt the assumption that collapsed (or undeveloped) separation of powers are at the root of many of the political or societal ills that they describe, the precise mechanisms by which institutions are controlled or manipulated tend not to be the subject of sustained analysis.[20] This is especially true for discussions of 'the rule of law' as an independent variable (Kahn 2010). A few general words about key institutions important to the administration of justice – abuses by legislatures, courts and prosecutors – are therefore useful.

Legislatures

This most political branch of any government by definition passes laws favouring a political majority. That fact remains acceptable, even to the losing minority, so long as the opportunity of minorities to regroup and displace reigning majorities remains plausible (Linz and Stepan 1996). The essence of a constitutional democracy, however, is to prohibit some majoritarian actions deemed so oppressive as to be unacceptable

---

[20] See, for example, Gel'man (2015: 72), who describes the first eight years of Putin's reign as enabled by 'the puppet-like parliament, ... powerless political parties, which played no role in government and policy formation; loyal and subordinated nonstate actors, such as business agents, major media outlets, and most of the NGOs; arbitrary use of the economic power of the state; and a politically dependent and rubber-stamped judiciary'; Shevtsova (2003: 194), who states, 'In the absence of independent institutions, the vacuum was filled by groups of influence, and the struggle among them for political clout and property was the major substance of politics in Russia ... The problem in Russia was that neither the rule of law nor independent institutions constrained clan wars;' and Dawisha (2014: 8): 'The internal logic of this system has strengthened the power of Putin over the rest; of "manual control" over institutions; of instructions and "understandings" (*ponyatiya*) over law; and of money over everything.' Dawisha describes Putin as showing 'clear disdain for the normal system of laws and checks and balances that stabilize and maintain a democratic regime over time' (2014: 236).

no matter the likelihood of political turnover; indeed, they may be prohibited because they are often designed to thwart such turnover.

However, such protections are not so hard to evade when the separation of powers is weak. Vladimir Putin's first major political actions as president were directed at strengthening the 'executive vertical' by reducing the power of the upper chamber of the Federal Assembly and constraining the previously uncontrolled autonomy of the federal regions – especially the ethnic republics – composing the Russian Federation (Kahn 1999). Control of the lower chamber, the State Duma, followed soon after (see Dawisha 2014: 270–272; Gel'man 2015: 78–79). A legislature whose members are beholden to the executive or his 'party of power' is unlikely to guard the institution's jurisdiction against executive encroachment. When power does not come from position, but rather positions are gifts from those in power, the institutional check is gone.

COURTS

The judiciary – famously described in the American context as 'the least dangerous branch' (Hamilton 1788)[21] – can also be a potent instrument of power and, in the right hands, a more pointed political tool. Yale Kamisar noted the long acceptance in the United States of a criminal justice system that tolerated (if it did not depend upon) aggressive police practices at the police station that circumvented the rights protected in the courtroom (Kamisar 1965).[22] The result when conditions of separation are *not* existent (or nominally existent but not enforced) is far worse: a powerful weapon to destroy or control one's political opponents. Lenin knew this well. He experienced its Tsarist variant and implemented its Soviet successor system, the abuses of both of which have been widely documented (for an overview with sources see Kahn 2006). Until the new Soviet leaders came to value efficient state administration (a value that percolated above state consolidation

---

[21] 'in a government in which they are separated from each other, the judiciary, from the nature of its functions, will always be the least dangerous to the political rights of the constitution; because it will be least in a capacity to annoy or injure them' (Hamilton 1788).

[22] Kamisar concluded on a note of despair: 'I suspect it is not so much that society knows and approves of the show in the gatehouse, but that society does not know or care' (1965: 19–20).

and political repression in fits and starts), any concept remotely akin to the principle of separation of powers was absolutely rejected (Gsovski 1948).

In an environment with no separation of powers, the protections of procedural or evidentiary rules (among the few instruments of power within the judiciary's control) are paltry, a fact exemplified by the show trial of Nikolai Bukharin, which preceded his execution by hours.[23] Stalin's Commissar of Justice, Nikolai Krylenko, summed this power up nicely:

> The court is, and still remains, the only thing it can be by its nature as an organ of the government power – a weapon for the safeguarding of the interests of a given ruling class ... A club is a primitive weapon, a rifle is a more efficient one, the most efficient is the court ... The court is an organ of State administration and as such does not differ in its nature from any other organs of administration which are designed, as the court is, to carry out one and the same governmental policy ... our judge is above all a politician, a worker in the political field.
>
> (Gsovski 1948: 241)[24]

---

[23] This exchange, between the accused and the prosecutor, speaks volumes:

BUKHARIN: I was not asked a single word about this during the preliminary investigation and you, Citizen Procurator, did not question me for three months, not a single word.
VYSHINSKY: I am questioning you now. This is my right.
BUKHARIN: But at the preliminary investigation ...
VYSHINSKY: Be so kind as not to instruct me how to conduct a preliminary investigation, the more so since you do not understand a thing about it. You understand more about the affairs for which you find yourself in the dock.
BUKHARIN: Possibly (Katkov 1969: 208).

[24] Gsovski (1948: 241) (quoting Н.В. Крыленко, Судоустройство РСФСР – лекции по теории и истории судоустройство – 1923 г.). A rare survivor of the purges, Mikhail Iakubovich, provided this account of how Krylenko, the prosecutor in his trial in 1931, put this theory into practice: 'Offering me a seat, Krylenko said: "I have no doubt that you personally are not guilty of anything. We are both performing our duty to the Party – I have considered and consider you a Communist. I will be the prosecutor at the trial, you will confirm the testimony given during the investigation. This is our duty to the Party, yours and mine. Unforeseen complications may arise at the trial. I will count on you. If the need should arise, I will ask the presiding judge to call on you. And you will find the right words"' (Medvedev 1971: 130). Krylenko himself was eventually arrested and, following his torture and false confession implicating others, convicted and shot (1971: 197, 268).

The Russian Constitution (Articles 120–122) provides assurances of independence, life tenure and immunity to judges. Yet, as with claims of fidelity to the principle of separation of powers, the reality for judicial independence may well be demonstrably improved from Soviet times but still 'restrained by the bureaucratic hierarchy in the judicial system, reluctance of the government to lose control over the judiciary, and, in many instances, [the judge's] own indifference to the principle of independence' (Kovalev 2010: 144).

PROSECUTORS

Stalinist show trials (like Richelieu's manipulations) are rather obvious examples of an idea – the instrumental use of the judiciary by the executive – that has undergone considerable refinement in the last century or so. Comparing Putin to Stalin or Richelieu is, in one sense, hyperbolic. There is no comparison between the purges and executions to the 'velvet repression' that Daniel Treisman and others have identified in Putin's Russia: 'Rather than putting many people in jail, the authorities aimed to intimidate and distract the opposition with drawn-out investigations, searches, and interviews. Still, a few arrests and trials were staged to publicize the new order and disable protest organizers' (2013: 255).

On the civil side, the political uses of a lawsuit are legion. Lawsuits are expensive, time-consuming and spirit-sapping.[25] Thus, for example, political suits for defamation may be used to bankrupt opponents and (if defamation is also a criminal offense) imprison them. In such a context, the plaintiff in an ostensible civil suit becomes a sort of prosecutor. Typically, such a plaintiff is a powerful political leader (perhaps even *the* leader) who declares the suit essential to vouchsafe his public honour and, vicariously, the honour of his office. Some states recognise this danger by decriminalising defamation and establishing nearly insurmountable bars for public officials to make use of civil lawsuits against their opponents in the press or other public forums. Other states are infamous for the opposite approach. Slander was recriminalised in Russia shortly after Putin's election to a third term as president.[26]

---

[25] Hand (1921). 'After now some dozen years of experience I must say that as a litigant I should dread a lawsuit beyond almost anything else short of sickness and death' (Hand 1926: 105).

[26] Федеральный закон от 28 июля 2012 г. N 141-ФЗ «О внесении изменений в Уголовный кодекс Российской Федерации и отдельные законодательные акты

On the criminal side, where the state is a necessary participant, the power of the prosecutor – this time the official representative of the executive branch in the courts – is even greater. The least dangerous branch has little control over what the prosecutor may do on his way to court and limited powers to control the forum itself.[27] Reliance on the good character of prosecutors, as Richelieu's example attests, is a weak defence. Here, too, the protection is primarily one of separation of powers. The Russian Constitution (Article 129, §§ 2–3) requires the agreement of both the president and the Council of the Federation for the appointment and removal of the Procurator-General; the top regional prosecutors are selected by the president and the Procurator-General with the agreement of the region; removal is the president's prerogative alone.

The removal of investigative powers from the Procuracy by a 2007 federal law creating a separate, insulated Investigative Committee, weakens even that relatively weak protection. The president 'directs the activities of the Investigative Committee' and has sole power to appoint and dismiss its Chairman without any legislative oversight at all.[28] Although the Russian criminal justice system embraces the doctrine of legality by which *all* plausible complaints of violation of law must be prosecuted, in reality what is a complaint worth investigating in Russia is now a presidential prerogative beyond the protection of any separation of powers that might remain there.

CONCLUSION

In his most recent study of Vladimir Putin, Vladimir Gel'man (2015: 81) asserts, 'All rulers in the world would like to govern their respective countries without checks and balances.' A consequence of such ambition, if sufficiently realised, is the Richelieu Effect. The erosion (or prevention) of robust separation of powers between governing institutions is possible because the foundations of justice are not hard marble,

---

Российской Федерации» (inserting Article 128.1 («Клевета») into the RF Criminal Code).

[27] In the United States, Justice Jackson's description of this power is famous, concluding: 'While the prosecutor at his best is one of the most beneficent forces in our society, when he acts from malice or other base motives, he is one of the worst' (Jackson 1940–1941: 3).

[28] Федеральный закон от 28 декабря 2010 г. N 403-ФЗ 'О Следственном комитете Российской Федерации,' Ст. 1(3) и Ст.13(2).

like the pillars or pediments of halls of justice. They are malleable human beings susceptible to pressure and temptation. This truth has long been known: 'Ambition must be made to counteract ambition. The interest of the man must be connected with the constitutional rights of the place' (Madison 1788).[29] Mikhail Gorbachev recognised this truth, too, as he struggled to install more robust separation of powers in a Soviet space that had categorically rejected it for as long as anyone could remember.[30] In Putin's Russia, the Richelieu Effect is not hard to detect in cases that matter to those in positions of sufficient power to exert their will on select cases before the judiciary.

At President Medvedev's last meeting with the Council, held on 28 April 2012, Medvedev referenced the Khodorkovsky case one last time:

> Secondly, very often we came back to cases that resonate but are isolated. We don't have to go far for examples: the criminal cases of Khodorkovsky, Magnitsky. In many cases this can be entirely justified but, on the whole, sometimes this created a feeling that the Council is interested only in the decision of problems in high profile, well publicized cases.
>
> With regard to that I would like to note the following. There is a much larger number of persons with respect to whom doubts arise as to their guilt in the commission of crimes or other circumstances of their cases. And you and I understand that pretty well.
>
> I received appeals from very different places, including, naturally, from behind bars. And there was one question: "Why do you deal with only several known cases, who is going to take care of us, of other prisoners, of those, who, let's say, believe that they suffered at the hands

---

[29] Madison (1788) continues: 'It may be a reflection on human nature, that such devices should be necessary to control the abuses of government. But what is government itself but the greatest of all reflections on human nature? If men were angels, no government would be necessary.'

[30] In his memoirs, Gorbachev notes his reluctance to intrude into the decision-making authority of the Constitutional Oversight Committee: 'The passivity of the committee was the source of many complaints, but I did not think I could interfere since I genuinely believed in the principle of separation of powers' (Gorbachev 1996: 324). Evidence that Gorbachev was sincere in expressing this belief may be taken from comments he made less than an hour after his inauguration as the first (and last) President of the Soviet Union on 15 March 1990: 'some stupid people believe that I need the presidency so that I can order people around ... If that was what I wanted I would have just remained general secretary and could have ordered people around for another ten or fifteen years!' (Brown 1996: 205).

of law enforcement agencies?" It seems to me, this is something to keep in mind even while understanding that some cases are symbolic and, probably, determine the general level of law and order in the country.[31]

A review of the transcript suggests that Khodorkovsky's name was mentioned only once more at that meeting, by Council member Mara Polyakova, who noted that the Council took up the Khodorkovsky and Magnitsky cases 'namely because their resonance helped to show, through their problems, those that exist in our judicial and law enforcement systems'.[32]

References
Anon (1744) *A Select Collection of Singular and Interesting Histories*. London.
Balmforth, T. (2013) 'Critics of Khodorkovsky verdict in Kremlin crosshairs', *Radio Free Eur/Radio Liberty*, 28 March, www.rferl.org/content/khodor kovsky-crime-trial/24940316.html.
BBC News (2007) 'New fraud charges in Yukos case', *BBC News*, 5 February.
Brown, A. (1996) *The Gorbachev Factor*. Oxford: Oxford University Press.
Dawisha, K. (2014) *Putin's Kleptocracy: Who Owns Russia?* New York: Simon and Schuster.
Der Spiegel (2013b) 'Bundesregierung verweigert Russland Kooperation im Fall Chodorkowski', *Der Spiegel*, 20 October.
(2013a) 'Exiled economic advisor: "Putin is afraid of the public"', *Der Spiegel*, 13 June.
Fournier, E. (1882) *L'Esprit dans l'Histoire: Recherches et Curiosités sur les Mots Historiques*. Paris: Dentu (4th edn).
Gel'man, V. (2015) *Authoritarian Russia: Analyzing Post-Soviet Regime Changes*. Pittsburgh: University of Pittsburgh Press.
Gorbachev, M. (1996) *Memoirs*. New York: Doubleday.
Gridasov, A. and Petelin, H. (2012) 'Yukos affair to be reconsidered: experts estimate Mikhail Khodorkovsky's chances to be set free as slim', *Izvestia*, 06 March (reproduced on Johnson's Russia List, # 42).

---

[31] http://president-sovet.ru/meeting_with_president_of_russia/vstrecha_soveta_s_prezi dentom_rf_d_medvedevym_28_04_2012_v_gorkakh/stenogramma/. Tamara Morshchakova does not appear to have attended the meeting. http://president-sovet.ru/ meeting_with_president_of_russia/vstrecha_soveta_s_prezidentom_rf_d_medvede vym_28_04_2012_v_gorkakh/uchastniki_zasedaniya/.
[32] http://president-sovet.ru/meeting_with_president_of_russia/vstrecha_soveta_s_prezi dentom_rf_d_medvedevym_28_04_2012_v_gorkakh/stenogramma/. Tamara Morshchakova does not appear to have attended the meeting. http://president-sovet.ru/ meeting_with_president_of_russia/vstrecha_soveta_s_prezidentom_rf_d_medvede vym_28_04_2012_v_gorkakh/uchastniki_zasedaniya/.

Gsovski, V. (1948) *Soviet Civil Law*. Ann Arbor: University of Michigan Law School.
Guriev, S. (2013) 'Why I am not returning to Russia', *New York Times*, 05 June.
Hamilton, A. (1788) 'The Judiciary Department', *The Federalist* # 78.
Hand, L. (1921) The Deficiencies of Trials to Reach the Heart of the Matter. New York: Lecture delivered before the Association of the Bar of the City of New York, 17 November.
  (1926) *3 Lectures on Legal Topics*. New York: Macmillan.
Henderson, J. (2011) *The Constitution of the Russian Federation: A Contextual Analysis*. Oxford: Hart.
Hoffman, D. E. (2011) *The Oligarchs: Wealth and Power in the New Russia*. New York: Public Affairs.
Interfax (2012a) 'Putin says there is no political content in Khodorkovsky case', *Interfax*, 07 March (reproduced on Johnson's Russia List, # 43).
  (2012b) 'Экспертиза дела "ЮКОСа"', *Interfax*, 01 April, www.interfax.ru/russia/238759.
  (2012c) 'Федотов о заявлении СК РФ по экспертизе дела ЮКОСа: "учите матчасть"', *Interfax*, 01 April, www.interfax.ru/news.asp?id=238756.
Jackson, R. H. (1940–1941) 'The federal prosecutor', *Journal of the American Institute of Criminal Law and Criminology*, 31(1): 3–6.
Kahn, J. (1999) *Federalism, Democratization, and the Rule of Law in Russia*. Oxford: Oxford University Press.
  (2013a) 'Freedom of expression in post-Soviet Russia', *Journal of International Law and Foreign Affairs*, 18.
  (2013b) 'In Putin's Russia, shooting the messenger', *New York Times*, 25 February.
  (2011) 'Report on the verdict against M. B. Khodorkovsky and P. L. Lebedev', *Journal of Eurasian Law*, 4(3): 321–332.
  (2010) 'The rule-of-law factor', in Newton, J. and Tompson, W. (eds.) *Institutions, Ideas and Leadership in Russian Politics*. Basingstoke: Palgrave Macmillan, 159–183.
  (2006) 'The search for the rule of law in Russia', *Georgetown Journal of International Law*, 37(2): 353–409.
Kamisar, Y. (1965) 'Equal justice in the gatehouses and mansions of American criminal procedure: from Powell to Gideon, from Escobedo to … ', in Howard, A. E. R. (ed.) *Criminal Justice in our Time*. Charlottesville: University of Virginia Press, 25–96.
Katkov, G. (1969) *The Trial of Bukharin*. New York: Stein and Day.
Kovalev, N. (2010) *Criminal Justice Reform in Russia, Ukraine, and the Former Republics of the Soviet Union*. Lampeter: Edwin Mellen Press.
Leutheusser-Schnarrenberger, S. (Rapporteur) (2009) *Document 11993, Report of the Committee on Legal Affairs and Human Rights*, 7 August, para. 99.

Linz, J. J. and Stepan, A. (1996) *Problems of Democratic Transition and Consolidation: Southern Europe, South America, and Post-Communist Europe*. Baltimore: The Johns Hopkins University Press.

Madison, J. (aka Publius) (1788) 'The structure of the government must furnish the proper checks and balances between the different departments', *The Federalist # 51*.

Medvedev, R. A. (1971) *Let History Judge: The Origins and Consequences of Stalinism*. New York: Columbia University Press.

Muižnieks, N. (2013) 'Report by the Commissioner for Human Rights of the Council of Europe, following his visit to the Russian Federation from 3 to 12 April 2013', *CommDH(2013)21*, 12 November, 42.

Nemtsova, A. (2010) 'Ella Pamfilova: a "hopeless cause"', *Newsweek* (International edition), 16 August.

Price, E. C. (1912) *Cardinal de Richelieu*. London: Methuen, 287–289.

RIA-Novosti (2010) 'Announcement of Khodorkovsky verdict postponed till Dec. 27', *Sputnik*, 15 December.

(2012) 'Kremlin experts deny taking Yukos money', *RIA-Novosti*, 01 April, 10.44 pm, http://en.ria.ru/russia/20120401/172538752.html.

Roberts, P. (2011) 'Does Article 6 of the European Convention on Human Rights require reasoned verdicts in criminal trials?' *Human Rights Law Review*, 11(2): 213–235.

Sakwa, R. (2014) *Putin and the Oligarch: The Khodorkovsky – Yukos Affair*. London: I.B. Tauris.

Schwirtz, M. (2012) 'Russian leader orders review of oil tycoon's conviction', *New York Times*, 06 March, A10.

Shevtsova, L. (2003) *Putin's Russia*. Washington, DC: Carnegie Endowment for International Peace.

Sputnik International (2013) 'Former Russian judge called in for questioning over Yukos', *Sputnik International*, 25 June, http://sputniknews.com/russia/20130625/181853411/Former-Russian-Judge-Called-In-for-Questioning-Over-Yukos.html.

Subbotin, M. (2013) 'Разбитые зеркала', *Gazeta.ru*, 8 February.

Trechsel, S. (2005) *Human Rights in Criminal Proceedings*. Oxford: Oxford University Press.

Treisman, D. (2013) 'Can Putin keep his grip on power?', *Current History*, 112 (756): 255.

White, G. L. (2013) 'Russia probes experts critical of oil baron trial', *Wall Street Journal*, 31 May.

Zheleznova (2013) 'Экспертов привлекли к делу ЮКОСа', *Ведомости (Vedomosti)*, 30 May.

CHAPTER ELEVEN

ADMINISTERIAL JUSTICE
Concluding Remarks on the Russian Legal Tradition

Marina Kurkchiyan and Agnieszka Kubal

Our basic intention in the way in which this book has been arranged is to introduce the reader to the multicoloured palette displayed by the provision of justice in Russia. The issues at stake in our collection of court cases range across several continuums: from the routine prosecution of petty criminals all the way to highly politicised cases swamped in publicity; from disagreements between neighbours about litter or noise to serious threats made by one business partner to another about the ownership of a considerable fortune; and from unpaid utility bills to the most serious life-or-death judgments determining the fate of the most vulnerable people, such as migrants or victims of trafficking. Beyond the display of this variation, we had a further goal in our compilation of such diverse case studies. We were aiming to trace a pattern in them and show how the legal institution really works in Russia. Furthermore, we hope that our case analyses will throw some light on the even deeper question of what law means in the Russian societal context.

The relationship between law and everyday life in Russia has evolved through many centuries, being shaped, reshaped and, on occasion, wholly transformed by radical political shifts. Contemporary ways of thinking, acting and feeling, both in relation to law and to society at large, cannot be understood without referring back to this intricate past. As is argued by Kurkchiyan, it is not helpful to treat the Russian legal tradition uncritically as one that belongs to the Romano-Germanic tradition while simultaneously placing it on the periphery of that tradition. The closeness of the two systems, Roman law and

Russian law, should not be allowed to obscure the differences between them and thereby distract us from gaining an understanding of Russian legal culture in its own right – a culture which has emerged from a complicated interplay between the original native customary law, the Roman law that was superimposed on it in early modern history, add-ons and modifications resulting from the extensive borrowing of Western forms and principles over subsequent centuries and the severe disruption caused by the lengthy twentieth-century experiment with communism. The result of all this is a legal culture that can be seen as one that contains similar forms to the Western traditional forms, with diverse meanings and identical meanings expressed in different forms. The contributions to this volume allow us to see specific examples of how this works out in the various sectors of law.

THE INDISTINCT BOUNDARIES OF THE REALM OF LAW

Tracing the evolution of the law through history, Kurkchiyan argues that, in the Russian legal tradition, there is no accumulated experience of a full-hearted professionalisation of law and no formation of a sufficiently autonomous legal institution that could claim 'ownership' over law. Such a development would require a consolidated group of professionals who would stake out their own social space by setting up a visible social purpose, taking control of a field of knowledge, cultivating a set of shared values, agreeing to a code of conduct, developing a specialised language, adopting distinctive symbols and safeguarding their group's boundaries. An institutional structure has unquestionably been in place since Imperial times, albeit with some ups and downs. It consists of a constitutionally defined structure of courts, provision for legal education, qualifications for lawyers and a judiciary that is expected to act independently. Yet there has never been a period in Russian history in which legal actors managed to monopolise the interpretation and implementation of law and project their own norms and professional standards effectively. Today, law in Russia is still midway between a 'lay' conception and a professionalised form. This state of affairs has important implications for the public perception of law, for inter-institutional relationships within the Russian polity and for the law's capacity to resist external meddling in its affairs.

In the general legal culture, the 'lay' notion of law is deemed to produce popular distrust and an incurable cynicism in relation to the delivery of justice and to all the legal actors involved in the process. Such an attitude was strongly expressed in the focus groups conducted by Hendley. Faced with a consumer dispute, people would dismiss the idea of consulting a lawyer unless the lawyer happened to be a trusted friend. If law is not seen as a professional matter, it becomes a mere text that can be interpreted by any literate person. The effect is not only that everyone becomes confident in his or her judgment of what a lawful outcome ought to look like, but is also that doubt is cast on any formal judgment that happens to not correspond to their expectation. Evidence of such confidence has also been observed in Hendley's focus groups. Pointing out the 'skin deep' knowledge of her focus group members about whatever legal issue was under discussion, she reports how lay participants became energetically engaged in a lengthy debate on the legal nuances of consumer rights and the issue of the burden of proof. She relates how people self-confidently offered advice on how to build a case and suggested what kind of evidence would or would not work in court. Hendley observed how 'The participants did not hesitate to put forward their views of the law as gospel.' She quotes a woman, aged 56, who was challenged on her interpretation of a particular law and responded 'This is not my opinion; it is the law.'

Andrianova exposes the lack of appreciation of the legal aid in most of the cases heard by Justices of the Peace, and the preference instead for relying on informal communication with the judges. Popova tells us about the ease with which journalists wander across the boundary between reporting and the legal domain when they describe issues that are properly a matter for legal investigation and judicial determination. She reminds us of 'the Russian media's general disregard for the difference between allegations and established facts'. The bizarre involvement of language experts in libel cases is clear evidence of the blurred boundaries between professional and lay takes on law. Within this mindset, there is no room for the delegation of decision-making to legal actors or the decisive exercise of judicial discretion. The very concept of 'expertise' becomes inapplicable in such a social environment. The pattern of amateurish involvement in the courtroom results in an atmosphere in which the legitimacy of the institution of justice itself comes into question, and the 'negative myth' about law becomes a dominant view: the belief that law cannot be relied upon to work in Russia and therefore that justice is never delivered.

Analytically, it is clear that it is the ramshackle nature of the fence around the legal domain that prevents the legal institution from gaining strength and developing its resistance to external influence. The lawyers' professional associations have never managed to raise the threshold that entrants to the profession have to step over – if, indeed, there is any threshold at all. In this 'open door' context, described by Kurkchiyan, we should not be surprised by the patent unevenness in the distribution of legal resources across the institution. As Andrianova points out, low-quality support, or no support at all, is available to ordinary people in the great majority of cases that go to the lower courts. However, a powerful contrast to that situation can be seen in the Arbitrazh Court, scrutinised by Bocharov and Titaev. This court displays a high level of legal sophistication in dealing with the contractual and large-scale financial disputes that make up its case load. Of course, the concentration of expertise at the well-paid end of the spectrum of legal services is common, and can be found in any society anywhere. What is distinctive is the strong probability of coming across a lawyer who is formally qualified but who, nevertheless, lacks the requisite skills and most of the basic knowledge. As Kurkchiyan was told by respondents during her research on this topic, the inability of the professional groups to exert a monopoly over legal services, combined with the unregulated entry into their profession, prevents Russian lawyers as a group from building up the binding common identity that they need.

However, as Kurkchiyan suggests, the degree of institutional build-up should be assessed in historical perspective. The stretch of time over which the professionalisation of law has been underway in Russia has been short. From this point of view, the achievements are significant: legal education is regulated and the standard is improving; the bar is being extended and strengthened continuously, if slowly; and, as Bocharov and Titaev report, the appreciation of legal professionalism is firming up in the highly influential economic sector. Our analysis indicates that the need for professionalism is starting to be more appreciated by laypeople and their reliance on a lawyer for advice is increasing. This perception is made clear in the interviews conducted by Andrianova and in the focus group discussions reported by Hendley. People really do want good advice, even though, as one focus group participant pointed out, most people are likely not to trust any one lawyer and will seek the opinion of several of them before making up their mind.

Such is the situation at present. Whether the Russian legal tradition will continue to evolve towards greater professionalism, what particular forms the interplay between the 'lay' and the 'professional' consumption of law will take and how long it will be before Russian law is fully professionalised, if ever, remain open questions.

INSTITUTIONAL VULNERABILITY

Any major social institution that is not sufficiently professionalised is predestined to have weak internal resistance against external interference. This should not be interpreted as an assertion that interference is indeed explicit, still less that it is inevitable or common. There is no empirical verification to support such an assertion. On the contrary, as the various authors of this volume have demonstrated with their disciplined observations, the outcomes of most cases are far from predictable. In particular, Bocharov and Titaev, after watching high-stake economic disputes pass through the courts, are very doubtful that the common stereotype of the courts being corrupt has any empirical grounding. They point out that a number of institutional arrangements combine to make extralegal influences most unlikely. The examples they give are the geographic locations of courts within the Arbitrazh hierarchy and the financial security and high prestige of the judges. On the other hand, in the numerous mundane cases that the courts deal with on a daily basis, external intervention would not make sense because there is so little to be gained.

Despite this, a close analysis of the data that the authors of this volume collected for the full range of criminal, administrative and civil cases in the main structure of the institution of justice does reveal various forms of institutional bias that need to be explained. Examining the outcomes of libel cases in Russian courts, Popova convincingly argues that there is no indication that decisions favour litigants who have an affiliation to the political party in power. However, the data do reveal a rather different bias, one towards people with strong personal connections that might give them access to so-called administrative resources. At the opposite end of the social spectrum, Kubal studied how the Russian legal system deals with people who have no resources of any kind whatsoever: immigrants, of which Russia has the world's third-largest group. She reports that judges rely heavily on the documents contained in the files presented to them, without proper questioning of either whatever is in any particular document or, still less, of the migrants themselves. There is, of course, a vastly asymmetric power relationship between the state law enforcement agency and the migrants, so whatever goes into the file determines the outcome. Kubal suggests that this explains the strongly predictable pattern that she observed in case outcomes: the judgment usually goes against the migrant.

Solomon, on the basis of a comparative scrutiny of various jurisdictions, points out that the low rate of acquittals in Russian courts is not, in itself, an indicator of accusatorial bias in Russian criminal justice. The rate is in line with some other Western countries. However, if, in the West, a low rate of acquittal is the result of a pre-trial assessment of the strength of evidence by the prosecutors, in Russia the pre-trial machinery has a different internal institutional logic. Solomon points to some of the pre-trial procedures, such as the practice of plea bargaining, that have little or nothing to do with pre-trial filtering in terms of critical examination of the evidence. Also, although the Western and Russian numbers might end up close together, the statistics are not comparable in substance. As Solomon demonstrates, low acquittals in criminal cases in the Russian courts *do* amount to an accusatorial bias, explained by the inter-institutional relationships between investigators, prosecutors and judges.

However, the most visible and least subtle problem in Russian court cases arises when the legal institution suffers from the 'Richelieu Effect', as Khan puts it when referring to cases in which a highly placed politician steps in to ensure the preferred outcome. Such cases are rarer, in fact, than Russia's shady reputation might suggest, but it is definitely the case that, when they occur, there are no countervailing institutional forces in the system, such as a sense of professional autonomy, identity and integrity among the lawyers and judges, to resist the corroding interference.

If the incomplete nature of the professionalisation of law within the Russian legal tradition is viewed within a societal context, it can also be seen as a reflection of a broader political tradition. In Russia there is insufficient separation and balance between the major branches of power – executive, legislative and judicial. Looking back over history, Russia has never experienced a redistribution of power between these institutions on a scale that would create a system of mutual checks and balances. Once again, we observe that the crucial issue in contemporary politics boils down to the question: What direction is Russia taking?

In contemporary Russia, a separation of powers is now set out constitutionally, and a set of reforms aimed at creating a basic legal framework that will achieve this outcome is formally in place. The judicial branch has effectively been upgraded in status. In particular, the remuneration and working conditions are now such that judges ought to be able to act independently and the authority of the institution of justice is being steadily reinforced. However, on the other hand, as Khan shows us, several badly distorted cases in recent years did take place and they reveal incontestable political interference in the delivery of justice. Such cases are few in number but the damage is significant. Regardless of the actual guilt or innocence of the accused in these cases, the visible evidence that powerful forces are at play sends a warning message right across the entire legal system. This frustrates everyone involved and inhibits the development of a fully autonomous internal legal culture that underpins the way the law works in practice. As long as politicians can pervert the course of justice, they block any growth in the public's appreciation of the law as a common good to be rightly protected by the professionals who serve it. The effect is that the autonomy that is necessary to support the authority of the institution of justice cannot be taken for granted.

THE FILE-DRIVEN PROCEDURE

One of the clear themes that flows through all the chapters in this volume is the role of case files in handling litigations; the default position of any Russian court seems to be to rely on written documents. As Kurkchiyan points out, this phenomenon is not a contemporary development nor even a legacy from Soviet times. The use of written papers as the sole basis for a court judgment goes back in history, when the earliest judges were essentially restricted to a clerical role. Their job was to write down all the testimonies and then send the whole set to a superior, who would make a judgment. Imperial courts were also in the habit of treating their civil service files as true representations of the facts, without much questioning. One can speculate that this side of the Russian legal tradition is the result of the absence of professional lawyers in the process. Without active lawyers in court – who could challenge the files, bring in other factual material, cross-examine witnesses in open court, and then argue in defence of the truthfulness of evidence that contradicts the files – the logical and easy solution for a judge is to take whatever is written in the file as solid 'evidence'.

The practice of file dependency was observed in close detail by Kubal and constitutes the basis for one of the main arguments in her contribution. She tells us about migrants who are unlucky enough to be accused of minor administrative violations and have to face the unshakeable faith of judges in the integrity of the officers in the migration service. Their protocols and reports on immigration raids sit unchallenged on the judges' desks, regardless of how (un)believable and (un)reliable the evidence contained in those files might be. Kubal infers from her observations in court that, in Russia, 'proof' is normally limited to formal documentary evidence. Even an appeal to a higher court on the procedural grounds that a file has been inadequately considered would most probably fail because the judge at the appeal hearing also takes whatever is in the file at face value. Kubal cites the case of a migrant from Uzbekistan who was photographed at a particular address during a raid, and the picture was submitted as proof that he was living there. His defence was that he merely happened to have visited the place that day. His poor command of the Russian language, however, prevented him from making sense of a document that he was pressed into signing without explanation. In court, he was not listened to and no attempt was made to check the accuracy of the evidence presented in the file.

The theme of 'paper evidence' as a decisive factor in judicial decision-making is also picked up by Popova in libel cases, leading her to conclude that 'The typical defamation case in Russia revolves around the collection of written documents ... court documents, linguistic experts, medical opinions and psychologists' reports'. In her observations, this procedure significantly reduces the capacity of a reporter to produce 'concrete' proof in their defence, while the usually well-connected plaintiff has no difficulty in building up a 'convincing' file. For instance, medical notes on high blood pressure, loss of appetite and sleep deterioration will be accepted as proof of emotional suffering. This finding would then be translated into significant financial damages. The only evidence that might succeed in showing that the report in question was well grounded would be a prior court decision on it.

Reliance on written documents is also apparent in criminal cases. A guilty or innocent verdict depends heavily on the content of the file that ends up in front of the judge. While probing what is meant in practice by a plea of guilty and examining how it tends to be achieved, Solomon comments that whatever may have happened before the trial, the existence of a plea simplifies the role of the judge. Plea agreements have been available in Russian pre-trial proceedings since 2001, and judges are obliged to work with the file and check that it contains the supporting 'evidence' without the need to question it. If an agreed plea of guilty is in the file, conviction follows automatically. If, however, the case becomes complicated and no straightforward document can be produced as evidence, as often happens in cases involving organised groups engaged in human trafficking, judges tend to ignore the obvious facts unless they are duly recorded. They often dismiss arguments made by prosecutors about the aggravating factors of group actions, as McCarthy illustrates with the case from Saransk.

One could argue that it is the weight given to the volume of the text, rather than to its content, that allowed the judge in the Khodorkovsky case to produce a verdict of 689 pages, but as Khan grasped in the course of a careful reading of the judgement, that judge did not provide a factual reason for his decision. Instead of bringing in what a Western observer would accept as factual evidence, the judgement offered an assertion of fact without linking it to any piece of evidence. The reasoning behind the judgment was explained by reference to another lengthy document, the indictment. In a number of places, the text was simply copied by the cut-and-paste technique.

Could this way of writing a judgment be explained by the intrusion of powerful political forces into the legal game? Probably not. After all, politically determined judgments do not need to be so obviously of poor quality by Western standards. Besides, the cut-and-paste technique of justifying a decision is an established practice in Russian courts. As an indicator of the superior professional qualifications of the kind of lawyers who are typically involved in commercial cases, Bocharov and Titaev tell us that judges in the Arbitrazh courts routinely ask lawyers to send them an electronic version of their arguments so that they can cut and paste helpful passages into their verdict. Nevertheless, it must be emphasised that the habit of giving priority to the file despite the presence of a disconnection between the evidence it contains and the factual evidence in the case obviously leaves the institution of justice vulnerable to unrestricted manipulation, if politics should choose to step in.

Hendley's records of a series of focus group debates show that, in Russia, the public understands very well the need for a written document in order to advance a case, regardless of how absurd the request for any particular document might be. In one example involving a hypothetical consumer dispute in which the store refuses to take back a faulty product, a discussant with experience of litigation noted how difficult it would be to prepare the case. She explained that before the case could be accepted for a hearing, the court would require evidence in the form of a written defence by the store about its refusal to take back the item. The effect of that would be a catch-22 situation: without a written document there could be no court case, and without a court case there could be no pressure to produce the document. This explains why the people interviewed by Andrianova said that they would take great care to take instruction directly from the Justice of the Peace in order to make quite sure that their case file contained all the paperwork that the judge might need as evidence.

EXTREME FORMALISM

A characteristic Russian pattern of thinking about what law is and how it should be applied emerges from all the cases presented in this volume. The manner in which the law is interpreted is formalistic in the extreme; law in practice is expected to be equated with the letter of the law. In other words, the characteristic Russian vision of law does not allow space for interpretations that would give prominence not so much to what the law actually says, as to what its makers intended to bring about, with an appreciation that any given legal principle or stipulation should be adjusted to fit the circumstances. However, in extreme formalism, the legal space of law is restricted to the law as it is written down. It is assumed that if the law is a good law, it must be applicable to any relevant circumstances just as it is written; when the time comes to implement the law there can be no legitimate requirement for flexibility or adjustment. It follows that there is very limited provision for a judge to exercise discretion and adapt the content of the law to the specific circumstances of a particular situation, as judges do in many other jurisdictions.

The reluctance of judges to exercise any discretion and to take responsibility for an interpretation of the law that would go beyond the letter of the text is evidenced in the chapters by Kubal, Popova and McCarthy. They report on cases as diverse as the deportation of economic migrants in administrative courts, libel suits in civil courts and charges of human trafficking in criminal courts. The most common strategy of judicial decision-making is to match, as strictly as possible, whatever evidence is available to the judge to the conditions as they are prescribed in the legal code.

The flaw in this technique is, of course, that real life is too complex and messy to be tidily squeezed into the rigid frame of any legal code, however well drafted. In real life there is always a need to interpret both law and evidence, but as Kubal, in particular, found out, such an approach occurs only on the rarest of occasions. However, when there is an undeniable need for at least some interpretation of the evidence, as there is in many libel cases, 'experts' such as linguists are called in. Their task is to provide the grounds to which the judge can refer when she or he is assembling the reasons for his or her judgment. In this way the judges are relieved of any duty to use their own professional instinct and straightforward common sense to interpret whether a given phrase is incriminating or whether a statement is a passive opinion or an active assertion. As Popova notes, this system of relying on expert witnesses is clearly a self-protective measure that allows the judges to be seen as objective and guided by law. She further points out that the requirement to operate within such a restricted legal space diminishes the option of using value-based reasoning, such as 'the public interest' or 'the common good'. These arguments have no legitimacy in the positivistic formalism of judicial decision-making and are not used in Russian libel cases. As a consequence, both free speech and investigative journalism are effectively unprotected.

When it comes to the interpretation of new laws, as happened when legislation criminalising human trafficking was passed in 2003, the reluctance of judges to use discretion and to offer novel interpretations has prevented the legislation from serving the purpose for which it was introduced. McCarthy points out that the lack of judicial willingness to step outside the comfort zone of simply matching the evidence to the legal code has resulted in a watering down of the new legislation.

Even so, to put the Russian attitudes towards judicial decision-making in perspective, it should be recalled that there is a tendency towards formalism right across Continental Europe and all the way to the shores of the English Channel. The common-law tradition works quite differently. However, it does seem that Russia has developed an extreme regime of formalism under which judicial discretion and a 'soft law' approach to reasoning come close to being perceived as illegitimate and are seen as too risky to be exercised.

ADMINISTERIAL TRIALS

The possible models of trial that are known, discussed and contrasted in relation to courtroom trials in Western jurisdictions in both common-law and continental-law traditions come down to two: the adversarial and the inquisitorial. They differ in the role repertoires of the actors during the hearing and the character of the interactions in the courtroom. In the adversarial model, the judge takes up the role of impartial and independent arbiter whose responsibilities are to safeguard the principles of fairness and equality. The respective representatives of the parties (prosecutor and defendant in criminal cases and litigants in civil cases) take up the active roles and argue their cases in order to uncover the truth. It is the responsibility of the two parties, not of the judge, to determine what points to raise, what evidence to produce, what arguments to put forward and which witnesses to bring in. In the inquisitorial model, by contrast, the judge becomes the central figure. He has an active role in posing questions, requesting evidence and using the court procedure to dig out the truth. Despite the differences in procedural technique between the two models, the end goal is the same. The courtroom is the forum where the truth is expected to be revealed and fully explained before sentence is passed.

In respect of its formal procedures, Russian courtroom practice has been following Western principles, shifting from one model to the other over different historical periods. Although the late Imperial courts began to endorse adversarial procedures in their final decades, Soviet practices were defined as inquisitorial. Thereafter, post-Soviet reforms brought adversarial procedural requirements back into most courtrooms. However, a careful reading of the case studies gathered in this volume tends to cast doubt on whether the actual practices really conform to either of the classic models, or even to a combination of them. In-depth empirical examination of courts suggests a different pattern, more in line with the Russian tradition of the role played by the judge. This is not to deny that elements of both adversarial and inquisitorial models are present in Russian courts today, but to argue instead, that the native model, one that could be described as the 'administerial' model of a trial, is the dominant form in Russian courtrooms most of the time.

Earlier, we commented on the patterns in Russian courts of file-driven procedures, the heavy use of administrative records as evidence, the reluctance of the judiciary to question the content of a case file even when the 'evidence' included in it is doubtful and the tendency to minimise discretion. Almost all the researchers who have contributed to this volume have made the point that the judges do not lead an inquiry to get to the bottom of their cases, as they would be expected to do under the inquisitorial model. However, at the same time, the lawyers in the same courtroom do not have the necessary procedural infrastructure and opportunity to make their case and engage in the fierce arguments that are fundamental if the adversarial rules of the game are to apply. The file-reliance mentality of the judges discourages adversarial confrontation. In addition, the inadequate professionalism of many of the lawyers working at the less lucrative end of the court spectrum does not equip them to lead the process. This situation applies to the majority of criminal cases and also to non-economic civil disputes.

How, then, should we interpret what actually happens in a typical Russian courtroom, in terms of the legal role performance of the actors and the interactions between them? To address this question, it is helpful to survey the case studies contributed to this volume with a view to exploring the meaning of a 'trial' within the entire process of legal procedure.

Studying the cases coming before a selection of Justices of the Peace, Andrianova observed that there were two stages in procedure: an informal one, followed by a much stricter formal trial. The informal pre-trial stage, which is a legitimate part of the overall process, allows for an unlimited number of meetings between the litigant and the judge. In the same manner as one might visit any government department office with a request or complaint, people can go to the courthouse to talk to the judge. In so doing, the litigants can get advice on the merits of the issue, discover what documents they need to add to the file, and also build the kind of personal relationship with the judge that is widely considered to be important for success in a formal trial. These informal sessions are noted in the file but no transcript of the conversation is provided. At this stage, the judge performs multiple roles: that of adviser, of educator, of mediator as a go-between, of mediator for reconciliation and – bizarrely – of the clerk who keeps the file up to date. Meanwhile, the judge familiarises herself with the case and its participants long before it reaches the courtroom.

At the next stage the case moves into a courtroom and is rigidly choreographed by the formal rules of due process. However, in spite of the ritualistic format of the trial, Andrianova's respondents told her that most cases are not decided in the courtroom. Usually the judge already has in mind what the verdict will be. Indeed, more often than not, the judge comes to the hearing with a draft of the judgment fully prepared so that it can be read out in public. In this scenario, the courtroom becomes the forum where the case is aired formally and the verdict is officially announced. The courtroom, then, is not the place where the truth is unearthed; that will have been determined at the pre-trial stage. The courtroom endows the judgment with legitimacy.

In various district and regional courts, Kubal witnessed the hearing of appeals against earlier judgments that had been brought to court by migrants from former Soviet countries. In this category, only one party was present and the procedure was expected to be inquisitorial. However, Kubal tells us that the judge tended not to question the evidence presented in the file. The objections of the appealing party did not lead to any attempt by the judge to determine the facts, with the effect that most of the appeals were rejected. It seems that what was happening in the courtroom was mainly a final authorisation of the findings that had been established in the earlier stages of fact collection.

Solomon has identified much the same way of determining the truth in the pre-trial stage in criminal cases, which are nevertheless officially supposed to identify the truth by holding the trial in adversarial style. He points out that most cases that reach a criminal court have already passed along an elaborate journey: investigation, prosecutor assessments with the case being sent back and forth for further investigations, negotiations, plea bargaining, etc. Cases that reach the court are assumed to be already in a shape such that the judge can feel confident in approving the work that has been done in the pre-trial stage. The judge has only to confirm the conviction and decide on the strength of the punishment. Within the institution, the public trial itself is not perceived as a definitive search for the truth. It is seen more as a way to evaluate the structures that have been putting the case together before it comes to court.

In other words, the Russian view is that the responsibility to deliver justice is not performed by hearings in a courtroom but accumulated gradually through the various stages of law enforcement. It starts when the police or another administrative agency forms a suspicion and begins to investigate, and continues through the several phases by which the procuracy are eventually persuaded that it makes sense to trigger court proceedings. The courtroom in this administerial model is merely the final point in the chain.

McCarthy also sees justice as a slowly developing product of the institutional interdependency of structures within the institution of law enforcement. Examining the ongoing attempt to co-ordinate outputs at each level, she explains how easy it is for the procurators and judges to slide into conservative and well-tested interpretations of the new laws on human trafficking when, in theory, they could devise and apply more appropriate and forward-looking ways that would actually fulfil the intention of the legislation. Khan, too, shows that, in politically charged cases, no serious attempt is made to test facts and find out the truth.

The procedures used in the Arbitrazh courts are distinctive and deserve special attention. Bocharov and Titaev comment that litigations of major economic disputes are run in an indisputably adversarial format. Yet, as their research reveals, only a small number of the cases can be described as genuine economic conflicts in the full sense of the term. For the rest of the time, the courtrooms are used for purposes far removed from fact-finding missions and the delivery of justice. For example, both state entities and private corporations sometimes file court cases in the Arbitrazh courts in order to produce bureaucratic records for internal use, to report to the tax authorities, to demonstrate the high productivity of the company's legal department or to use a particular judgment as a guarantee for the fulfilment of the contract in future (although that contract is not disputed), or, in effect, to delegate to the court the task of regulating the flow of insignificant and unchallenged administrative penalties. In other words, in addition to the purpose that judges serve in any Western jurisdiction, their opposite numbers in the Russian economic courts spend a significant proportion of their time on straightforward administrative matters.

Taken together, these observations from different corners of the Russian institution of justice lay a solid foundation on which to build an argument that, within this legal tradition, the meaning of a courtroom and the purpose that it actually serves cannot be fully understood when looked at through the lens of Western expectations of law. Contrasting Russian courtrooms with Western models of fact-finding and truth-determining can easily and consistently result in a frustrated and critical conclusion. Instead, it might be more productive to acknowledge that the traditionally developed administerial model for delivering justice exists and is routinely used. This acknowledgement would first require a reconceptualisation of the entire delivery of justice in Russia, complete with a better understanding of the place of non-judicial structures in determining the final outcome.

ADMINISTERIAL COURT ROUTINE

The administerial model of justice delivery and the image that it projects to people who happen to go to court have shaped the daily routine of the Russian courts. Bureaucracy is an integral part of that model. As Hendley's data suggest, the time and energy required to satisfy the court's bureaucratic appetite for paperwork form a significant deterrent to ordinary people who might otherwise decide to use litigation to resolve their disputes and remedy their grievances. As one of her informants put it, one would need the strength of 'reinforced concrete' to survive the tedious ordeal. Ethnographic observations by Andrianova provide confirmation of these focus group remarks. She paints a vivid picture of the public's experience of the Justices of the Peace courts, where more than 90 per cent of all cases are initiated. She describes lengthy periods of waiting in the low-ceilinged, windowless corridors of undistinguished buildings that were built for residential purposes but are now used as courthouses. She notes that the necessity of making a number of visits to the court before a trial can actually leave people with the impression that they are dealing with a tedious government department, such as a visa office or a driver licencing agency. This image is reinforced by the absence of proper clerical support for the courts, which adds the performance of clerical tasks to the judicial role of the Justices of the Peace.

Kubal observed a similar pattern in the district and regional courts at one level up, although in a better organised environment. She was puzzled to discover a practice of overbooking, in which two or three cases are routinely scheduled for the same time slot just in case one party does not show up. In fact, most people do show up most of the time. This creates long and frustrated queues in corridors. As one would expect in such circumstances, the comments of the frustrated users extend to the entire system of the delivery of justice.

Even in the very different case discussed by Khan, a highly politicised criminal trial, the procedural tedium of hearing the final judgment is inescapable. One can only imagine the atmosphere in the courtroom during the hours in which the judge reads out his excessively long judgment. Typically the judge rushes through it at breathless speed, never pausing, never looking up and not expecting the listeners to follow the reasoning behind his verdict – which, as Khan demonstrates, was not necessarily there in the first place.

However, this picture contrasts with the much more efficient Arbitrazh courts, a new branch of the legal system which has emerged in response to market need and which is not burdened by the legacy of the past. As reported in the Bacharev and Titaev study, the Arbitrazh courts are run efficiently, are well supported by their clerical staff and make full use of contemporary technology. Necessary information is easily accessible, the filing of a case can be done online and the entire process is transparent. The authors convincingly argue that this sharp contrast with the other courts is a reflection of the tension between an established mindset that is deeply rooted in the past and the newly emerging market-oriented attitude. If this analysis is correct, then there is a contemporary battle within the Russian legal culture between traditional and newly injected influences, swinging back and forth. Bacharev and Titaev do express concern that the trend nowadays is back towards the more traditional practices. However, at this stage of institution-building, it is difficult to predict which set of forces are likely to take over the evolving Russian legal culture in the future.

*****

In conclusion, what can we make of the peculiarities of Russian legal practice? The conventional way to answer this question is to judge the institution by contrasting it with the Western model. From this viewpoint, a Western-minded observer can point out that the judiciary is weak, conservative and formalistic in interpreting the law, that the courtrooms are not used to determine the truth and are not the place where justice is served, only the place in which it is published. They can point out that file logic requires an unjustifiable reliance on the pre-trial fact findings, that the institution is not sufficiently autonomous and is vulnerable to different forms of implicit and, in politicised cases, explicit biases, that the legal profession is not regulated and that the quality of service it provides is uneven and that, overall, with only a few exceptions, a Russian court behaves as if it were just another government department. This viewpoint carries the expectation that, if the Russian legal system is to be approved of, it must work in line with the Western model and, moreover, that it is possible to convert it to the Western model if the right reforms are passed and enforced.

However, to put on glasses containing Western lenses while looking at the Russian legal landscape would be a mistake. It would obscure various important facts. These include the fact that the outcome of each case is far from being predetermined, that justice is delivered most of the time, that there is no basis for the assumption that the case files and pre-trial assessments on which the judges rely so persistently are inaccurate most of the time and that the lawyers are generally incompetent (some are quite the opposite, even though their profession is not yet consolidated and the culture of law is not fully professionalised).

An alternative approach is to examine the internal logic of the Russian model of delivering justice, which can be done by adopting a standpoint *inside* the system. This requires the viewer to re-examine three things: the meanings behind the familiar forms, the role repertoire of the whole set of legal actors and the functions of the various structures in the overall system. With this re-examination achieved, we arrive at what is tentatively called the 'administerial' model. Under this model, the importance neither of the judiciary nor of the courtroom process should be overstated. Instead, if we direct intense attention to the pre-trial stages, the empirical observations reported throughout this book make sense.

As to judging the administerial model, the first question to be asked is not whether it is a good model or a bad one but how it works. Once this question is answered, it is reasonable to consider which aspects of it might realistically be changed in order to improve it. This whole approach is based on the principal finding of this book, which is that the administerial model exists in Russia, that it functions on its own terms and that it is the result not of any one design or political regime but of a complex interplay, over hundreds of years, between established native practices and intrinsic mentality and imported Western forms and principles. It is the product of the evolution of the local legal tradition and, as such, is rooted deeply in Russian history and culture. If we accept that the administerial system is likely to be here to stay, then the task of any reformer would have to be to review the entire process of building a case and to look for ways to improve the contribution of each substructure to the accumulation of facts found and file-building.

Finally, several features of the legal situation should be borne in mind: the legal culture is evolving, probably faster now than ever before, the professionalisation of the legal institution is building up and is clearly in line with Western development, the process of global integration is taking place continuously and inexorably and is having an influence in Russia, even if international conventions on topics such as human rights are resisted by the government and, overall, it is certain that these processes are slowly pushing the Russian legal tradition closer to the Western model. Nevertheless, despite this trend, the question of whether it will eventually result in squeezing out the administerial model and replacing it with the more familiar Western model of the delivery of justice is still an open question. History tells us that, in Russia, the traditional stream of legal culture has remained strong in the face of greater challenges than it now has to deal with. It is, therefore, likely that the administerial model will continue to dominate society and, under pressure from reformist measures, it will probably improve its own logic and procedures. However, as yet, we cannot be sure of this – for anyone interested in Russia, there will continue to be much to study.

INDEX

academic freedom, expert testimony and, 148–149
Academy of Science, 19
accusatorial bias, 9, 190–193
  criminal justice and, 170–197, 263–264
  Lebedev, V., and, 175–176
  Medvedev and, 175–176
acquittal rates, 9, 170–171, 185–191, 196, 227
  adversarial systems and, 170–171
  Canada and, 177–178, 189
  Europe and, 171, 180–182
  France and, 180–183, 189
  Germany and, 180–182, 189
  glasnost and, 170, 174
  human trafficking cases and, 219–220
  inquisitorial systems and, 170–171
  Japan and, 171, 189
  judges and, 173
  jury trials and, 190
  Netherlands, 180–182
  personal accusation cases and, 174
  post-Soviet countries and, 173
  pre-trial screenings and, 9–10, 171, 176–183, 264
  rehabilitative reasons, cases stopped for, and, 174–175
  Russia, Soviet, and, 171–174
  Sweden and, 189–190
  UK and, 171, 178
acquittals, conservatism and, 218
administrative cases, Justice of the Peace courts and, 70, 72
administrative independence, Arbitrazh courts and, 121
administrative resources
  defamation cases and, 156, 161–165, 167–168, 263
  moral compensation and, 165
administrative staff, Arbitrazh courts and, 131
adversarial systems, 183
  acquittal rates and, 170–171
  Imperial courts and, 270
  judges and, 270
Advocacy Act, 30–31

advocacy bar, 262. *See also advokatura*
  Arbitrazh courts and, 130–131
  identity and, 35, 262
  judicial reforms, 1864 and, 19–20
  Russia, Soviet, and, 21
advocates, criminal cases and,130. *See also* Colleges of Accusers and Defenders; colleges of advocates; Colleges of Defenders; private advocates
advokatura. See also colleges of advocates
  informal norms and, 32–35
  lawyers practicing outside of, 31–32
  normative vision of, 35–36
  professionalisation, post-Soviet Russian and, 29–35
  Russia, Soviet, and, 24
  self-governance and, 29
affidavits, immigration cases and, 93, 101–105, 113
aggravating factors, human trafficking laws and, 214–216. *See also* organised groups
appeals
  Arbitrazh courts and, 125–126, 134
  CAO and, 99
  courtroom proceedings and, 272
  human trafficking cases and, 214
  humanitarian logic and, 108–112, 115
  immigration cases and, 100–116, 272
  judges and, 219–220, 223–224
  Justice of the Peace courts and, 80
  Khodorkovsky case and, 235
Arbitrazh courts, 274–275. *See also* Economic Chamber of the Supreme Court; Gosarbitrazh; Supreme Arbitrazh Court
  administrative independence and, 121
  administrative staff and, 131
  advocacy bar and, 130–131
  appeals and, 125–126, 134
  architecture and, 131–132
  case file logic and, 267
  caseloads and, 123–124, 126–127
  commercial disputes and, 7–8, 118–139
  contractual petty disputes and, 124–126
  corruption and, 133–135, 263

INDEX

courtroom proceedings and, 273
courts of general jurisdiction and, 121–122, 131–133
court-users and, 131–132, 136
culture of, 132–133
delays and, 132
evidence and, 131
financial independence and, 121
financial value of cases in, 124, 126–128, 135
formalism and, 132–133
information technology and, 121–122, 139, 274–275
institutional structure of, 119–122
judges and, 130–131, 135
judicial independence and, 7–8, 118, 128–129
jurisdiction and, 120–123
justice for business and, 136–139
lawyers and, 130
origin of, 119–120
outcomes in, 128–129
precedents introduced by, 136–139
professionalisation and, 262
professionalism and, 130–131, 139
random distribution of cases in, 134–135
records of proceedings and, 132
Russian Federation territorial structure, outside of, 120–121
specialisation and, 131
state, disputes with and, 126–129
state and, 123
state entities and, 124–125, 138
substantive commercial cases and, 129–133
summary proceedings and, 127–128
architecture
   Arbitrazh courts and, 131–132
   courts of general jurisdiction and, 131–132
   Justice of the Peace courts and, 73–75, 274
asylum-seekers
   deportation, 108
   humanitarian logic and, 108–112
   labour and, 108
authoritarian regimes, lawyers and, 17

Berman, H.J., 16
bias, defamation cases and, 162–165, 263. *See also* accusatorial bias
Blumberg, A., 94, 113
Bourdieu, P., 12, 37
Brundage, J.A., 14
bureaucracy, justice, administerial model of, and, 274. *See also* state bureaucratic institutions
byudzhetniki
   defamation cases and, 156–159, 161–165
   moral compensation and, 160–161, 165
Byzantium, Kiev Rus' and, 15–16

Canada. *See also R. v Boucher*
   acquittal rates and, 177–178, 189
   charges, withdrawal of, and, 177–179
   criminal justice and, 177–180
   discharges and, 179
   diversion programmes and, 178–179
   guilty pleas and, 177
   pre-trial dispositions and, 176–180, 185
   prosecutorial discretion and, 179–180, 183
   prosecutors and, 177–180, 184
CAO. *See* Code of Administrative Offences
case file logic, 265–268
   Arbitrazh courts and, 267
   consumer disputes and, 267–268
   criminal cases and, 266–267
   defamation cases and, 266
   evidence and, 266
   formalism and, 102
   immigration law and, 7, 92–93, 99–107, 114–116, 263–266
   Imperial courts and, 265
   judges and, 100–101, 103–106, 111–112
   Justice of the Peace courts and, 268
   Khodorkovsky case and, 267
   lawyers, absence of, and, 265
   laypeople and, 267–268
   political interference and, 267
case outcomes, court-users reactions to, 86–90
case processing, Germany and, 180–183, 185
caseloads
   Arbitrazh courts and, 123–124, 126–127
   Justice of the Peace courts and, 71–72, 90
charges, withdrawal of, Canada and, 177–179
checks and balances, 232–233, 254–255. *See also* judicial independence; reasoned judgment, right to
   Constitution, Russian, 1993, and, 232–233
   professionalisation and, 264
   Russia, Soviet, and, 232–233
child trafficking, 215. *See also* illegal adoption
Church of Rus', Roman law and, 16
CIS. *See* Commonwealth of Independent States
Civic Assistance Committee, 98–99
civil cases, Justice of the Peace courts and, 70–72. *See also* consumer disputes; inheritance disputes; lawsuits
Civil Code, 53
   defamation cases and, 149–150
   freedom of contract and, 54
   moral compensation and, 161
client, commitment to, lawyers, post-Soviet Russian and, 32–33
Code of Administrative Offences (CAO), 92, 97
   appeals and, 99
   residence registration and, 99

279

INDEX

Colleges of Accusers and Defenders, 22
colleges of advocates, Russia, post-Soviet and, 29
Colleges of Defenders, 22–23
commercial disputes, Arbitrazh courts and, 7–8, 118–139. *See also* contractual petty disputes; substantive commercial cases
common-law countries, defamation cases and, 144, 147, 151–152. *See also* Canada; United Kingdom; United States
Commonwealth of Independent States (CIS), 110
communism, law and, 21
competence
  legal education and, 26–29
  professionalisation, post-Soviet Russian and, 26–29
complaint books, consumer disputes and, 45
Conception of Judicial Reform, 1991, 174
conservatism, 220
  acquittals and, 218
  human trafficking cases and, 216–224, 272–273
  judges and, 216–219, 223–224, 226, 272–273
  procurators and, 272–273
Constitution, Russian, 1993,
  checks and balances and, 232–233
  judiciary and, 252–253
  procurators and, 254
  prosecutors and, 254
Constitution, Soviet, 1936, 23–24
Constitution, Soviet, 1977, 232–233
consumer disputes, 43–51, 261
  case file logic and, 267–268
  complaint books and, 45
  consumer rights centres and, 48–49
  cost and, 59
  delays and, 58–59
  doing nothing about, 44–45
  education and, 47
  ekspertiz and, 47–49
  legal literacy and, 61–62
  litigation and, 49–51, 61
  stores, seeking recompense from, and, 45–48
consumer law, 42
consumer rights centres, 63
  consumer disputes and, 48–49
  fees and, 49
contractual petty disputes, Arbitrazh courts and, 124–126
corruption, 1, 33–34
  Arbitrazh courts and, 133–135, 263
  judges and, 135
  judicial discretion and, 3
  Justice of the Peace courts and, 79
  lawyers and, 133–134
  pre-trial sessions and, 79

cost. *See also* litigation, emotional cost of
  consumer disputes and, 59
  inheritance disputes and, 59
  of lawyers, 59
  of litigation, 57–60
Council of the President of the Russian Federation on Development of Civil Society and Human Rights. *See* Human Rights Council
court decisions, defamation cases, as proof in, 145–146, 158–159, 266
courtroom proceedings
  appeals and, 272
  Arbitrazh courts and, 273
  criminal cases and, 272
  justice, administerial model of, and, 271–273
  Moscow City Court and, 95–96
courtroom procurators (*gosobvinitel'*)
  human trafficking laws and, 206, 211
  quantitative assessment system and, 221–223
courts of general jurisdiction
  Arbitrazh courts and, 121–122, 131–133
  architecture and, 131–132
  court-users and, 131–132
  culture of, 132–133
  delays and, 132
  immigration law and, 6–7, 92–116
  records of proceedings and, 132
court-users
  Arbitrazh courts and, 131–132, 136
  case outcomes, reactions to, 86–90
  courts of general jurisdiction and, 131–132
  JPs and, 76–83, 87
  Justice of the Peace court hearings and, 79–83, 274
  Justice of the Peace courts and, 6, 68–91
CPC. *See* Criminal Procedure Code
crimes, grave, 215
crimes, reported, criminal cases and, 186
criminal behaviour, defamation cases and, 145–147
criminal cases, 42, 274. *See also* Khodorkovsky case; non-rehabilitative reasons, cases stopped for; rehabilitative reasons, cases stopped for
  advocates and, 130
  case file logic and, 266–267
  courtroom proceedings and, 272
  crimes, reported and, 186
  Justice of the Peace courts and, 70, 72
  political interference and, 254
  pre-trial screenings and, 272
  reconciliation and, 175
  repentance and, 175
Criminal Code
  human trafficking laws and, 205, 207–211

280

INDEX

organised groups and, 215–216
slave labour and, 208–210
criminal justice
  accusatorial bias and, 170–197, 263–264
  Canada and, 177–180
  Germany and, 180–182
  imbalance of power within, 191–193, 196–197
  Criminal Procedure Code (CPC), 174–175, 187–188
  indictments and, 239
  reasoned judgment, right to, and, 236
crown attorneys. *See* prosecutors
culture. *See also* legal culture, internal
  of Arbitrazh courts, 132–133
  of courts of general jurisdiction, 132–133
customary law, *Volost'* courts and, 20

dacha, 52
decision-making, legal positivism and, 205. *See also* pre-trial decision making
defamation cases, 141–168. *See also New York Times v Sullivan*; slander, criminalisation of; Supreme Court Explanation, 2005
  administrative resources and, 156, 161–165, 167–168, 263
  bias and, 162–165, 263
  byudzhetniki and, 156–159, 161–165
  case file logic and, 266
  civil, 143
  Civil Code and, 149–150
  common-law countries and, 144, 147, 151–152
  court decisions as proof in, 145–146, 158–159, 266
  criminal, 143
  criminal behaviour and, 145–147
  discrediting information and, 144–145
  dissemination and, 144–145, 150–151
  ECHR and, 142–151
  expert testimony and, 148–149
  fact-opinion distinction and, 150–152
  fair comment privilege and, 152
  fair report privilege and, 151–152
  federal officials and, 156–158
  formalism and, 142, 148, 165–168, 269
  free speech and, 141, 151
  journalism and, 145–147, 158–159
  judicial independence and, 8–9, 142–143, 167–168
  lawyers and, 162, 164
  linguists and, 148–149, 261, 269
  media competition and, 152–153
  media outlets and, 143, 152–153, 158–159, 168

  moral compensation and, 8, 149–150, 159–162
  motivations for, 158–159
  municipal officials and, 156–158
  outcomes of, 142, 159–165
  plaintiff success rate in, 155–156, 164–165
  plaintiffs in, 153–159
  political interference and, 253
  politicisation and, 8–9
  proof and, 143–146, 266
  public interest privilege and, 152, 168
  Putin and, 143, 152
  regional distribution of, 144–154
  regional officials and, 156–158
  Russia, high number in, 141, 143
  siloviki and, 156–159
  state officials and, 142–151, 161–165, 167–168
  success rate of, 8
  UK and, 141
  US and, 144, 149
delays
  Arbitrazh courts and, 132
  consumer disputes and, 58–59
  courts of general jurisdiction and, 132
  inheritance disputes and, 58–59
  judges and, 58
  justice, administerial model of, and, 274
  litigation and, 58–59
  Moscow City Court and, 95
deportation
  asylum-seekers, 108
  immigration law and, 97, 99, 112–113
de-professionalisation. *See* professionalisation
developers, inheritance disputes and, 55–56
discharges, Canada and, 179
discrediting information, defamation cases and, 144–145
disputes, 40–64. *See also* commercial disputes, Arbitrazh courts and; consumer disputes; contractual petty disputes, Arbitrazh courts and; inheritance disputes; state, disputes with
  laypeople and, 10
disputing, pyramid of, 42–43
dissemination, defamation cases and, 144–145, 150–151
diversion programmes, 178–179, 187, 193

ECHR. *See* European Court of Human Rights
Economic Chamber of the Supreme Court, 120, 138
education, consumer disputes and, 47. *See also* legal education
Ekaterina II (Imperatrice), 17
ekspertiz (expertise process), consumer disputes and, 47–49

281

INDEX

electronic case files, 121–122
Ellickson, R., 54
estrangement, inheritance disputes and, 60–61
ethnicity, immigration law and, 7
Europe
  acquittal rates and, 171, 180–182
  formalism and, 269
  prosecutorial adjudication and, 184
Europe, Western, professionalisation and, 12, 16
European Convention of Human Rights, 108, 111, 115
  reasoned judgment, right to, and, 236–237
European Court of Human Rights (ECHR), 96
  defamation cases and, 142–151
  Khodorkovsky case and, 236
Everyday Practices and Trouble Cases (Sarat), 94
evidence. *See also ekspertiz* (expertise process), consumer disputes and; proof
  Arbitrazh courts and, 131
  case file logic and, 266
  FMS presenting, 97–98, 100–107, 111–113, 115
  Khodorkovsky case and, 267
  Khodorkovsky second trial verdict and, 237–244
  migrant litigants and, 107, 266
Evroset, 43, 45–46
exceptionalism, Russian, 4
expert testimony. *See also* linguists
  academic freedom and, 148–149
  defamation cases and, 148–149
  formalism and, 148
  US and, 149

fact-opinion distinction, defamation cases and, 150–152
fair comment privilege, defamation cases and, 152
fair report privilege, defamation cases and, 151–152
fairness, prosecutorial adjudication and, 184–185
Federal Migration Service (FMS), 7, 93, 95, 99
  evidence presented by, 97–98, 100–107, 111–113, 115
  judges and, 111–112
  Ukrainians and, 111
federal officials, defamation cases and, 156–158
Federal Security Service (FSB), 216
Fedotov, Mikhail, 236–247
fees, 49, 59, 62
Felstiner, W.L.F., 42–44, 52
fieldwork, 4
financial independence, Arbitrazh courts and, 121

FMS. *See* Federal Migration Service
focus groups, 41
formalism, 268–269. *See also* conservatism
  Arbitrazh courts and, 132–133
  case file logic and, 102
  defamation cases and, 142, 148, 165–168, 269
  Europe and, 269
  expert testimony and, 148
  informality and, 2–3
  judges and, 148, 168, 268
  judicial discretion and, 268
formality, public hearings and, 79–83
France
  acquittal rates and, 180–183, 189
  prosecutorial discretion and, 182–183
free speech, defamation cases and, 141, 151
freedom of contract, Civil Code and, 54
freedom of expression, Russian Constitution and, 151
Friedman, L.M., 12
Fries, B.W., 13–14
FSB. *See* Federal Security Service

Garth, Bryan, 102
GDF. *See* Glasnost Defence Foundation
Gel'man, Vladimir, 250, 254
generalisation, Russian justice system and, 1–2
Germany
  acquittal rates and, 180–182, 189
  case processing and, 180–183, 185
  criminal justice and, 180–182
  pre-trial screenings and, 9
  prosecutorial discretion and, 181, 183
Glasgow University, 19
glasnost, acquittal rates and, 170, 174. *See also* Russia, Soviet
Glasnost Defence Foundation (GDF), 142, 153–160
Gorbachev, Mikhail, 232–233, 255
Gosarbitrazh (State Arbitrazh System), 119
gosobvinitel'. See courtroom procurators
guilty pleas, Canada and, 177
Guriev, Sergei, 247–248
GUVM, MVD. *See* Main Directorate for Migration Affairs of the Russian Federation, Ministry of Internal Affairs

human rights, 1. *See also* European Court of Human Rights; free speech; freedom of expression
Human Rights Council (Council of the President of the Russian Federation on Development of Civil Society and Human Rights), 10, 233
  Investigative Committee and, 248

INDEX

Khodorkovsky case, recommendations on, 245–246
Khodorkovsky case, repercussions for report on, 246–250
Khodorkovsky case and, 244–250
Medvedev and, 236–245
human trafficking cases, 208–224
 acquittal rates and, 219–220
 appeals and, 214
 conservatism and, 216–224, 272–273
 Investigative Committee and, 211
 investigators and, 211–213, 224
 judges and, 211, 215–220, 223–224, 226, 267, 269
 jurisdiction and, 211
 labour trafficking and, 213, 217–218
 organised groups and, 214–216
 pre-trial screenings and, 219–224
 procurators and, 211, 218–223, 226
 quantitative assessment system and, 219–224
 sex trafficking and, 212–214, 217, 224
 slave labour and, 217–218
 UN Protocol and, 213–214
human trafficking laws, 206–228
 aggravating factors and, 214–216
 courtroom procurators and, 206, 211
 Criminal Code and, 205, 207–211
 interpretation and, 211–219
 judges and, 206
 judges interpreting, 212
 pre-trial decision making and, 10
 procurators and, 205–206
 procurators interpreting, 212–216
 slave labour and, 208–210
humanitarian logic
 appeals and, 108–112, 115
 asylum-seekers and, 108–112
 geographic distribution of, 108
 immigration law and, 93, 107–112
Huskey, E., 22–24

identity
 advocacy bar and, 35, 262
 as moral calling, 36
 professionalisation, post-Soviet Russian and, 35–36
 solidarity and, 36
illegal adoption, 207
immigration cases. *See also* asylum-seekers
 affidavits and, 93, 101–105, 113
 appeals and, 100–116, 272
 increase in, 97–98
 labour and, 102–105
 Moscow City Court and, 95–96
 pre-trial stage and, 113–114
 trouble cases and, 93–94, 113–116

UK and, 114
Ukrainians and, 110–112
immigration law. *See also* Code of Administrative Offences
 case file logic and, 7, 92–93, 99–107, 114–116, 263–266
 courts of general jurisdiction and, 6–7, 92–116
 deportation and, 97, 99, 112–113
 ethnicity and, 7
 humanitarian logic and, 93, 107–112
 immigration status and, 7
 judges as enforcers of, 92–93, 97
immigration status, immigration law and, 7
Imperial courts
 adversarial systems and, 270
 case file logic and, 265
indictments
 CPC and, 239
 Khodorkovsky case and, 239–240
informal norms, *advokatura* and, 32–35
informality
 formalism and, 2–3
 Justice of the Peace courts and, 6, 86, 90–91, 133
information technology, Arbitrazh courts and, 121–122, 139, 274–275. *See also* electronic case files; internet; websites, Justice of the Peace courts and
inheritance disputes, 57
 cost and, 59
 delays and, 58–59
 developers and, 55–56
 doing nothing about, 52–53
 estrangement and, 60–61
 judges and, 57, 60
 legal literacy and, 62
 litigation and, 56–57, 60–61
 negotiated settlements and, 53–56
 notaries and, 56–57
 real estate and, 51–57
 theft and, 53
inheritance law, 42
inquisitorial systems, 183
 acquittal rates and, 170–171
 judges and, 270
institutional vulnerability
 political interference and, 263–265
 professionalisation and, 263–265
integrity, legality and, 2
international law, 1
internet, laypeople and, 50–51
interpretation, human trafficking laws and, 211–219
Investigative Committee, 211, 254
 Human Rights Council and, 248
 human trafficking cases and, 211

283

INDEX

investigators, 191, 211
  human trafficking cases and, 211–213, 224
  lawyers and, 193
  pre-trial dispositions and, 193–195
  pre-trial screenings and, 185–186
  prosecutors and, 25
  quantitative assessment system and, 220–221, 226

Japan, acquittal rates and, 171, 189
journalism, 145–147, 158–159, 261
JPs. *See* Justices of the Peace
judges. *See also* Justices of the Peace; Law on the Status of Judges, 1992
  acquittal rates and, 173
  adversarial systems and, 270
  appeals and, 219–220, 223–224
  Arbitrazh courts and, 130–131, 135
  case file logic and, 100–101, 103–106, 111–112
  conservatism and, 216–219, 223–224, 226, 272–273
  corruption and, 135
  delays and, 58
  FMS and, 111–112
  formalism and, 148, 168, 268
  human trafficking cases and, 211, 215–220, 223–224, 226, 267, 269
  human trafficking laws and, 206
  human trafficking laws interpreted by, 212
  immigration law, enforcers of, 92–93, 97
  inheritance disputes and, 57, 60
  inquisitorial systems and, 270
  justice, administerial model of, and, 270–273
  Moscow City Court and, 95, 100, 106
  plea agreements and, 266–267
  procurators and, 174
  prosecutors as, 183–185
  quantitative assessment system and, 220, 223–224, 226
  Russia, post-Soviet and, 25
  Russia, Soviet, and, 173, 196
  sentences, stability of, evaluated by, 195–196, 223
judicial discretion
  corruption and, 3
  formalism and, 268
  pre-trial decision making and, 10
judicial independence, 195–196, 251–253, 265
  Arbitrazh courts and, 7–8, 118, 128–129
  defamation cases and, 8–9, 142–143, 167–168
judicial reforms, 1864
  advocacy bar and, 19–20
  Justice of the Peace courts and, 69
  professionalisation and, 18–19
judiciary, 251
  Constitution, Russian, 1993, and, 252–253

political interference and, 251–253, 265
presidential authority and, 254
prosecutors and, 254
Russia, Soviet, and, 251–252
juge d'instruction, 183–184, 194
jurisdiction
  Arbitrazh courts and, 120–123
  human trafficking cases and, 211
  Justice of the Peace courts and, 70
jurists, Russia, Soviet, and, 24
jury trials
  acquittal rates and, 190
  Lebedev, V., and, 190
  Putin and, 190
  Ukraine and, 190
justice, administerial model of, 10, 269–277
  bureaucracy and, 274
  courtroom proceedings and, 271–273
  delays and, 274
  judges and, 270–273
  justice, Western model of, and, 275–277
  lawyers and, 270–271
  pre-trial stage and, 276
  reform of, 276–277
justice, duality of, Russia, post-Soviet and, 135–139
justice, Western model of, justice, administerial model of, and, 275–277. *See also* rule of law, Western
justice for business, Arbitrazh courts and, 136–139
justice for citizens, 136, 138–139
Justice of the Peace courts, 72–73, 133
  administration of, 76
  administrative cases and, 70, 72
  appeals and, 80
  architecture of, 73–75, 274
  case file logic and, 268
  caseloads and, 71–72, 90
  civil cases and, 70–72
  corruption and, 79
  court-users and, 6, 68–91, 274
  criminal cases and, 70, 72
  everyday experiences of, 68–91
  informality and, 6, 86, 90–91, 133
  institutional setting of, 69–70
  judicial reforms, 1864 and, 69
  jurisdiction and, 70
  lawyers and, 83–86
  legal assistance and, 83–86
  negativity towards, 86–90
  pre-trial decision making and, 80–81, 90
  pre-trial sessions and, 6, 76–79, 84–86, 88–91, 268, 271
  private citizens and, 71–72
  public hearings and, 79–83, 90–91, 271–272

284

INDEX

public image of, 73–75
records of proceedings in, 80
Russia, post-Soviet and, 70
Russia, Soviet, and, 69, 75
state and, 72
as state bureaucratic institutions, 75, 90–91
websites of, 75–76
justice system, Russian. *See specific topics*
Justices of the Peace (JPs)
court-users and, 76–83, 87
legal advice and, 77, 85
legal education and, 70
responsibilities of, 70–71, 76, 90

Kamisar, Yale, 251
Khodorkovsky, Mikhail, 10, 64
Khodorkovsky case, 231, 233–256. *See also* Yukos Oil
appeals in, 235
case file logic and, 267
ECHR and, 236
evidence and, 267
first trial in, 234–235
Human Rights Council and, 244–250
Human Rights Council recommendations on, 245–246
Human Rights Council repercussions for report on, 246–250
Medvedev and, 244, 246, 255–256
Putin and, 236, 246
reasoned judgment, right to, and, 236–244
Richelieu Effect and, 236–244, 254–256
second trial in, 235–239
verdict, second trial, in, 235, 239
evidence in, 237–244
indictment used in, 239–240
narrative-rationale of, 237–238
Kiev Rus'. *See also* Church of Rus', Roman law and
Byzantium and, 15–16
legal profession and, 15
Roman law and, 15–17
treaties and, 15–16

labour. *See also* slave labour
asylum-seekers and, 108
immigration cases and, 102–105
labour trafficking, 207, 213, 215, 217–218
law. *See also* customary law; human trafficking laws; immigration law; politically motivated laws; Roman law; *specific topics*
communism and, 21
laypeople and, 18, 54–55, 260–261
legal theory, Marxist and, 250
legitimacy of, 18, 261
Law on the Status of Judges, 1992, 25
law without lawyers, 15–18

laws, new. *See also* human trafficking laws
institutional resistance to, 226, 269
US and, 225
lawsuits, 253–254
lawyers. *See also* advocacy bar; advocates; law without lawyers; legal profession
advokatura, practicing outside of, 31–32
Arbitrazh courts and, 130
authoritarian regimes and, 17
case file logic and, 265
client, commitment to, and, 32–33
corruption and, 133–134
cost of, 59
defamation cases and, 162, 164
increasing use of, 85
investigators and, 193
justice, administerial model of, and, 270–271
Justice of the Peace courts and, 83–86
negativity towards, 51, 56
pocket, 34
pre-trial sessions and, 84–86
Roman law and, 13–14
Russia, Soviet, and, 21–25
society, commitment to, and, 32–34
sovereigns, Russian and, 17
Western, 33
laypeople. *See also byudzhetniki; podpol'nie*
case file logic and, 267–268
disputes and, 10
internet and, 50–51
law and, 18, 54–55, 260–261
professionalisation and, 262
Russia, post-Soviet and, 27–28, 37
Lebedev, Platon Leonidovich, 234–236, 240
Lebedev, Viacheslav
accusatorial bias and, 175–176
jury trials and, 190
pre-trial dispositions and, 194
legal advice, JPs and, 77, 85
legal assistance, 261. *See also* lawyers
free, 84
Justice of the Peace courts and, 83–86
legal culture, internal, 12
legal education
competence and, 26–29
JPs and, 70
professionalisation and, 18–19
Russia, post-Soviet and, 26–29
Russia, Soviet, and, 21, 24
legal literacy, 62. *See also* laypeople, law and
consumer disputes and, 61–62
inheritance disputes and, 62
litigation and, 61–62
pre-trial sessions and, 77–78
legal nihilism
Russia, post-Soviet and, 30
Russia, Soviet, and, 23–24

285

INDEX

legal positivism, 10
  decision-making and, 205
legal profession, 10, 15
legal theory, Marxist, law and, 250
legality
  integrity and, 2
  political intervention and, 10
legislatures
  political interference and, 250–251
  Putin and, 251
legitimacy, law and, 18, 261
Lenin, Vladimir, 251
linguists, defamation cases and, 148–149, 261, 269
litigation, 56–63
  avoidance of, 10, 40–41, 43, 49–51, 56, 63–64
  consumer disputes and, 49–51, 61
  cost of, 57–60
  delays and, 58–59
  emotional cost of, 50, 59–61
  inheritance disputes and, 56–57, 60–61
  legal literacy and, 61–62
  likely outcomes of, 57–58
  personal experiences with, 62–63
  political intervention and, 63–64
  proof and, 50
  rise in civil, 57
  social distance and, 42, 60–61

Madison, James, 255
Magnitsky case, 255–256
Main Directorate for Migration Affairs of the Russian Federation, Ministry of Internal Affairs (GUVM, MVD), 93
media competition, defamation cases and, 152–153
media outlets, defamation cases and, 143, 152–153, 158–159, 168. *See also* journalism
mediation, 41
Medvedev, Dmitrii, 10
  accusatorial bias and, 175–176
  Human Rights Council and, 236–245
  Khodorkovsky case and, 244, 246, 255–256
Middle Ages, professionalisation and, 12, 14–15
migrant litigants, 96, 107, 266
migration cards, 109
Moiseeva, E., 31
moral compensation
  administrative resources and, 165
  byudzhetniki and, 160–161, 165
  Civil Code and, 161
  defamation cases and, 8, 149–150, 159–162
  state officials and, 160–161, 165, 167–168
Morshchakova, Tamara, 173, 244–245, 247–248

Moscow City Court
  courtroom proceedings of, 95–96
  delays and, 95
  immigration cases in, 95–96
  judges and, 95, 100, 106
Moscow court, 68. *See also* Justice of the Peace courts
Moscow University, 19
municipal officials, defamation cases and, 156–158

negotiated settlements, inheritance disputes and, 53–56
Netherlands
  acquittal rates, 180–182
  prosecutorial discretion, 182
New York Times v Sullivan, 144
'no win no fee,' 134
non-rehabilitative reasons, cases stopped for, 175, 186
notaries, inheritance disputes and, 56–57

organised groups
  Criminal Code and, 215–216
  human trafficking cases and, 214–216

PACER. *See* Public Access to Court Electronic Records
people, ordinary. *See* laypeople; private citizens, Justice of the Peace courts and
People's Courts, 21–22
periodisation, Russian justice system and, 3
personal accusation cases, acquittal rates and, 174
Peter the Great (Emperor), 15, 17
Petrukhin, Igor, 173
plea agreements, 175, 187–189, 266–267. *See also* guilty pleas, Canada and
podpol'nie, 20
police
  quantitative assessment system and, 225
  US and, 251
political interference, 250–256. *See also* Khodorkovsky case; Richelieu Effect
  case file logic and, 267
  criminal cases and, 254
  defamation cases and, 253
  institutional vulnerability and, 263–265
  judiciary and, 251–253, 265
  lawsuits and, 253–254
  legislatures and, 250–251
  prosecutors and, 253–254
  Putin and, 250
political intervention, 64
  legality and, 10
  litigation and, 63–64
politically motivated cases, 206

politically motivated laws, 206
politicisation, defamation cases and, 8–9
post-Soviet countries, acquittal rates and, 173
precedents, Arbitrazh courts introducing, 136–139
pre-programming, 3
presidential authority, judiciary and, 254
pre-trial decision making, 10
  human trafficking laws and, 10
  judicial discretion and, 10
  Justice of the Peace courts and, 80–81, 90
pre-trial dispositions, 193–196
  Canada and, 176–180, 185
  investigators and, 193–195
  Lebedev, V., and, 194
  Putin and, 195
pre-trial screenings, 172, 185–191, 196.
      See also case processing;
      non-rehabilitative reasons, cases
      stopped for; prosecutorial adjudication;
      prosecutorial discretion; rehabilitative
      reasons, cases stopped for
  acquittal rates and, 9–10, 171, 176–183, 264
  criminal cases and, 272
  Germany and, 9
  human trafficking cases and, 219–224
  investigators and, 185–186
  procurators supervising, 186–187, 194–195
  reform through, 193–196
  Russia, Soviet, and, 185–186
pre-trial sessions
  corruption and, 79
  Justice of the Peace courts and, 6, 76–79, 84–86, 88–91, 268, 271
  lawyers and, 84–86
  legal literacy and, 77–78
pre-trial stage
  immigration cases and, 113–114
  justice, administerial model of, and, 276
private advocates, professionalisation and, 20
private citizens, Justice of the Peace courts and, 71–72
procuracy, return to, 187–188
procurators, 22–23, 205, 221. See also courtroom procurators
  accountability of, 195–196
  conservatism and, 272–273
  Constitution, Russian, 1993, and, 254
  human trafficking cases and, 211, 218–223, 226
  human trafficking laws and, 205–206
  human trafficking laws interpreted by, 212–216
  judges and, 174
  pre-trial screenings supervised by, 186–187, 194–195
  quantitative assessment system and, 219–224, 226

professionalisation, 12–37, 260–263. See also legal culture, internal; legal profession
  advokatura and, 29–35
  Arbitrazh courts and, 262
  checks and balances and, 264
  competence and, 26–29
  Europe, Western, and, 12, 16
  identity and, 35–36
  institutional vulnerability and, 263–265
  judicial reforms, 1864 and, 18–19
  laypeople and, 262
  legal education and, 18–19
  Middle Ages and, 12, 14–15
  Peter the Great (Emperor) and, 17
  private advocates and, 20
  Roman law and, 12
  rule of law, Western and, 15
  Russia, Soviet, and, 21–25
professionalism, Arbitrazh courts and, 130–131, 139
proof. See also *ekspertiz* (expertise process), consumer disputes and
  defamation cases, court decisions as proof in, 145–146, 158–159, 266
  defamation cases and, 143–146, 266
  litigation and, 50
prosecutorial adjudication, 183–185
  Europe and, 184
  fairness and, 184–185
prosecutorial discretion
  Canada and, 179–180, 183
  France and, 182–183
  Germany and, 181, 183
  Netherlands, 182
prosecutors. See also courtroom procurators
  Canada and, 177–180, 184
  Constitution, Russian, 1993, and, 254
  investigators and, 25
  as judges, 183–185
  judiciary and, 254
  political interference and, 253–254
  Putin and, 253–254
  quantitative assessment system and, 225–226
  US and, 183–184, 225
Public Access to Court Electronic Records (PACER), 121
public hearings
  formality and, 79–83
  Justice of the Peace courts and, 79–83, 90–91, 271–272
public interest privilege, defamation cases and, 152, 168
Putin, Vladimir, 64
  defamation cases and, 143, 152
  jury trials and, 190
  Khodorkovsky case and, 236, 246
  legislatures and, 251

Putin, Vladimir, (cont.)
  political interference and, 250
  pre-trial dispositions and, 195
  prosecutors and, 253–254

qualitative data, quantitative data and, 4
quantitative assessment system, 226–228.
    See also sentences, stability of, judges
    evaluated by
  courtroom procurators and, 221–223
  human trafficking cases and, 219–224
  innovation hindered by, 227–228
  investigators and, 220–221, 226
  judges and, 220, 223–224, 226
  police and, 225
  popular perceptions impacted by, 227
  procurators and, 219–224, 226
  prosecutors and, 225–226
quantitative data, qualitative data and, 4

R. v Boucher, 180
real estate, 51–57
reasoned judgment, right to
  CPC and, 236
  European Convention of Human Rights
    and, 236–237
  Khodorkovsky case and, 236–244
reconciliation, criminal cases and, 175
records of proceedings
  Arbitrazh courts and, 132
  courts of general jurisdiction and, 132
  in Justice of the Peace courts, 80
regional officials, defamation cases and,
    156–158
rehabilitative reasons, cases stopped for,
    174–175, 186
repentance, criminal cases and, 175
residence registration, CAO and, 99
Revolutionary Decree on the Courts, 21
Reynolds, S., 14
Richelieu Effect, 231–233, 236–244, 254–256,
    264
Roman law, 12–18, 259–260
  Church of Rus' and, 16
  Kiev Rus' and, 15–17
  lawyers and, 13–14
  professionalisation and, 12
rule of law, Western, 3–4, 13, 15, 250
Russia. *See specific topics*
Russia, post-Soviet. *See specific topics*
Russia, Soviet. *See also* Colleges of Accusers
    and Defenders; Constitution, Soviet,
    1936; Constitution, Soviet, 1977;
    People's Courts; Revolutionary Decree
    on the Courts
  acquittal rates and, 171–174
  advocacy bar and, 21
  advokatura and, 24

checks and balances and, 232–233
judges and, 173, 196
judiciary and, 251–252
jurists and, 24
Justice of the Peace courts and, 69, 75
lawyers and, 21–25
legal education and, 21, 24
legal nihilism and, 23–24
pre-trial screenings and, 185–186
professionalisation and, 21–25
Russian Constitution, freedom of expression
    and, 151

Sakharov, Andrei, 248
samosud (self-help solutions), 55
Sarat, Austin, 94, 113
self-governance, *advokatura* and, 29
sentences, stability of, judges evaluated by,
    195–196, 223
separation of powers. *See* checks and balances;
    political interference
sex trafficking, 207
  human trafficking cases and, 212–214, 217,
    224
siloviki, defamation cases and, 156–159
slander, criminalisation of, 253
slave labour
  Criminal Code and, 208–210
  human trafficking cases and, 217–218
  human trafficking laws and, 208–210
social distance, litigation and, 42, 60–61
society, commitment to, lawyers, post-Soviet
    Russian and, 32–34
sociology of justice, 4–5
solidarity, identity and, 36
South Korea, 152
sovereigns, Russian, lawyers and, 17. *See also*
    Ekaterina II (Imperatrice); Peter the
    Great
special procedure. *See* plea agreements
specialisation, Arbitrazh courts and, 131
state
  Arbitrazh courts and, 123
  Justice of the Peace courts and, 72
state, disputes with, Arbitrazh courts and,
    126–129
State Arbitrazh System. *See* Gosarbitrazh
state bureaucratic institutions, Justice of the
    Peace courts as, 75, 90–91
state entities, 124
  Arbitrazh courts and, 124–125, 138
state officials. *See also* federal officials;
    municipal officials; regional officials;
    siloviki
  defamation cases and, 142–151, 161–165,
    167–168
  moral compensation and, 160–161, 165,
    167–168

288

stores, seeking recompense from, consumer disputes and, 45–48
Subbotin, Mikhail, 248–250
substantive commercial cases, Arbitrazh courts and, 129–133
Sudebnik, 16–17
summary proceedings, Arbitrazh courts and, 127–128
Supreme Arbitrazh Court, 119–122, 134, 136–138. *See also* Economic Chamber of the Supreme Court
Supreme Court Explanation, 2005, 150–152, 161
Sweden, acquittal rates and, 189–190

tax evasion. *See* Khodorkovsky case
Thaman, S., 183
theft, inheritance disputes and, 53
thick description, 4
Travers, Max, 114
treaties, Kiev Rus' and, 15–16
trouble cases, immigration cases and, 93–94, 113–116

UK. *See* United Kingdom
Ukraine, jury trials and, 190

Ukrainians
  FMS and, 111
  immigration cases and, 110–112
UN Protocol, human trafficking cases and, 213–214
UN Transnational Organized Crime Convention, 208
United Kingdom (UK), 184
  acquittal rates and, 171, 178
  defamation cases and, 141
  immigration cases and, 114
United States (US)
  defamation cases and, 144, 149
  expert testimony and, 149
  laws, new and, 225
  police and, 251
  prosecutors and, 183–184, 225

Volost' courts, customary law and, 20

warranties, 44
websites, Justice of the Peace courts and, 75–76

Yngvesson, B., 61, 94
Yukos Oil, 1, 233–234. *See also* Khodorkovsky case

CAMBRIDGE STUDIES IN LAW AND SOCIETY

Books in the Series

Diseases of the Will: Alcohol and the Dilemmas of Freedom
Mariana Valverde

The Politics of Truth and Reconciliation in South Africa: Legitimizing the Post-Apartheid State
Richard A. Wilson

Modernism and the Grounds of Law
Peter Fitzpatrick

Unemployment and Government: Genealogies of the Social
William Walters

Autonomy and Ethnicity: Negotiating Competing Claims in Multi-Ethnic States
Yash Ghai

Constituting Democracy: Law, Globalism and South Africa's Political Reconstruction
Heinz Klug

The Ritual of Rights in Japan: Law, Society, and Health Policy
Eric A. Feldman

Governing Morals: A Social History of Moral Regulation
Alan Hunt

The Colonies of Law: Colonialism, Zionism and Law in Early Mandate Palestine
Ronen Shamir

Law and Nature
David Delaney

Social Citizenship and Workfare in the United States and Western Europe: The Paradox of Inclusion
Joel F. Handler

Law, Anthropology, and the Constitution of the Social: Making Persons and Things
Edited by Alain Pottage and Martha Mundy

Judicial Review and Bureaucratic Impact: International and Interdisciplinary Perspectives
Edited by Marc Hertogh and Simon Halliday

Immigrants at the Margins: Law, Race, and Exclusion in Southern Europe
Kitty Calavita

Lawyers and Regulation: The Politics of the Administrative Process
Patrick Schmidt

Law and Globalization from Below: Toward a Cosmopolitan Legality
Edited by Boaventura de Sousa Santos and Cesar A. Rodriguez-Garavito

Public Accountability: Designs, Dilemmas and Experiences
Edited by Michael W. Dowdle,

Law, Violence and Sovereignty among West Bank Palestinians
Tobias Kelly

Legal Reform and Administrative Detention Powers in China
Sarah Biddulph

The Practice of Human Rights: Tracking Law between the Global and the Local
Edited by Mark Goodale and Sally Engle Merry

Judges beyond Politics in Democracy and Dictatorship: Lessons from Chile
Lisa Hilbink

Paths to International Justice: Social and Legal Perspectives
Edited by Marie-Bénédicte Dembour and Tobias Kelly

Law and Society in Vietnam: The Transition from Socialism in Comparative Perspective
Mark Sidel

Constitutionalizing Economic Globalization: Investment Rules and Democracy's Promise
David Schneiderman

The New World Trade Organization Knowledge Agreements: 2nd Edition
Christopher Arup

Justice and Reconciliation in Post-Apartheid South Africa
Edited by François du Bois and Antje du Bois-Pedain

Militarization and Violence against Women in Conflict Zones in the Middle East: A Palestinian Case-Study
Nadera Shalhoub-Kevorkian

Child Pornography and Sexual Grooming: Legal and Societal Responses
Suzanne Ost

Darfur and the Crime of Genocide
John Hagan and Wenona Rymond-Richmond

Fictions of Justice: The International Criminal Court and the Challenge of Legal Pluralism in Sub-Saharan Africa
Kamari Maxine Clarke

Conducting Law and Society Research: Reflections on Methods and Practices
Simon Halliday and Patrick Schmidt

Planted Flags: Trees, Land, and Law in Israel/Palestine
Irus Braverman

Culture under Cross-Examination: International Justice and the Special Court for Sierra Leone
Tim Kelsall

Cultures of Legality: Judicialization and Political Activism in Latin America
Javier Couso, Alexandra Huneeus, and Rachel Sieder

Courting Democracy in Bosnia and Herzegovina: The Hague Tribunal's Impact in a Postwar State
Lara J. Nettelfield

The Gacaca Courts, Post-Genocide Justice and Reconciliation in Rwanda: Justice without Lawyers
Phil Clark

Law, Society, and History: Themes in the Legal Sociology and Legal History of Lawrence M. Friedman
Edited by Robert W. Gordon and Morton J. Horwitz

After Abu Ghraib: Exploring Human Rights in America and the Middle East
Shadi Mokhtari

Adjudication in Religious Family Laws: Cultural Accommodation, Legal Pluralism, and Gender Equality in India
Gopika Solanki

Water on Tap: Rights and Regulation in the Transnational Governance of Urban Water Services
Bronwen Morgan

Elements of Moral Cognition: Rawls' Linguistic Analogy and the Cognitive Science of Moral and Legal Judgment
John Mikhail

Mitigation and Aggravation at Sentencing
Edited by Julian V. Roberts,

Institutional Inequality and the Mobilization of the Family and Medical Leave Act: Rights on Leave
Catherine R. Albiston

Authoritarian Rule of Law: Legislation, Discourse and Legitimacy in Singapore
Jothie Rajah

Law and Development and the Global Discourses of Legal Transfers
Edited by John Gillespie and Pip Nicholson

Law against the State: Ethnographic Forays into Law's Transformations
Edited by Julia Eckert, Brian Donahoe, Christian Strümpell and Zerrin Özlem Biner

Transnational Legal Ordering and State Change
Edited by Gregory C. Shaffer

Legal Mobilization under Authoritarianism: The Case of Post-Colonial Hong Kong
Waikeung Tam

Complementarity in the Line of Fire: The Catalysing Effect of the International Criminal Court in Uganda and Sudan
Sarah M. H. Nouwen

Political and Legal Transformations of an Indonesian Polity: The Nagari from Colonisation to Decentralisation
Franz von Benda-Beckmann and Keebet von Benda-Beckmann

Pakistan's Experience with Formal Law: An Alien Justice
Osama Siddique

Human Rights under State-Enforced Religious Family Laws in Israel, Egypt, and India
Yüksel Sezgin

Why Prison?
Edited by David Scott

Law's Fragile State: Colonial, Authoritarian, and Humanitarian Legacies in Sudan
Mark Fathi Massoud

Rights for Others: The Slow Home-Coming of Human Rights in the Netherlands
Barbara Oomen

European States and Their Muslim Citizens: The Impact of Institutions on Perceptions and Boundaries
Edited by John R. Bowen, Christophe Bertossi, Jan Willem Duyvendak, and Mona Lena Krook

Environmental Litigation in China: A Study in Political Ambivalence
Rachel E. Stern

Indigeneity and Legal Pluralism in India: Claims, Histories, Meanings
Pooja Parmar

Paper Tiger: Law, Bureaucracy and the Developmental State in Himalayan India
Nayanika Mathur

Religion, Law and Society
Russell Sandberg

The Experiences of Face Veil Wearers in Europe and the Law
Edited by Eva Brems

The Contentious History of the International Bill of Human Rights
Christopher N. J. Roberts

Transnational Legal Orders
Edited by Terence C. Halliday and Gregory Shaffer

Lost in China? Law, Culture and Society in Post-1997 Hong Kong
Carol A. G. Jones

Security Theology, Surveillance and the Politics of Fear
Nadera Shalhoub-Kevorkian

Opposing the Rule of Law: How Myanmar's Courts Make Law and Order
Nick Cheesman

The Ironies of Colonial Governance: Law, Custom and Justice in Colonial India
James Jaffe

The Clinic and the Court: Law, Medicine and Anthropology
Edited by Ian Harper, Tobias Kelly, and Akshay Khanna

A World of Indicators: The Making of Government Knowledge through Quantification
Edited by Richard Rottenburg, Sally Engle Merry, Sung-Joon Park, and Johanna Mugler

Contesting Immigration Policy in Court: Legal Activism and Its Radiating Effects in the United States and France
Leila Kawar

The Quiet Power of Indicators: Measuring Governance, Corruption, and Rule of Law
Edited by Sally Engle Merry, Kevin Davis, and Benedict Kingsbury

Investing in Authoritarian Rule: Punishment and Patronage in Rwanda's Gacaca Courts for Genocide Crimes
Anuradha Chakravarty

Contractual Knowledge: One Hundred Years of Legal Experimentation in Global Markets
Edited by Grégoire Mallard and Jérôme Sgard

Iraq and the Crimes of Aggressive War: The Legal Cynicism of Criminal Militarism
John Hagan, Joshua Kaiser, and Anna Hanson

Culture in the Domains of Law
Edited by René Provost

China and Islam: The Prophet, the Party, and Law
Matthew S. Erie

Diversity in Practice: Race, Gender, and Class in Legal and Professional Careers
Edited by Spencer Headworth and Robert Nelson

A Sociology of Constitutions: Constitutions and State Legitimacy in Historical-Sociological Perspective
Chris Thornhill

A Sociology of Transnational Constitutions: Social Foundations of the Post-National Legal Structure
Chris Thornhill

Shifting Legal Visions: Judicial Change and Human Rights Trials in Latin America
Ezequiel A. González Ocantos

The Demographic Transformations of Citizenship
Heli Askola

Criminal Defense in China: The Politics of Lawyers at Work
Sida Liu and
Terence C. Halliday

Contesting Economic and Social Rights in Ireland: Constitution, State and Society, 1848–2016
Thomas Murray

Buried in the Heart: Women, Complex Victimhood and the War in Northern Uganda
Erin Baines

Palaces of Hope: The Anthropology of Global Organizations
Edited by Ronald Niezen and Maria Sapignoli

The Politics of Bureaucratic Corruption in Post-Transitional Eastern Europe
Marina Zaloznaya

Revisiting the Law and Governance of Trafficking, Forced Labor and Modern Slavery
Edited by Prabha Kotiswaran

Incitement on Trial: Prosecuting International Speech Crimes
Richard Ashby Wilson

Criminalizing Children: Welfare and the State in Australia
David McCallum

Global Lawmakers: International Organizations in the Crafting of World Markets
Susan Block-Lieb and Terence C. Halliday

Duties to Care: Dementia, Relationality and Law
Rosie Harding

Insiders, Outsiders, Injuries, and Law: Revisiting "The Oven Bird's Song"
Edited by Mary Nell Trautner

Hunting Justice: Displacement, Law, and Activism in the Kalahari
Maria Sapignoli

Injury and Injustice: The Cultural Politics of Harm and Redress
Edited by Anne Bloom, David M. Engel, and Michael McCann

Ruling Before the Law: The Politics of Legal Regimes in China and Indonesia
William Hurst

The Powers of Law: A Comparative Analysis of Sociopolitical Legal Studies
Mauricio García-Villegas

A Sociology of Justice in Russia
Edited by Marina Kurkchiyan and Agnieszka Kubal

Constituting Religion: Islam, Liberal Rights, and the Malaysian State
Tamir Moustafa

The Invention of the Passport: Surveillance, Citizenship and the State, 2nd Edition
John C. Torpey

Law's Trials: The Performance of Legal Institutions in the US "War on Terror"
Richard L. Abel

Law's Wars: The Fate of the Rule of Law in the US "War on Terror"
Richard L. Abel

Transforming Gender Citizenship: The Irresistible Rise of Gender Quotas in Europe
Edited by Eléonore Lépinard and Ruth Rubio-Marín

Muslim Women's Quest for Justice: Gender, Law and Activism in India
Mengia Hong Tschalaer

CPSIA information can be obtained
at www.ICGtesting.com
Printed in the USA
LVHW041011051221
705332LV00012B/1510